WOMEN AS HAMLET

The first Hamlet on film was Sarah Bernhardt. Probably the first Hamlet on radio was Eve Donne. Ever since the late eighteenth century, leading actresses have demanded the right to play the role – Western drama's greatest symbol of active consciousness and conscience. Their iconoclasm, and Hamlet's alleged 'femininity', have fascinated playwrights, painters, novelists and film-makers from Eugène Delacroix and the Victorian novelist Mary Braddon to Angela Carter and Robert Lepage. Crossing national and media boundaries, this book addresses the history and the shifting iconic status of the female Hamlet in writing and performance. Many of the performers were also involved in radical politics: from Stalinist Russia to Poland under martial law, actresses made Hamlet a symbol of transformation or crisis in the body politic. On stage and film, women reinvented Hamlet from Weimar Germany to the end of the Cold War. This book aims to put their half-forgotten achievements centre-stage.

TONY HOWARD lectures in English at the University of Warwick. In 2000 he was the International Shakespeare Fellow at Shakespeare's Globe. He has worked in the professional theatre in several capacities, with plays performed by Covent Garden Community Theatre, Theatre Royal Stratford East / Royal Court Theatre and Major Road. He is the author of *A Short Sharp Shock* (with Howard Brenton, 1980) and, with John Stokes, is the co-editor of *Acts of War: The Representation of Military Conflict on the British Stage and Television Since 1945* (1996). Performed translations, with Barbara Bogoczek, include works by Mikhail Bulgakov, Tadeusz Różewicz and Jan Brzechwa. His essays on Shakespeare, film and theatre have appeared in many books and journals including *New Theatre Quarterly* and *Around the Globe*.

WOMEN AS HAMLET

Performance and Interpretation in Theatre,
Film and Fiction

TONY HOWARD

CAMBRIDGE
UNIVERSITY PRESS

CAMBRIDGE UNIVERSITY PRESS
Cambridge, New York, Melbourne, Madrid, Cape Town, Singapore, São Paulo, Delhi

Cambridge University Press
The Edinburgh Building, Cambridge CB2 8RU, UK

Published in the United States of America by Cambridge University Press, New York

www.cambridge.org
Information on this title: www.cambridge.org/9780521864664

First published 2007
Third printing 2008

Printed in the United Kingdom at the University Press, Cambridge

A catalogue record for this publication is available from the British Library

Library of Congress Cataloguing in Publication Data
Howard, Tony, 1947–
Women as Hamlet: Performance and interpretation in theatre, film and literature/Tony Howard.
p. cm.
ISBN-13: 978-0-521-86466-4
ISBN-10: 0-521-86466-6
1. Shakespeare, William, 1564-1616. Hamlet. 2. Breeches parts. 3. Shakespeare, William, 1564-1616 --
Dramatic production. 4. Shakespeare, William, 1564-1616--Stage history. 5. Shakespeare, William,
1564-1616--Film and video adaptations. I. Title.

PR2807. H59 2007
822.3'3–dc22
2006036489

ISBN 978-0-521-86466-4 HARDBACK

Contents

v

List of illustrations

Preface

This book has its origins in 1990 when thanks to the Artistic Director of Kraków's Stary Theatre I was fortunate enough to see Teresa Budzisz-Kryżanowska in *Hamlet* (*IV*), directed by Andrzej Wajda. A decade earlier, I had seen Frances de la Tour's Hamlet at the Half Moon Theatre in London while working with her director Robert Walker and her Gertrude, Maggie Steed, on an anti-Thatcher satire in which, reversing *Hamlet*, all but two of the cast were women and most cross-dressed as men. I admired Frances de la Tour's scorching, sad performance, but it was not until Kraków that I appreciated the extraordinary creative daring such a performance could involve, nor the new levels of meaning an actress playing Hamlet might open up. This led me to seek out Asta Nielsen's silent film *Hamlet* (1920) at the National Film and Television Archive in London, and to examine reviews of Sarah Bernhardt's 1899 production. It became clear that not only had a great many actresses played this role over the centuries, sometimes brilliantly, but that the idea of the female Hamlet had fascinated painters, novelists, playwrights and film-makers too – both women and men, and in many countries. Here was a Shakespearean subculture, inseparable from shifting attitudes to gender and political identity.

For a while this project aimed to be encyclopaedic, but so many professional actresses have played Hamlet that this proved impossible. What I have tried to do is to sketch the territory, and retrieve the stories of just a few remarkable performances. The extraordinary thing was not that so many great actresses had played Hamlet but that most were comprehensively forgotten. Treva Rose Tumbleson's unpublished 1981 PhD thesis was an indispensable guide (sadly she died while this book was taking shape); fortunately several of those careers have lately received acute scholarly attention, and more will follow.

This is a study of a tradition that has run alongside the 'official' fortunes of *Hamlet* for over two centuries. After the Introduction, the first two chapters explore the emergence of that tradition from the late eighteenth century to the end of the nineteenth, and the growing connections between the female Hamlet and the politics of enfranchisement. This leads to a study of Bernhardt's legendary transitional *Hamlet* and some aspects of her international legacy. Chapters 5 to 8 focus on key productions/performances – from World War I to the end of the Cold War – in Germany, the USSR, Poland, Spain, Turkey and Eire; these sections consider some of the ways Hamlet's body has been reshaped by changing attitudes to gender, repression and political control. Chapter 9 looks at female Hamlets in sound film and fiction, permeating our imagination in contradictory ways. Chapter 10 samples the explosion of Shakespearean cross-gender experiments in Britain and the USA since the late 1970s. The concluding chapter considers the complex iconic status of the female Hamlet in recent writing and performance. The early chapters focus on the work of individual actresses, and on the creative feminisation of Hamlet by the painter Eugène Delacroix and the novelist Mary Braddon. The later sections explore the relationship between artists, cultural movements and power in specific national situations; the female Hamlet has been an elusive signifier of both schism and possibility.

Most of the modern (1979 and after) stage productions discussed in detail in this book, I saw either in person or on tape; the one exception was *Hamlet's Nightmare* at the Project Theatre, Dublin, so I am especially grateful to the production staff who obtained information for me. There is no space to acknowledge all those to whom I am indebted but I must thank Teresa Budzisz-Kryżanowska, Frances de la Tour, Olwen Foure, Fiona Shaw, Tadeusz Bradecki of the Stary Theatre, and very many at Shakespeare's Globe – especially Patrick Spottiswoode who arranged a special screening of Asta Nielsen's *Hamlet* at the National Film Theatre, and Claire van Kampen who composed a new live score for it. I have been generously helped by the staff of the Theatre Museum, the British Library, the Folger Shakespeare Library, the Museo Nacional del Teatro, the National Film and Television Archive, New York Public Library, the Shakespeare Centre, Birmingham Shakespeare Library, and the University of Warwick Library. My debt to those who helped with access to and translation of archive materials, films and videos is immense, including Ania Barwinska, Rowland Cotterill, Maria Delgado, José Ramón Díaz Fernandez, Dilek Inan, Russell Jackson, Lasse Kekki, Jennifer Lorch, Kirsten Ludwig, Luke McTiernan, Lawrence Raw, Monika Siedel,

Ruth Vaughan, and the British Council in Ankara and Istanbul. I must also thank Dora Schweitzer, designer of the Wilde Thyme *Hamlet* (London 2003) and Tina Jones of Brit-Pol Theatre. I benefited hugely from the advice of Maggie Gale and the late Clive Barker, who both commissioned early versions of some of these chapters; from Kate Chedgzoy, who directed me towards work on Vestvali; from the participants in the "*Hamlet* on Film" conference (Shakespeare's Globe, 2001); and from the encouragement of Susan Bassnett, Jeremy Treglown, and CUP's editors. The comments of Ann Thompson and Stanley Wells were invaluable. Very special thanks to Carol Rutter and John Stokes.

All of that however pales beside the contribution and patience of Barbara Bogoczek, without whom it would never have been finished, or begun.

CHAPTER I

Introduction: *The drama of questions and the mystery of Hamlet*

> How can woman put herself into the text – into the world and into
> history?
>> Helène Cixous, 'The Laugh of the Medusa', 1975[1]

The first Hamlet on film was a woman, Sarah Bernhardt (1900). Probably
the first Hamlet on radio was a woman, Eve Donne (1923). The 'observed
of all observers', the 'glass of fashion and the mould of form', the 'hoop
through which every actor must jump' according to Max Beerbohm,
Hamlet is also the role that has since the late eighteenth century most
inspired tragic actresses to challenge expectations and cross gender lines.
Several of the most brilliant performances of the part in our time have
been by women, and the issue of Hamlet's 'femininity' has fascinated
artists in all media. Crossing boundaries, contesting convention, disrupting or reflecting the dominant sexual politics, this regendering of Hamlet
has involved repeated investigations into the nature of subjectivity, articulacy, and action – investigations with radically different consequences
depending on the cultural situation. It has been an extraordinary history,
but until recently, with the re-evaluation of such unconventional actresses
as Charlotte Charke, Charlotte Cushman, Asta Nielsen and Eva Le
Gallienne, it was largely ignored. Why, at certain points, was it thought
appropriate for women to play this role, and why were many other artists,
male and female, fascinated by them? To establish some parameters we
begin with a German actress, a French painter, and an amateur American
critic who each in different ways and for different reasons explored what
has been seen as the femininity of Hamlet.

I

Performance: Hamlet 2000

Hamlet raises all the questions that human beings ask throughout their
lives . . . Today, in a world in which science and politics want to make us believe

that all questions can be answered, our instincts tell us that this is all wrong. . . What will this 'Hamlet 2000' be like? What will be his questions to the world, on the eve of the new millennium?[2]

Angela Winkler, one of Germany's leading actresses, played Hamlet at the Hanover Schauspielhaus as part of the millennial Expo 2000. Best known internationally for her role in the film *The Lost Honour of Katherina Blum* (1975) as an innocent bystander embroiled in state terror, she won Germany's Best Actress award as Hamlet. The director was Peter Zadek. '*Hamlet 2000*' was tied into the politics of Germany and Europe after the Wall; few performances have carried such symbolic weight. It was a Berlin Schaubühne production but it was co-financed by Expo 2000 and the Avignon Festival, rehearsed in Strasbourg, premiered in Vienna in 1999, and climaxed its Berlin run that December, the week the world's leaders assembled in the reunified city to mark the rebuilding of the Reichstag.[3] In response to the end of a brutal century, Angela Winkler made Hamlet an embodiment of bruised hope. If Hamlet always shows 'the very age and body of the time his true form and feature' (and many saw the advice to the Players as the key to her contained realism), after such an age of violence must not the 'form and feature' of consciousness itself, which Hamlet has for so long represented, be refigured? Zadek said he sensed 'instinctively' that at that moment a woman must ask 'the questions', and the androgyny of Winkler's Hamlet had collective resonance.

Angela Winkler was fifty-five, the same age as Bernhardt when she played Hamlet a century earlier. 'I didn't set out to play a man', Winkler said, 'I don't find that interesting.'[4] Rather, she saw theatre as 'a different way of living' – 'It's very important for me that the work corresponds to a precise moment in my life.' She had four children and rationed herself ('I couldn't act all the time. I had to have pauses, to be with my family') and in the 1990s she chose to collaborate with particular directors on major projects. 'Why did Zadek want a woman to play Hamlet?' she was asked: 'Why did he choose me? I don't know. I never ask directors to explain.' She had had no driving interest in *Hamlet* ('I'd only seen the play once, in 1977, I hadn't read it, and I've never played Shakespeare') but its difficulty attracted her ('If it's not a struggle, I don't accept') and there were private echoes. Late in World War II Winkler's father was shot and assumed dead on the Russian Front; when she was six like a ghost he returned to Germany. As we shall see, any effective performance of Hamlet, by man or woman, resonates with autobiography. Angela Winkler made Hamlet emotionally raw and

Figure 1   Angela Winkler as Hamlet, Berlin 1999; director: Peter Zadek.
(*Photo*: Roswitha Hecke).

unprotected, consumed by an insatiable hunger for truth, observing history with amazement (see Figure 1)

Somewhere near 'the end of history' on an empty windswept stage, a
modern soldier wrapped in leather and furs kept watch (NATO's bombing

of Belgrade began during rehearsals). In an age of grand architectural statements like the new Reichstag, Elsinore was a metal box, a giant version of the portakabins® seen on building sites everywhere. Its blank impermanence made European critics think of migrant workers, refugees, and the construction of false realities: 'What symbolizes postmodern randomness better?'[5] As nervous guards clicked their rifles, the container opened, and to murmurs of ecclesiastical music from a distant time of belief, the Ghost emerged rattling bells and beads and toting a ring-binder ledger of sins. It ignored the soldiers and locked itself back in: there was no dialogue between numb present and grotesque past. Then a business-suited new Court emerged from the box for a photocall; Claudius' white uniform unified elements from East and West Germany. Otto Sadler made him a canny working-class politician who easily solved the Norway problem and smiled, complacent as Clinton, Blair and Schröder in the post-ideological age. Women's condition however had not altered – Ophelia was a timid doll and Gertrude a scarlet woman forever in red. Elizabeth Plessen's translation interlaced Schlegel's Romantic rhetoric with everyday idioms and the acting veered between the conversational and caricature. Dressed in 1940s fashions, Ophelia and her fighter-pilot brother were what Claudius and Gertrude might once have been: time slipped; people coexisted with their own past; *Hamlet* was haunted by memories from Germany's postwar reconstruction and from Angela Winkler's life.

Hamlet arrived late, in black tunic and hose, disrupting everything and taking all the culture's contradictions and suppressed anxieties into his/her self. Winkler pushed through to the front, slammed down a kitchen chair and sat taut and sullen, unable to stay still, shaking her long dark hair, fingers drumming. Everyone tried to ignore her till she laughed out loud to hear of Laertes' escape. Gertrude came over from the party but Hamlet could hardly speak: 'I know not seems . . .' The production made nothing of Winkler's gender, nor did she 'play a man': rather, as Michael Billington observed, 'she absorbs Hamlet's emotions into her own personality' and crucially, like Sarah Bernhardt, she played a child. Hamlet became pre-gendered – 'the problem child', Roland Koberg said, 'at a dinner party, whose behaviour is disturbed . . . And all simultaneously stare, perplexed, and shy away because they cannot deal with it.' Claudius delivered a pep-talk. In *Hamlet* – and this was one reason why the role beckoned many actresses – there is no division between history and the private sphere.

Winkler was one of many actresses who played Hamlet in the 1990s. In Stockholm (1996) and Cincinnati (1997), the character was made female (Princess Hamlet) while in other cases (e.g. London, 1992) there was a thorough male impersonation. The experience varied from country to country. For example specific languages are more or less gendered so there were no personal pronouns to define Leea Klemola's Finnish punk Hamlet (1995) as either 'he' or 'she': Hamlet was '*han*'. Cultural contexts varied, sometimes unpredictably. In Giles Block's 1995 Japanese production (Shochiku Theatre, Tokyo) Hamlet was Rei Asami, from the all-female Takorasaka company who were reversing the centuries-old *onnagata* tradition of all-male casting. Takorasaka implicitly critiqued a society that had clung to conventions of gender representation from a distant age; yet a group of actresses had staged *Hamlet* in Japan as early as 1907 and the kabuki-trained actress Yaeko Mizutani played Hamlet successfully in 1933 and 1935. Block's 1995 production was less revolutionary than it sounded and, he said, 'As soon as rehearsals started everyone forgot about the sex of the person, she was like any other performer, playing Hamlet.'[6] All cross-cast *Hamlet*s involve decisions regarding the nature of gender – biologically or culturally determined? learned, improvised or imposed? – and may universalise the character or focus on *difference*. But what most female Hamlets have in common is that they are catalysts – inassimilable figures alien to the norms around them. The paradoxes and dissident intensities of Hamlet's beliefs and language become sharper through the figure of an actress/prince whose very presence exposes artifice – the theatrical conventions we might otherwise not question, the political banalities masking Elsinore's lies, and the structures of power and gender that normally trap women in *Hamlet* in the roles of Mother, Virgin and Whore. The female Hamlet is a walking, speaking alienation effect. Angela Winkler confronted the fact that Hamlet embodies contradiction.

In public Winkler was scarcely audible, but alone with the audience tempestuous energy burst through. She punched the air ('Hercules!'), hit her shoe thinking of Gertrude's new ones, jumped into the audience to explain incest ('My father's brother!'), but retreated to the lonely stage and blew her nose on her sleeve. Horatio delighted her with magic tricks but she confided in the spectators, almost naively: 'It is not nor it cannot come to good.' Winkler made the famous pronouncements seem simple, even trite ('Frailty thy name is woman,' 'To be or not to be, that is the question') but new and astonishing to Hamlet, who was so intrigued by the 'vicious mole of nature' that s/he nearly missed the Ghost.

Winkler showed that each individual encounters life and death as if for the first time, and the fact that women cannot normally speak this text in public intensified the effect: she gave Hamlet a compulsive need for knowledge, and articulation. Reviewers spoke of *The Little Prince* and *Peter Pan*. As Koberg noted, everyone suppressed their past except Winkler's Hamlet, who 'believes in the past, corresponds with it . . . Hamlet has the longest memory and the shortest life'.

We shall see that when gender is put in question, so is genre. Farce and tragedy overlapped: Winkler pulled a gun on Marcellus and Horatio to comic effect; seeing the Ghost on its knees in shame – 'Strange, tattered, half-shaman half fool,' (Kolberg) – Hamlet gave it a chair, but it fell off. 'My uncle?' expressed amazement. Winkler was volatile: 'Oh but there is, Horatio!' was a mature explosion of rage, but then she banged on the stage ('Swear!') like a six-year-old whose father had returned from the dead, and told Horatio in all simplicity that there are lots of things in heaven and earth. At the 2000 Edinburgh Festival some British reviewers complained that Zadek was identifying femininity with immaturity, but this ignored Winkler's force and intellect. There was a profound visible disparity between her *performance* – variously a disturbed adolescent, a college rebel, and Pippi Longstocking – and her *physical self*. There were superficial similarities, for example, to Rebecca Hall's Hamlet (Soho Theatre Company 1997) in a production aimed at London teenagers that addressed questions of alienation and self-harm among adolescent girls (Hall yelled the soliloquies as if confiding in her pals at a disco) but Winkler's Hamlet was multi-dimensional: lost child and experienced woman, past and present overlaid. In action she created a restless, ebullient figure of 'childlike radiance', yet photographs showed her mature features and haunted eyes. She created a post-Brechtian collage of clashing but truthful emotional moments: 'Not male, not female, not boyish, . . . simply a person, who happens to be an actress', said *Le Pais*, and *Le Monde* added: 'A child, neither girl nor boy.'[7] But to be a child in this smug Denmark was to be the one person observing life as an outsider – that is, *truthfully* – 'cold reality seen through the eyes of a child'. Winkler made *Hamlet* about individuation, the forging of a consciousness over three hours and a lifetime.

Her encounter with Polonius was uniquely pointed. He was played by Ulrich Wildgrüber, who had been Zadek's Hamlet in 1977 in an iconoclastic but outrageously pre-feminist production where Gertrude was half-naked with painted breasts, Ophelia was a sex-toy, and women played Claudius' parasites (Polonius, Rosencrantz, Guildenstern).

Now Wildgrüber's fat, scant of breath, myopic and flustered Polonius was the male Hamlet tradition gone rotten – 'a large pompous duck flapping his wings inconsequentially, darting his beady eyes left and right to emphasise his regurgitation of chewed-over nostrums and common-places'.[8] He gabbled and interrupted himself, frustrated by his inability to find the *mot juste*, distracted by his own false gestures. He shrieked when crossed. Written into the man's body was 'disastrous uncertainty' (Koberg), the loss of the postwar generation's promise. (Wildgrüber died during the run.) Twenty years on, Hamlet was in Claudius' pay, but Winkler and Katherina Blum had not lapsed – 'The face is unaffected, betrays no age'[9] – and the radical spirit – greasy-haired and dishevelled, laughing at third-hand 'words, words, words' – was younger than ever.

So Angela Winkler's Hamlet negotiated her identity in relation to gross middle-aged men: Rosencrantz and Guildenstern were faded chorus boys dancing to 'Singing in the Rain' and the Players were bored, camp exhibitionists whose show featured onstage sex and a murderer who spewed on his audience. Their Voice Beautiful star ruined the Hecuba speech, but Hamlet's heartfelt version crystallised a young person's first discovery that art might transfigure pain. In 'O what a rogue and peasant slave am I' Winkler used her rich natural voice for the first time. The actor acts out true 'dreams', she stressed, and raking the fully-lit auditorium with her eyes, 'addressing flaming words clearly and directly to the public'[10], she challenged them to consider their relationship to this play: what was Hecuba to *them*? Then she was back in infancy, scuffing the floor and confiding what she'd heard about Theatre – that it touches the guilty. . . . She ran out. It was the first of two intervals, and before each break Hamlet confronted the audience of this expensive 'festival production'. Faced with Elsinore's bland meritocracy, German critics admitted 'these are people like you and I, petty plotters, inconspicuous and interchangeable'.[11] When Winkler rushed back, she was murmuring 'To be or not to be'. She spoke the soliloquies directly but drifted into introspection; her unprotected face was 'an open book'.[12] With the last lines ('. . . lose the name of action,') Hamlet understood the appalling complexity of existence for the first time and lapsed into shocked isolation.

For the psychologist Nancy Chodorow, the 'masculine sense of self' is separate, the 'feminine sense of self remains connected to others in the world'.[13] Hamlet's struggle for individuation occupied both grounds. Noticing Ophelia, Winkler smiled at their comic disparateness – Ophelia was a prim 1950s *debutante* clutching a handbag, Hamlet now resembled a drowned rat – but identified a potential ally. In all productions where an actress plays Hamlet, the clashes with Ophelia and Gertrude gain importance; even if there has been a suspension of disbelief, it now becomes impossible to ignore the leading artist's gender. The Nunnery and Closet scenes comment on choice and female identity in a patriarchal world. All Hamlets are surrounded by models of masculinity, from the Ghost to Fortinbras, Laertes, Horatio and even Claudius, but this Hamlet's psyche incorporated fragments of Ophelia and Gertrude too. Annet Renneberg's Ophelia, trapped in a time-warp of domestic conformity, shocked by Hamlet's slovenly disrespect, returned the gifts robotically and horrified Hamlet, who had never before experienced rejection, only false grins. Winkler ripped the letters to pieces and hurled the scraps in Ophelia's face; all Hamlet's pain erupted – '*Dummkopf!!*' – and was misdirected at her: Hamlet emptied Ophelia's handbag on the floor and drew a knife on her in a scene of great physical violence, but at the end the young people's shared tragedy was shocking. Both actresses crawled on the floor as Ophelia spoke her soliloquy, 'Blasted with ecstasy', and Hamlet scrabbled wretchedly for the letters. Not only did the politicians ignore Ophelia's pain, they actually planned Hamlet's removal with Winkler at their feet: a child was not worth lying to, nor a woman. Hamlet was totally alienated, even from the Self ('Now I am alone!'), but as she gathered the last letters Winkler spoke 'Speak the speech . . .' half to herself: 'Suit the action to the word . . . obey the modesty of nature.' Can art offer answers? The decadent play-within-the-play was a travesty of Shakespeare, but alongside it Angela Winkler's reanimated *travesti*, the tradition of female-to-male cross-dressing, presenting it as an exploration of identity, not the jaded replication of roles.

The Prayer scene focused the production's dialectic onto Winkler's Hamlet and Sadler's King. Hamlet writhed as she imagined Claudius' torment, he mocked his own glib prayers; it was disturbing to register Hamlet's naivety against his cynical intimacy with corruption. A total pragmatist, he used whatever means a situation required – kindness, diplomacy, religious mantras, murder – while Gertrude inhabited a fantasy world. Eve Mattes was Zadek's Queen in 1977; two decades later she showed her still clinging to the sensual illusion that luxury meant fulfilment. Frustrated, unable to articulate anything but adoration for the dead and hatred for the living, Hamlet beat and dragged her across the floor; but when the Ghost entered, Gertrude put on 1940s dance music and swayed to it, and the dead man joined her, escaping into nostalgia too. Mother and child sat close in exhausted silence, and Winkler became gentler. What followed was unexpected. Claudius invaded the bedroom,

Hamlet hid under the bed, the pain of psychological separation unresolved; but s/he re-emerged to confront the King, and grew up. Claudius sank on the mattress, convinced life was a sty where only violence worked ('No-one is monstrous. Everyone is wretched. They are all fatalists' [*Le Monde*]) but Angela Winkler stepped in front of the stage curtain in a beret and leather jacket, an image of the Baader-Meinhof era. Costumes had subtly taken Winkler from her 1940s childhood to the 70s and her own identification with the cinema of conscience. 'What is a man/If his chief good and marker of his time/Be but to sleep and feed?': surveying the audience on their little patch of EU ground, Hamlet transcended the immediate moment for the first time, and committed to action.

William Hazlitt wrote, 'It is we who are Hamlet.' Women who take the role pose recurrent questions. Is Hamlet a 'universal' figure whose dilemmas everyone shares, male or female? Is Hamlet a 'feminine' character whose words invite a woman's voice? What is the relationship between Shakespeare's all-male theatre and the conventions that have succeeded it? How may the sexual and state politics of an English Renaissance play relate to the time and place of its re-enactment? *Hamlet 2000* for example was typical of its period in its inventive treatment of Ophelia and the fact that in madness – here signified by the loss of one glove, shocking in this coded world – she became a second Hamlet. Winkler shaped the production even in her absence: she unleashed energy. Ophelia's hair went awry, she played off the kitchen chair like Winkler, stalked Gertrude, and when Claudius shook her she shook him back. But unlike Hamlet she empathised with Gertrude, wept for her, stared inside the older woman's handbag and saw nightmares there. Laertes blamed his sister for his shame, hitting her viciously till she let out frightening birdlike cries. She ripped her flowers and scattered them as Hamlet had the letters. Then Gertrude described Ophelia's death *to the audience*, beginning her own awkward journey in Winkler's footsteps, from female Sign to female Subject.[14]

The graveyard scene laid social corruption bare. Hamlet and Horatio stood on the roof of the steel container while down below gravedigger-clowns in masked fumigation suits waded through mountains of rubbish and found human remains. Some read this as a scene of ecological disaster, a mass exhumation after ethnic cleansing, or the excavation of Germany's secrets.[15] Winkler covered her mouth against the stench and descended, forcing Horatio – the increasingly terrified Intellectual – to follow the woman's lead. The rest tried to deny reality, so perversely this became the only spectacular scene: the container opened, revealing a shrine and the royal party in Victorian mourning. Ophelia's coffin was metal; she was toxic. The clowns robbed graves and men played tug-of-war with her corpse. Laertes and Hamlet collapsed, victims who had forgotten their real enemies.

Winkler's Prince always retained something of the child – Rosencrantz and Guildenstern had to die because they broke the rules – but the play's final movement began with a farcical *anagnorisis*: when Osric entered he was Polonius in a long blond wig, one last degenerate recycling of 'Hamlet 1977'. The 'fall of a sparrow' speech was calm and happy; Hamlet could see through masks now, yet was not tainted. Winkler embraced Laertes. To quote Heilig, she made Hamlet 'addicted to life', a feeling intelligence who 'hangs on to life by every fibre of the senses. . . The world has disappointed Hamlet beyond measure, more than the heart can bear' but 'the heart remains the most reliable, the only interlocutor'.[16] In a tatty jumper, Winkler fought the duel like a talented novice with infectious humour. *Hamlet* is theatre's greatest meditation on death, and Zadek's production opposed four perspectives. Gertrude drank the poison as an instinctive act of rebellion. Laertes died bitterly. Claudius, the absolute materialist, studied a tiny fatal scratch on his forearm, chuckling at its absurdity. Only Hamlet, though regretful, accepted death. Winkler arranged herself carefully on her kitchen chair, there was a comic interruption when Osric announced Fortinbras, and suddenly mid-sentence Hamlet was dead. Whatever answers to 'The Questions' s/he had learnt, they were not for spectators: 'The rest is silence.' To drums, Fortinbras entered in a greatcoat and helmet. It was Ophelia. But Ophelia turned hectoring tyrant – Zadek short-circuited any feminist reading or sense of collectivity. The humanity of Angela Winkler's Hamlet was unique.

Reviewers across Europe were lyrical in their attempt to define Winkler's achievement. Gerhard Stadelmaier argued that the twentieth century's Hamlets had stood for partial visions – the intellectual, the Oedipal, the existential – but 'now this century is almost ended' so on this emptied millennial stage Winkler's Prince 'for the first time bears the memories of not just one sector, but of the whole world'. Hamlet's androgyny meant amplitude, and for Michael Billington 'What Winkler brings out – in a way that no man I have ever seen quite has – is Hamlet's enormous capacity for love, a capacity that is constantly baffled and frustrated.'[17] Stadelmaier honoured her 'beautiful seriousness': 'Hamlet's death is a miracle, a smile in sleep. . . [Winkler] burns out like a holy candle – the child's dream was to create beauty and reason in a mad and ugly world . . . The attempt failed . . . It was nevertheless a wonderful children's game.'[18] Roland Koberg praised Winkler for reinventing the heroic: 'One wants to live in the country from which Angela Winkler comes.'

In one sense that country has been densely populated. Amongst many others Hamlet has been played by Judith Anderson, Sarah Bernhardt, Charlotte Cushman, Alla Demidova, Nuria Espert, Olwen Fouere, Fatma Girik, Clare Howard, Elizabeth Inchbald, Mme. Judith, Bertha Kalisch, Eva Le Gallienne, Siobahn McKenna, Asta Nielsen, Nance O'Neil, Giacinta Pezzana, Anna Maria Quinn, Julianna Ramaker, Sarah Siddons, Frances de la Tour, Diane Venora, Angela Winkler, Margarita Xirgu, Clara Ziegler.[19] Over the past century and a half, Hamlet has been played by women in Britain, the USA, Australia, Eire, Russia, France, Italy, Japan, Germany, Spain, Sweden, Denmark, Poland, Finland, Mexico and elsewhere. The list could be expanded to include the names of at least two hundred professional actresses but would still be incomplete, and out of date within months. Some, like Bernhardt, essayed it because Hamlet is Everest, the part male actors traditionally *must* play, and these women declined to be excluded. Some had specific professional, personal or political agendas while others, like Winkler, were cast by male directors. Many appeared in low-status fringe or provincial theatres, others on the most distinguished stages in the world; some caused little stir because theatrical cross-dressing was at that time commonplace, others were denounced. In the 1950s the English theatre historians Mander and Mitcheson categorised female Hamlets alongside children and trained dogs, but in Germany, Turkey and Canada women played Hamlet in full-length films; many movies told of fictional actresses who long for the role; and the female Hamlet surfaced in novels and plays. What might playing Hamlet have meant to an actress and her public in Regency Dublin, Victorian London, Berlin in the 1920s, or Manhattan at the height of the Women's Movement? It was sometimes an act of transgression and it always involved empowerment of a kind. This book tries to tell some of those stories.

Hamlet 2000 raised questions of authorship in the relation between male director and female performer; it was not untypical that Zadek theorised the production while Winkler declined to: 'How do I work? I read, I read, I read. Always read. Then when I'm on stage I do it. What do I do? I don't know but I do it.'[20] She and Zadek made *Hamlet* a collective biography of her generation – a legacy of guilt, the

battle between feeling, conviction and complacency, the dream of reinventing identity through a unification of extremes. And she appropriated
the role: though postwar German theatre has been director-dominated,
'the new Zadek', as one critic said, was actually the 'new Winkler'. The
female Hamlet puts the actress centre-stage. Theatre history has often
been placed in a political and social vacuum; contemporary performance
is often discussed in isolation from the traditions that shaped it or against
which it rebels; drama, film, fiction and the visual arts are usually listed as
unrelated phenomena, and the gulf between High Art and popular entertainment sometimes seems unbridgeable. With all due wariness, this book
is a small attempt to cross boundaries. I hope that some of the radically
shifting meanings of the figure of the female Hamlet will emerge through
a study of cultural practices. Just as Winkler's androgynous Hamlet embodied a wealth of contradictory experiences, her act of gender–redefinition
suggested – for individuals and the body politic – the possibility of change.
Despite the charge in Britain that it equated femininity with immaturity,
on the Continent her conversation between the Actress, Hamlet and the
Child was read as a study of active innocence, and growth; she put herself,
as Cixous had written, 'into the text' and 'into history'. And it is important
to stress that 'Hamlet's gender' has intrigued us for centuries.

II

Representation: 'The woman will be out'

His Hamlet was always very much the same: rather slight of figure, with a fine
head, long and oval, thick dark hair, swept forward over delicately arched brows;
a slender Grecian nose; a straight sensitive mouth . . .[21]

In the early 1830s Eugène Delacroix created a number of lithographs
inspired by *Hamlet* and in 1835 he painted a startling vision of Hamlet
in the grave, which by borrowing Resurrection iconography offered
Hamlet as a secular Christ. Louise Colet wrote a verse eulogy of 'the
Hamlet Shakespeare dreamed of', but the Academy rejected the painting.
Delacroix created a new version in 1839 and in 1843 took his vision of
Hamlet to the general public by publishing a set of thirteen old
and new lithographs, to which he later added three more.[22] 'They had
no success', Delacroix wrote, 'It's no use', the French would never be
'partisans of Shakespeare'; but after his death they were republished
for the 1864 Shakespeare Tercentenary and worked their way into the

Figure 2   Eugène Delacroix, 'Hamlet and Horatio at the Grave', 1839, oils
(Louvre Museum, Photo © RMN).

collective imagination.[23] George Sand said, 'No one has framed in a more
poetic light or posed in an attitude more real, that hero of suffering,
indignation, doubt, and irony.'[24] Delacroix's images haunted French
writers, partly via Baudelaire, who decorated his apartment with them
and was obsessed by that 'delicate, pallid Hamlet' – 'soft and slightly
hesitant, with an almost expressionless eye'. Here was the 'exquisite'
ideal, 'the fusion of drama and dream'.[25] Delacroix's imagery registers

to this day. It is intriguing, then, that the model for many of the illustrations was his friend Marguerite Pierret. The iconic Hamlet most of us have inherited from the Late Romantics actually was a woman (see Figure 2).

In the 1839 painting Hamlet's femininity is unmistakable: a feather in the bonnet stands in for long windswept hair and as Hamlet's delicate fingers recoil from the skull and tug at his cloak, they expose a slender leg and garter-like trunk hose. The right hand is cradled on the belly almost as if s/he were pregnant. Marguerite Pierret (*née* Heydinger) began in Delacroix's letters and journals as a true-life Ophelia. She was pregnant when her lover Charles Pierret (Delacroix's close companion) lost his father. He shied from marrying her and Delacroix described the situation as a tormented variation on *Hamlet*, 'engraved in your mind's eye': 'That bed, those lights, that midnight silence by your father's corpse' . . . Pierret must marry 'the poor girl, whom I pity' . . . 'It's all driving him crazy. Loneliness into the bargain'.[26] In due course Marguerite became Delacroix's Hamlet and like modern theatre directors he paralleled the Prince and Ophelia, though he gave Hamlet Ophelia's vulnerability rather than, like Peter Zadek, bequeathing Ophelia Hamlet's anger. Delacroix made their eroticised deaths closely similar, both lying bodies twisted as in an embrace, their faces sculpted masks half turned to the ground, their chests half bared.

Though capable of sternness, Delacroix's Hamlet is usually a fragile dreamer, a stranger in a late-medieval world of brazen muscularity and violence. All the other men, even Horatio, might have burst from Raphael canvases. Elsewhere Delacroix expressed the 'exotic' genius of Shakespeare through orientalism (e.g. *Othello*, *Antony and Cleopatra*), ecstatic turmoil and even horror (*Macbeth*), but Hamlet was all grace and, especially in the 1830s pictures, gazelle-like delicacy. Only on seeing the Ghost does Hamlet burst into uncontainable life as the men strain to stop him embracing the Sublime, for this *gamine* creature with doe eyes is the Romantic artist's surrogate, the ideal union, to quote Delacroix on Chopin, of 'strength of mind and frailty of body'. (Coleridge argued that 'a great mind must be androgynous' and later Tennyson would write of the androgyny of the Artist, and of Christ.[27])

As well as sustaining the affinity with Ophelia, Delacroix created a tactile bond between Hamlet and Gertrude, who cling together like Graces in a common anguish. However he also presented Hamlet's inconsistencies through shifts in gender: in 1843 he reworked the 1839 Graveyard painting as a lithograph and transformed Hamlet into a bearded

Figure 3   Eugène Delacroix, 'Hamlet Reading', pencil drawing (Musée Bonnat).

saturnine hero, the calves muscular, the pose dynamic, even the feather masculinised into a kind of cock's comb. Several 1843 designs shared these qualities, so that across the whole sequence Hamlet became a malleable body – childlike or athletic, vulnerable, aggressive or wild from frame to frame – but two of his very last reasserted femininity. A pencil treatment of Hamlet reading preserves the process of creating androgyny: (see Figure 3, the print Delacroix slightly restyled his female model's hair and used light to slim the face and create radiance. He hid the shape of her hips and legs with a bunched cloak. Conversely, however, he used the cloak in the Recorders scene to *heighten* femininity, surreptitiously suggesting a bustle – a trick he used for the fight in the grave (1843) to hint at a sexual violence where the female force is stronger. In an essay, 'Realism and Idealism', Delacroix stressed that life models were important but were 'a slave to the imagination'. Composition involved the 'liaison' of observation, memory and fancy because art like thought 'idealises and selects'. Thus he created a double androgyny in *Hamlet* – some pictures featured the idealised figure, the spiritual/physical fusion ('in apprehension how like an angel') of Female and Male, while the series overall made Hamlet a complicated montage of feminine and masculine impulses – the heterogeneous body.

Along with an element of self-portraiture – Delacroix also painted himself as Hamlet, at a time when he was preoccupied with his own physical frailty – his androgynous Prince drew on several points of inspiration. Firstly he was influenced by the Kembles, London's leading theatre dynasty – by the grace of Charles Kemble's Hamlet (whom he drew spying from behind a lady's fan) and by Sir Thomas Lawrence's portraits of the family: 'Nobody', said Delacroix, 'has ever made eyes, especially women's eyes, as Lawrence does, and those mouths, partly open and perfect in their charm.'[28] Kemble's sister Sarah Siddons was the first established actress to play Hamlet. There were also affinities between Delacroix's *Hamlet* and the views of several literary women: Mme de Staël, one of the first French critics to see it as a philosophical text, anticipated his vision of a sensitive spirit misplaced in the world of matter and corruption, and there was a strong connection with George Sand (Aurore Dudevant), who asked why Shakespeare invites every man and woman to identify with Hamlet: we 'vibrate around him like so many echoes of his mysterious complaint'.[29] She believed his pain – 'that drying up within you of all the springs of life, love, trust and kindness' – is universal and paradoxical: 'It is that very love of truth and justice that condemns you to become stupid or mean; and not being able to be one or the other, you feel yourself going mad.' The heroine of her novel *Lelia* has been called a female Hamlet, and Sand adapted *As You Like It* for the Paris stage, exploring themes of cross-dressing and self-redefinition that made her own life scandalous.[30]

Sand had begun to appear in men's clothes around 1830, provoking doubts even in Bohemian circles, and explained cross-dressing as a bridge between psychological polarities: 'Look upon me as being at the same time . . . a brother, in order to render you the services which you might expect from a man, [and] a sister, so as to listen to and understand the delicate feelings of your heart.'[31] She points to the mid-century connection between the androgynous image and the emergence on most radical agendas of women's rights:

I intend to possess, now and ever, the full and proud independence which you men believe you have alone the right to enjoy. . . Therefore consider me as a man or as a woman, as you please . . . I am a *being*.[32]

As women asserted the right to participate in all aspects of intellectual life, theatre was a public part of this process. In 1867 Mme Judith played Hamlet and established a Parisian tradition that continued well into the twentieth century. In Britain the practice was almost a century older, but was often attacked. Delacroix and Winkler were in fact unusual in making the androgynous Hamlet an ideal synthesis of female and male; others found the concept difficult and when many women donned his mantle – or a man argued for Hamlet's 'femininity' – there was often a sense that dominant sureties were threatened. For the female Hamlet lays claim to the central text of Western theatre, and often exposes prejudices embedded in language itself:

Zadek and Winkler make no discernible effort to emphasise the so-called 'feminine' characteristics of Hamlet. Winkler's Hamlet is the most sensitive, the most vulnerable character at the Danish Court but *this Hamlet is neither weak nor indecisive*.[33]

III

Definition I: 1603–4 – 'Unmanly grief'

The self is gender-amorphous, holding within itself the potential for many different and changing gender and sexual identities. (Philip Auslander, 1997[34])

On one level *Hamlet* is a map of gender, from the Ghost – the armoured emblem of patriarchy Hamlet can never match – to Ophelia, the

virginal sacrifice to father, brother, lover and King. Further, the presence
of the Player Queen, a transvestite male actor, reminds us that Ophelia
and Gertrude too are only fictional *presentations* of the Female on a
single-sex stage from which women were banned. This self-consciousness
throws performance conventions and notions of gender into question,
more thoroughly than in Shakespeare's other tragedies (until Cleopatra
derides the squeaking boy who plays her) and the main focus of confusion is 'sweet', 'gentle', 'piteous' Hamlet himself. He denounces women
as performers – 'ambling', 'lisping', disguised as 'Niobe, all tears' – but
sees himself as woman-like in his grief and his failure to achieve revenge.
He self-diagnoses 'my weakness and my melancholy', and melancholia,
said Burton's *Anatomy of Melancholy*, 'turns a man into a woman'.[35]

Burton referred to Dürer's portrait of Melancholia (1514) – 'a sad
woman leaning on her arm with fixed looks' and 'neglected habit' –
and saw 'my mistress Melancholy' as an effeminising condition ('soft,
sottish or half-mad') which attacked intellectual men 'of a deep reach,
excellent apprehension'.[36] Thomas Nashe (1594) had called melancholy
'the mother of dreams' and 'terrors' and Claudius says Hamlet's 'melancholy sits on brood' hatching 'danger'.[37] Juliana Schiesari has argued that
Renaissance Melancholy represented 'the "feminine" within man'.[38]
Hamlet damns his own eloquence as womanly, disgusted 'that I, the
son of a dear father murdered. . . /Must like a whore unpack my heart
with words/And fall a-cursing like a very drab.' He dismisses his intuition
before the duel as 'such a kind of gain-giving as perhaps would trouble a
woman' and speaks of himself as a battleground contested by female
forces – 'my dear soul' ('mistress of her choice') versus Fortune (playing
on blood and judgement like a pipe 'to sound what stop she please').[39]
Gertrude clings to a positive faith in her son's femininity, 'As patient as
the female dove',[40] but the satyr Claudius despises his 'unmanly grief'
(and Norway's 'impotent' King) so when Hamlet has no weapons but
words he undermines Claudius with sexual sarcasm: 'Farewell dear
mother.' Hamlet's struggle against his femininity is duplicated in
Laertes, who is ashamed of his tears – 'The woman will be out'[41] – and
their ranting over Ophelia's body shows them both overlaying natural
grief with a berserk male persona. (Burton's *Anatomy* condemned mour-
ners' 'unmanly wailing'.)[42] Though much theatrical culture has suggested
that 'Men and women were fundamentally different species, in habits
of thought, feeling and action separated by a deep and unbridgeable
divide',[43] *Hamlet* disproves Hamlet's belief that male identity depends
on Herculean violence. The rage he directs at the women is inseparable

from his loathing of the woman in himself, yet what he hates is precisely what made *Hamlet* enduring.

Notions of gender are culturally constructed. Cross-dressing exposes this, but Shakespeare's play both challenged and reinforced stereotyping. Strangely, the earliest surviving text of *Hamlet*, the so-called 'bad' Quarto of 1603, gave more scope to the woman's voice than the authorised Second Quarto (1604) and Folio (1623) which make fundamental cuts to Gertrude: in the Q1 Closet scene she states, 'I never knew of this most horrid murder' and proves it by allying herself with her son and Horatio, plotting against Claudius, and inheriting Hamlet's role of actor/observer:

> Then I perceive there's treason in his looks
> That seem to sugar o'er his villainy:
> But I will sooth and please him for a time,
> For murderous minds are always jealous.[44]

Q2 removes this thread, reducing her to an enigma, unable to demonstrate loyalty, innocence, agency or insight: Shakespeare forced audiences to see her through Hamlet's tormented eyes. In 1603 she witnessed the confrontation when Claudius sends Hamlet to England, and Ophelia had to listen while her father read out Hamlet's love letters. In both these public scenes the women were silent, but that dramatically registered their helplessness and in fact though the language in Q1's pirated text is obviously unreliable, Ophelia's speeches here have an animation that she later loses. In Q1 her first words after seeing Hamlet's distraction are:

> Oh my dear father, such a change in nature,
> So great an alteration in a prince,
> So pitiful to him, fearful to me,
> A maiden's eye ne'er looked on . . .
> Oh young prince Hamlet, the only flower of Denmark,
> He is bereft of all the wealth he had,
> The jewel that adorn'd his features most,
> Is filched and stol'n away, his wit's bereft him [.][45]

In Q2 this becomes, 'Oh my lord, my lord, I have been so affrighted!' (II.i) And madness gave her power: Ophelia dominated her Q1 mad scenes through the music, singing in both scenes and playing the lute in the first. Shockingly she sang 'Let in a maid who out a maid/Never departed more' to her brother. Though many actresses have intuitively restored some of these lost qualities, Shakespeare left them little to work on; after 1603 the two women were effectively reduced to the body, to objectified figures unable to articulate ethical understanding or even their own distress. Hamlet meanwhile became far more reflective, more melancholic; since his 'feminisation' was accompanied by the simplification of the women, there would be a natural justice centuries later when Delacroix incorporated the woman's body into Hamlet and the actresses who played him reintroduced female consciousness to the play. Thus Mercedes Salvador and Rafael Portillo have argued that in Spain – where women did perform in the Golden Age – several leading actresses have played Hamlet out of frustration with Shakespeare's gender balance (the 'female roles were not important enough').[46]

IV

Definition II: 1881–2000 – 'Within man's discourse'

In 1989 the director Richard Eyre, who was fascinated by the affinity between Hamlet and Dürer's 'androgynous' Melancholia, said:

I've come more and more to see the play as a war between the female, the feminine, within a man and the masculine within a man; and the story is effectively how you drive out the woman from a man. And in order to deal with the world which he occupies, the world of the Court, the exclusively male-dominated world where military values and the values of *realpolitik* are held as absolutes, he has to drive out the woman in him . . . And I think that's the tragedy.[47]

Hamlet's 'femininity' has shifted in and out of favour. When Garrick played him in the eighteenth century he was faulted for demeaning 'the dignity, solemnity, and manhood of the character, by giving a kind of feminine sorrow to it'; but Edmund Kean, the Romantics' Hamlet, was admired for 'a cry of nature so exquisite that it could only be compared to the stifled sob of a fainting woman'.[48] In 1866 the *Atlantic Monthly* praised Edwin Booth's genius as feminine, and therefore peculiarly suited to Hamlet – 'that lithe and sinuous figure, elegant in the solemn garb of sables . . . the pallor of his face and hands, the darkness of his hair, those eyes that can be so melancholy-sweet, yet ever look beyond and deeper than the things around him'.[49] But it was therefore self-evident that he could not play Othello, Macbeth or Coriolanus properly: they are 'essentially masculine, and we connect their ideals with the stately figure, the deep chest-utterance, the slow, enduring majesty of men.' Booth explained, 'I have always endeavoured to make prominent the femininity of Hamlet's character . . . I doubt if ever a robust and masculine treatment of the character will be accepted so generally as the more womanly and refined interpretation. I know that frequently I fall into effeminacy, but we can't always hit the proper key-note.'[50] The spectre of 'effeminacy' distressed many nineteenth-century commentators, including French and German critics cited in Edward P. Vining's book *The Mystery of Hamlet* (Philadelphia 1881). Courdaveaux: Hamlet is 'faint-hearted' and eaten by 'effeminacy'. Rohtbach: 'He is a weakling. When he says, "Frailty, thy name is woman," he might have used his own name.'[51] Hazlitt – who defined 'effeminacy of character' as the 'prevalence of sensibility over will', marked by 'self-love' and 'want of energy' – called Hamlet 'as little of the hero as a man can well be'.[52] Edward Vining, who was a railroad systems expert, pushed the attitude to an extreme. His study of *Hamlet*, rather outside his field, was subtitled *An Attempt to Solve an Old Problem*, which was precisely that 'Hamlet lacks the energy, the conscious strength, the readiness for action that inhere in the perfect manly character.' In which case, 'how comes it that humanity still admires him?'[53] His answer was that Hamlet is a princess in disguise.

She has been secretly raised as a boy for reasons of state and is trapped in that fiction. 'Smile with disdain or laugh in ridicule if to you it seem good', Vining wrote, but 'the new may still be true.'[54] The play was packed with clues. Why does the Ghost never call Hamlet 'My son'? Why can he out-fence Laertes but is 'instantly overcome' in a brawl? If thirty, why is he called 'young Hamlet'? – 'Is not Hamlet's extreme maturity of mind, combined with his youthfulness of appearance . . . strong proof that here was a woman masquerading in a manly part? A very plain-looking woman will pass for a very handsome man, when suitably attired; and the natural brightness and freshness of her complexion, combined with absence of beard, will give her a boyish appearance.' Hamlet, he said, is tearful, impulsive, disgusted by drink, feels the cold, shudders at the thought of death, faints, is sensitive to smells, and indulges in 'wordy warfare' – all 'traits more characteristic of the gentler sex'.[55] Edward Vining was bewildered by Hamlet's sensibility: 'When God created man in his own image, male and female created he them', and there must be no overlapping. His biblical logic might have suggested that actually God's own image is androgynous, but the ideal Vining sought in Shakespeare was the opposite of Delacroix's. He was disturbed because even in a world of binary stability, literature – where he sought the exemplary, not confusion – let deviants in. Lady Macbeth was monstrously masculine and Hamlet seemed her weird antitype, a 'fundamentally feminine' man. Two aspects particularly distressed him. Firstly no man 'possessing any real nobility of character' could so insult a lady; but Viola and Rosalind – both cross-dressed – chide Olivia and Phoebe in terms that resemble Hamlet's attacks on Ophelia and the Queen. Did not Hamlet's words similarly suggest 'the bitterness of one woman against the feelings of another', not 'the half compassion, "more in sorrow than in anger", with which a man regards a feminine weakness'? *Ergo*, Hamlet is a woman too. The second problem was Horatio, held by Hamlet 'in my heart of heart' with 'a warmth of fondness and admiration far greater than is natural between friends of the same sex'. Lesbian actresses had already played Hamlet, and though the term 'homosexual' was not yet current, Wilde would soon suggest the sonnets were inspired by Shakespeare's love for a boy player. By listing Hamlet's crimes against masculinity, labelling them 'feminine weakness' and then transferring them to a masquerading lady, Vining exorcised the spectre of inversion. Passive qualities contemptible in a Victorian man became delightful in a tragic heroine, and 'the pangs of disprised love' now indicated Hamlet's unspoken but *normal* longing for Horatio.[56]

Thus Vining saved Hamlet's reputation. 'Am I a coward?' – no, simply 'a woman incapable of accomplishing the revenge . . . imposed upon her', wracked by 'a hopeless love that she might never reveal, tortured by jealousy, sorely sensitive to all a woman's natural faults, and incensed . . . at the sacrifice of personal purity made by her mother.' 'Shrinking from the mortal struggle with the King, fearing bloodshed, viewing the possibility of her own death with a shuddering horror', she sought 'some escape, some easier method of fulfilling her duty.'[57] And Vining was polite: 'No slur is meant in saying that this . . . is what we should expect from a gently-nurtured woman.' However his essentialism allowed no alternative to Victorian myths of industrious masculinity. Hamlet is 'plump', 'dainty' and 'hysterical' – 'Are not these characteristics thoroughly feminine?'[58] The fact that several actresses were currently playing the part made his theory more viable. So did the fact that he *was* responding to currents in Shakespeare's text. As he noted, Hamlet believes his 'disposition to extend deliberation in words is womanish', and Vining took seriously the differences between the First Quarto and subsequent texts. He traced the shift from Q1's avenger to a more melancholic and reflective figure – 'the gradual evolution of the feminine element' – until making the dizzying claim that obviously it 'occurred to the dramatist that so might a woman act and feel, if educated from infancy to play a prince's part.' Reclassifying Hamlet as female acquitted the character (and the empathising reader) from charges of abnormality or arrested development.

'Aside from the absurdity of the writer's theory', Edwin Booth recommended *The Mystery of Hamlet* to the critic William Winter: 'It is very ingenious.' 'I agree with much that he urges in support of it . . . You must see the book – it will amuse & I think it will interest you too.'[59] In fact it did the opposite; Winter went on to wage a campaign against actresses who dared play Hamlet, whom he *did* see as an ideal masculine force – 'a man of originally sweet, gentle, affectionate nature, and in no way feminine'. Female Hamlets, he claimed, were all 'unpleasingly mannish' or 'experimental, confused, indefinite and insignificant. It was a bad day for "the glass of fashion" when some misguided essayists began to call him "feminine" and the ladies heard of it.' Winter's misogynist position was that women neither should nor could play Hamlet, who is 'supereminently distinguished by a characteristic rarely, if ever, distinguished in women: namely, that of "thinking too precisely on the event" '.[60] What these late nineteenth-century controversies half-concealed was a confused response to the rise of women's rights and education. In different ways Vining and Winter both projected current male anxieties onto Shakespeare. And yet the importance of the gendered psychological struggle in *Hamlet*, the men's attempt to deny their femininity, explains why Vining's book did not quite vanish. Joyce discussed it in *Ulysses*, as did the Freudian Ernest Jones in *Hamlet and Oedipus*, and in 1920 the great actress Asta Nielsen based a film on it.[61] It prompted Jones to praise *Hamlet*'s analysis of the 'strikingly tender feminine side' of men with an 'abnormal' attachment to the mother.[62] In *The Interpretation of Dreams* Freud defined Hamlet as an hysteric – a disorder, he said, involving bisexual symptoms.[63] Jones equated 'femininity' with hysteria and dependency but also quoted Frank Harris: 'Whenever we get under the skin, it is Shakespeare's femininity that startles us.'[64] Could androgyny, as Delacroix had indicated, be linked to genius? Edward Vining merely took the discomfort with Hamlet's lack of overt masculinity to an extreme, and in the process showed why actresses have found the role magnetic – not simply in order to play feminine qualities, however, but to lay claim to the supposedly male ones. Bernhardt played Hamlet, she said, because writers so rarely created female roles exploring intellect: 'This is the secret of my preference. No female character has opened up a field so large for the exploration of sensations and human sorrows as that of Hamlet.'[65]

One legacy of Shakespeare's single-sex theatre was the prioritisation of male experience; the Russian actress Alla Nazimova in 1907 called

Shakespeare's women 'more like types, ideals...either good or bad...and what they are at the beginning of the play that they stay till the curtain falls'.[66] 'Ophelia brought nothing new to me', said Bernhardt. When actresses with strong personalities played Ophelia and Gertrude, the results could be strained: for example the response to Glenda Jackson's angry Ophelia (RSC 1965) was hostile and she left the cast. The critic Penelope Gilliatt said Jackson made Ophelia the play's protagonist and she should play Hamlet; at least two international offers to do so followed, but at that time cross-dressing was substantially seen as a joke and Jackson never did it.[67] But 'It is we who are Hamlet' and, especially at the end of the nineteenth and twentieth centuries, in tune with the Suffrage movement and Second Wave feminism, many actresses did claim the right to be included and wear the language as well as the cloak; as several have said, 'I wanted to speak those words.' In 1992 Sue Parrish directed an all-female *Hamlet* as an act of historical and political reclamation: 'Everyone in the world', she argued, 'knows Hamlet. Women have no equivalent character. The famous...quotation "It is we who are Hamlet" makes me think: hang on, we women don't get a go at doing this creature.' 'There are two roles for women', she said, 'Ophelia is iconised as the Madonna and Gertrude is demonised as the Whore.' Parrish wished to explore the nature of Hamlet's subjectivity and specifically the coexistence of femininity and masculinity in 'his inner life': 'It is this "femininity" which has drawn many actresses, from the nineteenth century onwards, to play Hamlet.'[68] Margery Garber's *Vested Interests: Cross-dressing and Cultural Anxiety* appeared the same year and argued that *travesti* is at the heart of the psyche, the act of theatre, and dissent: 'Transvestism was located at the juncture of "class" and "gender"...To transgress against one set of boundaries was to call into question the inviolability of both, and of the social codes by which such categories were policed and maintained.'[69]

However, just as the Victorians argued whether women should be permitted to play Hamlet, there were now feminist debates as to whether they should want to. For some, *Hamlet* was a misogynist text so central to the patriarchal tradition that leading actresses' interest in it was suspect. Erika Munk argued that *travesti* here reinforced the old stereotypes of female hysteria and passivity that can be traced back to Aristotle ('Woman is...more easily moved to tears...more prone to despondency and less hopeful...'). Hélène Cixous wrote in 1975, 'If woman has always functioned "within" the discourse of man...it is time for her to dislocate this "within", to explode it, turn it around and seize it; to make it hers',[70] but for example Teresa Dobson – in *New Theatre Quarterly*, which devoted many essays to these issues in the 1990s – argued that cross-dressing Shakespeare for feminist purposes was 'futile'. Though 'the aim is to give woman voice', the practice accepted the primacy of male canonical texts and defined 'women as mouthpieces rather than articulate beings – as objects rather than subjects'.[71] Contesting the notion of the 'master-piece', Sue-Ellen Case objected that traditionally 'women are called upon to identify with Hamlet, Oedipus, Faust and other male characters imbued with specifically male psychosexual anxieties. The idea that these are "universal" characters represses the gender inscription in the notion of the self.'[72] Does a woman's voice give Hamlet's misogyny spurious authority? Is an actress who plays him colonised? Fiona Shaw played Richard II in 1995 but turned down several offers of Hamlet, feeling excluded from this 'male consciousness', and warned that tragic cross-dressing, the search for 'the natural androgyne' within, can involve actresses' suppression of aspects of themselves rather than personal discovery.[73] Yet in Angela Winkler's case, cross-casting was corrective – she refocused Hamlet's verbal fusillades as precise critiques of Ophelia and Gertrude's self-image and not an assault on 'Woman'. 'She proves that solitude, despair, ethical doubts about revenge and a sense of betrayed love are qualities that transcend gender.'[74]

Once Hamlet was accepted as the greatest role in Western drama, some independent actresses were bound to attempt it, and when they did it became a war zone, because the great 'feminine' protagonist was male property – the role that legitimised the two-dimensionality of the Mother/Whore and Virgin by annexing 'feminine' sensibilities and psychological complexities into a hero. Great acting involves more than immersion in character: it entails understanding of the politics of writing, personality and performance; it is a dialogue between the actor and the role, and it communicates a sense of the play's significance here and now. As we shall see, the *Hamlet* gender debates have been complex and their foundations moved; to quote John Stokes (1994), 'It is precisely because theatrical cross-dressing is always "culture-specific" that it has been historically and geographically so widespread. Furthermore, the recurrence of cross-dressing will always relate, though not always in some easily quantifiable way, not only to the social structure in question, but to theatre's place within it.'[75] The issue of reception is still more pointed. 'Depending on each individual's gender and sexual preference, each spectator will have their own personal response to such a performance', Lizbeth Goodman commented (1998): 'Theatre is a site of desire.'[76] No single theory could encompass all the performances in this book, let alone the novels and films which have built or interrogated the myth of the female Hamlet; yet if there could be one principle at work it would be this, that theatre is the site of paradox and s/he draws us towards its centre. Tragic acting simultaneously demonstrates death's dominance and asserts life; transsexual acting simultaneously presents 'male' and 'female' as opposites *and* denies their separation; to play Hamlet's contradictions and indeed magnify them, as cross-casting does, is to enquire into human diversity and explore the meaning of intellect and agency – areas from which, as Gertrude's opacity and Ophelia's humiliation show, women have so often been excluded and not least by Shakespeare.

In 1995 Leea Klemola, 'one of Finland's most promising actresses', played Hamlet in Helsinki, the first woman to do so in that country since Elli Tompuri in the 1900s.[77] 'Being a woman is itself a restricting role', Klemola said, 'Many women can, I can, recognise a man inside ourselves. . . For a woman, theatre offers very few opportunities to play a human being.' But 'theatre is a game based on roles', she added, so 'it doesn't matter whether you play a part which is older than you, or younger, or the opposite sex. Hamlet was human.' Klemola did not sentimentalise Hamlet – 'His image of himself is unbalanced, he starts to destroy the environment around him. He's a human being, but not a very good one' – and there was one area where she found identification difficult, the hunger for revenge: 'Maybe it's easier for men to think that way.' Yet this very obstacle led her to reassess the meaning of the play: 'I've been thinking that beneath the revenge there's another, deeper, motive and that's a journey towards the mother's love.' *Hamlet* is a journey where, whether in front of a postmodern metal box or in sixteen lithographed tableaux, Hamlet must pass from the Court to the battlements, through Gertrude's bedroom to Ophelia's grave, from speech to violence to silence. Two hundred actresses, and counting, elected to tread this path.[78]

Notes

1. Hélène Cixous, 'The Laugh of the Medusa'. See Kelly Oliver, *French Feminism Reader* (Lanham: Rowman and Littlefield, 2000), p. 257.
2. 1999 Vienna Festival publicity.
3. Premiere: Volkstheater, Vienna, 21 May.
4. *Le Monde* 12 May 1999. The following account is based on performance notes made in Hamburg. Journalists consulted: Barbara Villiger Heilig, *Neue Zürcher Zeitung* (25 May); Gerhard Stadelmaier, *Frankfurter Allgemeine Zeitung* (25 May); Roland Koberg, *Berliner Zeitung* (26 May),

Reinhold Reiterer, *Berliner Morgenpost* (26 May); Lothar Sträter, *Nürnburger Zeitung* (27 May); Gerhard Jörder, *Die Zeit* (27 May); Urs Jenny, *Der Spiegel* (31 May); Stefan Steinberg, *World Socialist Website*, (30 September 1999).
5. Steinberg, *World Socialist Website*.
6. Giles Block 'In Conversation' on Shakespeare's Globe website 1999 discussing his all-male *Antony and Cleopatra*, 1999. For earlier Japanese performances see Takashi Sasayama, JR Mulryne and Margaret Shewring, *Shakespeare on the Japanese Stage* (Cambridge: Cambridge University Press, 1998).
7. 11 and 12 May 1999.
8. Steinberg.
9. *Le Pais*, 11 May 1999.
10. Barbara Villiger Heilig.
11. Lothar Sträter.
12. Barbara Villiger Heilig.
13. Nancy Chodorow, *The Reproduction of Mothering: Psychoanalysis and the Sociology of Gender* (Berkley: University of California Press, 1978), p. 169.
14. Sue-Ellen Case, *Feminism and Theatre* (London and New York: Methuen, 1988), pp. 112–17.
15. *Le Pais*, 11 May 1999.
16. Barbara Villiger Heilig.
17. *Guardian*, 23 August 2000.
18. Gerhard Stadelmaier.
19. Gerda Taranow, *The Bernhardt Hamlet* (New York: Lang, 1996), p. 123.
20. Interviewed, *Le Monde*, 12 May 1999.
21. Helen Phelps Bailey, *Hamlet in France from Voltaire to Laforgue* (Geneva: Librarie Droz, 1964), p. 62.
22. He followed it with three more to create the full series: Hamlet and the Queen in Act 1; Hamlet pursuing the Ghost; Hamlet with the Ghost; Hamlet and Polonius; Hamlet and Ophelia; the Play Scene; Hamlet with the recorders; the Prayer scene; Polonius' death; the discovery of Polonius' body; Hamlet and Gertrude with the portrait of his father; Ophelia's madness; Ophelia's death; Hamlet with the skull; the fight in the grave; and the death of Hamlet. See Catherine Belsey's essay, ' "Was Hamlet a Man or a Woman?": The Prince in the Graveyard, 1800–1920', in Arthur Kinney, ed., *'Hamlet': New Critical Essays* (New York: Routledge, 2002), pp. 134–58. Belsey shows Delacroix's influence by reproducing Viktor Müller's 1868 painting 'Hamlet and Horatio at the Grave of Ophelia': Hamlet has the yearning features and naked, exposed neck of the conventional Ophelia.
23. Eugène Delacroix, *Selected Letters: 1813–1863* (London: Eyre and Spottiswoode, 1971), pp. 301, 375, 210: 'The whole thing cost me five or six hundred francs, and I did not recoup half my expenses. See Arlette Sérulaz and Yves Bonnefoy, *Delacroix & Hamlet* (Paris: Editions de la Réunion des Musées Nationaux, 1993).
24. Bailey, *Hamlet in France*, p. 64.

25. Baudelaire, 'Curiosités Esthétiques', *Oeuvres Complètes* (Paris: Pléiade, 1954), pp. 705–9.
26. Delacroix, *Selected Letters*, pp. 58, 61–2. Later she accepted Delacroix's illegitimate child into their household.
27. See Carolyn G Heilbron, *Towards Androgyny* (London: Gollancz, 1975), For a rebuttal of Heilbron's arguments see Kari Weil, *Androgyny and the Denial of Difference* (Charlottesville: University Press of Virginia, 1992).
28. Delacroix, *Selected Letters*, pp. 55–6. The 1827 Parisian engagement by Charles Kemble's company, with *Hamlet*, triggered an explosion of interest in Shakespeare. Like Berlioz – who married the Ophelia, Hariett Smithson – Delacroix dedicated himself to the challenge of reshaping the *Hamlet* legend for a different medium. Though conservatives condemned Kemble's lapses of taste, the man with Ophelia's fan became almost as defining an image as Hamlet with the skull. For Dumas it suggested intelligence, realism, and 'a certain wholly English grace'. In 1847 Dumas and Paul Meurice incorporated the fan into their adaptation of *Hamlet* and it became emblematic. Even in 1886, though Mounet Sully's stocky, bearded Prince was far from the Delacroix model, he still used the fan and made Hamlet a 'gentle, pensive, languid', sobbing 'sick child'; 'perhaps, indeed, he has emphasised a trifle overmuch the almost feminine gentleness', Jules Lemaître, *Theatrical Impressions* (London: Herbert Jenkins, 1924), p. 231.
29. Bailey, *Hamlet in France*, p. 73.
30. Donna Dickenson, *George Sand: A Brave Man, the Most Womanly Woman* (Leamington Spa: Berg, 1988).
31. *Letters of George Sand*, vol. 1 (London: Ward and Downey, 1886), p. 199. Delacroix's idealised portrait of Sand in male dress (1840) resembled his early Hamlets and shaped her public image. He warned her to steer between the vices of both women ('the terrible tenacity of the sex to which, charming as it is, you no longer wish to belong') and men ('Try not to become a man either, they are horrid creatures'). Delacroix, *Selected Letters*, p. 210.
32. Sand, *Letters*, I, pp. 198–9.
33. Steinberg, *World Socialist Website*. [Italics mine].
34. Philip Auslander, *From Acting to Performance: Essays in Modernism and Postmodernism* (London: Routledge, 1997) p. 136.
35. Robert Burton, *The Anatomy of Melancholy* (London: Dent, 1932) vol. 3, p. 142 – on love-melancholy. Juliana Schiesari argues that melancholy was 'a malady whose initial disempowerment potentially afflicts exceptional men, especially men of letters, who walk a delicate line between something fatal and something transcendant'. Juliana Schiesari, *The Gendering of Melancholia: Feminism, Psychoanalysis, and the Symbolics of Loss in Renaissance Literature* (Ithaca: Cornell University Press, 1992), p. 235. Melancholy in women however was a destructive condition – 'brutish', 'foolish', 'stupified' and the reverse of Hamlet's hyper-articulacy: 'many of them cannot tell how to express themselves in words, or well tell what to make of their sayings'.

36. Burton, *Anatomy* vol. 1, p. 392.
37. Thomas Nashe, *Selected Works* (London: Edward Arnold, 1967), p. 155; *Hamlet* III, i, 160–1.
38. And 'the appropriation of femininity' by men from culturally silenced women: Schiesari, *The Gendering of Melancholia*, pp. 253–4.
39. *Hamlet* III, ii, 53–61.
40. *Ibid.*, II. ii. 586–90; V. ii. 161–2; V. i. 282–3.
41. *Ibid.*, IV. vii. 163.
42. Burton, *Anatomy* vol. 2, p. 180.
43. Marybeth Hamilton discussing female impersonation in 1920s America, Lesley Ferris (ed.) *Crossing the Stage: Controversies on Cross-dressing* (London and New York: Routledge, 1993), p. 111
44. *The Tragicall Historie of Hamlet Prince of Denmarke*, eds Graham Holderness and Bryan Loughrey (London: Harvester Wheatsheaf, 1992), p. 88. Spelling modernised here.
45. *Ibid.*, p. 56.
46. 'Spanish Productions of *Hamlet* in the Twentieth Century,' in A Luis Pujante and Ton Hoenselaars (eds.), *Four Hundred Years of Shakespeare in Europe* (Newark: University of Delaware Press, 2003), p. 193.
47. *South Bank Show*, London Weekend Television, 2 April 1989.
48. William Ackerman Buell, *The Hamlets of the Theatre* (New York: Astor-Horner, 1968), pp. 22, 51.
49. EC Stedman on Booth, *Atlantic Monthly*, May 1866.
50. Booth to William Winter (9 February 1882): Daniel J Watermeier (ed.), *Between Actor and Critic: Selected Letters of Edwin Booth and William Winter* (Princeton: Princeton University Press, 1971), p. 81.
51. Cited Edward P Vining, *The Mystery of Hamlet* (Philadelphia: Lippincott, 1881), p. 38.
52. William Hazlitt, *Table-Talk* (London: Dent, 1921), pp. 248–55.
53. Vining, *Mystery of Hamlet*, p. 46.
54. *Ibid.*, p. 5.
55. *Ibid.*, p. 55.
56. The *Oxford English Dictionary* did not include *homosexual* until its later Supplement, citing Havelock Ellis' 1897 apology for using this 'barbarously hybrid' word. The past was a cryptogram for Edward Vining. In *An Inglorious Columbus* (1885) he claimed that America was discovered by Afghanistani Buddhist monks, and his *Israel* (1908) proved the truth of the Pentateuch.
57. Vining, *Mystery of Hamlet*, pp. 74–5.
58. In 1881 at a time of profound social advances for women, Vining's theory was driven by a distrust of unleashed femininity. In the *OED*, work on which began five years earlier, *Femininitude* was equated with 'spite', and a high proportion of the *feminine* entries were deprecatory: 'feminine usurpation', 'feminine persecution', 'the whole feminine army, envy, avarice, pride, &c', and 'feminine' as a synonym for weak or fearful. *Effeminate* meant

'Womanish, unmanly, enervated, feeble, self-indulgent, voluptuous; unbeco-mingly delicate or over-refined': e.g. 'false politeness and effeminacy' or (*Samson Agonistes*) plain 'foul effeminacy'. Of course femininity was also equated with tenderness, compassion and sensibility, but it was essentially the opposite of whatever currently seemed 'the perfect manly character' (Vining). The language of Vining's day was inscribed with anxieties about the twin dangers of decadence and female emancipation: the *OED* cited Lord Lytton (1881) on 'our present somewhat effeminised civilisation', and Henry James (1886) on the advance of 'damnable feminisation'. Cultural and nationalistic factors conditioned the reception of Shakespearean acting, and the French actor Charles Fechter's Othello was called a whining affront to the British stage: 'Mr Fechter's pathos is certainly not that of a Moor; it is scarcely that of a *man*' (the *Daily Telegraph* said in November 1862): 'There is nothing masculine about it, nothing which stirs the soul, nothing which commands respect and inspires sympathy.'

59. Watermeier, *Between Actor and Critic*, p. 81.

60. William Winter, *Shakespeare on the Stage* (New York: Blom, 1911–16), pp. 427–8; 437–8. See below, p. 112.

61. Vining quoted the pioneer psychologist Henry Maudsley: 'We not uncom-monly observe the character of the mother, with her emotional impulses and subtle but scarce conscious shifts, in the individual when young, while the calm deliberation and conscious determination of the father come out more plainly as he grows older.'

62. Ernest Jones, *Hamlet and Oedipus* (London: Gollancz, 1949), pp. 77–8.

63. Sigmund Freud, *The Interpretation of Dreams, Complete Psychological Works*, vol. 4 (London: Hogarth Press and the Institute of Psycho-Analysis, 1954), p. 265.

64. Jones, *Hamlet and Oedipus*, pp. 93, 273.

65. Sarah Bernhardt, *The Art of the Theatre* (London: Bles, 1923), p. 137.

66. Nazimova, 'Ibsen's Women', *Independent*, 17 October 1907.

67. At Joseph Papp's Public Theater, New York and (for Anthony Page) pre-revolutionary Iran. See Ian Woodward, *Glenda Jackson* (London: Weidenfeld and Nicolson, 1985), p. 45.

68. The *Roaring Girl's Hamlet* programme.

69. Marjorie Garber, *Vested Interests: Cross-dressing and Cultural Anxiety* (New York and London: Routledge, 1992).

70. Cixous, 'Laugh of the Medusa'.

71. See Teresa Dobson, '"High-Engendered Battles": Gender and Power in *Queen Lear*', *New Theatre Quarterly* 14, 2 (May 1998), pp. 139–45.

72. Case, *Feminism and Theatre*, p. 121.

73. Fiona Shaw, Foreword to Lizbeth Goodman and Jane de Gay, eds., *The Routledge Reader in Gender and Performance* (London: Routledge, 1998), pp. xxiii–xxv.

74. Billington, *Guardian* 23 August 2000.

75. Review of Ferris, *Crossing the Stage in Women and Theatre Occasional Papers* 2 (1994), p. 143
76. *Routledge Reader*, p. 168.
77. *Helsingin Sanomat* 1 February 1995. Klemola was a founder-member of Q-Theatre, formed by recent graduates five years earlier. I am indebted to Lasse Kekki for these references and translations.
78. Recent scholarship suggests that the First Quarter of *Hamlet* is a free acting version adapted from an original which was closer to Q2. If this were true, it would indicate that performers were dissatisfied with the representation of the women from an early date, and expanded their roles. The older theory – that Q1's structure predates the later versions – still has much logic to commend it, however. See the new Arden two-volume edition of *Hamlet* (2006) for a rich discussion of the issues.

I

The women in black

CHAPTER 2

Playing Hamlet, writing the self

> For days I could think of nothing but the pale face and inky
> cloak of the melancholy prince. The old red volume had suddenly
> become like a casket filled with jewels, whose fame and flashes,
> I thought, might glorify a life. I often stopped to look at it with
> longing eyes, and one day could not resist climbing up to take it
> from its shelf. . .
>
> Mary Anderson[1]

One day in 1871 in California, Dr Hamilton Griffin showed his twelve-
year-old stepdaughter a large gilded red tome: 'This', he said, 'contains
all the plays of William Shakespeare, and I mean to read to you the great
master's masterpiece, *Hamlet.*' Griffin put Shakespeare on a par with the
Scriptures, and years later the actress Mary Anderson recalled it as her life-
defining moment. In the illicit act of entering her stepfather's study and
taking the book herself, she tried to 'glorify' her life and some nights later
startled the family by appearing 'wrapped in one of Dr Griffin's army
cloaks':

> Angels and ministers of grace defend us!
> Be thou a spirit of grace, or goblin damned. . . .[2]

When the adults laughed at her, 'I indignantly quitted the room, falling
over the cumbersome cloak in what was meant to be a majestic exit.'
Other careers, perhaps, died in the bud at such moments. But across
the centuries many actresses have remembered Hamlet as a formative
influence on their ambitions and sense of identity, and Mary Anderson,
with her imagination fired by the part and with no notion that gender
might limit self-expression, began to work in secret on the roles that
energised her. The penetration of the father's library, the appropriation
of the clothes, the forbidden text, these images of transgression will recur
throughout this study.

I

Denmark's daughters: 1741–1820

It was in the eighteenth century that Shakespeare's emergence as the
embodiment of Genius first encouraged actresses to aspire to be the
protagonist of the 'master's masterpiece' – as, on a practical level,
did *Hamlet*'s commercial appeal. Determined to offer a personal vision,
several classical actresses of extraordinary ability, most notably Sarah
Siddons (Figure 4) and fifty years later Charlotte Cushman, laid claim
to the role and to equality of intellectual opportunity. For women had few
tailor-made chances to play 'Genius'. As a result, many actresses would
use their power within the system to play Hamlet at a time when definitions of theatrical realism were still far less circumscribing than
they would become in the age of Ibsen, and when the right of the
performer – male or female – to dictate the nature of the theatre event
was uncontested. It was only at the end of the century – when Sarah
Bernhardt led a third, international wave – that male critics tried concert-
edly to undermine the actresses playing Hamlet and a new elite,
the directors, for the most part declined to cast them. Headlines like
'A She-Hamlet' made a pathological oddity out of a tradition of work
which had flourished on the margins for a century. However – and this is
apparent in the earliest account of all – a quality of rebelliousness was also
attached to the *travesti* Hamlet, and Bernhardt's success threatened to
bring the margins into the centre of British theatrical life. During the
nineteenth century, female Hamlets became identified with the *popular*,
the anti-traditional and indeed the principle of social change, for many
actresses in this role were known for their dedication to progressive causes.
Even where we have information – at best generally anecdotal – there
is little uniformity of motive; the early history of female Hamlets is a
collage of images, hints and narratives that show how complexly the figure
began to function. Nonetheless, they set up issues that would remain
central.

The first first-hand account of a woman playing Hamlet was explicitly
oppositional and carnivalesque, and appears in one of the earliest, most
outrageous, autobiographies of any English actress: *A Narrative of the Life
of Mrs Charlotte Charke, Youngest Daughter of Colly Cibber, Esq.: Written
by Herself* (1755). Charlotte Charke (1713–60) recorded her Hamlet in a
spirit of burlesque, explaining that she played the part somewhere in the
provinces with her small touring company simply, she said, 'for want of

Figure 4   Sarah Siddons as Hamlet: 'Aye madam, it is common', Dublin, 27 July 1802.
Watercolour by Mary Hamilton (Copyright the Trustees of the British Museum).

a better' – because there were no half-competent men around. She
attacked male Hamlets who sounded 'like a cat in labour' but derided
the 'low understanding' of her own admirers, including a country gentleman who 'was pleased to express his approbation of me, by saying no
man could possibly do it better, because "I so frequently broke out in

fresh places" '.[3] Reducing her Hamlet to a *double entendre*, she made no claims for it. Her *Narrative* was a weapon in a public conflict with her father, the actor/manager/playwright/Poet Laureate Colley Cibber, whose own memoirs had included one of the founding texts of British theatre history, a careful description of Betterton's Hamlet.[4] At the opposite extreme Charlotte described her decision to play Hamlet herself as flippantly as possible. This was consistent with a book which celebrated marginality in every way; the *Narrative* (a model for Angela Carter's *Wise Children*, the most dazzling modern meditation on the female Hamlet) is a picaresque extravaganza where triumph, disaster, confessional and tall tales are indistinguishable.[5] It was consistent with her career, which took in fairground stages, puppet shows and debtor's prison. And it was consistent with Charke's love of *travesti*, whether in such roles as Macheath, Ancient Pistol and Pope Joan, or in offstage streets and bedrooms. Charke claimed she often cheated poverty by masquerading as men – a waiter, a proof-reader, a sausage-maker – so perfectly that women wooed and tried to wed her, though 'the players cannot keep counsel' and often revealed her secret (Charke liked to quote Hamlet inappropriately). She traced her love of cross-dressing back to her childhood and her parodic relationship with her father to the age of four, when she dressed in his clothes, 'taking it into my small pate that by dint of a wig or a waistcoat, I should be the perfect representation of my Sire'.[6]

For all the alleged liaisons with women, she was contemptuous of male homosexuality and shrouded her 'original' motive for cross-dressing in dark hints: 'I rather choose to undergo the worst imputation that can be laid on me on that account, than unravel the secret.' 'Trembling' to hold a 'female pen', describing herself as an 'oddity', Charke published her autobiography in instalments and included updates on her father's refusal to pay her off to prevent new revelations: it was a perfect revenge text. Dressing as 'the glass of fashion and the mould of form' was a minor transgression by Charlotte Charke's standards; but whenever a woman embodied Hamlet's 'noble *mind*' there was a perceived element of provocation. This ensured that most of Charke's successors – some of them also writers, all of them highly independent – performed the role far from London, in comparative obscurity but relative freedom. The first female Hamlet in the official records, Fanny Furnival (d. 1752), played Hamlet at the Smock Alley Theatre, Dublin on 28 April 1741.

Said to be 'far superior to any of her predecessors, possessing an elegant figure, an uncommon share of beauty, a perfect knowledge of every part she undertook, and an execution scarcely excelled by any actress of that day'[7],

Fanny Furnival faced entrenched competition when she worked at Drury Lane: 'The parts in tragedy were so taken up, that her talent that way was never once try'd.' So in 1739 she and her husband moved to Dublin, where she played tragic leads and a wide spectrum of *travesti* roles. During a financial crisis which passed greater powers to Smock Alley's actors, Mrs Furnival proposed herself as Hamlet and the innovation attracted such attention that she repeated it for her benefit performance a week later, took it to Belfast, and reprised it in Dublin the next year.[8] In 1775 the young Sarah Siddons (1755–1831) – whose father had been trained by Fanny Furnival and was even rumoured to have married her – was spotted in Worcester by the Rev. Henry Bate, who wrote to David Garrick that 'the woman Siddons' was a startling talent with 'a good breeches figure' and amazing cultural pretensions: 'Nay, beware yourself, Great Little Man, for she plays Hamlet to the satisfaction of the Worcestershire critics.'[9] (She used Garrick's own version of the play, which cut 'Now might I do it pat.') She played Hamlet in 1776 in Birmingham and Manchester and was later seen for example in Liverpool (1778), Edinburgh, Bristol (1781) and Dublin (1802).[10] It was inspirational.

On 8 April 1780, Siddons' friend Elizabeth Inchbald (1753–1821), the Manchester Gertrude, herself played Hamlet; this was an extraordinarily intense event because she was a Hamlet in true mourning – her husband (twice her age when she married) had suddenly died in what she termed 'a week of grief, horror, and despair', and she played Hamlet as a benefit for her stepson George, who was Horatio: 'I shall not look upon his like again.'[11] Neither she nor Siddons ever risked the part publicly in London but in 1785 the royal family did Siddons 'the honour to hear her read the part of Hamlet'.[12] Other actresses began to emulate her, including Mrs Balkley in Edinburgh that year and Mrs Edmead in York (1792). In 1796 at Drury Lane, Jane Powell (c.1761–1831) became probably the first actress to play Hamlet in London, presented by Siddons' younger brother John Philip Kemble. Powell was visibly nervous. 'If we make allowances for embarrassment and imperfect study,' said the *Morning Post*, 'the performance of Mrs Powell was by no means indifferent.' She 'looked the character remarkably well; that is, according to the general idea of the personal requisitions of the part', and repeated it at Drury Lane (1802) a few weeks before Sarah Siddons revived her own Hamlet in Ireland.[13]

Siddons' mould-breaking role in all this was crucial. Respected for her neo-classical poise, often painted as one of the Muses, she had done more than any other single figure to establish the stage as a dignified calling for women; her decision to play Hamlet both at the start and the peak of her career was a thrilling precedent. It should be stressed that she was uncomfortable with the cross-dressing tradition dating back to the first Restoration actresses, where *travesti* was a complex erotic game in which gender was assumed, concealed and exposed. While the actress assumed male manners, the costume revealed her own 'shape'; the cross-dresser could be an identification-figure for women in the audience, acting out fantasies of empowerment, but she was also a source of visual pleasures for women and men, and many (male) comments on early female Hamlets assessed them in erotic terms. Even when Mrs Inchbald played Hamlet while grieving, blurring the line between fiction and personal pain, 'Denmark's Prince was not by any means destitute of grace and elegance.'[14] Inchbald made her name in comic and sentimental cross-dressing (though playing Hamlet was a step on a journey which led to her abandoning acting to become an influential dramatist, editor and translator); Mrs Siddons however felt such physical embarrassment as Rosalind/Ganymede that she hid herself in a long cloak. Her Hamlet attempted to reinvent *travesti*, prioritising an androgyny not of the eroticised body but of the mind. This was difficult.

For at twenty even Sarah Siddons was defined as a marketable 'breeches figure', and when Garrick hired her in 1776 she walked into a controversy over the politics of cross-dressing. He cast her in *Epicoene* as Morose's termagant wife, who is actually a disguised boy player. Garrick tried to update *travesti* conventions (to the point of dizziness – Jonson gave us a boy playing a woman, here is a woman played by a woman playing a boy), but critics demanded 'a young smooth-faced man'.[15] Siddons was hissed; her body was literally the focus of a controversy which became so abusive that she was replaced and left London. She returned to her provincial apprenticeship, to greater control of her career and to Hamlet, where her dignity and classicism were unconstrained. Siddon's model of tragic cross-dressing aspired to make gender irrelevant, not the point of the game.

Like Furnival and many of her successors, Mrs Siddons often played Hamlet on a benefit night, a crucial part of the freelance actors' economy when they could try parts denied them by the casting system and novelty might boost their earnings. There were risks, though, and after the *Epicoene* debacle *Hamlet*'s success took Siddons by surprise: 'I played Hamlet in Liverpool to near a hundred pounds' she told Elizabeth Inchbald, 'and wish I had taken it to myself; but the fear of charges, which, you know, are most tremendous circumstances, persuaded me to take a benefit with Barry, for which I have since been very much blamed.'[16] In 1802 the Dublin theatre 'groaned under the weight of spectators' but even then she was uneasy as Hamlet, 'oppressed by the novelty of her appearance'. As with Rosalind, she concealed herself in a cloak, a strange 'long black scarf' which created a statuesque image but provoked catcalls. In her first scene, playing the son, she was scarcely audible; but when Horatio told her of the Ghost, Siddons, confronting the Sublime, took control. First came 'astonishment', then Hamlet was 'lost in thought': 'You might trace in imagination the progress of his wonder, and his half formed suspicions, till roused from his reverie by the sudden idea of personally communicating with the Spectre, he declared his purpose.' She played Hamlet rarely; not even her colleague and biographer James Boaden caught up with it, but he knew admirers wanted details – her intensely subjective response to Horatio's story, her blazing determination to see the Ghost, and their 'breathless', 'transcendent' encounter. Siddons was, he said, a brilliantly *reactive* performer and therefore well-matched to the role. Intriguingly, her brother John Kemble played Laertes to her Prince before becoming the Hamlet of his generation; but Boaden said he declaimed 'To be or not to be' in 'the higher tones of his voice, and lost the cast of thought', whereas Siddons would make the soliloquy 'like audible rumination'. In Dublin she entered 'with wonderful judgement' into the sentiments of 'this very difficult character'.[17] For Boaden, gender created barriers even genius could not cross – 'Were she *but* man, she would exceed all that man has ever achieved in Hamlet'[18] – but Siddons startled Dublin with a 'capital' duel for which she had trained intensively with her Laertes, Mr Galindo. With this athletic climax she won against the odds, but there were bitter consequences. It was when she played Hamlet that she found herself accused for the only time in her life of sexual license.

In 1809 Catherine Galindo, the wife of the Dublin Laertes, published *Mrs Galindo's Letter to Mrs Siddons*, exposing the only 'true' reason why any woman could want to play, let alone train for, Hamlet:

[Y]ou proposed to Mr Jones to perform Hamlet, I now believe for no other purpose than to be taught fencing by Mr G. for by so doing you had an excuse to have him constantly with you, to the exclusion of my company, as you said you could not be instructed while any person looked on.[19]

She claimed Siddons seduced Galindo as they rehearsed and acted in Limerick, Cork and Dublin. Then when Mrs Galindo confided that she felt neglected, the star humiliated her. 'You proposed to read

Hamlet for my benefit', buying her off with the very play that gave her power over the husband: 'Not a shilling of the money did I receive.' As incriminating evidence she published a letter Siddons wrote Galindo (1803) in a moment of depression: 'About this time last summer, we used to be practising the noble science of defence, it served the purpose of the moment very well, very well indeed – and I wish all your scholars would do you as much credit, as so poor a man as Hamlet was.' He knew 'how to keep me "up up up" '.[20] The Galindoes were both opportunists; the scandal proved the difficulty Sarah Siddons faced as an independent woman needing male collaborators; when she tried to extend her range, training and creative freedom, she put herself in compromising situations.

The problems opened up by tragic cross-dressing were fraught and the women who followed Siddons as Hamlet needed a degree of courage as well as enterprise. Boaden condemned *travesti*'s 'vile and beastly trans-formations' and the York theatre manager Tate Wilkinson sniped at actresses who enjoyed dressing as men – 'a failing which has seldom added to female reputation'.[21] When Mrs Edmead was 'tempted, for her own amusement, to perform Hamlet' ('How a woman of good sense could be so determinedly wrong is to me inconceivable') she forfeited her right to politeness: 'Her features are by no means handsome', Wilkinson joked, 'and her mouth is not one of the least apertures.' His priorities were financial, though, and female Hamlets were a novelty, so he presented her with a shrug, 'Not that I approve such innovations and experiments'. *Travesti* was delightful when it met male expectations, distasteful when it challenged them; an actress as Hamlet was uniquely confrontational because the soliloquies broke through the spectacle and required audiences to identify with the character's/the actress's mind. So it was not surprising that when Jane Powell and Julia Glover (Lyceum Theatre, 1820) brought the female Hamlet to London, they were ill at ease.

Like Siddons and many of their successors, Jane Powell and Julia Glover (née Betterton, c.1779–1850) were known for dominant roles where 'power and experience are the most necessary qualifications'. Glover later played Falstaff. Though Siddons and Inchbald first acted Hamlet in their twenties, the role became associated with mature leading ladies who faced the perennial shortage of major leading roles and were bold enough to experiment. It was often said Powell lacked pathos, but she surprised the press and was criticised for making Hamlet 'a very young man', opening the debate about *Hamlet*, maturity and gender that has lasted for centuries. Precisely because the Georgian tragic repertoire encouraged actresses to play for *force*, one attraction of Hamlet was that it was a rare chance to explore sensitivity without drowning in victimised sentiment. Julia Glover was known for 'force and breadth', but she was a subtle actress with 'a special air of spontaneity': 'It was difficult to believe that she was simply repeating the words she had beforehand learned by heart', and 'when silent her looks and movements, her persistent attention to the scene, greatly aided the representation'. After early problems (her father, who claimed descent from the great Betterton, gave her an education but was said to have sold her in marriage for £1,000), she became a leading light of the profession and Hamlet was a personal triumph: 'Her noble figure, handsome and expressive face, rich and powerful voice, all contributed to rivet the attention of the elite assembled on this occasion.' Repeatedly 'bursts of applause greeted her finished elocution as she delivered the soliloquies'.[22] For the first time a female *Hamlet* was a gala metropolitan event, but she distrusted her reception (when Edmund Kean congratulated her backstage, she accused him of coming 'in mockery to scorn and scoff') and some actresses drawn to Hamlet had already searched much further afield for an unprejudiced response.

II

Undiscovered country

After the War of Independence and the War of 1812, some London stars were offered lucrative contracts in America. Politics, cultural snobbery and sheer distance deterred them, but in 1818 New York's Park Theatre made a 'Talent Raid' on London.[23] Kean refused but several younger actors took the risk and laid the foundations for new American theatrical dynasties – and new freedoms for actresses who faced fewer entrenched conventions there. Audiences were hungry for sensation and the female Hamlet was an instant attraction. Mrs Bartley (1783–1850) and her husband sailed to New York and on 29 March 1819 at the Park Theatre, she became probably the first actress to play Hamlet in America. As Miss Smith she had played Ophelia opposite Kean and some ranked her second to Siddons, 'formed by nature for the higher walk of her profession'. 'She had a noble and expressive face, full, strong, and melodious voice, capable of any intonation, and an original conception of her author.'[24] The Park's leading lady Mrs John Barnes (Mary Greenhill, 1780–1864) played Hamlet some months later and made it one of her main roles.[25] In 1822 Mrs Battersby played Hamlet soon after her own New York debut.

A prude in Hannah Webster Foster's 1797 novel *The Coquette* condemned America's theatrical fashions and especially cross-dressing: 'To see a woman depart so far from the female character, as to assume the masculine habit and attitudes, and appear entirely indifferent, even to the externals of modesty, is truly disgusting.'[26] But female-to-male cross-dressing in all its forms soon became a tradition, especially in New York and at the Park. T Allstone Brown's *History of the New York Stage* listed thirty male parts not uncommonly played by women there, including scapegraces like the thief Jack Sheppard, gymnastic heroes (the bareback rider Mazeppa) and historical and Shakespearean figures, especially Romeo (e.g. Mrs Barnes, Mrs FB Conway, Charlotte Cushman, Susan Denin, Mrs John Drew, Mrs Thomas Hamblin, Mrs Henry Lewis, Mme Ponisi, Mrs Coleman Pope, Mrs William Setton, Caroline Viet, Mrs James Wallace, and Ann Duff Waring).[27] For many actresses cross-dressing involved 'immature' boys' roles, but Elizabeth Reitz Mullenix sees the 1830s as the period when American female Hamlets began to be common. The Park Theatre star Mrs Shaw (Eliza Trewar), 'a lady who did Hamlet', played it there between 1838 and 1840.[28] In 1843 and '45 Mrs Brougham (Annette Nelson) – 'stalwart', 'formidable', 'an imperial beauty'[29] – chose Hamlet for benefit nights.

> 'On Mrs Barnes' Hamlet'[30]
> Strange, Mrs Barnes so much bewitches,
> Because, forsooth, she wears the breeches;
> Strange, that so many husbands roam
> To see – what they endure at home.

Apart from the sense of openness, the great difference between the reception of female Hamlets in Britain and America was that, however satirically, it was quickly sensed in the new republic that there were links between the play and social changes. William Hill Brown's novel *The Power of Sympathy* (1789) told of 'Ophelia', a young New Englander seduced, abandoned, and driven to suicide by 'paternal power', and her tragedy proved 'the Advantages of Female Education'. America's Ophelias must be allowed to develop a careful independence, and 'the duty of a child to her parents will be in proportion to the attention paid to her education'.[31] The daughters of America's new theatrical dynasties gained an unusual education on the stage and inherited the custom of tragic cross-dressing. 'Graceful, spirited, pretty,' 'extremely picturesque in attitude and action', Fanny Wallack (1822–56) was the niece of JH Wallack who arrived in 1818.[32] She – 'the reigning Transatlantic woman Hamlet' – played Hamlet frequently in New York after 1849 and became the leading lady at the Broadway, a theatre with a vast 4,500 capacity.[33]

Mrs John Barnes' daughter, Charlotte Barnes (1818–63) first acted at the age of three, played Juliet to her mother's Romeo, and graduated like her to Hamlet. 'With her frail physique and mournful, wandering eyes', she gave the role a 'languishing', haunted quality and 'an impression of refinement and poetic sensibility.'[34] Charlotte Barnes in fact became one of America's first substantial playwrights and dramatic theorists: she believed tragedy must 'display the emotions and passions of which we have all been conscious'.[35] She wrote historical dramas but believed classical conflicts of love and duty were being fought out in the contemporary world; in her verse tragedy *Octavia Bragaldi* (1837) which was set in the Renaissance but dramatised a recent American scandal, she showed 'the futile and lamentable results of revenge, even under circumstances which in the world's opinion serve in some degree to palliate it'. She believed pathos was important, but less so than a sense of tragic *responsibility*: 'It is always more instructive when a person has been *himself* the cause of his misfortune, and when his misfortune is occasioned by the violence of passion, or by some weakness incident to human nature.'[36] Hence perhaps her own progress from Ophelia to Hamlet. She was an early feminist and insisted women must share their experiences; in her updated *Canterbury Tales* a group of American women exchanged stories, and in a dramatic monologue entering Queen Victoria's mind on the eve of her coronation Barnes wrote: 'Woman is woman everywhere; on England's throne,/Or tideless Mississippi's banks, she's still the same.' Just as Hamlet wipes the past clean by sharing forgiveness with Laertes, Barnes demanded an escape from 'memories of former bitterness': 'Two nations speak one language.'[37]

If Hamlet was the performance for which Charlotte Barnes was most remembered, by the 1860s Hamlet was so important for Charlotte Cushman (1816–76) that the sculptor Emma Stebbins would argue that *only* a woman could play him.

Charlotte Cushman: Samson, Ruth and Hamlet

I was born a tomboy. My earliest recollections are of doll's heads ruthlessly cracked open to see what they were thinking about; I was possessed with the idea that dolls could and did think. I had no faculty for making dolls' clothes. But their furniture I could make skilfully. I could do anything with tools. (Cushman, notes for an autobiography[38])

At her death the stage historian WJ Lawrence described Cushman as 'the one outstanding actress of her time most frequently seen in male roles.' She was great in 'the illustration of Shakespeare', creating characters 'at once human and poetic' – 'white marble suffused with fire'.[39] One of the most respected actors of the nineteenth century, she has come to be recognised as a key figure in the cultural emancipation of American women; always a moral and professional model, in the late twentieth century she became a lesbian icon. Famous for her monumental Lady Macbeth, she also played over thirty male roles including three Shakespearean parts especially identified with her – Romeo, Cardinal Wolsey, and her Hamlet which, 'within the bounds of a studiously conventional reading', Lawrence judged 'astonishingly fine'.[40] A clergyman put gender at the heart of his funeral eulogy: 'She seemed to stand complete in nature, with the finest qualities of either sex. Her strength was that of a man, her tenderness was that of a woman. She was a Samson and Ruth in one.'[41] However she never ceased to be controversial. Emma Stebbins drew attention to Cushman's 'I was born a tomboy' because it was a derogatory term – 'the advance-guard of that army of opprobrious epithets which has since been lavished so freely upon the pioneers of woman's advancement. . . [T]he ugly little phrase had power to keep the dangerous feminine element within what was considered to be the due bounds of propriety.'[42] Stebbins insisted that posterity remember the 'many years of prejudice' Charlotte Cushman faced.

Square-faced (with features like an owl, she said), statuesque, and in many respects staidly respectable, Cushman formed intense female friendships. 'Miss Cushman possessed in a remarkable degree the power of attaching women to her', wrote one obituarist carefully: 'They loved her with utter devotion, and she repaid their love with the wealth of her great, warm heart.'[43] Itinerant actors depended on networks of personal and professional relationships; Cushman enlarged this into a feminist principle and in time founded an artistic colony for women artists in Italy. Success freed her to live to some extent by her own rules, and for women like young Harriet Hosmer (another sculptor) Cushman's Hamlet was inspirational, launching a lifelong friendship: 'You have no idea how splendid Hamlet was!'[44] Emma Stebbins recalled Cushman's 'intense pleasure' in the role: 'She alludes to it in some of her letters as the very highest effort she had ever made, and the most exhausting; of all her parts, this one seemed to fill out most completely the entire range of her powers.'[45]

Born in Boston, Cushman originally aspired to write or sing. She made her first public appearance in Mozart and was trained by James Maeder and his wife Clara Fisher, but Cushman's contralto voice was strained and damaged, so she turned to acting.[46] She benefited, though, from the Maeders' belief that the performer must be able to communicate forcefully without gestures – this demanded close preparation, inner discipline, vocal clarity, and the rejection of rhetoric, all of which would mark Cushman's Hamlet. The fact that cross-dressing was now commonplace in American theatre was crucial to her apprenticeship: she was encouraged to become a singer by Mary Wood (who acted with Julia Glover's Falstaff), was trained by Clara Fisher (who played Hamlet as a child star), filled in male roles in New Orleans, played Romeo for the Wallacks, and made a name as 'a lady-actor of gentlemen'. In New York she was in Mrs Barnes' 1837 benefit *Hamlet* and next year played Gertrude to Mrs Shaw's Prince.[47] These events were formative. At the Park she played Viola to her sister Susan's Olivia, and she was Oberon in 1840, the year that Madame Vestris' London production redefined Oberon as a female role. Above all, the Cushman sisters formed a partnership as Romeo and Juliet that won Charlotte international fame when they visited London in 1845.

Like Hamlet, the role of Romeo interrogates masculinity's contradictions: when Mercutio dies, Romeo exclaims that Juliet's beauty 'hath made me effeminate', and his frenzy after killing Tybalt compels the Friar to ask 'Art thou a man?': 'Thy form cries out thou art' but 'Thy tears are womanish' and 'thy wild acts denote/The unreasonable fury of a beast':

> Unseemly woman in beseeming man;
> Or ill-beseeming beast in seeming both:
> Thou hast amaz'd me.[48]

Romeo had begun to attract actresses because it was felt they could explore this tragic 'effeminacy' and alleged hysteria, while giving the romance an idealised colouring. Cushman persuaded the Haymarket Theatre that to establish herself in England she must appear in unconventional roles, but she provoked a company revolt by replacing Garrick's sentimental ending with Shakespeare's. London's unpreparedness for the force and emotional realism of her Romeo – 'No thought, no interest, no feeling, seems to actuate her, except what might be looked for in Romeo himself, were Romeo reality' – was typified by Sheridan Knowles: 'I listened and groaned and held my breath, while my blood

ran hot and cold . . . every scene exhibited the same truthfulness . . .
My heart and mind are so full of this extraordinary – most extraordinary
performance – that I declare I know not where to stop or how to go on!'[49]
As Faye E Dudden argues, Cushman's harsh intensity turned
travesti inside out so that it in no sense offered woman as a commodity.[50]
The sensation caused by her 'top-most passion! – not simulated passion –
no such thing – real, palpably real', emboldened her to work on
Hamlet, which became Romeo's companion piece, her tragic study of
restraint.

In February 1847, after playing Hamlet during a provincial tour including Manchester and Dublin, she put together a promptbook with inter-
leaved comments for an unknown correspondent.[51] This is the first time
we can see inside the mind of an actress playing Hamlet. In 1851 she
took the part to Boston and New York.[52] Cushman made the standard
expurgations – bawdry, incest, violations of religious taste – but her devotion to the play was remarkable: her British text was longer than the
American one, which itself ran three hours and forty minutes till
she was forced to cut.[53] Like Siddons she kept *Hamlet* from London
reviewers, some of whom habitually called her work primitive ('rude'
and 'violent': *Spectator*). Even at home some responses to her Hamlet
were harsh ('bizarre'[54]) but admirers like Harriet Hosmer were ecstatic:
'I used to think Lady Macbeth was the finest thing that could be done, but
Queen Katherine shook my foundations and Hamlet overturned it!'[55]
One paper called it 'unusually subtle and complete' and not simply
'very fine for a woman'; its 'great absolute excellence' was never external:
'She enters into his melancholy, his poetic philosophy, his resolution
and his impulsiveness.'[56]

'Such is Miss Cushman's Hamlet', a critic wrote – 'a sensitive, young,
and retired man of virtuous feelings', shocked by bereavement, who
'broods in loneliness over his sorrows until the manliness of his character
is affected, and he becomes worn and lachrymose.' The Ghost 'brings
dismay and bitterness into a bosom where before gloom and sadness were
the only tenant' and 'his assumed madness and real distraction . . . so
commingle and run into light and shade as scarcely to be distinguished'.[57]

'Remember it is a woman': Cushman in action, 1847
From the first, Cushman stressed the painful intensity of the bond
between mother and bereaved child, describing how, during Gertrude's
'Cast thy nighted colour off' speech, Hamlet 'gradually withdraws his
gaze from her, drooping the head. On the word *common* he suddenly

meets her eye and fixes it until he has, in a very marked manner, repeated the word *common*, as if to say, "You have indeed, as well as the Court, treated my father's death as an ordinary affair."' As the Court left, Hamlet followed 'mechanically with drooping head, lifts his head with a sigh', but suddenly stopped, compelled to unpack his thoughts (as a Victorian she cut the brooding on incest). The decision to seek the Ghost 'should be spoken with great intensity, "not loud but deep"'.[58] Cushman's style was formal and slow. She used much traditional business but all her comments indicate her wish to avoid melodrama and express Hamlet's intimacy with his father, Ophelia and Gertrude. The Ghost entered behind Cushman's back; Horatio cried out and the spirit came as close to her as possible 'without touching'. Hamlet's 'attitude', she wrote, 'must be anything but forceful – the head and body shrinking back as much as possible' and 'Hamlet's eye should not leave the Ghost during the scene.' She used her sword to denote shifting emotion: Hamlet 'impulsively' drew it 'as a brave' to warn off Horatio and Marcellus, but at 'Horrible, most horrible' leant on it in shock. At 'bear it not', he 'recovers + holds sword in a most menacing attitude'; until, learning of his mother's 'falling off', he ('mournful') relaxed his grip. When the Ghost began to leave, Hamlet dropped the sword and knelt for a blessing. As they swore their oaths Cushman held it as a cross.

To quote Treva Rose Tumbleson's pioneering study, Cushman's approach was progressive 'in restoring as much as currently feasible of the text, [and in] her attempts to abolish melodramatic effects, and to present a saddened but vigorous prince without sentimentality' – this 'courtly', 'vigorous' Hamlet 'reacted strongly to events, but did not attitudinize'.[59] Not only did Cushman try to remove melodrama from the play, which had become as much a cascade of Gothic thrills as a philosophical drama, her performance was a conscious critique of what many men had done with it, especially America's leading tragedian Edwin Forrest. Cushman was preoccupied with Hamlet's relationships with the women. Some thought her most successful male role was Cardinal Wolsey, but she found Hamlet more congenial because Wolsey fights to dominate *Henry VIII* – forcing Cushman to *outdo* every man onstage in terms of 'voice, bearing, and impression' – whereas Hamlet toys easily with everyone but the women.[60] Wolsey's viciousness towards Queen Catherine disgusted her; Cushman approached Hamlet's scenes with Gertrude and Ophelia very differently, giving them dignity and stressing Hamlet's duty to sharpen their consciences. She had a feminist agenda grounded in – her word – 'respect'.

She was also profoundly religious. In the Nunnery scene Ophelia knelt before a crucifix, signifying the issue of honesty and what was for Cushman the *Christian* gravity of 'To be or not to be'. She lessened Hamlet's fear of the afterlife, cutting 'But in that sleep of death what dreams may come/When we have shuffled off this mortal coil/Must give us pause.'[61] Her letters and journals show she believed each soul was assigned 'one spot which we have been destined to fill worthily, highly, perfectly, without flaw', and so the whips and scourges had a purpose – to inspire 'the determination to be worthy in spite of lets and hindrances': 'The small conquest over the self to-day, shall lead to the larger to-morrow.'[62] Her Hamlet made to leave Ophelia, 'rejecting the gifts', but caught a glimpse of the King ('oh oh – you are there sir') and the scene became confessional: as near the audience as possible, Hamlet 'leads her forward and utters "are you honest" most significantly'. Ophelia panicked: 'Her exclamation of surprise startles him + puts him on the qui vive, he then puts "on his antic disposition" speaks the following speeches rather playfully than violently until "Go thy ways to a nun-nery".' Then he saw Polonius.

He turns then suddenly and asks seriously for her father, as a test of her knowl-edge of their being there. On her uttering the falsehood which her manner betrays she knows to be one, he looks at her with contempt and replys [sic] to her indignantly. Saying farewell very seriously – the <u>following</u> speeches both with regard to <u>matter</u> and <u>manner</u> have a warranty for violence.

Whereas Forrest's Hamlet projected generalised aggression against the women, this became Ophelia's 'test', which tragically she failed, unleash-ing the anger Cushman had kept in check: she left at 'To a nunnery go,' but ran back and relaunched the tirade. Cushman let her fellow-actress keep her soliloquy ('Oh what a noble mind') and protected her from the men's brutal unconcern by getting her offstage before they returned. 'I acted the scene in this way at Manchester Theatre Royal', she wrote, and was 'much praised for it.'

Cushman's Hamlet despised Rosencrantz and Guildenstern, greeting them 'in high pitched tones of mimic rapture – as a satire on his <u>friends</u>,' but was at ease with the Players. She sat for 'Speak the speech', which was 'quiet and unaffected'.[63] She included several rarely-heard passages and was especially interested in 'Denmark's a prison . . .': 'I think the resto-ration of this will be much approved of.' She stressed that 'My young lady and mistress' must be a boy player, and her careful sifting of tradition was clear during *The Mousetrap*. During Lucianus' speech Hamlet 'in agitation crawls imperceptibly towards the King – at "he poisons him" is close to him' – but despite this familiar move Cushman kept the acting muted and led everything towards *Gertrude's* response:

The pouring it into the ear, and the cautious exit of Lucianus should fascinate the King, who does not perceive that Hamlet is standing over him until he hears the words '<u>murtherer</u> <u>gets</u> the <u>love</u> of Gonzago's <u>wife</u>!' at that the King's eye encounters him as also does his mother's who shrieks on the word <u>Wife</u>.

The Court fled, Hamlet exulted – 'The grand climax is made here' – but Cushman dropped much stock bravura business: 'Don't throw away the pipe – (poor thing!) nor do not snatch the wand from Polonius (that's vulgar) but point to the cloud with the pipe'. Her underplaying ('Places the pipe, without any apparent intention in Pol.'s hand') set up the confrontation with Gertrude; she ended the scene on 'I will speak daggers to her but use none', cut the Prayer scene (which was usual, though she considered including it), and moved straight to what she feelingly called the Queen's 'agony' – few previous Hamlets, after all, had played Gertrude first.

Forrest had established the custom that Hamlet must 'rave and rant at the Queen like a drunken potboy'.[64] Cushman strained to awaken the mother's conscience; it was by far the most carefully annotated scene. Hamlet entered and stood by the door, keeping distant until –

Mother, you have my father much offended: Hamlet 'advances, takes her hand and looks her severely in the face'. Gertrude fails to respond; Hamlet 'puts her hand from him'.

You are the queen, your husband's brother's wife;/And – would it were not so! – you are my mother. 'This is spoken rapidly and sarcastically until "not so," bethinks himself of the respect due to his mother, and repeats, "You are" with much feeling and respect.'

Is it the King?: Hamlet backed away from the arras, turned, 'observes her agony, and shrieks frensidly [*sic*]'. 'The dialogue rapidly carried on, Hamlet's fiercely, until the Queen says "as kill a King!" '– Hamlet 'takes her <u>L</u> hand with his <u>L</u> hand, looks her in the face and utters "Ay lady" with great solemnity'.[65]

Leave wringing of your hands. Peace, sit you down: 'Ham should remember; it is a woman that he invites or requests to be seated . . . he should not through [*sic*] her about too much.'

Look here upon this picture and on this was intimate. Gertrude's miniature became 'exposed, as tho it had escaped from her bosom in the late struggle – his seeing it, suggest the following speech'.

Enter Ghost: Cushman rejected violent effects – 'the kicking of the chair', 'the Queen's sprawling on the ground' – and sought psychological truth: 'On seeing his father, he becomes, as it were, <u>paralysed</u>. No start into a graceful or wide spreading attitude. The form and feature become anything but agreeable in aspect under such <u>shocking</u> surprises.' Hamlet froze. *On him, on him:* 'Still motionless'. *How is't with you lady?:* 'Moves but his lips'. . . .

Do you see nothing there?: The Ghost drew mother and child strangely together, into a sculptural grouping. Hamlet 'expresses wonder, puts his left hand across his person and takes her <u>L</u> hand'; he 'bends his body forward, extends his right arm and points emphatically to Ghost'. She saw nothing. Hamlet, confused, 'stands back, loosens her hand' but then 'seizes her <u>L</u> hand with his right hand as he follows Ghost draws her after him'.

Look where he goes: The Ghost 'waves his truncheon as if forbidding Hamlet's further advancing. . . . Hamlet trembles violently + staggers into the chair he had occupied – and the Queen into hers.' They were back exhausted in their domestic scene, but with a new poignancy: *Mother, for love of grace* became an appeal: *Mother, Mother*. . .

Confess yourself to heaven: 'Hamlet induces her to look him in the face – he then clasps his hands and utters the following <u>Confess yr</u>. most beseechingly.' Cushman cut the harsh aftermath, the sexual taunts, but showed Gertrude's love and Hamlet's confusion through broken gestures: Gertrude 'offers to embrace he waves her off'; she 'offers to embrace he puts her from him'. Yet finally there was tenderness: Hamlet 'leads her to door, takes both her hands with his left hand'. The last line was *Thus bad begins and worse remains behind.*

In the arrest scene 'Hamlet enters wildly' and 'Exits rapidly'. In Act IV Cushman decimated the King's speeches but overall cut less than most actor-managers, favouring Gertrude and Ophelia. In the graveyard Hamlet was dignified: she disliked the stage direction to throw down Yorick's skull, doubting it was genuine. She allowed no doubt about the sincerity of Hamlet's love: 'Bursts into a passionate fit of tears before he speaks – "I loved her".' Cushman turned on Laertes 'with great violence'.

Cushman made her deep Christianity clear. She divided the last scene in two, creating a separate philosophical dialogue with Horatio. She cut Hamlet's killing of Rosencrantz and Guildenstern but inserted 'There's a divinity that shapes our ends' into her meditation on the fall of the sparrow: 'What is't to leave betimes?' *Curtain.*

As Siddons had proved, actresses could challenge expectations in the duel scene; Emma Stebbins pointed out that in the mid-nineteenth century even girls' right to play sports – 'which were considered strictly and exclusively masculine' – had to be fought for. Audiences were always astonished by Cushman's athleticism and as Romeo she made stage combat express emotion: 'Tybalt is struck dead as lightning strikes the pine; one blow beats down his guard, and one lunge closes the fray; indignation has for a moment the soul of Romeo. With Paris there is more display of swordsmanship: he falls by the hand of the lover.'[66] But in *Hamlet* Cushman was concerned with the emotional action *around* the duel. The last scene was a rush of movement held together by Hamlet's selflessness. He took Laertes' hand. When Gertrude collapsed Hamlet was weakened, leaning on his sword, but – 'Recovering himself as she speaks' – her plight electrified him: 'On the word "poisoned" he shrieks out "O"'; on '"Let the doors [be shut]", is rushing up when Laertes speaks and stops him.' At 'I follow thee', Cushman began to fall. Horatio caught her and helped her to the floor, but she sprang up to prevent his suicide ('snatches the cup'). She spoke the last words holding onto Horatio, who lowered her 'gently'. Cushman demanded tact to the last: 'A violent fall in this or any other scene in which Hamlet is engaged' would be 'atrocious'. A dead march played behind the scene.

Charlotte Cushman's health deteriorated. She began a long fight against breast cancer and for what was expected to be her farewell tour (1861) returned to Hamlet. When she played it in Philadelphia on 28 January it was 'most awfully exhausting', physically and mentally. 'But darling,' she wrote to Emma Crow, 'it is such a magnificent character and I can assure you that though I was nervous lest all the words should not be right, I acted the part so much better than anything else I have done here that I am amazed at myself and wonder whether the spirit of the Dane was not with me and around me last night.'[67] A group of 'Senators, Representatives and Citizens' appealed, 'This being announced as your farewell engagement in Washington, and consequently the last opportunity many of our citizens and sojourners may ever have of witnessing the impersonation of a lady universally acknowledged as the greatest living tragic actress, we, the undersigned, respectfully solicit you to appear some evening as Hamlet, a part wherein you have lately created such a profound sensation, and one so beautifully suited to your refined and undoubted genius.' The playbills promised 'Three of her Most Artistic Impersonations' including, on Saturday night, her 'Sublime Rendition of HAMLET!' A silk programme commemorated the occasion.[68]

Cushman was friendly with the rising star Edwin Booth and his wife Mary Devlin, who had been her Juliet. She borrowed his Hamlet costume for the tour, but for the first time there was rivalry between a leading actor and actress over Hamlet. Booth wrote from New York, 'She is down on me as an actor; says I don't know anything at all about Hamlet, so she is going to play it here in February'; she complained that 'My engagement was cut short . . . I was to have acted *Hamlet* there but they prevented it because Edwin was going to do it.' She thanked the Booths (she 'would never have been able to act Hamlet so well' except in his 'mantle and draperies') but the wrangling reflected its importance for her circle.[69]

Emma Stebbins argued that Cushman had proved only a woman could play Romeo plausibly: 'When a man has achieved the experience requisite to *act* Romeo, he has ceased to be young enough to *look* it; the discrepancy is felt to be unendurable.'[70] Since Cushman gave Romeo 'gentleness', 'grace of deportment' and enough 'chivalrous gallantry . . . to make the *vraisemblance* perfect', then the same argument applied to 'young Hamlet': 'Her commanding and well-made figure appeared to advantage in the dress of the princely Dane; and her long experience in the assumption of male parts took from her appearance all sense of incongruity.'[71] But more significantly, Stebbins claimed Cushman brought intellectual and moral qualities to Hamlet that no youth could:

A crude Hamlet is insufferable; an old Hamlet is equally incongruous; in this respect Miss Cushman satisfied the eye, in all others she gratified the mind. The matchless delivery of that immortal language, no word or sentence slurred over or 'come tardy off', no delicate intricacies of thought left obscure, but all illuminated by a genius created for such interpretation, was alone a treat beyond comparison.

'We never saw Hamlet until it was done by Cushman', a journalist agreed, but despite much enthusiasm audiences on her 1861 tour were 'so-so'.[72] America like Elsinore echoed with rumours of war. She wondered whether tragedy was appropriate at such a time but she had faith in catharsis: perhaps 'with all the bad blood let out of the land, we shall be better, stronger, happier'.[73] She believed that on the personal level too life depended on conflict, and Hamlet's dilemmas and soul-searching related strongly to her own strict morality. She believed sin was only weakness (hence her sympathy for Gertrude) but that it faces us with 'evils we have to combat'.[74] She believed profoundly in the importance of conscience and Christian self-examination, in life as a 'test': 'There are few entirely perfect characters, few souls so white as to bear full sunshine.'[75] Believing herself deeply flawed, Cushman expressed her ethical vision through her art, and Shakespearean issues of guilt and consequence preoccupied her: 'We cannot commit a wrong without its punishment following closely at the heels; we cannot break a law of eternal justice, however ignorantly, but throughout the entire universe will there be a jar of discord which will so trouble the divine harmonies that in the rebound we shall find each man his own hell!'

Cushman had her own Ophelia. During the 1846–7 British tour in which she played Hamlet, news came that the young artist Rosalie Sully, 'the one bright spot in my existence', had died in America. During her first voyage to England Cushman wrote that she could not sleep, wracked because she was abandoning her dearest friend for family duties and perhaps ambition: 'The memory of all that I had left, pouring upon me words of regret at the steps I had taken. . . Such wretched thoughts that it were better I could not think. . . I hear her sigh for her absent friend. I feel almost her arms about me and then weep again.'[76] Cushman had hoped to earn enough 'to have her with me always', but as time passed Sully sent distraught letters that 'break my heart'. The actress saw herself as a 'backslider', a breaker of promises to herself and God, and like Hamlet asked herself if she was a coward: 'I shall be less a coward day by day as I bring myself face to face with my soul, and God help me to see better as I "learn to labour and to *wait*." Ah, what profound wisdom is in that little sentence! . . . How hard it is to wait!' 'Patience', she said on her deathbed, was 'all the passion of great hearts!'[77] Readiness was all. 'I found life sadly real and intensely earnest', Cushman explained when she finally retired in 1874. 'I resolved to take therefrom my text and my watchword. To be thoroughly *in earnest*, intensely in earnest in all my thoughts and in all my actions, whether *in* my profession or *out* of it, became my one single idea.'[78]

Cushman won her way into literary elites and progressive circles. Her admirers included Lincoln and Disraeli; Whitman, whom she regarded as America's most truthful poet, called her the greatest actor 'in any hemisphere' and a pointer to the intellectual future.[79] Cushman and her Italian artists' colony became magnets for independent young women. In England, Matilda Hays, her Juliet, joined her in a 'female marriage': they 'made vows of celibacy and eternal attachment to each other – they live together, dress alike'.[80] Cushman became the visible hub of a subculture where her public transvestism – and her long exploration of 'male' tragic passions – became inseparable from her role as model and resource for women of talent. Iconically, her Hamlet linked intellect, resolve, love of women, and compassion. The writer Anne Brewster called her 'the one passionate love of my life' – ' "the ever fixed mark" to my "wandering bark" on the Ocean of Thought'.[81] Julia Ward Howe simply said that thanks to her 'I feel much better about womankind.'[82] Cushman's example made many things possible.

III

Felicita von Vestvali: 'I am the way I am'

In Germany a dying actress-Hamlet wrote 'Horatio' a last letter:

> My nervous disease, which is terrible, has been softened by G.'s presence . . . I love her passionately and I want to do something nice for her day in and day out. Now it doesn't matter whether it happened under the peach or the apple tree, whether she seduced me or I her – we love each other passionately. I just wish you were here, dear Horatio . . .[83]

'The World-Renowned Shakspearian [*sic*] Tragic Actress' Felicita von Vestvali (1829–80) 'from the imperial theatres of Paris and other cities',[84] was born Anna Marie Staegemann in Stettin (now Szcezcin, Poland). Like Cushman, Vestvali trained as a singer – she sang baritone in *Ernani* – but unlike her, Vestvali enjoyed an international *travesti* opera career from Germany to Mexico. The Emperor Napoleon rewarded her with a suit of silver armour. In 1855 she sang Orfeo in the American premiere of Gluck's *Orfeo and Euridice* and flourished there until 1865 when a season in San Francisco collapsed in acrimony. She sued the manager for breach of contract and for threatening her: 'You damned fiend of a woman (repeated three times, with violence and gesticulations), take care, you have come to the right man. I'll prove that you have bones in your flesh, and before you leave the country I'll break every bone in your body.'[85] 'In order to recuperate', wrote her friend the actress Rosa von Braunschweig, Vestvali 'studied the part of Hamlet'. She took 'both this play and the *Romeo* of the great British playwright on all her trips' and had stepped in as Shakespeare's Romeo in San Francisco. Now her career changed direction. She played Hamlet in America and Britain, appearing at the Lyceum in London as Romeo in 1867. She performed in English with local actors; and a fashionable audience, at first merely 'patient', were won over by her authority, her 'eloquent' eyes, and above all her voice – 'strong and deep and manly in tone'.[86] She 'made a decidedly good impression'.[87] Vestvali's season ('Continued success!') ran four weeks, and in 1868 she returned as Petruchio and Hamlet (twenty performances). Queen Victoria received her and she was called a female Kean. She was also an unusually visible lesbian.

For some time Vestvali avoided playing Hamlet in Germany – 'the country', Braunschweig said, 'which least gives licence to the extraordinary'.[88] When she finally did so in Hamburg, Berlin, and Leipzig, the press reported that most of the audience 'came merely for strangeness' sake and in part even to destroy a lady who was brave enough to play Hamlet'. But Vestvali won respectful silence:

The noble figure, who surpassed the king and many of the other 'heroics' in height and all of them in nobility of posture, her expressive face turned toward the floor, already disarmed all prejudice. The second doubt was dissipated when she began to speak. Her sonorous alto voice, her clear declamation which showed no trace of dialect indicated that the artist was equal to her task. . . The power of her genius caused all scruples against women acting male parts to be forgotten.[89]

Vestvali made Hamlet blond and Nordic – a youth with a 'fresh, healthy colouring, although from birth a little hypochondriacal': 'For the outward representation of a female Hamlet, Mother Nature probably had not gifted any other woman, none, with such splendid genius and specifically "masculine" traits. Her physique alone reminds one of the – so-called – Lord of creation [i.e. men].'[90] Vestvali's Hamlet was 'not only a dreamer. . . vacillating until the moment of the execution'; she made him heroic and 'vividly represented his energetic will, his pressing, piercing decision toward action. The most important scene was probably the struggle at Ophelia's grave and the eruption of his love for her.'[91] One Berlin critic rated hers the most original conception of the two dozen Hamlets he had seen, and 'We have never witnessed better fencing on stage.'

Though Vestvali had a child, exotic rumours about her sexuality included the claim that she was an hermaphrodite. After her death her friends made her lesbianism public. In 1900 Rosa von Braunschweig explained in a pioneering journal of sexual psychology how Vestvali's sexuality found artistic expression in her Hamlet: 'The female Uranian usually combines specifically feminine traits, such as sensitivity and depth of feeling, with masculine energy, drive, and goal-oriented striving.' 'The combination of masculine and feminine qualities', she argued, 'quite often makes for beings whose talents far surpass those of mother-women,

and who contribute to the arts and sciences just as valuable services.'
Vestvali's symbolic attachment to Hamlet – the tragic/romantic/heroic
role that allowed her best to express her 'genius' – suggested new definitions, and like Emma Stebbins, Braunschweig used the career of an actress
who played Hamlet to demand a revolution in education, in this case sex
education. 'The ignorant masses brand their inclination usually as base
sexuality. How different it would be if parents became enlightened about
the nature of homosexuality and learned to reckon that it is imparted by
nature.' 'How often girls are driven into a marriage', she added, 'in which
not only they but a second person becomes unhappy. If parents would
learn to recognise their children's sexual tendency. . .much misery
would be prevented in the world.'[92] Concentrating on Hamlet, she
revealed Vestvali's self-discoveries, her ethics and her inner struggles:
'She painfully felt the conflict with all existing moral laws, but truth
towards her self was for her more important than a moral code which
was made without consideration for the third sex, whose existence cannot
be denied.' And for Vestvali's circle *Hamlet* also offered a model for
same-sex emotional friendship. 'She often called herself "Hamlet"',
Braunschweig explained, and called one young actress 'Horatio': 'I am
that actress.'

The uniqueness of Hamlet is that the part's parameters are so broad
and the writing so malleable that, deliberately or unconsciously, all performers expose aspects of themselves in it. Playing Hamlet is autobiographical because, as Angela Winkler was to show, Hamlet is the process of
individuation. His starting-point is the desire *not* to be ('O that this too
too solid flesh. . .'), not to conform, not to betray the inner self, not
to speak: 'Then hold my thought for I must hold my tongue.' It is the
desire to withdraw, back to Wittenberg. It is attachment to the past,
devotion to idealised memories of the Father and horror at the independence of the Mother. But its closing-point is both death and succession,
the control of the future. The end is silence, but the interim is language,
and the astonishing complexity of the landscape of words; Hamlet is
impossible to map. Playing Hamlet was a way to choose whether to
express dissidence or authority, ennui or action, desperation or wit, and
to replace the unread book patriarchy plants in Ophelia's hand with
the red and gold volume from Dr Hamilton Griffin's study, and the
books Hamlet feeds on ('reading the book of himself' – Mallarmé[93]).
Cushman played Hamlet because of her concern with the tragedy's ethics
and spirituality; other actresses found, as most Hamlets do, that lines and
situations resonated with their own experience, and for Vestvali the points

of contact were painful as well as assertive. 'Adventure simply appeals to me – I am the way I am', she said, but her achievements were won at great nervous expense; she regretted the rootlessness of the travelling player's life, wandering between countries 'with the collection bag': 'That's a fine attitude for an idealistic *bel esprit,* isn't it, Horatio?' Ill from 'the great strain', she went into semi-retirement. 'Absent thee from felicity awhile. . ./To tell my story': keeping faith, Braunschweig told this Hamlet's story to educate and to honour Vestvali as a model, an 'extraordinary being': 'She filled the Old and the New World with her fame, and it was mostly due to her Uranian nature that she knew how to overcome all obstacles with masculine energy and that her boundless striving allowed her to achieve the goal to which her genius had predestined her.'[94]

For these actresses, Hamlet had moved from being a 'benefit freak' to a role women were asked to enact before heads of state and which often attained a more private significance. For young Mary Anderson, opening *Hamlet* not only involved a passage from (step-) fatherly authority to self-definition, but also entry into a world of female support. She persuaded her mother, who identified theatre with immorality, to take her to meet Charlotte Cushman. Mary told her the roles, all transgressive, she was secretly preparing – Joan of Arc, Richelieu, Richard III and Hamlet. Cushman gave her the encouragement, and her mother the moral reassurance, she needed to go on.

Notes

1. Mary Anderson, *A Few Memories* (London: Osgood, McIlvaine, 1896), p 23–25. Anderson starred in a rare revival of Webster's *Duchess of Malfi,* where 'his master's masterpiece' means 'the work of Heaven'.
2. Actually, she substituted *goblin's dame!* for the 'swear' *damned.* For a modern equivalent: 'I remember doing Hamlet soliloquies in the living room for my mother when I was about thirteen. Dad was trying to watch football on TV and kept telling me to shut up. But my mother was thrilled. . . I don't know why, but when he died I knew I had to act.' (Andrea Hart, *Guardian* 1998.)
3. *A Narrative of the Life of Mrs Charlotte Charke (Youngest Daughter of Colly Cibber Esquire), Written by Herself,* 1755 (London: Constable, 1929), pp. 167–8. See Philip E Baruth, ed., *Introducing Charlotte Charke: Actress, Author, Enigma* (Urbana: University of Illinois Press, 1998), p. 110.
4. *An Apology for the Life of Colly Cibber, Actor. . . With an Historical Account of the Stage During his Own Time* (London 1740).
5. Charke: 'I have promised to conceal nothing that might raise a laugh'.

6. Charke, *Narrative*, pp. 17–18. See Kristina Straub, *Sexual Suspects: Eighteenth-century Players and Sexual Ideology* (Princeton: Princeton University Press, 1992), p. 139; Felicity A Nussbaum, *The Autobiographical Subject; Gender and Ideology in Eighteenth-century England* (Baltimore: Johns Hopkins, 1989), *passim*.

7. Lee Lewes, quoted, Philip H Highfill, *A Biographical Dictionary of Actors, Actresses, Musicians, Dancers, Managers and Other Stage Personnel in London, 1660–1800*, vol. V (Carbondale: S. Ill. University Press, 1978), p. 429; WR Chetwood, *A General History of the Stage* (Dublin 1749), p. 157.

8. Dublin, 28 April 1741; Belfast, 1 July 1741; Dublin, 1 August 1742.

9. David Garrick *Letters*, ed. David M Little and George M Kahrl (London: Oxford University Press, 1963), p. 1028. Her body was already a commodity: she was pregnant and Garrick worried that her 'big belly' would interfere with her availability for *travesti* roles in male 'shape'. Furnival coached her father Roger Kemble in male roles when he was a trainee in 1751 ('No woman on the British stage was better qualified for giving instructions'.)

10. Bristol: 23 and 30 June 1781

11. *Memoirs of Mrs Inchbald*, ed. James Boaden (London 1853), vol I, p. 95. See Annibell Jenkins, *I'll Tell You What: The Life of Elizabeth Inchbald* (Lexington: University Press of Kentucky, 2003), p. 63.

12. Roger Manvell, *Sarah Siddons, Portrait of an Actress* (London: Heinemann, 1970), p. 329.

13. 12 and 27 May 1796; 25 May 1797; in 1802 Dorothy Jordan was her Ophelia. Originally the *Monthly Mirror* noted her embarrassment and some problems with lines; although a year later she was more assured, this benefit *Hamlet* lost her £133. But in 1804 Thomas Gilliland said Hamlet was the role that best expressed 'the vigour of her genius'. He praised her discrimination here, her 'correct emphasis' and pathos, and said her delivery was so natural that she seemed to rely 'upon the feelings of the moment to prompt her'. (See Highfill, *Biographical Dictionary*, vol. XII, p. 148.)

14. Tate Wilkinson, *The Wandering Patentee* (York 1795), pp. 116–17.

15. See Kalman A Burnim, *David Garrick Director* (Pittsburgh: University of Pittsburgh Press, 1961), p. 29.

16. Manvell, *Sarah Siddons*, p. 50.

17. William Smith Clark, '"The Siddons" in Dublin', *Theatre Notebook* IX (1954–5), pp. 103–10.

18. James Boaden, *Memoirs of Mrs Siddons* (London 1827) I, pp. 282–3. Apparently from embarrassment, she wrapped herself in a cloak. Did she help mould the image of the huddled, classical-Romantic Hamlet Thomas Lawrence would immortalise in his portrait of her brother (who had acted Laertes to her Prince)?

19. *Mrs Galindo's Letter to Mrs Siddons.* (London 1809), pp. 6–7.

20. *Ibid.*, pp. 8, 61. Mrs Galindo claimed they had been discovered together in bedrooms and committing unspecified acts in a carriage. Presenting Siddons as an Iago, she added details of an incriminating handkerchief. The *Dublin Satirist* picked up the story in its January 1810 issue.

21. Boaden, *Memoirs of John Philip Kemble* (London 1825) II, p. 334; Wilkinson, *Wandering Patentee*, pp. 116–17.

22. The 'ringing distinctiveness of her tones, her prompt and voluble utterance, her vivacity of action, told irresistibly upon the house'. Walter Donaldson, *Recollections of an Actor* (London: Maxwell, 1865), pp. 137–8.

23. See Joseph W Donohue Jr, *The Theatrical Manager in England and America* (Princeton: Princeton University Press, 1971), pp. 87–110. The indispensable study of these issues is now Elizabeth Reitz Mullenix, *Wearing the Breeches: Gender on the Antebellum Stage* (New York: St Martin's Press, 2000). This contains details of the performances by Mary Barnes, Cushman, Dickinson and Marie Prescott.

24. Walter Donaldson, *Recollections of an Actor*, p. 95.

25. 22 May: apparently she was less successful. See Richard Hutton, *Curiosities of the American Stage* (New York: Harper, 1891). Another early Hamlet, Mrs Cleveland, had first appeared in New York in 1776.

26. Quoted from William Hill Brown, *The Power of Sympathy* and Hannah Webster Foster, *The Coquette* (Harmondsworth: Penguin Books, 1996), pp. 195 6.

27. T Allstone Brown, *History of the New York Stage* (New York: Dodd, Mead and Co, 1903), vol. 3, p. 67.

28. Mullenix, *Wearing the Breeches*, p. 29: Treva Rose Tumbleson, *Three Female Hamlets: Charlotte Cushman, Sarah Bernhardt and Eva Le Gallienne* (PhD University of Oregon, 1981), p. 78. William Winter thought Mrs Shaw's Hamlet better than Cushman's: Winter, *Shakespeare on the Stage* (New York: Moffat, 1914), p. 429.

29. William Winter, *Other Days* (New York: Moffat, Yard, 1908), pp. 120–1. She returned to Britain; she played Hamlet in Liverpool in 1847.

30. Boston press quoted William W Clapp Jr, *A Record of the Boston Stage* (Boston: Munroe, 1853), p. 163. Mrs Barnes retired from the American stage in 1841 but in 1842 her Hamlet was 'well received' in England. See *Dictionary of American biography*.

31. Brown, *The Power of Sympathy*, p. 43.

32. Montrose J Moses, *Famous Actor-Families in America* (New York: Crowell, 1906), p. 213.

33. WJ Lawrence, *Illustrated London News*, 17 June 1899. She played Hamlet at the Astor Palace in 1850.

34. Winter, *Shakespeare on the Stage*, p. 429.

35. From the 'laconic quotation' with which she introduced *Octavia Bragaldi*.

36. Charlotte Barnes, *Plays, Prose and Poetry* (Philadelphia: Butler, 1848), pp. iii–iv.

37. *Ibid.*, p. 133. She 'could play nothing tolerably save the Prince,' (Lawrence, *ILN*).

38. Quoted Emma Stebbins, *Charlotte Cushman: Her Letters and Memoirs of Her Life* (Boston: Houghton, Osgood, 1879), p. 13.

39. *New York Tribune*, quoted Stebbins, p. 296.

40. Outside *travesti*, one male critic said, her *forte* was the 'woman where most of the softer traits of womanhood are wanting' or who is driven 'by some earnest and long cherished determination' to assume 'the power and energy of manhood'. See Oral S Coad and Edwin Mims Jr, *The American Stage* (New Haven, 1929), p. 75.

41. Sarah Foose Parrott, 'Networking in Italy: Charlotte Cushman and "The White Marmorean Flock"', *Women's Studies* XIV (1988), p. 319.

42. Stebbins, *Cushman*, p. 12.

43. *Boston Advertiser*, 19 February 1876.

44. Harriet Hosmer, *Letters and Memories* (London: Moffat, Yard, 1913), p. 17.

45. Stebbins, *Cushman*, p. 217.

46. Fisher had been a child prodigy in London and New York playing Shylock and Hamlet. See Clara Fisher Maeder, *Autobiography of Clara Fisher Maeder* (New York: Dunlap Society, 1897).

47. WT Price, *A Life of Charlotte Cushman* (New York: Brentano, 1894), p. 127.

48. *Romeo and Juliet*, II. i. 120–1; III. iii. 108–13.

49. Knowles quoted Stebbins, *Charlotte Cushman*, p. 63.

50. See Faye E Dudden, *Women in the American Theatre: Actresses and Audiences 1790–1870* (New Haven: Yale, 1994).

51. From September 1846 she and Susan toured Liverpool, Dublin, Limerick, Cork, Glasgow, Edinburgh, Perth, Dundee, Leeds, Newcastle, Sheffield, Hull, Birmingham and Manchester. She became ill at the end of the tour.

52. Boston, 21 November; New York, 24 November. For these performances she compiled a new promptbook, now in the Library of Congress.

53. She cut 1,098 lines in 1847; 1,455 in 1851 (Tumbleson). In 1847 she kept many references to the politics and Fortinbras (though he did not appear).

54. Leach, *Bright Particular Star: The Life and Times of Charlotte Cushman* (New Haven: Yale University Press, 1970), p. 241.

55. Hosmer, *Letters*, p. 17.

56. Review (16 February 1861), cited Lisa Merrill, *When Romeo was a Woman: Charlotte Cushman and her Circle of Female Spectators* (Anne Arbor: University of Michigan Press, 1999), p. 132.

57. Review quoted Tumbleson, *Three Female Hamlets*, pp. 153–4.

58. Promptbook in the Folger Shakespeare Library, pp. 153–4.

59. Tumbleson, *Three Female Hamlets*, p. 181.

60. Stebbins, *Charlotte Cushman*, p. 218.

61. She also cut 'There's the respect/That makes calamity of so long life'. Many cuts in her Folger promptbook concerned standard questions of taste and practicality. Rhetoric was trimmed, for example the Player King's

speech by about 50 per cent. Cushman's acting version was loyal to the shape of the play save for heavy cuts to the King's role (his 'conscience' aside in the Nunnery scene, his prayer scene, and most of his lines in Act IV).

62. Cushman to Emma Crowe, 1861, quoted Leach, *Bright Particular Star*, p. 314.

63. Tumbleson, *Three Female Hamlets*, pp. 153–4.

64. *Tribune*, 27 November 1860, reviewing Booth, who like Cushman chose 'to conduct himself like a gentleman and not a blackguard' here.

65. Cushman: 'I have seen a painting of Talma in this passage – the first time I acted the part I took this view of it – it was much admired.'

66. Stebbins, *Cushman,* p. 60.

67. Letter to Emma Crowe, quoted Merrill, *When Romeo Was a Woman*, p. 132.

68. 16 February 1861. Mary Shaw played Ophelia.

69. Letters to Mary Devlin. See Yvonne Shafer, 'Women in Male Roles: Charlotte Cushman and Others', Helen Krich Chinoy and Linda Walsh Jenkins, *Women in American Theatre* (New York: Theatre Communications Group, 1987), p. 78; Merrill, *When Romeo was a Woman*, p. 132.

70. Stebbins, *Charlotte Cushman*, p. 60.

71. *Ibid.*, pp. 217–18.

72. Booth. See Merrill, *When Romeo was a Woman*, p. 132.

73. Leach, *Bright Particular Star*, p. 309.

74. *Ibid.*, p. 314.

75. Letter to Emma Crow, August 1861.

76. Diary quoted Lillian Faderman, *Surpassing the Love of Men* (New York: Morrow, 1981), pp. 222–3.

77. Quoting James Russell Lowell's 'Columbus'. See Leach, *Bright Particular Star*, p. 395.

78. *Ibid.*, p. 377.

79. Walt Whitman, *The Gathering of the Forces* (New York: Putnam's, 1920), p. 344.

80. Elizabeth Barrett Browning writing to her sister in 1852, quoted Leach, *Bright Particular Star*, p. 210.

81. Parrott, 'Networking in Italy', p. 334.

82. Leach, *Bright Particular Star*, p. 278. Cushman appeared slightly fictionalised as an inspirational figure in Louisa May Alcott's *Joe's Boys* and Geraldine Jewsbury's *The Half Sister*.

83. 'Yours, *Hammel-fett* (Mutton-fat).'

84. 18 November playbill, and *Illustrated London News* 16 November 1867. Most of the following information is cited from Rosa von Braunschweig, 'Felicita von Vestvali', *Yearbook of Intermediate Sexual Types*, vol. 1 (1903), reprinted in Lillian Faderman and Brigitte Erikson (eds.) *Lesbians in Germany: 1890s–1920s* (Tallahassee: Naiad, 1990). I am grateful to Kate Chedgzoy for this reference.

85. Edmund M Gagey, *The San Francisco Stage: A History* (New York: Columbia University Press, 1950), pp. 119–21. Vestvali was contracted for 100 nights, including a share of profits plus benefit performances. She acted with the Anglo-German Daniel Bandmann, whose own Hamlet was Fechterian and who married Millicent (Lily) Palmer, later England's leading female Hamlet.

86. *Athenaeum*, 23 October 1867.

87. *Athenaeum*, 21 December 1867.

88. Braunschweig, 'Vestvali', p. 78.

89. 'The well-known Leipzig critic Gottschell', *ibid.*, p. 78.

90. Berlin critic, *ibid.*, p. 79.

91. Gottschell, *ibid.*, p. 78.

92. *Ibid.*, pp. 73–4.

93. See Martin Scofield, *The Ghosts of Hamlet: The Play and Modern Writers* (Cambridge: Cambridge University Press, 1980), chapter nine, *passim*.

94. Braunschweig, 'Vestvali', pp. 74–5. By August 1860 Charles Dickens could refer idiomatically to his mother 'got up in sables like a female Hamlet.' This allusion was complex, though, touching areas of pain and black comedy: Dickens was writing privately, stating that he had found his mother - who would die in 1863 - 'in the strangest state of mind from senile decay'. Her appearance and 'the impossibility of getting her to understand what is the matter' created a 'dreary scene' lit by 'ghastly absurdity'. Walter Dexter, ed., *The Letters of Charles Dickens* (London: Nonesuch, 1938), vol. 3, 172. Thanks to John Stokes for this reference.

CHAPTER 3

'Is this womanly?'

There should be a law against such perversions; they are high crimes and misdemeanours against truth, taste, and aesthetic principles of art, as well as offences against propriety, and desecrations of Shakspere [sic]. In his time women did not appear on the stage at all; now they usurp men's parts, and 'push us from our stools'.

George Vandenhoff, *Leaves from an Actor's Notebook*, 1860[1]

It is an uncommon event to meet a woman that at some period of her life, she had not wished she had been a boy.

Mary Virginia Terhune, *Eve's Daughters*, 1882[2]

I

Frances Anne Kemble and the throne of self

In 1848 Fanny, the daughter of Charles Kemble and niece of Sarah Siddons, found herself brooding on Hamlet: 'The only thought that makes me shrink from the notion of suicide is the apprehension that to this life another *might* succeed, as full of storm, of strife, of disappointment, difficulty and unrest as this; and with that uncertainty overshadowing it, death has not much to recommend it. It is poor Hamlet's "perchance" that is the knot of the whole question.'[3] To universal astonishment, Fanny Kemble (1809–93) had given up acting to marry Pierce Butler, the owner of a slave-plantation in Georgia. The marriage however degenerated and she recorded her alienation in her diaries: 'I still feel a stranger here', she wrote after five years, 'and fear I shall continue to do so until I die.' In 1848 she was in England again and Butler sued her for desertion. Fighting for access to her children, Kemble felt herself caught in a tragedy: 'Well is it with those who quietly reach the fifth act of their lives . . . The sudden catastrophe of adverse circumstances, wrecking a whole existence in the very middle of its course, is a more terrible thing than death.'[4] Her response transformed her career and opened new options for nineteenth-century actresses.

A few months after Charlotte Cushman's English tour as Hamlet, Fanny Kemble began to raise funds for the divorce with a series of solo Shakespeare readings. These phenomenally successful events symbolised her struggle for independence and were welcomed as practical proof that an educated woman could succeed alone. To prepare, she commandeered reading-texts that her father had put together for recitals. He began his readings at Buckingham Palace, but Fanny declined a similar royal invitation and started her new career in a hall in Highgate. On the first three nights she read her most popular Shakespearean roles – Juliet, Lady Macbeth and Ophelia – but now the woman's voice controlled every play. In his solo *Hamlet* her father was nervous of assuming Ophelia's voice; he kept her out till the Nunnery scene and cut her madness to one short page. Fanny conversely embraced the possibilities of androgyny, offering 'myriad voices and faces condensed into one' – 'sweet', 'hoarse', 'tender', 'burly and deep-chested'. 'How shall I describe the immense animal spirits, the utter transformation of voice, face and gesture', wrote one spectator, of 'this extraordinary woman?'[5] Forced to return to America to contest Butler's charges, she made Shakespeare her main financial weapon. In January 1849 she read *Hamlet* to a crowded hall in Boston and the poet Longfellow recorded: '*Hamlet* sublimely read; with the only true comprehension and expression of the melancholy Dane I have had the good fortune to hear.'[6]

Fanny Kemble had gained an objective perspective on Hamlet from an early age through playing Ophelia, and in her 1832 journal – en route to America to act with her father – analysed the character at length, apparently identifying strongly with his 'impatience at his own dependent position'. For her, Hamlet was 'gloomy, despondent, ambitious and disappointed in his ambition, full of sorrow for a dead father, of shame for a living mother' – a 'questioning spirit, looking with timid boldness from the riddles of earth and life to those of death and the mysterious land beyond it'. 'Weary of existence', he was yet kept 'from self-destruction by religious awe'. Until events disturbed a delicately balanced personality, she found Hamlet 'sad and dreamy in his affections', with 'not enough of absolute passion in his love to make it a powerful and engrossing interest'. But 'then see what follows': 'a horrible and sudden revelation' pits his innate 'want of resolution and activity' against 'burning hatred' and 'imperative duty'. Fanny Kemble – whose own watchfulness and self-awareness were demonstrated when she published her intimate journals – stressed 'the vigilant and circumspect guard he is forced to keep upon every word, look and action . . ., his constant watchfulness', until violent events crowded in, culminating in 'the miserable death of poor Ophelia'. Given 'all these – the man's own nature, sad and desponding, reasoning and metaphysical, and the nature he acquires from the tutelage of events, bitter, dark, amazed, uncertain' – her interpretation became inevitable: 'I am surprised at anybody's ever questioning the real madness of Hamlet.'

Fanny believed 'the great beauty' of her father's Hamlet, which so inspired Delacroix, was 'a wonderful accuracy in the detail' – 'the finer and more fleeting shades of character, the more graceful and delicate manifestations of feeling' – but she criticised 'a weakness of voice . . . a want of intensity'.[7] She was equally suspicious of Kean's Hamlet – 'an eye like an orb of light, a voice, exquisitely touching and melodious in its tenderness, and in the harsh dissonance of passion, terribly true' – because he fragmented the part, 'acting detached passages alone and leaving all the others, and the entire character indeed, utterly destitute of unity'.[8] Convinced 'the highest walks of tragedy' were unreachable without 'startling and tremendous bursts of passion' but meaningless without form, Fanny Kemble put both men in the second rank: 'I fancy my aunt Siddons united the excellencies of both these styles.'

She sat, Longfellow said, at 'a reading-desk covered with red, on a platform, like the gory block on the scaffold; upon which the magnificent Fanny bowed her head in tears and great emotion. But in a moment it became her triumphal chariot'.[9] He honoured her with a sonnet, climaxing:

> Oh happy Poet! by no critic vext!
> How must thy listening spirit now rejoice
> To be interpreted by such a voice!

Kemble read the plays in two-hour versions sitting at a table backed by crimson screens. She wore a different dress for each play and, lit by candelabra with a large volume of Shakespeare on a lectern (feminised by her into what Longfellow called a 'sybilline' 'magic book'), she fabricated a situation giving her easy authority – part educational, part domestic, part devotional. Her countless male roles provoked controversy. The *Athenaeum* detected strain 'in the violent changes and the counterfeit tone which more reluctantly obey her strong dramatic will, when a Lear or a Falstaff are to be made to speak', and the actress Ellen Tree wrote, 'I do not think it possible for a woman to read comic male characters in Shakespeare and avoid a tinge of vulgarity or grossness.'[10] Fanny herself used to mock Shakespeare recitals, especially the idea a man 'might get up and start reciting the balcony scene in *Romeo and Juliet*', but now when she read Falstaff, she 'forgot herself'.[11] Even Tree conceded, 'She read the men *best*.' One of her reasons for abandoning the stage had been her intense self-consciousness, her sense of the falsity of the illusions around her; a reviewer concluded she had found a 'subjective' form to liberate her intelligence: 'The reflective consciousness which will not allow the actress to forget her mind in her character becomes an admirable quality in the dramatic expositor.'[12]

'What nights these are!' Longfellow wrote, 'With Shakespeare and such a reader.' 'What a marvellous era in the world's history is this we are living in!' wrote Fanny Kemble, who knew that her situation had a larger resonance. 1848 was the year of revolutions: 'Kings, princes and potentates flying dismayed to the right and left, and nation after nation rising up, demanding a freedom which God knows how few of them seem capable of using.'[13] When she read Shylock that spring she made him a thoughtful man of 'settled convictions' who 'personified the sufferings of his nation'.[14] It was in 1848, too, that her friend Lucretia Mott organised a convention at Seneca Falls, New York State, that formulated the *Declaration of Sentiments*, a founding text for suffragist thought: 'We hold these truths to be self-evident; that all men and women are created equal.' The *Declaration* condemned patriarchal control of the divorce laws and called for women to speak in public: man 'has usurped the prerogative of Jehovah himself, claiming it as his right to assign for her a sphere of action'.[15] In September 1849 the Butlers were divorced. He won custody of the children but Kemble used her Shakespeare readings to raise funds for women's organisations and the Abolitionists. Her *Journal of a Residence on a Georgian Plantation*, published in 1863, had a startling effect on both sides of the Atlantic. It contributed to a climate of opinion that prevented British intervention to aid the Confederacy and when extracts were published in London as *The Essence of Slavery*, much was made of the moment when a group of black nursing mothers came to Kemble for help. When they compared their experiences with her own, 'I held the table before me so hard, in order not to cry, that I think my fingers ought to have left a mark on it.'[16] When she gave birth herself she had written, 'I was at first a little disappointed that my baby was not a man-child, for the lot of woman is seldom happy, owing principally, I think, to the many serious mistakes which have obtained universal sway in female education. I do not believe that the just Creator intended one part of His creatures to lead the sort of lives that many women do . . . [17]

She kept up her readings for twenty years, and with her essays on Shakespeare's characters (especially the women) she became an acknowledged authority. Many actresses followed her lead as readers/lecturers, from Eleanor Glyn to Charlotte Cushman who pointed out that readings let actresses extend their working lives; she credited Fanny Kemble with revolutionising the status and self-image of the actress, and indeed the profession increasingly shone out in a world where most girls were denied educational opportunities. Several suffragist writers saw the situations actresses confronted nightly as metaphors for repression and self-abnegation, for the discomfort facing the woman who aspired beyond the home. One of Kemble's closest American friends, the novelist Catherine Maria Sedgewick described a young woman's agony when she wins a composition prize and has to appear on a stage. The curtain draws and exposes her dressed in black, seated on a throne – what another writer Mary Terhune called the unreachable 'throne of Self' and 'intellectual strivings'. Looking like a 'meek usurper', she can hardly speak under the public gaze and in 'a low and faltering voice' reads her piece – called 'Gratitude.'[18] And when Caroline Howard Gilman first saw her own work in print she felt ashamed, 'as if I had been detected in man's apparel'.[19] Actresses faced the reverse challenge, to establish personal integrity despite their immodest visibility. *Hamlet* traces the psychological and political obstacles blocking the path to 'the throne of self', and Hamlet's death on the throne became the iconic climax of many performances by actresses, from Millicent Bandmann-Palmer to Eva Le Gallienne. Liberty, Fanny Kemble often insisted, was a matter of education, the attainment and use of knowledge. Late in life, addressing an audience of young American teachers, 700 men and women with the future in their hands, she began with *Hamlet*: 'Speak the speech I pray you, as I foretold you . . . '[20]

II

Mary Braddon and the domestic Hamlet

The feminised prince became increasingly familiar within the two new domains of suffrage politics and popular culture. In 1863, alongside the publication of Kemble's *Georgian Plantation* journal, Alice Marriott, the most acclaimed Victorian female Hamlet, took over Sadlers Wells

Theatre in Islington, Oliph Webb played Hamlet at the Britannia Theatre in the East End, and the 'sensation' novel *Eleanor's Victory* by Mary Braddon appeared in serial form. Mrs Braddon, 'the Queen of the circulating libraries',[21] wrote over eighty tales of – in her words – 'mystery and murder & so on' aimed at the popular and especially the female 'market'.[22] In *Eleanor's Victory* she rewrote *Hamlet* as the story of a Victorian woman in her teens.

Braddon's heroine is Eleanor, the youngest daughter of George Vane, an old drinking crony of the Prince of Wales but fallen on hard times. She is fifteen and perhaps touched by 'that rare tropical blossom, that mental once-in-a-century flourishing aloe, which men call Genius'. In Paris, however, her father is poisoned and in Shakespearean pastiche he is buried wretchedly, laid barefaced in the Morgue till 'they placed him amongst a cluster of neglected graves, in a patch of ground . . . where the bones of the departed were . . . stirred up out of their coffins periodically to make room for new-comers'.[23] Ophelia's fate beckons; 'This poor lonely child of fifteen might go melancholy mad, perhaps, in her grief', her imagination haunted by images of Ophelia filtered through Gothic novels: 'the dreary river bank', 'the drowned young women'.[24] She dons white muslin and 'her highly nervous and imaginative nature' succumbs to delirium. But then Eleanor discovers that her father killed himself because an unknown villain ruined him at the gaming tables, and Mrs Braddon updated the Ghost as a suicide note torn into cryptic poetry:

> *forget, Eleanor, never forget Robert Lan*
> *a cheat and a villain who*
> *some day live to revenge the fate*
> *poor old father*[25]

From then on Eleanor is Hamlet, 'gloomily absorbed': 'I remember nothing, except that my father tells me to revenge his murder.' Her few friends are appalled by the 'horrible discrepancy between this girl's innocent youthful beauty and all this determined talk of fierce and eager vengeance' – 'Are you mad?' – but her emotional trajectory follows Hamlet's: 'After the first burst of passionate vehemence . . . her manner had grown almost unnaturally calm . . . She kept silence, brooding.'[26] 'I don't know who he is', she murmurs, 'or where he comes from, but sooner or later I swear to be revenged upon him for my father's cruel death.'

'I don't know whether it is womanly or Christian-like,' she said, 'but I know it is henceforward the purpose of my life, and that it is stronger than myself.'[27]

'Human nature is made up of contradictions', Braddon wrote, and Eleanor Vane embodies Hamlet's contradictions: remorseless dedication to revenge versus despairing enervation. By re-imagining Hamlet as a bereaved young Victorian woman, she gave the pain a precise objective correlative. The loss of the Father, whom Eleanor expected to nurse for years, is cataclysmic for her sense of self: 'Every link that had bound her to life, and love, and happiness, seemed suddenly severed, and she stood alone, groping blindly in the thick darkness of a new and dreary world.' Denied her future, she enters a state of spiritual alienation: 'There was only the sad, desolate present, – a dreary spot in the great desert of life, bounded by a yawning grave.'[28]

She is sent back to England like Hamlet in the hope that its sights and impressions will cure her melancholia; they do not, but Braddon reminded her readers that 'classic vows of vengeance were all very well in the days when a Medea rode upon flying dragons', but not in Brixton and Bloomsbury.[29] Moreover Eleanor does not know her enemy's identity and a solitary woman in her position has no way of ever discovering it: she must find herself employment, security and probably a husband. Not only did *Eleanor's Victory* insist that a young Victorian woman can experience Hamlet's sufferings, it argued that she will feel them more appallingly, because she is denied Hamlet's hopes of redress. Eleanor assumes a false name and becomes a lady's paid companion near Windsor (Braddon loathed 'the wearisome dull slavery of a governess', from personal experience). There she stumbles across a listless would-be painter named Launcelot Darrell; he, she realises, is the man who drove her father to his death. They were competing for the same legacy. Melodramatic coincidence was one of Braddon's key resources, as if to say that her heroines had no chance of changing their situation without incredible luck. But like Hamlet, Eleanor must find evidence – if she cannot, 'I will try and believe that I have been deluded by some foolish fancy of my own.'[30] And so Mary Braddon's female Hamlet also becomes one of fiction's first female detectives.

Braddon had few literary pretensions, she described herself as 'not great but popular'. Detractors accused her of presenting 'wicked women' sympathetically, exploiting 'that half-serious, half-smiling curiosity with which the world is at present watching the efforts of the female sex to take up a stronger position'. [31]A hack in her 1864 novel *The Doctor's Wife* (inspired by *Madam Bovary*) admitted, 'The next best thing to do if you haven't got ideas of your own is to steal other people's ideas in an impartial manner',[32] but the *Hamlet* borrowings in *Eleanor's Victory* were more than a convenience. Braddon populates the novel with characters who see themselves and others in terms shaped by Shakespeare.[33] It was her comment on Shakespeare's growing presence in Victorian consciousness on the eve of his Tercentenary, and on the human tendency to self-dramatise and reduce others – in this book particularly women – to stereotypes. George Vane, for example, 'was wont to lament his daughter's cruel lack of affection in very bitter language, freely interspersed with quotations from *King Lear*' –

ignoring the one rather important fact that, whereas Lear's folly had been the too generous division of his own fortune between his recreant daughters, *his* weakness had been the reckless waste and expenditure of the portions which his children had inherited from their mother.[34]

The Horatio character, Dick Thornton, is a theatrical scene-painter and melodrama writer who imagines Eleanor as Juliet; Laura, Eleanor's charge at Windsor, falls for Darrell and fantasises, 'I could live for ever and ever near him, and be content to see him sometimes, or to hear his voice, even if I did not see him. I should like to wear boy's clothes and be his page, like Viola.'[35] The characters see themselves or each other as Cleopatra, Caesar, Antony, Jessica, Celia and Rosalind, and with profound irony Darrell himself is a would-be Hamlet. Brooding on uncles, inheritance and his mother, and – marked by 'an almost feminine softness' – he is the image of Delacroix's Prince:

The dark eyes had a lazy light in them, and were half hidden by the listless droop of the black lashes that fringed their full white lids. The straight nose, low forehead, and delicately moulded mouth, were almost classical in their physical perfection, but there was something wanting in the lower part of the face; the chin receded a little where it should have projected; the handsome mouth was weak and undecided in expression.[36]

A child of the Regency period ('the men of that frivolous era seem to have abandoned themselves to unmanly weakness'), this 'sulky', 'irresolute' and self-pitying poseur is a decadent travesty of the hero who is actually incarnated in the woman he stares at and sketches but cannot *see*. This conflict between potential female and male Hamlets would be common in later fiction inspired by the play. But having placed a girl in the role, Braddon tested its viability. If the perennial *Hamlet* question was 'Why does he delay?' she gave two reasons why Eleanor cannot avenge her father, one social, one psychological, and both issues of gender.

The first concerns status and marriage. Unaware who Eleanor is, Darrell proposes to her. A true Gothic avenger might accept in order to unlock his secrets; her sense of 'womanly honour' prevents her, but when the local lawyer Gilbert Monckton also asks for her hand – which would allow her to stay in Windsor and spy on Darrell – her dead father breaks into her thoughts: 'Have you so little memory of my wrongs and my sorrows that you can shrink from any means of avenging me?'[37] With the Ghost rationalised as part of her consciousness, she accepts Monckton – and traps herself in a loveless marriage. Within a page her jealous husband recasts her as Desdemona.[38] Each time Eleanor leaves the house to pursue her investigations, he sees proof of her adultery, reducing her from agent to object as he peers at her from behind a handkerchief. If Denmark was a prison, marriage in the 1860s is worse.[39] Braddon's subversive twist to *Hamlet* was that tragedy actually liberated Eleanor Vane: her father's death saved her from her fate as an unpaid nurse and forced her to redefine herself, unlike the trapped women of Windsor: 'shallow' Laura, Darrell's insulted mother, and two spinster neighbours turned by domestic servitude into Goneril and Regan. But now Hamlet and Horatio's roles become reversed: the trapped Mrs Eleanor Monckton can only watch Darrell, looking for signs of conscience, while Dick the melodrama writer scours Windsor Castle's corridors for proof.

To that extent Mary Braddon rewrote *Hamlet* as a feminist social critique. However her psychological perspective was less radical; she conceded that placing a woman in the Hamlet role violated certain assumptions about female emotional and intellectual resources. Braddon copied Wilkie Collins' *The Woman in White* (1860) which also used a pair of female and male investigators, but Collins' novel is 'the story of what a woman's patience can endure, and what a man's resolution can achieve' and Braddon accepted the formula – 'Your brain is clearer, your perceptions quicker, than mine':

'I must obey you, Dick,' Eleanor said, 'because you are good to me, and have done so much to prove that you are a great deal wiser than I am.'[40]

Braddon abandoned *Hamlet*'s time-scheme and years pass as Mrs Monckton struggles with depression and her predicament. Braddon presents this as a failure of temperament and when it comes to action as opposed to suffering, Eleanor is not equipped for her role. Braddon praises Dick's 'deliberate policy, as compared with the impulsive and unconsidered course of action recklessly followed by a headstrong girl'; and when Eleanor tries to engineer Darrell's punishment the result is disastrous. One dark night she sees two villains plant a forged will, so she re-enacts Hamlet's defeat of Rosencrantz and Guildenstern by switching documents. She stage-manages a public *coup de théâtre* in which she denounces Darrell as a murderer and reveals her identity – 'I am Eleanor Vane,' – but Braddon twisted the plot again. The incriminating papers have vanished. Eleanor is humiliated, and everything she has achieved is destroyed. She runs away.

Mary Braddon insisted that sensational literature like hers was a poor guide to life and that her readers – predominantly homebound women – must resist the temptation to escape into fantasy. She pitied 'those poor foolish girls who read nothing else, and think that their lives are to be paraphrases of their favourite books'.[41] Like Hamlet, Eleanor Vane usually has a book in her hand but her library is limited: 'Perhaps she formed her ideas of life from the numerous novels she had read, in which the villain was always confounded in the last chapter.' Darrell sneers at Eleanor's Will Scene ('an excellent paragraph for a hard-up penny-a-liner') and even Horatio warns, 'Life is not. . .a five-act play.'[42] Braddon took her readers to the point where, if her modern *Hamlet* was not to end even more bleakly than Shakespeare's because women were not free agents, the model must be abandoned.

No-one articulates the central *Hamlet* parallel – least of all the modest Eleanor – until the finale, when she meets the motherly Mrs Lennard who calls her Hamlet.[43] This lady is Braddon's answer to Dickens' Miss Faversham, a woman who ditched her fiancé at the altar and has had a jolly time ever since, mocking 'with tragic rapture' the idea that anyone should live in thrall to the crimes of the past. Joking about 'great expectations', Mrs Lennard suddenly spins the plot to an amazing Dickensian resolution. The wicked are exposed, the good rewarded, everyone is reconciled, marries or inherits in a textbook reversal of *Hamlet* – and Eleanor forgives Launcelot Darrell. For she finally rethinks the loyalties underlying her tragic identity: 'Absorbed in her affection as a daughter', she 'had sacrificed the living to the dead.' Indeed, 'she had been wrong altogether. . .vengeance is the right of divinity alone'. 'Eleanor, Eleanor!' Dick's mother cried at the start of the book, shocked by her vengefulness, 'Is this womanly? Is this Christian-like?' Braddon finally concluded it was not.

She showed there could be no plausible justice for a Victorian Eleanor/Hamlet without a fairy-tale transformation, 'And after all, Eleanor's Victory was a proper womanly conquest, and not a stern, classical vengeance.' Despite her reputation for scandal, Braddon closed her *Hamlet* by absorbing Eleanor and her 'tender woman's heart' into domesticity. She saw that Hamlet was a protagonist with whose profound malaise, integrity and sense of helplessness women readers might, however secretly, identify; but finally she only allowed her heroine to be the passive, suffering Hamlet, not the philosopher, the satirist or the avenging agent. And yet it was possible to see Braddon's ending as progressive because she believed social values are ultimately shaped by mature women: Eleanor *outgrows* Hamlet's obsession with the Father. And after all, kingly George Vane was a lying wastrel who drank away two marriages and three fortunes. *Eleanor's Victory* was widely read in England and America; it contained a spirited defence of mass culture and the melodrama stage, and it showed a modern female Hamlet knocking at the door of suffrage politics and the popular imagination.

III

'Not great but popular'

Who were the women who played Hamlet? In the mid-nineteenth-century Shakespeare was not yet wholly a writer for the middle classes or the education system. Shakespeare could be seen in many 'minor' London theatres in poor districts – the Standard, Shoreditch; the Pavilion, Whitechapel ('Here is a remarkable circumstance: *Hamlet* has been played at the Pavilion more times in the course of one season than in all the leading theatres in the whole of London together'[44]); and especially at the Britannia, Hoxton, where in 1864 the manageress Sarah Lane organised the most substantial of all the Shakespeare Tercentenary Festivals, and then made it an annual event. In November 1863 Oliph Webb played a benefit Hamlet at the Britannia and a photograph, unusually, shows her reading in her 'mad' costume, with the cloak slung the wrong way, twisted round the front of her body. But there was little sense of comedy: the features were pale, pinched and staring, she stood unnaturally taut, as if sleep-walking; small hands made exact gestures; she wore her father's ring. The Britannia engaged female Hamlets for midweek midsummer nights in 1867, 1869, 1871 and 1873. In 1867 their leading actress, the 'brilliant, versatile' Sophie Miles, 'one of the most beautiful women who ever took to the art of acting', was Hamlet and in 1869 it was 'young and clever' Marie Henderson: 'Capital House. Total amount 383.3.0.' 'Possessed of a pleasing appearance, some command of passion and clear pronunciation, this lady is likely to become a very great favourite.'[45] Working-class taste prized diversity: Henderson shared the bill with *Falsely Accused, or the Boys of Bircham School* and a blackface minstrel.

Two years later she was Hamlet again alongside the melodrama *Black-Eyed Susan*, and was even more successful: 'Immense Pit and Gallery – filling out not only the Audience part of the house, but the passage as well – to the astonishment of all the actors & the management.'[46] (And it was Henderson's Hamlet that drew the crowd; receipts fell when *Black-Eyed Susan* was repeated without her.) The company were 'rough' – 'somewhat too loud and demonstrative for Shakespeare'. On such nights *Hamlet* was stripped to the plot: Miss Bellair (Britannia 1873) cut Act 2 – the 'antic disposition' scenes, Hecuba, and 'O what a rogue and peasant slave am I'.

The aura of scandal still clung to the female Hamlet. The legend of Charlotte Charke provoked 'disgust' amongst Victorian stage historians, and because the tragic cross-dresser – inseparable from an entertainment industry that increasingly provided spaces for male gratification – drew attention to her gender in the very act of playing against it, critics often subjected her to pseudo-medical inspection: 'Tall and masculine, though the head is rather small, and the face presents but a limited tablet for the expression of feeling,'. . . 'Quaint little movements, the lower limbs are apt to cling helplessly together, the knees are instinctively bowed inward'.[47] If she *was* physically convincing she was 'mannish'. Prurient rumours about Vestvali, or Cushman's leading ladies – even her sister was said to be her lover – typified the female Hamlet's reception, and tales circulated of actresses playing Hamlet at moments of moral breakdown. Days after Sophie Miles first played Hamlet at the Britannia in 1867 she abandoned her children and eloped to America; when she returned the company shunned her; two days after Marie Henderson's Britannia Hamlet (1869) she collapsed on stage, allegedly drunk. When the actor Walter Montague committed suicide after his wedding night, rumours hinted that he had discovered something unnatural about his wife Winetta and that she stole his costume to play a Hamlet of 'somewhat Romantic appearance'.[48]

However, unconventional actresses enjoyed increasing opportunities as new touring networks emerged and rail and steamship transport developed. For example Eleanor Goddard, 'the celebrated tragic actress', played Hamlet in the North of England, toured the American and Australian gold fields in the mid-1850s, then returned to England and was Hamlet in Northampton in 1862.[49] It was a two-way business; in 1870 the Canadian actress Julia Tremayne made her British debut as Hamlet in Southampton, and some Australian women took their Hamlet to America or Britain. Australian female Hamlets included Mrs Cleveland, Mrs Evans, Fanny Heir and Louise Pomeroy. *Hamlet* thrived within the

Figure 5   Charlotte Crampton as Hamlet. *Illustrated London News*, 17 June 1899.

popular entertainment industry and many little girls in theatrical families, infant phenomena, played the prince in condensed versions. PT Barnum brought the Shakespearean infant double-act of Ellen and Kate Bateman from America, and Ellen (1844–1936) later played Hamlet.[50] The most extravagant populist was Charlotte Crampton (1816–75) (see Figure 5).

Figure 6   Louise Pomeroy as Hamlet. *Illustrated London News*, 17 June 1899.

Born in Kentucky 'she excelled as Hamlet, Iago, Richard III and Shylock and was called 'a woman of Genius, wayward, dissolute and daring,' driven by a 'compelling fire that was akin to that which made Kean's performance so thrilling'.[51] In this case 'impersonate' was literal: though 'petite', she imitated the hyper-masculine Edwin Forrest, with a pencil-thin moustache and beard, wild eyes, upswept hair, a Van Dyke cape flung jauntily, and her sword ready to hand.[52] In 1859 in a two-week New York season she played Hamlet, Mazeppa, Shylock, Lady Macbeth, 'The French Spy', and Richard III on horseback with her trained steeds Alexander and Black Eagle. A fine fencer and reckless equestrian, she drew attention to her body in unpredictable ways, slung 'naked' across a horse as Mazeppa one night, bearded as Forrest-Hamlet the next. The Civil War brought her like many women into direct contact with violence; she enlisted in the Union army medical service and Laurence Selleneck has shown that women's experiences in the nursing corps and elsewhere inspired many kinds of cross-dressed entertainments.[53] Charlotte Crampton fused Shakespeare, fine verse-speaking and circus but was highly rated by sophisticates too; several critics ranked her Hamlet second to Cushman.[54]

   In actor-managerial theatre two factors always influenced the casting of Hamlet, novelty or seniority, and when women played him two broad approaches emerged – volatile young Eleanor Vane, as it were, versus

Figure 7   Alice Marriott as Hamlet, 1864, (© V & A Images / Victoria and Albert Museum London).

trapped Mrs Monckton. A drawing of Louise Pomeroy (d.1893) as Hamlet in the Play scene drew attention to the actress, not the character (see Figure 6). She was sketched reclining in long boots and a tunic like a very brief skirt; out of context it became a pin-up pose. Yet her image was subtle: Pomeroy was also a playwright and her Hamlet holds sheets of writing; the expression is cautiously watchful, she is object and subject, body and mind. Complex gazing offered complex pleasures. Nothing could be less like the upfront formal photographs commissioned by the respected Alice Marriott (1824–1900) (see Figure 7). Here were divergent idealisations of woman: late-Romantic liberated beauty, or matronly moral worth; their images of passion or probity reflected the attempt to fix Hamlet as the expression of 'feminine' feeling or 'masculine' will, as youth or wisdom, and also illustrated basic choices in Victorian theatrical cross-dressing – the erotic versus 'earnest' (Cushman's word) male impersonation. However the English actresses who made a reputation in the role – Alice Marriott, Julia Seaman and Millicent Bandmann-Palmer – were all in the second category. Hamlet was their passport to exploring the mind onstage with dignity, and indeed after a century of fugitive performances and *jeux d'esprits*, Alice Marriott made the female Hamlet respectable in England.

'Correct and careful': Alice Marriott

In 1859 Miss Marriott established herself as Hamlet in Glasgow, Bath, Birmingham, Dublin and Liverpool: 'Miss Marriott has done as much for Hamlet as Miss Cushman did for Romeo – she has made it a creation – a thing of beauty.'[55] 'A Playgoer for Thirty-Five Years' enthused, 'I have seen all the great actors since Kemble's time in the part, – *the most difficult one* in the whole range of Shakespeare's characters. *None of them* satisfied me . . . As regards Miss Marriott's portrayal of the young prince, I would almost be induced to say it was PERFECT.'[56] After this she outbid Siddons and Cushman and took Hamlet to London (Marylebone Theatre 1861). Victorian critics, used to middle-aged Hamlets like Macready, thought she was physically well cast: 'Her figure is imposing and her carriage is, if not quite masculine, sufficiently so for stage purposes.' Though Marriott made much of her income from melodrama her sober Hamlet, wearing the Order of the Elephant, was 'brought up on the dignity and refinement of a Court', with 'a cultivated mind and a sensitive temperament' and extraordinary gentleness. Critics praised her 'careful study' and elocutionary clarity, everyone remembered her voice. She gave 'fresh significance' to 'passages that might hitherto have escaped the notice of cursory students' and her 'To be or not to be' was often applauded – not for originality but for 'chasteness of expression'.[57] She won the respect of critics hostile to *travesti*; in fact in 1899 conservatives evoked the *gravitas* and musicality of Alice Marriott's Hamlet to attack Bernhardt.[58]

Equally significantly she and her husband took over Sadlers Wells, the most admired London theatre outside the West End, so in February 1864 an English actress for the first time played Hamlet not as a visiting star but in her own coherent 'archaeologically-correct' production, with 'New and Characteristic Scenery', 'New and Appropriate Costumes', new 'Elaborate Machinery', and 'Correct' armour – 'The whole produced under the immediate direction and superintendence of Miss Marriott'. Venue and moment were both significant: Samuel Phelps had made Sadlers Wells famous with his scrupulous productions of Shakespeare for working and lower-middle-class audiences, and the Tercentenary celebrated the incorporation of the Shakespeare Myth into the heart of the national identity. As the Victorians celebrated Shakespeare's place in the march of English history, productions like Charles Kean's increasingly advertised their 'accuracy' and research, turning theatres into educational *tableaux vivants*. For Alice Marriott's *Hamlet*, medieval documents, weapons and architecture 'have been copied with exactness . . . the result of long and anxious deliberation on the subject, assisted by such evidence as may be deemed authentic'. Intriguingly, she sensed the potential disparity between archaeological reconstruction and Shakespeare's fluidity. 'Great difficulty ensues', Sadlers Wells said, in reconciling 'the proper representation of the age depicted' with 'the various habits, styles, and costumes which are necessary for fulfilling the Poet's intentions', and inevitably her own cross-dressing – the fact that a 'reality' was being recreated with artifice at the heart of it – added to the difficulty. In the new positivist climate, *travesti* became aesthetically rather than morally problematic, so Alice Marriott tried to make the setting and her performance equally plausible.

The result was 'a most signal and unequivocal' success, 'a very singular result of talent, courage, and industry. 'Unbridled enthusiasm nightly': she would play Hamlet four times a week till further notice in a production praised for convincing settings and innovatory ghost effects. 'Nothing for years within the walls of a theatre could exceed the enthusiasm created by Miss Marriott's representation of *Hamlet*.' This was playbill hyperbole, but Marriott reprinted the long and enthusiastic *Times* review for a month: 'It is the Hamlet of Miss Marriott that will attract the Shakespeareans in this Shakespearean year.'[59] It became a national highlight of the celebrations. Liverpool invited her back for April 22nd, Birthday Eve, and the Mayor threw the theatre open so the city could see Marriott's Hamlet *gratis*. Her success was a gossip item in the provincial press: 'It has been said by critics that the part should always be played by a woman, Hamlet being more feminine than masculine in his nature. The worst of this experiment is that we may now expect to be inundated with female Hamlets. . .'[60]

One of these was Julia Seaman (1837–1909), who became Marriott's main competitor but brought a different mode of realism, behavioural realism, to bear. WJ Lawrence called her 'a pioneer of the new school in the provinces', and 'the first colloquial Hamlet' played by a woman.[61] This 'new school' grew from the visits to London (1861, 1864) by the Frenchman Charles Fechter, whose *Hamlet* set in the Viking period was revolutionary both visually and psychologically; hostile English journalists called his prince – 'lounging on tables and lolling against chairs'[62] – 'umanly'. But Julia Seaman promoted 'the Fechterian conception', the 'colloquial' aesthetic that drew Hamlet closer through casual physical details and unpredictable changes in tempo. Like Fechter, Seaman gave Hamlet unkempt long blond hair and wore 'that peculiar black dress. . .which became so famous' when Fechter wore it.[63] The 'new' actors tried to inhabit their environment; in contrast to Marriott's formality, Seaman slouched. Half-impatient, half-preoccupied, Hamlet's fingers played with the heavy belt holding her knife, echoing Fechter's 'To be or not to be' where he 'dreamily "thought" it out before you, toying the while with his little jewelled dagger', on the verge of onstage suicide (see Figure 8).[64] She played Hamlet at least 200 times and strongly defended her interpretation.

Such solid professionalism created a niche for tragic androgyny (honoured by Irving when he cast Marriott, Seaman and Aimé Desborough, another female Hamlet, as the witches to his Macbeth). The twin perspectives on *Hamlet* – the vendetta versus trapped dignity – continued in English popular theatre to the end of the century, and actresses continued to relate it to melodrama – an evolving form – whether sensational or sentimental. Clare Howard was the 'enormously popular' leading lady at the Pavilion Theatre, Whitechapel, playing 'heroines and 'adventuresses', 'virtuous damsels and vamps'.[65] In 1899 she played Hamlet across London (Theatre Royal, Stratford East and New Imperial Theatre, Westminster) and divided her week between *Hamlet* and *The Indian Mutiny*, a 'Great Historical Military Costume Play' by her husband

Figure 8   Julia Seaman as Hamlet: 'To be or not to be...'. *Illustrated London News*, 17 June 1899.

George Daventry, in which she played the British heroine and Daventry was a 'villain of the deepest dye'.[66] Their audiences hissed Claudius. WJ Lawrence protested that 'All the players in support laboured to drag down the tragedy to the level of the veriest transpontine sensational piece, underlining all the death and combat scenes, and acting with a stridency that became accentuated through the adventitious aid of commonplace melodrama music,' Howard's Hamlet 'spoke "through" sundry bars of pizzicato, agitato, and other such strains of music. At this or that situation there was heard a melodramatic "chord" or "crash", as well as "hurries"'; but Chance Newton defended her – 'I did not find this melos-setting

of our greatest tragedy at all disturbing' – and pointed out that she restored
'those extremely melodramatic passages' involving 'the hero's very thrillful
arrangement to have the spies Rosencrantz and Guildenstern murdered
on their arrival in England instead of himself.'

Clare Howard made her gender obvious – she was photographed in the
Ghost scene with her doublet undone, rearing back and clutching at her
flowing hair – and so did Millicent Bandmann-Palmer (1845–1926),
who was involved with *travesti* Shakespeare traditions from her youth
and committed herself to Hamlet more than any other actress. She
claimed to have played the part a thousand times. In photographs she
preserved the old Kemble/Siddons pose of the sensitive heroic prince in
the high-feathered bonnet, but the cloak Siddons hid in became a majestic
furred robe trailing the ground (see Figure 9). Two golden dagger-belts
accentuated her bust and waist, the hair was long, the gaze defiant, in a
fin-de-siècle image linking beauty, opulence and death. She merged several
traditions. As Milly Palmer in the 1860s she played Ophelia to Alice
Marriott and Juliet to Vestvali's Romeo; she married the Prussian actor
Daniel Bandmann whose own Hamlet was influenced by Fechter.[67]
Daniel Bandmann was prone to 'volcanic' violence against women, and
Jill Edmunds has suggested that taking over Hamlet after his death might
have been Millicent's act of revenge. Her theatre company toured widely,
especially round the north, and in November 1894 her week-long
Liverpool season included *East Lynne; Mary, Queen of Scots; Catherine
Howard*; and *Hamlet*: the play matched her canny taste for emotive
drama around a passionate but suffering protagonist. 'She could wring
dry the hearts of an audience with her pathos', wrote Whitford Kane,
her Fortinbras in 1902.[68] Her restoration of Fortinbras was significant
and Kane thought she played Hamlet 'with great seriousness and tragic
power'. *The Era* praised her 'strenuous study, womanly sympathy,
and bright intellect' in the role and offered an explanation:

The emotional actress always cherishes the notion of playing Juliet, so the
intellectual one longs to grapple with the philosophical problem which
has set so many great brains to work – to whit, the personality of the moody
Dane.[69]

Bandmann-Palmer had studied many *Hamlet* critics; she agreed with
Dowden that Hamlet remains 'always a mystery, and therefore not
always intelligible,' but she insisted he is not insane: ' "The burden and
the mystery of this unintelligible world" rests so heavily on his sensitive
spirit that it sometimes leads him to fits of passing frenzy.'

Figure 9   Millicent Bandmann-Palmer as Hamlet. *Illustrated London News*, 17 June 1899.

In happier days he would have been a beautiful young King with a taste and a talent for poesy. The pain and horror of the sorrow and sin by which he is surrounded make him a brooding, self-centred, self-tortured man . . .

She insisted that playing Hamlet was an *interior* experience; long after Cushman, she still criticised men 'who mouth and declaim the part. It should not be acted so much, she thinks, but thought aloud.' And this demanded immersion: 'The day before she is to play Hamlet she speaks to no-one. She tries to get into the spirit of the part ere getting up. She walks, talks, and thinks even like a man.' And, however 'intellectual', Hamlet was an emotional experience: in the wings a sudden noise 'will almost make her cry'. Her 405th Hamlet was immortalised in

Joyce's *Ulysses*. She played Hamlet at the Gaiety, Dublin, on 15th June 1904 and 'to say the least sustained it creditably'. Next day Leopold Bloom plans to see her in *Leah the Forsaken* as a Jewish Juliet, but across Dublin Stephen Daedelus and his cronies discuss the mystery of Shakespeare, inspired by Milly Palmer's odyssey.[70]

IV

New Hamlets / New Women

Clustered events mark shifts in culture. In 1867 Felicia von Vestvali played male roles in London, Mme Judith played Hamlet in Paris and Germany, and on the political stage of the House of Commons John Stuart Mill made what Simone de Beauvoir called 'the first speech ever officially presented in favour of votes for women'.[71] Two years later Alice Marriott made her debut as Hamlet in America, Susan B Anthony founded the National Association for Woman Suffrage, Wyoming gave women the vote, while in Germany Louise Otto founded a Women's Association and Leon Richier published *The Rights of Women*. Karl Marx's daughter Eleanor (born 1858) recalled that Shakespeare was 'the bible in our house', and for her the most important Marx family readings were those where she played Richard III and Hamlet, especially the Closet scene. She became an Ibsen pioneer and a teacher of Shakespeare as well as a political activist.[72] Activists and literary women laid claim to *Hamlet* as intellectual property: in 1874, when Julia Seaman made her American debut as the 'new' Hamlet, George Eliot (Mary Ann Evans) finished a dramatic poem which she had been writing for three years, involving a modern (male) Hamlet at Oxford, 'our English Wittenberg'.[73] She considered the impact of science and Darwinism on faith and turned *Hamlet*, purged of murder and revenge, into a dense symposium – an attempt at expressing the 'actual content of ideas'.[74] 'Blond, metaphysical and sensuous', Eliot's Hamlet grants some truth to all men's philosophies, dreams of transcending dialectics. Laertes, Horatio, the Priest and even Guildenstern, Rosencrantz and Osric duel with ideologies but Hamlet listens and finally opts for silence: 'He dreamed a dream so luminous/He woke(he says) convinced; but what it taught / Withholds as yet.'[75] Even as she rewrote Shakespeare, Eliot (who, TH Huxley joked, 'teaches the inferiority of men') placed faith in reticence and gave Hamlet the 'feminine' role of passive listener; but she did not change his gender – and indeed she could not, given its setting, since women were not admitted to Oxford examinations till 1885. For the most revolutionary aspect of the mid-Victorian female Hamlet was not that audiences saw an actress loving a woman or killing a man (many breeches characters did both) but that they saw a woman playing a university student.

No-one was further from silence than Anna Dickinson (1842–1932) who played Hamlet in New England and New York in 1882. Born a Quaker, supporting her widowed mother from an early age, she became a national celebrity at eighteen when she delivered such an eloquent anti-slavery speech in Connecticut 'that she revolutionized the politics of that State'.[76] An address to Congress and an audience with Lincoln cemented her reputation. Her short black hair, piercing grey eyes, and passionate delivery became famous across the country; calling for an emancipationist crusade, she became known as the 'Joan of Arc of the Unionist cause', or simply 'Anna'. Her candour was startling: at an 1863 assembly calling for more black troops, she accused the North of using them as cannon-fodder. After the war, Anna Dickinson became a professional speaker; she lectured across America with no less passion on 'The Rights and Wrongs of Women', called for universal education, and continued to demand racial equality, including inter-racial marriage. Then in 1878 she played Anne Boleyn in her own play *A Crown of Thorns*, but 'Anna Dickinson roasting the press' had become one of the symbols of American feminism and the New York papers took their revenge. After vicious reviews, the play lost her $60,000, yet she continued to write and threw down the gauntlet with *Hamlet*.[77] It was at this moment that Edward P Vining's book appeared and Edwin Booth linked them: 'Good for Anna!'[78] Dickinson's boyish Hamlet was iconoclastic at first sight.

Instead of black she wore purple and her hair looked modish (see Figure 10). William Winter complained that she had neither male 'dignity' nor womanly grace. He conceded that 'Her reading of the text was intelligent' but dismissed the famous voice as 'monotonous', 'unsympathetic' and 'feeble' in 'passages requiring fervour'. He said Dickinson did not seem interested in the whole play: 'Many words were clipped and slurred, and only a slight sense was signified of Hamlet's supernatural environment' and she was 'metallic, inflexible' towards Ophelia.' 'The killing of Polonius was done in a perfunctory way.' In fact Winter complained she was not acting at all – 'There was little or no impersonation, the performer, instead of the character, being conspicuous' – and he was angry because she made Hamlet her mouthpiece: 'Her delivery was

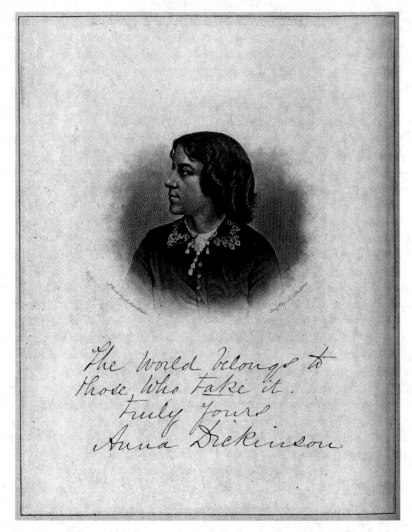

Figure 10 'The world belongs to those who take it.' Anna Dickinson, postcard in
extra-illustrated copy of Henry Phelps, *Hamlet from the Actor's Standpoint* (New York:
Werner, 1890). (Reproduced by permission of the Folger Shakespeare Library).

oratorical' with 'the twang of the conventicle'.[79] But then Hamlet
articulated many of Anna Dickinson's beliefs.

In her book *A Ragged Register*, her diagnosis of the dilemma of
contemporary women paraphrased Hamlet ('I do not know/Why yet
I live to say, This thing's to do,/Sith I have cause and will, and strength

and means/To do it,'): women must look inwards and say, 'I know what I want to do, and have a will to do it.'[80] Dickinson wrote that women, endowed with 'brains, culture, opportunity', must use them; they must fight inner 'idleness', and 'act'. She believed the end of the nineteenth century was a pivotal age that would witness an exchange of Masculine and Feminine in the service of justice. At last men might advance beyond their instinctive 'brute power' – 'The entire movement of civilization is marked by the ability of men to do without force' – while women who had never wielded a sword (Winter said Dickinson's Hamlet looked afraid of his) must fight the new battles, advancing the reforms for which they most sharply saw the need. 'Fortune', she said, did not exist except as 'the measure of intelligence': women must 'sit down with themselves alone, and make acquaintance of their own capacities', use their 'women's intelligence', and force themselves out of isolation into the public realm. For Mary Braddon's lonely female Hamlet in the 1860s 'there was only the sad, desolate present – a dreary spot in the great desert of life, bounded by a yawning grave'; 'At the grave's mouth', Anna Dickinson believed, 'We confess a common bond.'[81]

'Curiosity' was rife across America. 'She will do a large business,' the *Bohemian* (Ohio) predicted, commenting that images of her Hamlet resembled Wilde.[82] She had enthusiasts ('truly great and brilliant in the role'[83]) but was pilloried. 'We have insisted for years that Anna Dickinson was a man', said *Peck's Sun*, proposing that someone should put a spider in Yorick's skull: if Hamlet screamed, panicked and spat, 'then Miss Dickinson is a woman. The country will watch eagerly for the result of this test.'[84] Years later an admirer recalled being 'utterly disgusted' by the tiny attendance, which shrank 'as one by one the audience dwindled. . . But, with hardly more than a dozen others, I viewed the last tragic moments. . .and I still declare that Anna Dickinson was an ideal Hamlet, and that her performance was a great intellectual and artistic triumph.'[85]

'She had been trained to lecture, not to act', Winter complained, but she believed theatre was a forum for self-expression and praised the opera star Christina Nilsson for precisely that quality of 'self': 'The woman's supreme power lies in what permeates voice and action. As she comes down to her audience. . .before she sings a note or stirs a gesture, she conquers.'[86] When so political a figure as Anna Dickinson spoke Hamlet's words it was a complex intervention. There were sneers that she was begging for attention and that it indicated mental imbalance. In fact *Hamlet* effectively finished her stage career, and although she was fitfully involved with politics she distanced herself from the suffrage movement and suffered poverty and ill-health. In 1891 she was committed to a house for the insane after she spent a period in seclusion (for many women living 'retired lives', Harriet Beecher Stowe had written, 'thinking grew to be a disease'), but on her release Dickinson brought a suit for wrongful confinement, effectively putting her sanity on trial. After six years she won her case. 'Go with us to the crucifixion,' Mark Twain wrote to a friend before Anna Dickinson's acting debut; but on a portrait postcard Dickinson wrote, 'The world belongs to those who take it.'[87]

Hamlet permitted actresses to stretch the bounds of sanity and survive. When *fin-de-siècle* female Hamlets claimed their visible place in the public sphere, at the very heart of the repertoire, they were asserting a woman's right to experience and express extremes of consciousness. In contrast to the stock image of Ophelia's fey delirium so adored by Victorian painters, the female Hamlet – in what many suffragists regarded as 'rational' masculine dress – articulated a mind that was possibly 'antic' but also sublimely alert and sane. Via theatre and *Hamlet*, the arc of Dickinson's career represented a slide from participation in mass political movements into isolation, but some younger actresses moved in the opposite direction – like Janet Steer (Hamlet, 1899), an American who became prominent in the English suffrage movement. When William Archer first saw Steer in *An American Bride* (1893) he praised her 'presence and earnestness' but thought romantic drama was the wrong niche for someone with her 'harshness of voice and general hardness of contour'.[88] Six years later *The Times* welcomed her Hamlet, 'a part that has long had a fascination for actresses as well as actors. . . . Her appearance is in her favour, and her voice too, since its range is low and impressive. She has evidently studied the play closely and with intelligence, and her acting is decidedly clever. . . [T]he play certainly went well.'[89]

In her photographs Steer's Hamlet sat hunched and round-shouldered in the graveyard, dourly sunk in thought, one hand clenching the skull, conveying its dead weight. She wore a cloak and fur hat against the cold and her hair was hacked short. Dark make-up accentuated her eyes to match her prominent features (her Hamlet resembled Irving or Benson). Hamlet seemed near the end of his tether. Steer put together a strong company in Birmingham, then took the play to London (Crystal Palace Theatre), but after this made her mark as an activist.[90] She was involved with the Actresses' Franchise League (founded 1908) from the beginning when she arranged a meeting with Christabel Pankhurst, whose faction committed to direct action against private property and the government; in 1912 Steer was imprisoned. That autumn she was in the AFL delegation at a rally for Irish Home Rule and in 1914 she played Charlotte Corday in the Pageant of Great Women.[91] She was an AFL committee member during the Great War. Esmé Berenger, who fulfilled a long-held ambition by playing Hamlet years later, was also active in the League, where she taught fencing skills. Similarly the Birmingham-born Edith Wynne Matthison acted in Elizabeth Robins' *Votes for Women!* (1907) before going to America where she too played Hamlet.[92] If the female Hamlet in the mid 1800s embodied a woman's right to education, by the 1890s different words at the end of the play came into focus: 'He has my dying voice.' The final victory was to win, and use, the franchise.

Shakespearean *travesti* was a symbol of enfranchisement in 1893 when Mary Shaw was Rosalind in the Professional Women's League's *As You Like It* at the Palmer's Theatre, New York.[93] Nearly 150 women took part. However, *Hamlet* figured less in turn-of-the-century suffrage circles than earlier actresses might have predicted. The emergence of plays for New Women made seizing a male symbol increasingly peripheral; the immediate issue was to transform the real worlds of family and work. From the 1880s new regendered *Hamlets* emerged. Ibsen's Mrs Alving revealed the sins of the Father to the diseased Son, and *Hedda Gabler* – 'The female underground revolution in thought', said one of Ibsen's notes – became the modern actress's *Hamlet*: 'She is a very complex, very modern, very morbid type.' (AB Walkley) Hazlitt's 'It is we who are Hamlet' was supplanted the moment a woman at the English premiere told Elizabeth Robins 'Hedda is all of us.' Rebecca West in *Rosmersholm* was seen as a Hamlet figure, and in *Mrs Warren's Profession* Shaw modernised *Hamlet*'s structure – the educated young person returns home to discover the mother's sexual secret – but Vivie Warren with her bike and 'pile of serious-looking books' rationally *accepts* her legacy. Shaw wrote *Saint Joan* to rethink *travesti*, claiming 'It is quite likely that sixty years hence every great English and American actress will have a shot at St Joan, just as every great actor will have a shot at Hamlet.'[94]

It was significant that Elizabeth Robins – who played Hedda in London, explored the politics of hysteria in her play *Alan's Wife*, and put suffrage rallies on stage in *Votes for Women!* – was deeply critical of Sarah Bernhardt's Hamlet in 1899: 'However well she does it . . . there is no moment in the drama when the spectator is not fully and calmly conscious that the hero is a woman masquerading, or is jarred into sharp realisation of the fact by her doing something that is very like a man. It is a case where every approach to success is merely another insistence on failure.'[95] Noting that Bernhardt made Hamlet boyish, Robins defined a 'law': 'A woman, when she plays at being a man, may hope with some show of success, to climb to the height of twenty years, and then stops short, suffering, it would seem, from arrested development.' Writing two years before she gave up acting, she suggested that imitating male behaviour was a demeaning and irrelevant game, and her description of the older woman's Hamlet – 'her little runs and jumps', 'she laughs with all the keen enjoyment of a child' – is effectively of Ibsen's Nora before she sees the light. When, a century later, Harriet Walter led preliminary workshops for an all-female *Hamlet*, she was distrustful of cross-dressing: 'We may occasionally take on the great roles, but until the practice becomes widespread, it is bound to be more about the player than the play.'[96] From Cushman to Bernhardt this was no objection; the assertion of personal identity was the prime reason to break the rules, but Sarah Bernhard's version was not just the apotheosis of the traditional female Hamlet, she heralded its demise.

Notes

1. George Vandenhoff, *Leaves From an Actor's Notebook* (London: Cooper, 1860), pp. 202–3.
2. Mary Virginia Terhune, *Eve's Daughters* (New York: Anderson and Allen, 1882) p. 256.
3. Quoted Dorothea de Bear Bobbé, *Fanny Kemble* (London: Elkins, Mathews and Marrot 1931), p. 174.
4. *Ibid.*, pp. 151, 197.
5. See Georgianna Ziegler, 'The Actress as Shakespearean Critic: Three Nineteenth Century Portias', *Theatre Survey* XXX, nos. 1/2 (May/ November 1989), pp. 93–109. In New York she earned $8,000 in a month. See *Charles Kemble's Shakespere Readings: The Selected Plays Read by Him in Public* (Second ed. London: Bell, 1879).
6. Samuel L Longfellow, ed., *The Life of Henry Wadsworth Longfellow* (London: Kegan Paul, 1886), p. 134.
7. In a Hamlet defined by 'polished and refined tastes, an acute sense of the beauty of harmonious proportions, and a native grace, gentleness and refinement of mind and manner,' she wrote, 'Nothing to my mind can exceed the exquisite beauty of his last "Go on, I follow thee", to the Ghost. There is one thing in which I do not believe my father ever has been or ever will be excelled – his high and noble bearing, his gallant, graceful, courteous deportment, his perfect good breeding on the stage.'

8. Fanny Kemble, *Journal of a Young Actress*, ed. Monica Gough (New York: Columbia University Press, 1990), pp. 25–6.

9. Longfellow, *Life*, pp. 131–4.

10. *Athenaeum*, 7 May 1852; Ellen Tree, letter (1863), cited in Anne Russell's important 'Tragedy, Gender, Performance: Women as Tragic Heroes on the Nineteenth-Century Stage', *Comparative Drama* vol. 30 no. 2 (Summer 1996), p. 156. Longfellow – who found Kemble reading Queen Constance almost too painful, reflecting her fight for her children – thought that when playing male pain or anger, she drew on her own: she read *King Lear* 'wonderfully well; with great power and pathos. It was her best reading, so far'. In 1832 Tree had been offended when Covent Garden proposed she open the season as Romeo: 'If you intend me to do any good in the higher walk of the Drama it would be *ruin* for me to open in a male character'. Kemble played Juliet to Tree's Romeo for a benefit that year and thought Tree 'looked the part' – 'beautiful and not unmanly': Kemble, *Records of a Girlhood* (New York: Holte, 1885), p. 200.

11. In 1833 she was appalled when the anti-slavery campaigner William Channing suggested a new form of theatre (to heighten its 'intellectual pleasure and profit') and tried to persuade her 'to take detached passages and scenes from the finest dramatic writers, and have them well declaimed in comparatively private assemblies'. She rejected his idea of anthologised excerpts: 'What!' she wrote, 'Take one of Shakespeare's plays bit by bit, break it piece-meal, in order to make recitals of it! destroy the marvellous unity. . . to make patches of declamation!' Harmony was a watchword. Kemble, *Records of Later Life* (London: Bentley, 1882), I, p. 49.

12. *Athenaeum*.

13. Quoted Bobbé, *Fanny Kemble*, p. 228.

14. *Athenaeum* 3 April 1848. The critic was unsure, complaining that she underplayed Shylock's greed. He praised her Antonio and Bassanio more than Portia – too inelegant and bawdy.

15. See Judith Wellman, *The Road to Seneca Falls* (Urbana: University of Illinois Press, 2004).

16. *The Essence of Slavery* (London: The Ladies' London Emancipation Society, 1863), pp. 21–2.

17. Kemble, *Records of Later Life*, I, p. 41.

18. Catherine Maria Sedgewick, *A New England Tale* (1822), quoted Mary Kelley, *Private Woman, Public Stage: Literary Domesticity in Nineteenth-Century America* (New York and Oxford: Oxford University Press, 1984), p. 68. Terhune in *Eve's Daughters* attacked male fear of women's 'intellectual strivings'; see Kelley, p. 101.

19. Cited Kelly, *Private Woman*, p. 180.

20. Bobbé, *Fanny Kemble*, p. 265.

21. Quotation from *The World* used in publicity for Braddon's novels. 'The most tiresome journey is beguiled, and the most wearisome illness is brightened, by any one of her books'. See Gail Marshall and Adrian Poole, *Victorian*

Shakespeare (London: Palgrave, 2003) for comments on Braddon's use of Shakespeare.

22. Letter to Edward Bulwer-Lytton, 1864, quoted Robert Lee Wolff, *Sensational Victorian: The Life and Fiction of Mary Elizabeth Braddon* (New York: Garland, 1979), p. 168.

23. Mary Braddon *Eleanor's Victory* (1863): Cheap Uniform Edition (London: Maxwell, n.d.), p. 79.

24. *Ibid.*, p. 52.

25. *Ibid.*, p. 77.

26. *Ibid.*, p. 80.

27. *Ibid.*, pp. 77–8.

28. *Ibid.*, p. 82.

29. *Ibid.*, p. 341.

30. *Ibid.*, p. 168.

31. *New Review*, December 1863.

32. Braddon, *The Doctor's Wife* (London 1864), p. 41.

33. She explained in 1864 that she wished to explore character more.

34. *Eleanor's Victory*, p. 15.

35. *Ibid.*, p. 151

36. *Ibid.*, pp. 127–8.

37. *Ibid.*, p. 188.

38. *Ibid.*, p. 195. Monckton first sees Eleanor as Joan of Arc or (cf *Hamlet*) Jepthah's Daughter.

39. Monckton believes his wife is deceiving him because it is a social probability – the one revenge open to the victims of 'so many matrimonial bargains' like the 'sale of cattle': 'Who should know this better than Gilbert Monckton the solicitor'?

40. *Ibid.*, pp. 222, 236. Eleanor's loyalty to her father's appeal, 'Never forget,' makes her recognise Darrell, whom she glimpsed for a mere second in Paris. Otherwise she uncovers little herself except when she plays to male fantasies – as an abandoned maiden in a shipping office, needing protectors. See Elaine Showalter, *A Literature of Their Own: from Charlotte Brontë to Doris Lessing* (London: Virago, 1982), p. 163. See also Showalter's key essay, 'Representing Ophelia: Women, Madness, and the Responsibilities of Feminist Criticism,' in Patricia Parker and Geoffrey Hartman, eds., *Shakespeare and the Question of Theory* (New York: Routledge, 1993), pp. 77–94.

41. Braddon, *The Doctor's Wife*, p. 27.

42. *Eleanor's Victory*, pp. 303, 102.

43. *Ibid.*, p. 355. Braddon may have been circumspect in not advertising her use of *Hamlet*. The *Quarterly Review* mocked one 'sensation' writer for claiming that he drew the 'conception' of his heroine's character from Shakespeare, Byron, Goethe and Scott. See 'Sensation Novels', *Quarterly Review*, v. 113, no. 226 (April 1863), pp. 482–514.

44. AE Wilson, *East End Entertainment* (London: Barker, 1954), p. 79.

45. Note for 28 July in Frederick C Walton, *The Britannia Diaries 1863–75*, edited by Jim Davis (London: Society for Theatre Research, 1992), pp. 188, 162; *Sunday Times*, 1 December 1867, cited Davis. Miles was Australian. For valuable details of many Victorian actresses mentioned here see Jill Edmonds, 'Princess Hamlet', in Viv Gardner and Susan Rutherford, eds., *The New Woman and Her Sisters* (Hemel Hempstead: Harvester Wheatsheaf, 1992), pp. 59–76. This chapter also draws on contemporary surveys: Laurence Hutton, *Curiosities of the American Stage* (New York: Harper, 1891); WJ Lawrence, *Illustrated London News* 17 June 1899 (hereafter: Lawrence, *ILN*); and Henry Chance Newton, *Cues and Curtain-calls* (London: John Lane, 1927).

46. James Anderson *An Actor's Life* (1902), cited Davis.

47. *Athenaeum* on Vestvali's Romeo, 25 October 1867; John Coleman, *Fifty Years of an Actor's Life* (London: Hutchinson, 1904), p. 362.

48. See Lawrence, *ILN*, and Chance Newton. She played Hamlet in Albany and elsewhere in America and died in 1877.

49. Rosa Cooper played Romeo there five months later, followed in 1866 by Helen Clyde. In the 1850s Mrs Percy Knowles played Hamlet in Plymouth and on tour.

50. The Baltimore-based actress-playwright Sidney Bateman and the actor HL Bateman managed their daughters in both America and London, where Mr Bateman took over the Lyceum and hired the young Henry Irving. Ellen gave up acting early and Isabel became a nun, but their sister Kate continued successfully.

51. WT Price, *A Life of Charlotte Cushman* (New York: Brentano, 1894), p. 119.

52. Forrest glowered at Claudius in their first scene; the Ghost's story threw him into a rage. By the Closet scene he was at such a pitch that he fell to the floor when his father reappeared, and at the end of the scene he ran out, disgusted by his mother: AC Sprague, *Shakespeare and the Actors* (Cambridge, Mass.: Harvard University Press, 1944), pp. 133, 166, 169, 177.

53. After the Civil War Crampton abandoned the stage to lecture on temperance; but she returned and played supporting roles (including Gertrude) and character parts until her death.

54. See Price, *A Life of Charlotte Cushman*, p. 119.

55. *Liverpool Daily Post*, 29 November and 1 December 1859.

56. For this and the following quotations see Frank W Wandsworth, 'Hamlet and Iago: Nineteenth-Century Breeches Parts', *Shakespeare Quarterly* 42 (1966), pp. 129–39.

57. *Ibid.*, pp. 134–5.

58. But she was also praised for her 'power of facial expression' in Dublin, and London billed her as 'sustaining the character' and called Hamlet 'an impersonation'.

59. *The Times* 25 February 1864.

60. The *Mercury*, quoted in Lou Warwick, *Theatre Un-Royal* (Northampton: Lou Warwick, 1974), p. 198. Marriott chose Hamlet for her 1869

American debut. The *New York Times* thought it respectable enough to review twice but it had less novelty value there. Back home, Miss Marriott's Dramatic Company continued to tour and in 1875 the Dublin Gaiety promised 'Miss Marriott in her great impersonation of Hamlet'. Perhaps the image faded; a later photograph of her mildly dishevelled 'antic disposition' shows the face fleshier, the legs thinner, the stance more awkward. She looked ill. But here was the gentleness everyone cherished.

61. Lawrence, *ILN*.
62. GH Lewes, *On Actors and the Art of Acting* (London: Smith, Elder, 1875), p. 22.
63. *The Times* 21 May 1864.
64. Chance Newton, p. 191.
65. *Ibid.*, p. 215
66. 15 and 17 February 1899, Theatre Royal, Stratford East, then 24 February, 1899, New Imperial Theatre, Westminster.
67. Fechter presented Vestvali's London seasons. Bandmann restored some passages with a moral dimension ('Now might I do it pat') and saw the importance of Fortinbras. See *Athenaeum*, 15 February 1875. Jill Edmunds points out that Bandmann was physically aggressive in rehearsals, especially toward women: 'Was his wife's Hamlet an act of vengeance against her violent husband?'
68. Whitford Kane, *Are We All Met?* (London: Mathews and Marrot, 1931), pp. 59–63.
69. *Dundee Evening Telegraph* reprinted in the *Era* (21 January 1899).
70. James Joyce, *Ulysses* (New York: Random House, 1934), pp. 75, 196.
71. Simone de Beauvoir, *The Second Sex* (Harmondsworth: Penguin, 1970), p. 153.
72. She would look 'very pointedly' at Marx on 'Mother, you have my father much offended.' See Yvonne Knapp, *Eleanor Marx: Volume 1* (London: Laurence and Wishart, 1972), p. 58.
73. 'A College Breakfast Party', George Eliot, *Collected Poems*, ed. Lucien Jenkins (London: Skoob, 1989), p. 167. See Frederick Karl, *George Eliot* (London: Harper Collins, 1996), p. 586. Karl sees Eliot-Hamlet pinning faith in a transformational aestheticism: 'The ideal has discoveries which ask/No test, no faith, save that we joy in them:/A new-found continent'. This *Hamlet* dialogue, originally called 'A Symposium', was published by Macmillans, who wanted Eliot to write a life of Shakespeare. She did not wish to publish the poem and it did not appear till 1878.
74. Harriet Beecher Stowe wrote to George Eliot that sometimes she had read her books 'supposing you man'. (Kelley, *Private Woman, Public Stage*, p. 252). See Ellen Carol Du Bois, *Feminism and Suffrage: The Emergence of an Independent Women's Movement in America* (Ithaca: Cornell University Press, 1978) and Blanche Glassman Hersh, *The Slavery of Sex: Feminist-Abolitionists in America* (Urbana: University of Illinois Press, 1978).

75. 'A College Breakfast Party', p. 184.
76. T Allston Brown, *History of the New York Stage* (New York: Dodd, Mead, 1903), p. 239. See Chester Giraud, *Embattled Maiden: The Life of Anna Dickinson* (New York: Putnam, 1951).
77. Dickinson played Hamlet in Rochester (19 January), then at Haverly's Fifth Avenue Theatre, New York (20 March for a week). Her play *An American Girl* (1880) ran for six weeks – it was said to be popular with married women – starring Fanny Davenport. US publicity for Asta Nielsen's film linked Fanny Davenport with Bernhardt and Rachel as one of the 'great actresses who hold Hamlet was a woman'.
78. Daniel J Watermeier (ed.), *Between Actor and Critic: Selected Letters of Edwin Booth and William Winter* (Princeton: Princeton University Press, 1971), p. 81.
79. William Winter, *Shakespeare on the Stage* (New York: Moffat, Yard, 1911), pp. 430–1. Her rejection of traditional black for more impassioned colours was echoed by several twentieth-century actress-Hamlets in America, including Eva Le Gallienne, Siobhan McKenna and Judith Anderson.
80. Anna Dickinson, *A Ragged Register* (New York: Harper, 1879), p. 126.
81. *Eleanor's Victory*, p. 82; Dickinson, *A Paying Investment* (Boston: Osgood, 1876), pp. 105–16.
82. *Bohemian*, 18 March 1882.
83. *Buffalo Times* 26 May 1929.
84. *Peck's Weekly*, reprinted in George W Peck, *Peck's Compendium of Fun* (Chicago: Belford, Clarke, 1886.) Gutenberg Project: www.gutenberg.org/dirs/1/4/8/14815/14815-h/14815-htm.
85. *Buffalo Times*.
86. *Ragged Register*, p. 182.
87. Harriett Beecher Stowe, *Oldtown Folks* (Boston: n.p., 1869), p. 255; *Mark Twain's Letters*, ed. Albert Bigelow Paine (New York: Harper, 1917), p. 278.
88. *Theatrical World*, undated clipping, Theatre Museum.
89. *The Times* undated clipping, 1899.
90. In 1900 Steer took on the management of the Comedy Theatre and presented a bill including her Closet scene.
91. See Claire Hirshfield, 'The Actresses' Franchise League and the Campaign for Women's Suffrage: 1908–1914', *Theatre Research International* 10 no.2, pp. 129–53.
92. Matthison was born in Birmingham and worked with Ben Greet. 'She made a great success when she appeared as Hamlet' (1930) – *Who's Who in the Theatre* entry.
93. 21 November 1893. A similar British performance followed. In 1899 Mary Shaw spoke in London on 'The Stage as a Means of Livelihood in America'.
94. Shaw 1934, quoted Holly Hill, *Playing Joan* (New York: Theatre Communications Group, 1987), p. xi.
95. Elizabeth Robins, 'On Seeing Madame Bernhardt's Hamlet', *North American Review* 171 (December 1900), pp. 908–918.
96. Harriet Walter, *Other People's Shoes* (London: Viking, 1999), p. 223.

CHAPTER 4

Virile spirits: Bernhardt and her inheritance

The artist [playing Hamlet] must be divested of all virility. He must make us see a phantom compounded of the atoms of life and of the decay that leads to death. It is a brain ceaselessly warring against the reality of things. It is a soul that longs to escape from its carnal vestment. That is why I claim that these parts always gain when they are played by intellectual women, who alone are able to preserve their character of unsexed beings, and their perfume of mystery.

Sarah Bernhardt[1]

In 1867 the actress Mme Judith (Julie Bernat) was in dispute with the Comédie Française, due she believed to hostility to her intellectual and political connections. Having seen a *travesti* Hamlet in England, she tried out the role herself in a burlesque at the Varietés in Lyons. 'Shakespeare was right', she wrote, 'to weld together, as he did, the comic and the tragic, and Victor Hugo's claim that their fusion is the very essence of all true art is indeed well founded.'[2] She repeated it in Nantes and the composer Victorin Joncières asked her to include some of his *Hamlet* music, then 'the fame of my various appearances as the Prince of Denmark' led to an engagement at the Paris Gaieté in December 1867. She used the adaptation by Alexandre Dumas *père* and Paul Meurice, which was in alexandrines and originally very free: the first scene was cut, Dumas added a love-scene where Hamlet wrote poetry, his madness was clearly feigned, there was no voyage to England, Hamlet went into hiding, Fortinbras was omitted, and Hamlet survived. The Ghost decreed the characters' fates. Mme Judith appeared in a revised version (1864) which restored Shakespeare's start and finish, but not Fortinbras.[3] Meurice 'told me that my sex really helped me to express the melancholy and indecision of the character'. In her memoirs she argued that great acting is a matter of 'transformation' and 'the actor who gives free reign to his own personality always remains second-rate . . . Art does not consist in the commonplace reproduction of reality, but in a new creation in which the significant characteristics of the personality to be evoked are brought into prominence.' She praised the adaptable actor 'who from first to last realises the spirit of his part' over one 'who always remains himself'.[4] 'A little time afterwards', she added acidly, 'I met Madame Sarah Bernhardt, who declared that it was quite impossible for a woman to act Hamlet. This, I expect, is why she interpreted him herself several years later, and I have great pleasure in admitting that she made a simply adorable Prince!'[5]

I

'What exquisite ideas she had': Bernhardt

Sarah Bernhardt (1844–1923) was the greatest 'personality' actress of her age, as famous for her offstage life as her acting. Bernhardt established her early reputation not only as Phèdre and Andromache, for example, but also in *travesti* playing adolescent heroes. Working in an established French tradition, she took for granted the actress's right to appropriate roles across the divide and May Agate wrote, 'She was made for *le travesti* with her slight build and lyrical genius; for, mark you, it is only the poets and dreamers that fall into the category. . . It implies a certain sexlessness – an almost Pierrot-like quality.' 'It was not a question of becoming in any sense masculine', Agate said; Bernhardt could sublimate her 'glamour and feline grace, to give something which I believe to be on a much higher plane – that of the mind'.[6] Late in life she played both Portia and Shylock (she was Jewish) in extracts from the *Merchant*, and considered acting Romeo (opposite Maude Addams) but decided – despite Cushman and other precedents – that his passion was outside an actress's range. At the end of the century she played what she called her 'three Hamlets' – 'the black Hamlet of Shakespeare, the white Hamlet of Rostand's *L'Aiglon* and the Florentine Hamlet of Alfred de Musset's *Loranzaccio'* – each, in the Delacroix tradition, 'a strong mind in a weak body'. She had played Ophelia in 1886, but it 'brought nothing new to me in the study of character'. 'As a matter of fact', she stated, 'it is not male parts, but male brains that I prefer' – 'generally speaking male parts are more intellectual than female parts' and above all 'no female character has opened up a field so large for the exploration of sensations and human sorrows as that of Hamlet.'[7] In 1897 she commissioned the most faithful French translation to that date, by Marcel Schwob and Eugene Moraud, in prose; in 1899 she turned the Théâtre des Nations into the Théâtre Sarah Bernhardt, and opened *Hamlet* on 20 May amidst a torrent of publicity ranging from stories of duels fought over her ambitions to rumours that she prepared by sleeping in a coffin. Performances followed in London a month later, and New York (Christmas Day 1900), and though as we shall see she attracted torrents of criticism her *Hamlet* became legendary, the subject of the first Continental Shakespeare film (1900), an illustrated book in Spain (1905) and more recently Gerda Taranow's superb full-length study (1996).[8] She was received like royalty at a Stratford gala matinee, where she became the first (and still the only) woman to play Hamlet at the Memorial Theatre. It remains the critics' reference-point for almost all serious *travesti* to this day.

With her genius for publicity and friction, Bernhardt announced that she had examined acting-texts and promptbooks and rejected established British actors' interpretations. Like Cushman's supporters but more provocatively, Bernhardt at fifty-five upturned the cliché that no actress can play Juliet till she's too old by pronouncing that Hamlet is beyond any man: 'A boy of twenty cannot understand the philosophy of Hamlet' whereas the older actor 'does not look the boy, nor has he the ready adaptability of the woman, who can combine the light carriage of youth with. . . mature thought'. Bernhardt mocked the physiques of male Hamlets: 'He wants to play Hamlet when his appearance is more suitable to King Lear.'[9] How did ageing men suggest a mind and body 'haunted by doubt and despair', a heart 'ceaselessly tortured' by dreams, a soul that 'frets the body' and threatens 'to burst its tenement of clay'? By digging in the make-up box. Actors had perpetuated an absurd stage tradition: 'the noble Dane of stout proportions'. This 'absolute error' defaced Shakespeare's portrait of a 'a youth of twenty summers' – 'young Hamlet' even to his fellow-students – lacking the 'experience which would have led to different results'. He was 'a boy', she insisted, a creature of 'nerves and intellect, dramatic and passionate'. From the reactions, she said, 'It would appear that in England one must present Hamlet as a melancholy professor.'[10] Yet Bernhardt did not play the expected sentimental waif.

The *Daily Telegraph* admired her 'effervescent youthfulness' – 'impulsive and occasionally boisterous – prone to sudden waves and gusts of passion; eccentric and multi-changing. . . The boy with the flaxen hair is full of impetuousness and high feeling. His nobility of character, his love of truth and hatred of falsehood, are ever pronounced.' She made him 'volatile', 'impulsive and irrepressible – a torrent that must be let loose'.

Punch joked that she made him a spoilt royal brat but still judged Bernhardt, 'with all her *gaminerie*', preferable to those 'eccentric middle-aged-youths from thirty to fifty'. On the other hand JT Grein of the Independent Theatre complained, 'It was palpable from the first that Mme Bernhardt had entirely misconceived the character'. It was the era of Forbes Robertson's scholarly, sensitive Hamlet, and Grein complained that in her passion and gesticulation 'we miss the metaphysician'. Where the English tradition made the play a string of set-pieces where each star scored new points, Bernhardt stressed its overall dynamics. The excitement she and the clash of genders and cultures generated was so intense that much of her London performance can be recreated through the extraordinarily detailed reviews.[11]

II

Bernhardt in action: images

The son

On the Paris first night, *Hamlet* in fifteen scenes with musical interludes lasted almost five hours. For London's Adelphi Theatre there were twelve scenes. A furred and brocaded boyaresque Court was discovered, without a procession or a solitary star entry. Bernhardt did not signal Hamlet's melancholy; he seemed 'a pleasant, humorous, very gay Prince, who in happier circumstances would have been the life and soul of the Court' (*The Times*) and gave Horatio a 'hail-fellow-well-met reception' (Elizabeth Robins). But news of the ghost gave Hamlet a sense of purpose. There were 'keen, questioning looks', 'eager, disjointed questions' (*The Times*) and meditative pauses as she sat, legs crossed; Robins thought this her most collected, 'modern' moment – 'like a youthful Psychical Researcher, bent on employing scientific methods'. So, on the battlements, 'the Betterton tradition was cast to the winds,' as the *Stage* noted: 'Instead of a Hamlet crouching with fear, and bowed down with reverential awe, Madame Bernhardt gives us one who had made up his mind to encounter the Ghost of his dead father with no show of dread, and with the boldness that Hamlet's speech to Horatio and Marcellus would lead us to expect: "I'll speak to it though Hell itself should gape and bid me hold my peace."' 'These are not the words of a weak or languid person', Bernhardt insisted: 'I am reproached with not being sufficiently astonished, not sufficiently dumbfounded, when I see the ghost. But Hamlet comes expressly to see it; he awaits it.'

Her defining moment was both quasi-naturalistic and sculptural: sensing her father, she *turned her back on the audience*, caught sight of him on 'Angels and ministers of grace', flung off her cap, and froze. At several key moments she would rework this image, her body motionless, stretched by tension and exhilaration. 'As she stood with bared head and appealing, uplifted hands, the effect was so beautiful' that Robins was startled when Hamlet broke the mood by casually turning to his friends; yet 'one was made to feel the humanity' of Hamlet and his 'entire confidence' that his father would still be there when he looked again. 'I never got so vivid an impression of the warm, personal relation between the dead king and Hamlet before.' Hamlet's physical vulnerability came into focus as Bernhardt struggled with Horatio and Marcellus, but she saw him as anything but 'feeble': 'He draws his sword against his friends, and threatens to kill them if they will not let him pass.' And then – another sudden transition; 'What exquisite ideas she had!' (Clement Scott) – she crossed herself before following the Ghost.

Enfant terrible

'Mad,' said Sarah Bernhardt slowly, as she bent down and clasped her hands in her ruddy hair, and her voice was like that of one in a dream. 'What could those who say he was mad be thinking of? He feigned madness to effect his purpose. . . It is all as clear as day. . . insanity would give the lie to the very keynote of his character.' (*Daily Chronicle*)

Bernhardt saw Hamlet as a performer – 'all things to all men' but never himself except when alone. 'The most sensible' yet 'most unhappy of men' must speak, and speak constantly, to 'conceal his thought' in a tragedy of self-repression: 'As an avenger he must act a part and appear not to feel the storm of rage and indignation that runs riot', nor 'his strong suppressed love'. However, she played the boy's surface spriteliness so well that many saw nothing beneath; her energetic 'antic disposition' scenes, where she developed a vein of childish cruel comedy, were especially controversial. When jovial Polonius (who read the love-poetry through a magnifying glass) tried to look at Hamlet's book Bernhardt, seated on a settle, stuck her feet in the air, sprawled and turned away; 'The first *"Des mots"* he spoke with an absent-minded indifference. . .; in the second *"Des mots"* his answer seemed to catch his own attention; and the third *"Des mots"* was accompanied by a look, and charged with intense but fugitive attention, with a break in the intonation that clearly said: "Yes, it is words, and everything else in the whole world is only words, words, words." '[12] Later she 'buzzed' through Polonius' 'comical-tragical' speech, caught an imaginary fly on his nose, then opened her hand to show – nothing. 'What a world of meaning the actress puts into it!' (*Referee*) – 'See, old man, there is nothing more in all your talk than here in the palm of my hand.' Audiences applauded but many English critics were offended by such 'discourtesy' and contempt': 'It is not in Hamlet's character, as I understand it, or as Mr Forbes-Robertson, most courteous of Hamlets, understands it.' (*Referee*) Grein hated this 'enfant terrible who . . . made it his business to baffle his equals with ill-digested grandiloquence, and to worry his underlings with unbecoming chiding and outbursts of uncontrollable anger, or with impertinent jokes that were anything but princely.' Bernhardt countered that the lines are not polite, and besides her Hamlet, alert to the conspiracy threatening him, vented his frustration in these petty triumphs. Noticing Rosencrantz and Guildenstern conspiring, she thumped their heads together and showed, 'by one of those sudden fell looks which the actress has at command, that he sees through their game, and his tone changes at once. He lets them feel directly the force of his scorn and rage.' (*Morning Post*) In the midst of all the knockabout Robins was surprised by the 'very fine' and 'entirely beautiful' gravity of 'Except my life, except my life, except my life.'

The London press called her vocally 'harsh' and 'monotonous' (there was first-night vocal strain). Grein said Hamlet 'either rushes through a stream of words in almost inaudible accents, or he hurls the words at his bystanders in frantic howls', and the *Morning Leader* thought she was limiting her scale – 'so flexible, so eternally free' – to two notes suiting a man: 'languorous complaint' and a 'torrential rush of unhindered passion'. *The Star* complained that the soliloquies were 'not thought out but cried out', and Grein had a misogynist explanation: she spoke 'To be or not to be' 'without depth, without searching for the solution of the great problem' – 'in a true girlish manner'. But Bernhardt was annexing Hamlet for the declamatory *tirade* tradition, and did not see these speeches as ontological knots; rather 'Hamlet *dreams* when he is alone.'[13] She seems to have seen all the soliloquies as one continuous stream of thought, sound and imagery, carrying Hamlet from 'Oh that this too too solid flesh would melt' through to commitment to action: 'When he dreams it is of his plan – of his vengeance. If God had not forbidden suicide he would have killed himself in disgust of the world. But since he cannot kill himself he will kill!' Hamlet's mind ('the most original, the most subtle, the most tortuous') was also 'the most simple': 'This being who appears to be so complex has really only one idea: to avenge his father.' She saw him as a boy, 'heartbroken to see the mother he loves as the loving wife of his father's assassin', driven by a 'passion of hate' and a 'thirst for vengeance' from the first; but ('a thinker, not a madman') he thought before he acted, and set out on a painful quest for *proof*. For Bernhardt everything – 'The suspicions, the inquietudes, the remorse, the terrors of being the puppet of a malignant spirit' – revolved round 'this primary uncertainty', the modern mind's need for evidence. The *Star*: 'She has *seen* the part throughout', and 'it is intensely dramatic. It has passion and fire – too much passion and fire for Hamlet, I think, for it shows little if anything of his hesitations and perplexities, his malady of the will. This Hamlet is an avenger of consistent and firm purpose – which is just what Hamlet was not.' Bernhardt disagreed.

Asexual love

'To be or not to be' was 'pathetically chanted throughout in the *voix d'or*. (*Daily Telegraph*) Hamlet pressed his head against a doorway and one critic drew attention to a 'sweetly subtle change of inflection' at 'To die – to sleep'.[14] Scott said she had no rival in the following 'love scene' – 'the brain of the French actress is so quick, her changes so vivid' – and 'the mere presence of Ophelia makes Hamlet almost a saint. She has touched his bitter nature.' Scott paraphrased her 'nunnery' speech as 'Save yourself from the contact and contamination of man while you can!' She spoke gently, 'with streaming eyes and quivering lips', and even Grein thought this 'the one moment. . . when the voice sounded gloriously, and betrayed wealth of feeling and immensity of grief.' 'With Ophelia there is no feigning', Bernhardt said, 'he is always real with her.' 'Poor Ophelia' was 'the one tender spot in his seared heart' but therefore she threatened to 'turn him from the path of vengeance he has mapped out'. 'Hamlet loves Ophelia! He renounces his love! . . . He renounces everything – in order to gain his object.'[15] At first deeply involved with the Court world, Bernhardt's prince became more isolated scene by scene ('she detaches him in the most hopeless way'[16]) and love turned to poison when he glimpsed Polonius spying. Hamlet asked Ophelia where her father was 'with hesitation. . . with the utmost apprehension' and her lie destroyed his faith. 'His whole nature changes, his philosophy is soured. His sacred ideas become a mad whirl of emotion . . . He can scarcely express himself for indignation and disgust.' (Scott) Sneering sarcasm, 'hammered and hissed', reduced Ophelia to her father's level in Hamlet's mind, crushed her, and prepared for her public humiliation in the Play scene.[17] Drained, Hamlet left the stage with a whisper.

Death's body

'O what a rogue and peasant slave am I' was 'violent throughout,' 'snarled' with 'shrewd satisfaction; she enters with zest into the office of detective.' Robins described her 'ignoble cunning'. Bernhardt eased the tension briefly in her authoritative but conversational advice to the Players. A valet lit footlight candles for the small platform stage on which she spoke; Hamlet jumped down, laughing with excitement. The Players acted before a 'primitive' Tuscan landscape-backcloth and standing stylised trees. Musicians (flutes and recorders) sat on the floor. The royal party sat directly facing it on a balustraded gallery, so the 'real' and 'mock' Kings were opposed on twin platforms across the full width of the stage. Courtiers crammed in front of a corridor exit at the rear. Hamlet set Ophelia – her head bowed – on a chair centre-front, drawing attention to her humiliation, though her treatment was ambiguous: there was more vulgarity than usual, yet Hamlet 'pressed endearingly with his hand her fair head'. (*Globe*) 'Wormwood, wormwood' came at the top of Bernhardt's voice – or rather *'Absinthe, absinthe'*, 'like a call to an invisible waiter'. (After English complaints she changed it to *'Amertume, amertume'*.) Watching Claudius, her anxiety was 'impulsive and palpable'. (*Daily Telegraph*) 'Catlike', 'like a tiger' (Grein, Baring), she crept across and up to the dais as the King craned anxiously forward – 'and then it is that Hamlet reads the truth'. (*Daily Chronicle*) Bernhardt suddenly leapt onto a bench and shouted in his face. The King stood distracted, the confused Court rose, but this triggered the real climax. At 'Lights! Lights!' Bernhardt snatched a torch from the servants and 'thrusts it into the wretched man's pallid face to see the full effect' like 'an avenging angel'. (*The Times*, Baring) 'A finer display of passionate acting has seldom been witnessed' than this 'whirlwind of fury'. (*St James'*) She gave Hamlet 'energy and glorying malignity' (*Daily Telegraph*) and 'the triumphant exultation of certainty', (*Morning Post*) and in the recorders scene Hamlet still shook with excitement. 'What intense joy surges through him at the idea of being free', she said: 'The uncertainty had stifled the explosion of his vengeance. Now he is free.'[18] Now Bernhardt would be 'terrible with the King' and 'wicked' with his 'evil' pawns.

In London Bernhardt ran the Prayer and Closet scenes together in one set (see Figure 11). Hamlet paced behind Claudius (Kate Terry Gielgud: 'M Bremont interested me . . . he was a plausible villain, ingratiating'),

Scène de l'Oratoire

Figure 11 Sarah Bernhardt in the Prayer scene, Paris 1899. *Morning Leader,*
18 June 1899.

then came in close 'with blade upraised, as if to cut him down'. (*Standard*)
There was no self-doubt: 'He does not kill the King, not because he is
vacillating and weak, but because he is firm and logical. He wishes to
kill him in a state of sin, not of repentance; for he desires to send him to
hell.' (Bernhardt) Moments later, Polonius' cry behind the arras released
all inhibitions, and Bernhardt's body expressed a fierce catharsis: 'She
stood suddenly tiptoe, like a great black exclamation mark, her sword
glittering above her head, and a cry, '*C'est le roi!*' rang in our ears.' 'For a
tightening second', wrote Desmond MacCarthy, the play seemed over.
With his rapier left in the curtain, Hamlet dragged his 'unworthy
mother' (Bernhardt) through the 'indictment' – 'a coarse scene, terrifying

Figure 12 Bernhardt in action, 1899: 'Angels and ministers of grace defend us';
'Alas poor Yorick'; duel scene. Drawings from Gregorio Martinez Sierra,
Hamlet y el Cuerpo de Sarah Bernhardt (Madrid: n.p., 1905).

in its truth and savagery'. The emotional extremes she ran through were
remarkable. When the Ghost materialised within a painting on the
wall only to fade away, Bernhardt ran 'appealing dumbly for another
sign, and passing pathetic fluttering hands over the unresponsive surface,
groping piteously like a child in the dark'; yet there were protests
because she joked as she lugged out Polonius' guts.[19]

Her next scenes emphasised conflict and plot – Hamlet's defiance
of Claudius had a 'terrible force' (*Daily Chronicle*) and the account of
his fight with the pirates was unfamiliar on English stages – but it was
Bernhardt in the graveyard that became iconic, and spectators and artists
projected their own nuances on her. In one photograph she looks down
casually at a skull, with a hand on her waist and a detached half-smile;
Robins said she handled it 'callously' – 'as lightly as a lap-dog', but in
another she holds Yorick's skull close to her face, her finger touching its
teeth, and at 'Here hung those lips that I have kissed', one critic sensed
something unprecedented, 'a woman apostrophising the skull of a dead
lover'.[20] In drawings, paintings and cartoons the recurrent image is of
a slight, dark figure holding the skull high, intrigued and galvanised
by death (see Figure 12). Bernhardt made the funeral an opulently
morbid celebration of the feminine. Behind a great cross, hooded priests
bore Ophelia shoulder-high on a floral bier; young women scattered

blossoms on her; she held a flower. Hamlet and Laertes fought passionately (not in the grave) and Hamlet threw himself on the ground, finally
expressing his love (she 'tears the cat to pieces': *Referee*). Even then
Bernhardt insisted this 'is not grief, but still defiance'.

The boy grew into dignity and greeted Osric with studied politeness –
'There is no bantering, no jesting' now – and despite the 'underlying
certainty of doom' (Baring) she inflected 'It will come' with courage.
In the duel, Gertrude sat isolated in the royal gallery while Claudius
plotted in the crowd; when she drank the poison, he could only cry
'Do not drink!' across the width of the stage, and for the second time
he watched a poisoning scene helplessly. Bernhardt's death scene
was instantly famous: 'The actress allows you to see what is passing in
Hamlet's mind as no other Hamlet has done in my time.' (*Referee*) He felt
a sword-scratch, dismissed it, but removed a glove and saw blood.
He instantly struck Laertes' foil from his hand, stood over it and offered
his own. 'There is a deadly pause; Laertes takes the foil offered him,
and Hamlet picks up the other. In the next encounter he presses
Laertes and thrusts home.' (*Morning Post*) The Queen fell, Claudius
tried to flee, and Hamlet struck again, with a shout. Bernhardt showed
the poison scour through the veins. 'After the life-long storm comes
the dying calm' (*Birmingham Gazette*) and a 'touchingly beautiful'
death built of visual moments. 'He reverently kissed his dead mother's
flowing tresses', then at 'the rest is silence', 'Mme Bernhardt leaves the
final word unuttered, but indicates it with her pressed finger upon the
closing lips', the same touch she gave the skull.[21] She died standing, falling
back into the arms of Horatio and an attendant. Her body turned
instantly rigid and heavy as she sank back and was lowered as if from
the cross. Hamlet was lifted onto a shield and carried off through an arch
of weapons; these rites overlapped with Ophelia's, but it was a crown
Fortinbras placed on Bernhardt's body, not a flower. Her head hung back
over the shield.

The aesthetic disagreements in England were absolute:

The scenes are arranged with a fine regard for effect, and they give Mme
Bernhardt a series of triumphs, showing the different ranges of her power and
the variety of her style. She passes from height to height, irresistible always, and at
length reaches such a grand climax that the audience can only relieve their
feelings with loud and repeated '*Bravos*'. (*Birmingham Gazette*)

The melodramatic vein prevailed throughout; and when, in the duel
scene . . . Hamlet even slipped off his glove to display a gory hand, I saw clearly

what was amiss – Shakespeare had to give way to the author of *La Tosca*; Mme Bernhardt's Hamlet was conceived under the spiritual influence of Sardou. (*Grein*)

'One could never, even for a single instant', the *Sunday Times* said, 'escape from the consciousness that it was a man's part being rendered by a woman.' But that was of course the point. No-one at the Théâtre Sarah Bernhardt's *Hamlet* lost sight of Bernhardt. She was always herself, the startling actress/auteur displaying 'her wonderful art and wonderful personality' (*The Times*) even as she created a controversial characterisation. The power to transform yet proclaim the self was the doubleness of star acting. However it was significant that two of her harshest London critics were actresses. Kate Terry Gielgud ('she disappointed me utterly') thought she only created a portrait of 'an unmannerly youth; undignified, disrespectful, moody and short-tempered'. She was also much more specific than the male critics:

She handicapped herself from the start with her clothes. Her legs are not shapely, but she wore the traditional black tights, over which hung a short doublet, with the most unbecoming sleeves ever invented, a huge puff falling below the elbow producing an effect of enormous width from neck to waist and making her look as if her arms were glued to her sides. A white under-dress of elaborate make was worn, muffling her up to the chin, and she trailed . . . a long wide scarf over one shoulder, which got in her way and was not picturesque.

Terry thought it a crude attempt to look masculine; the crudity Elizabeth Robins complained of was a matter of vision: comparing Bernhardt unfavourably to Booth, she said 'the great tragedy has been drained of its dignity by her preoccupation with plot and behavioural realism'. Bernhardt's Hamlet belonged to the material world. On the other hand the *Morning Post* thanked 'the greatest artist of the modern stage' and even embraced her for the nation: she had rendered *Hamlet* the 'greatest service' – 'she has restored . . . the strong character which Goethe took away from him.'

III

'Report me and my cause aright'

European leading ladies hurried to play Hamlet as soon as rumours linked Bernhardt with the role. Mlle Dudlay of the Comédie Française launched a provincial *Hamlet* tour in March 1898, starting in Toulouse, and Mme Derigny played it weeks later in Paris at the Bouffes du Nord. Giacinto Pezzana was Hamlet in Italy. The same year, in a pre-emptive strike against Bernhardt, Adele Sandrock toured Germany, Holland, Belgium, Poland and Russia before coming home to act it in Vienna. She had made her reputation in Romantic drama, then in Ibsen and the plays of her lover Arthur Schnitzler, who based the Actress in *Reigen* on her, and she played the lesbian Countess in Wedekind's *Lulu* plays. Sandrock's pathos as Hamlet was praised but she complained that the press did not take it seriously. Her histrionic style was 'tense' and hysterical: 'No-one can come near her in the interpretation of the decadent, the perverse, the degenerate, those straying in senses and nerves,' one critic wrote, but 'classical parts are beyond her'.[22] At the Finish National Theatre Elli Tompuri played Hamlet. Agatha Bârsescu toured it in Romania in 1906–7. In the English-speaking world alongside Bandmann-Palmer, Howard and Steer, late-century Hamlets included Emelie Burke, Annette Dunne, Florrie Groves, Nellie Holbrook, Mrs Nunn, Eliza Warren and Viola Whitcomb.[23] In Australia, Virgie Vivienne played Hamlet and Ophelia in a highlights evening in 1898.[24] Ellen Terry thought Julia Jennings' version for one of the small fit-up companies that visited theatreless towns (Jennings Portable Theatre, Droitwich 1900) was 'excellent'.

In 1901 Bertha Kalisch (1874–1939) played Hamlet in Yiddish at the New York Yiddish Theatre. She had emigrated from Poland in 1896 and quickly earned star status in the Jewish community; emulating Bernhardt, her Hamlet won praise within and beyond it. The *New York Morning Journal* admired Kalisch's directness: 'There were no airs, there were no frills. There were no poses, no struggles for elusive effect.' She 'got down to the solid bedrock of the idea and hammered at it'. Only a month after Bernhardt's Hamlet opened on Christmas Day 1900, Kalisch imitated her appearance but added her own emotional highpoints: Ophelia was present praying during the Soliloquy and in the following scene Kalisch screamed at her; Hamlet drew a sword on Gertrude, only to repent immediately, and Ophelia's drowned body was carried onstage. The denouement came swiftly, in the graveyard. Kalisch regarded Hamlet as 'my greatest artistic success'. To quote Joel Berkowitz, this was true 'popular theatre – popular enough not only to remain in her repertoire as long as she remained in the Yiddish theatre, but also to appeal to the "uptown" critics'.[25] Kalisch appeared alongside several rewritings of Shakespeare, including *The Jewish Queen Lear* featuring the matriarch Mirele Efros, driven from her home and the family business by her daughter-in-law. Bertha Kalisch was the last of the great demotic Princess Hamlets, offering

an androgynous image of intellect and daring to a new community negotiating its relationship with the dominant culture.

Meanwhile, however, Bernhardt's challenge encouraged a backlash.
Genteel anti-Semitism offered one of many justifications for dismissing
her Hamlet: 'She had three things overwhelmingly against her – her sex,
her race, and her speech . . . You never ceased to feel for a moment that it
was a woman who was doing that melancholy Dane, and that the woman
was a Jewess, and the Jewess a French Jewess.'[26] Many London reviewers
were francophobic – in 1898 and early 1899 France and Britain were on the
brink of a colonial war over North Africa – and 'The French never
have and never will understand Hamlet. There are certain racial qualities
that are not to be cancelled even by the fullest culture.'[27] During her
London engagement Bernhardt – who was guest of honour at the
inaugural meeting of the Anglo-French Association formed to improve
relations – stressed that Hamlet was not English and Shakespeare
belonged to the world. The major debate, however, was of course about
gender. 'There is room – is there not?' asked the *Sunday Times*, 'for an
arabesque – a fantasia, played upon the themes of *Hamlet* by a woman
of genius.' *St James'* granted that she had more justification than most
'in her own personality' with its 'virility and a certain masculine robust-
ness' and noted Hamlet's 'weakness and vacillation almost feminine in
their nature'; but finally he 'possessed attributes which it may safely
be said stand entirely outside the power of any actress to portray'. For
the *Globe*, 'Female Hamlets . . . are, and always will be, a delusion and
a snare . . . The more inspired and divine a woman is, the less fitted she
is to play Hamlet', and the stage paper the *Era* was bluntest.
It condemned 'Shakespeare's great drama being used for purposes
which are served by the exhibition of a "freak" at Messrs. BARNUM
and BAILEY's show' – 'the unsexed woman, the woman, who, physically,
approaches to the masculine – the monstrosity in short.'[28] It focused
a growing misogyny.

In 1901 Laurence Hutton devoted a chapter in *Curiosities of the
American Stage* to 'mongrel Hamlets' and American writers fought over
Charlotte Cushman's posthumous reputation.[29] In 1894 WT Price's *Life
of Charlotte Cushman* dismissed the 'female biographers' including her
'intimate friend Miss Stebbins' who presented her as a feminist. Price
was perplexed by Cushman's interest in male characters. He granted
that it was delightful when Shakespeare's 'loveliest damsels' in 'trunk
and hose and booted', 'stand forth, playing with the fancy'; but
'a point is reached at which the question of taste arises. We may say

that it is impossible for a woman to act with sincerity, by reason of temperament and mental characteristics, and elemental nature, in certain roles essentially masculine.' When it came to Hamlet, 'Only eccentricity and a desire for notoriety can be at the bottom of such performances.' Cushman was the great exceptional American artist who proved the rule; Price praised her unique 'virile genius' and reinterpreted her support for other women as proof that she *transcended* the feminine: 'Playing the part of a man in these serious relations of life', she 'acquired a positive manner and direct way of dealing with affairs that told on her art,' and emulated the superior sex: 'She had cast behind her all of those disturbing concerns of feminine emotion.' Price celebrated Cushman as 'a woman with the strong intellect of a man, and without that obstinacy of mental apprehension that separates the ordinary woman from the concepts of the world, held by men of judgement, experience and sense'.[30]

William Winter's *Shakespeare on the Stage* (1911–16) broadened the attack by condemning 'unpleasingly mannish' and 'confused' female Hamlets. Dismissing Hamlet's alleged femininity as nonsense, he attacked women's inability to 'think precisely' and asserted that a 'sweet, gentle, affectionate' and 'exquisitely sensitive temperament' is by definition manly. As for love, 'It can be doubted whether woman is nearly as capable as man has often shown himself to have been, of forming and cherishing and adoring, even to idolatry, an ideal of celestial loveliness and excellence in a human being of the opposite sex.'[31] 'The emergence of a female as Hamlet has always had the effect of futile experiment'; some 'semi-masculine women, such as Charlotte Cushman, Miss Marriott, and Mrs Waller, could, and did, measurably, impart at least an impression of sincerity and weight;' but 'the female Hamlet must, of necessity, always suggest either an epicine hybrid or a paltry frivolity.' With 'the great, serious male incarnations of dramatic poetry', women were 'absurd and out of place'. To sharpen the point Winter rewrote his old review of Alice Marriott, making her 'gloomily comic': her 'impressive' (1869) figure was 'massive' now.[32]

In England the *Illustrated London News* responded to Bernhardt's visit with a judicious survey of female Hamlets by WJ Lawrence, and Chance Newton's memoirs celebrated the tradition in working-class theatres; but when Clement Scott included Bernhardt in his book *Some Notable Hamlets*, the *Athenaeum* – which had dismissed the work of Siddons, Cushman and Marriott as 'mere triumphs of posturing or elocution'[33] – said Scott had forfeited his professional credibility.

The most influential attack was Max Beerbohm's essay on Bernhardt's 'absurd', 'preposterous' 'aberration', the product of 'unreasoning vanity'.[34] Beerbohm also decried Mrs Bandmann-Palmer's version because whereas Rosalind charmingly deceives other characters, the Hamlet actress 'tries directly to illude the audience itself'. He claimed that men could cross-dress successfully but women could not: 'The explanation is simple... A man contains in himself the whole of a woman's nature *plus* certain other qualities which make the difference between him and her.' Indeed, 'Creative power, the power to conceive ideas and execute them, is an attribute of virility: women are denied it. In so far as they practise art at all, they are aping virility, exceeding their natural sphere. Never does one understand so well the failure of women in art as when one sees them deliberately impersonating men upon the stage.'[35] The erasure of female Hamlets from theatre history was guaranteed when George CD Odell's seminal *Shakespeare from Betterton to Irving* (1920) disposed of Bernhardt and the whole tradition with one sentence from the *Athenaeum*: 'Where everything is necessarily wrong, nothing can be right.'[36]

As Bernhardt toured *Hamlet* from Paris to London to New York – and on film through the world – she brought those arguments stringingly to life. Not only did she inspire some male critics to condemn her and several actresses to compete, a legend stamped itself in the minds of several girls born in the 1880s and '90s that remained with them throughout their lives.

IV

Bernhardt's inheritance

To see Hamlet's mind in action . . . To have that pure. (Siobhan McKenna, 1957)

In a time of profound changes that would eclipse the glory of the *fin de siècle* actress, the aesthetic and commercial conditions ended which for a century had allowed women to promote themselves as Hamlet. There was a revolution in theatrical thinking and the start of a shift from actor-managerial to 'directed', 'designed' and 'conceptual' Shakespeare; there was a new almost abstract concern with the body in theatrical space, as an open signifier with a wealth of potential meanings, and new power was given to the (usually male) director to define them. Edward Gordon Craig, the prophet of this transformation, tried to interest Bernhardt in his plans for *Hamlet* but she was bored by the prospect of posing in his palace of moving walls: 'He is showing me a lot of screens.'[37] The collaboration never took place, and so Bernhardt's *Hamlet* registered as a last flowering of the nineteenth-century vision of the play – the star-centred reconstruction of a medieval world – while Craig's (finally staged at the Moscow Arts Theatre in 1911) became the defining symbol of director-led Shakespeare, with everything integrated into a *mise en scène* where the actor ceased to command. Craig walked out of Bernhardt's *Hamlet* (she 'did not convince us') and criticised *travesti* casting in the role ('We do not know that the idea is exactly fascinating'): 'Women are all actresses, there is no subtlety they cannot compass provided they remain women, but to pretend to be a man is, in our opinion, never desirable nor successful.'[38] Yet he compared Hamlet to the Mona Lisa during his Moscow rehearsals and considered ('dreamed about', he said) giving him a female doppelganger – a 'bright golden figure', perhaps '*always* with Hamlet', representing the division of 'spirit and material': 'And I think that this figure. . .is death. But not dark and gloomy as she generally appears to people, but such as she appeared to Hamlet – bright, joyful, one who will free him.' Her first appearance must come during 'To be or not to be' – 'She must be beautiful, glowing, and during the reverie, she leans towards him and leans her head on his shoulder...'[39] In 1913 he granted a woman might reveal 'that *spiritual virility* which belongs to Hamlet and which all male actors miss'.[40] The history of female Hamlets had been a matter of performance and self-presentation, about the self-defining power of the Actress; now, with the rise of the Director, it became a question of interpretation. Male directors began to cast women as Hamlet for symbolic purposes, imposing particular meanings on the body, the voice, and on what they imagined was the essence of femininity. Bernhardt was halfway there already when she told the British press that playing Hamlet 'takes the brains of a man and the intuitive almost psychic power of a woman'[41] – here were Craig's 'material' and 'spirit'.

Spirit

Androgyny could stand with shifting inflections for human duality, for the opposition of reason and emotion or flesh and soul; Meyerhold in Russia and William Poel in England both cast actresses as the allegorical enchained heroes, half saint half beast, in Calderon's *Constant Prince* and *Life is a Dream*, and Poel chose Edith Wynne Matthison (who would later play Hamlet) as Everyman. In Poel's *Bacchae* (1908) Lillah McCarthy (his 1898 Romeo) played Dionysus because they were intrigued by 'the double meaning of this divine being' – an androgynous holy tyrant, both 'God' and 'child'[42] – and the word 'child' resonated when directors cross-cast actresses: was the supposed female principle uncorrupted, or incomplete? For Poel, realism negated 'the creative art of acting' and he was intrigued by *travesti* because he believed masculine psychology underwent such a transformation in the late seventeenth century that modern Englishmen could not access Shakespeare's sense of 'virility'.[43] Poel's experiments excited several figures in the French *avant-garde* who reshaped the Bernhardt legacy: in Paris, two cross-dressed *Hamlet*s opened a completely new era by asking what were the consequences if Hamlet really was an androgynous 'child': s/he became a soul on a spiritual quest.

Craig's discussion of Hamlet and gender was occasioned by the 1913 Théâtre Antoine production with Suzanne Desprès (1874–1931).[44] She was the wife of the Symbolist innovator Lugné-Poe, who was impressed by Poel's *Two Gentlemen of Verona* (with a woman as Valentine) and co-directed *Hamlet* with Firmin Gémier. It became a landmark in Continental Shakespeare, a demonstration of the power of economy, and proof that classical text and innovative production could support each other.

Suzanne Desprès was born Charlotte Bouvellet to a poor Verdun family and one of her greatest successes was as the male lead in Jules Renard's *Poil de Carrotte* (*Carrot-top*, 1900), a bitter peasant drama exploring a loveless relationship between a child and his mother. At the Théâtre de l'Oeuvre, which fostered an aesthetic of dreamlike muted lyricism and spareness of design and gesture, Desprès was in the forefront of the new drama, exploring a hinterland between naturalism and poetry as Solveig in *Peer Gynt* or Hilde Wangel in *The Master Builder*. Despite her achievements class prejudice dogged her critical reception; she was often accused of monotonous speech, dismissed as incapable of nobility, and Hamlet was her vindication – her 'victorious response' to both charges. In a lavish illustrated review *Le Théâtre* stressed that her Hamlet bore no relation to Bernhardesque *travesti*: her walk was masculine, not theatrical, 'she has taken care not to choose a skin tight costume' and 'never evokes memories of the masquerade or operetta'.[45] Though she presented an 'anxious adolescent', Desprès also seemed 'a being who is too intelligent'. Resembling a frail ecclesiastical scholar, her Hamlet was physically undeveloped: 'The head seems too heavy for the body. . . a predominance of brain . . . The brow is high and luminescent. The face is sick and pale. One senses that this person has spent a long time in the libraries meditating. The eyes are of an admirable purity . . .' She took the concern with Hamlet's intellect into unmapped territories.

Desprès' Hamlet was quietly sanctified, a figure of conscience in a listless primitive world. *Le Théâtre* praised her for rejecting Romantic theatre's clichés – 'declamation', 'gesticulation' and 'excessive lyricism'. Here was quiet, melodious understatement, she gave each phrase its own rhythm: 'There are no grimaces, no violent starts', and if Craig's 'spiritual virility' was an inner courage, her prince had it: 'She is concerned to show that Hamlet remains calm in the midst of the most tragic events.' The Ghost terrified the others but he 'overcomes his emotions', reciting the elaborate phrases – 'Be thou a spirit of health or goblin damned,/Bring with thee airs from heaven or blasts from hell . . .' – to distance himself; and as soon as the Ghost vanished he formulated philosophical objections. This might be some demonic deceit, so Desprès made the play an anti-melodramatic search for *spiritual* verification. 'Mme Suzanne Desprès is not concerned to catch the public's attention with serpentine movements. She never stops watching, observing,' until the message from the dead proved true. Hamlet's hurt, innocent eyes were opened to the crimes of which humanity was capable, from Gertrude's remarriage through to Laertes' treachery: 'Her eyes reveal so much to us!'

Desprès excelled in irony but 'when she jests. . . she is on the verge of tears'. She radiated generosity and 'childlike candour'; disarmed by scruples and conscience, her Hamlet trod a Symbolist pathway between fact and dream: 'She glides.' Gémier said that the greater the work, 'the closer it brings us to the sublime' and 'the less need it has of decor and pictorial production. The words carry the decor in themselves.'[46] Desprès' world was formalised and *faux-naïve* with religious overtones. A triptych of arches was surrounded by heraldic eagles; the large central arch could be curtained off for the palace or opened to reveal a painted scene. The critic Paul Grosfils appreciated the attempt to rescue Shakespeare from historical realism without mechanically reconstructing the Elizabethan stage: in this new century of 'lines, forms and colours', designers should 'situate a character in a milieu created for it. *Hamlet* gains from being presented in a *seule venue*, in unique decor.'[47] Some thought it too rudimentary, others mentioned Bakst,

118

Hamlet – which
Guildenstern
less terrifyin
a new har
a bench
confe
loc

Figure 13 Susan Desprès, Paris 1913; directors: Firmin Gémier and Lugné-Poe.
Le Théâtre, 11 October 1913.

and some found their imagination triggered by the frequent 'profound' darkness. The Ghost was a 'dark spectre'. Set, costumes and poses all echoed medieval art: the Queen was a Flemish image of piety, the graveyard echoed Breughel. But in her heavy academic gown Desprès was a figure from a later state of consciousness, the fellow of Montaigne and Descartes.

In many ways the production was a retort to Bernhardt who 'had no patience with the kind of play that is produced in the dark' and made Hamlet so unreflective and socially engaged.[48] The Desprès Hamlet was separated from the body of the play spatially as well as by time. In photographs, a visual narrative emerges where she is almost always at the edge of the central arch, in a margin between the eleventh century and the spectators' realm, in the space of tragedy (see Figure 13). At first Hamlet turned away in desperate isolation, pressed by grief against the left-hand arch while the others stood round blandly as if dropped by chance into their two-dimensional space. But after the Ghost, Desprès' isolation empowered her. While the Player recited, she sat half-attending, musing ahead; she watched the Court during the play with her back to the audience: the drunkard king was pictorially locked within the arch and his guilt became the focus of a double spectacle – *The Mousetrap* and

Després supervised. She mocked Rosencrantz and
ghtly, dismissed the gentle Ophelia with scorn, and was
in the Prayer scene than critics expected; but she revealed
hness in the Closet scene (staged with extreme formality, just
below a candelabra). Though Hamlet tried to extract Gertrude's
sion, the Queen turned elaborately away – a sculpture of penitence
ng herself in silence. After exile, Hamlet returned to penetrate the
ntral arch and enter Golgotha (painted crosses evoked the Passion) but
Després still kept off-centre, the focal point was the grave: 'The scenes
in the graveyard have never seemed so deeply disturbing. We truly have
a charnel house vision. The ground . . . has an odour of death.' In the duel
the King and Queen stood inertly, imitations of life, but Hamlet was
physically transformed: agile, darting, literally freed from the cloak of
introspection and finally centre-stage. And then? Having cleansed the
world-stage, she left it: 'How to forget the looks with which she gazes
into the distance', said *Le Théâtre*, 'and already sees beyond death?'
The 1913 *Hamlet* was a triple success. It was a personal triumph
('She seems to be playing a piece she wrote herself'), pointed to a new
French Shakespearean style defined by simplicity, and encouraged
Hamlet's assimilation into French culture:

The immaculate soul of Hamlet is a precious treasure. Madame Suzanne Després
teaches us to cherish it. Other interpretations have emphasized the character's
peculiarities for us. Thanks to Mme Suzanne Després he no longer seems strange
or fantastic. We can love him.

'I will never be able to express sufficiently how much I love this
tormented face.'

Blood and Hamlet

'Of course it's Hamlet I am longing to do', the young Sybil Thorndike
wrote in 1904. 'Really he's not more male than female – he's everybody
who has got things they want to do and keep failing.'[49] After playing roles
like Brutus at a new girls' grammar school and training with Ben Greet's
companies (where women often played male walk-ons and she was
the Player Lucianus), Thorndike believed theatre was not a place for
mere illusion, a feeling strengthened by encounters with Greek drama
and Chinese theatre: 'You don't want actual life, you want a more
concentrated thing, a life that you don't see really because eyes are
not clear and hearing not acute.' Hamlet remained the one great
Shakespeare role she wished and failed to play, but when war broke out

in 1914 Lilian Baylis' Old Vic mobilised women to take on male roles, insisting that actresses understood men. Thorndike played Everyman, Lear's Fool, Prince Hal and Launcelot Gobbo alongside the female leads and admitted to feeling hampered, even 'jealous', in normal Shakespearean companies. 'There should be no sex in acting', Baylis insisted, 'you ought to be able to understand men as well as women.'[50] Temporarily, cross-dressed women in Shakespeare were patriots, and when troops returned the practice often continued in repertory. In 1920 (Strand Theatre, London) in the presence of the Duchess of Argyle, Eve Donne played Hamlet with an all-female cast for the British Empire Shakespeare Society. Donne's husband and director Acton Bond took Shakespeare to British troops in France, and the Society (founded 1901) also worked with amateurs, targeting 'the rank and file of the people' with the aim of 'making Shakespeare a vital force of the English-speaking race'.[51] Then on 23 April 1923 Eve Donne became probably the first Hamlet on radio. A few months after its launch, the London Station of the British Broadcasting Corporation celebrated Shakespeare's birthday and the First Folio's tercentenary with 'A Shakespeare Night' featuring the BESS in two programmes of songs, scenes, and 'Hamlet's Soliloquy: Miss Eve M Donne'.[52] It was an extraordinary moment and in no way transgressive – a concert included 'Merrie England' and 'Land of Hope and Glory'. In France, however, the war darkened *Hamlet* and the Delacroix vision. It had been 'a poem of death' for the Symbolists and now, as Valéry said, 'our European Hamlet contemplates millions of spectres'.[53] The Trenches were a prophecy come true, 'a little patch of ground which cannot hide the number of the slain,' and from that ground came the Hamlet of Marguerite Jamois (1901–64).

In 1928 Jamois played Hamlet at the Théâtre Montparnasse directed by Gaston Baty, one of the group of directors known as 'The Cartel' – Baty, Jacques Copeau, Louis Jouvet and Georges Pitoëff – whose fusion of classical and experimental disciplines dominated interwar Parisian theatre. Just as Expressionism shattered beauty and logic in response to the carnage, Baty rejected the traditional legitimacy of the 'bare word'. After 1918 language in the theatre could only be a starting-point for 'collective hallucinations':

The poet dreams up a play. He puts on paper whatever is reducable to words. But they can only express part of his dream . . . It is for the director to restore to the poet's work what was lost on the road from dream to manuscript.[54]

Extending the 1913 experiment, they tried to combine neo-Renaissance stagecraft, historical knowledge, and modem symbolism – Marguerite Jamois' Hamlet inhabited a mortuary:

The medieval courtyard was the heart of the castle, like the great hall for the Elizabethans, where soldiers guard the living and the dead are ever present. Here ambassadors are received, here is the chapel, and beside the chapel the charnel house. It is there that the old king is buried; Claudius goes to pray on the tomb; Hamlet takes the Queen to the tomb...[55]

Ophelia's burial was her homecoming. The permanent courtyard set was a deep cubist pit dominated by power and *momento mori*. There was no sky. Like Desprès', the Jamois Hamlet was born out of time: 'He represents civilisation amongst semi-barbarians', Baty said, 'an intellec- tual' in a world 'where only force counts,' but now that world was more brutal. Characters passed beneath a stone arch carved with a massive effigy of the dead ruler, with his tomb slab at its feet; spotlit, the statue became the Ghost; the Father was inescapable, literally holding up Elsinore's prison walls like one of Craig's *über-marionettes*. In contrast to 1913, everything was asymmetrical, an out-of-joint brutalist place of chunks and fragments; figures emerged from a maze of mismatched doorways and the exits led to tombs. Claudius masked this truth by dropping in a massive tapestry of St George and the dragon – sanctified violence – for ceremonial scenes. Romantic melancholy was banished from this hard environment, where soldiers in stewpan helmets lounged easily but the news of the Ghost pushed Hamlet back into a corner. Yet Jamois was not traumatised; she dressed for action and had the bobbed hair of Saint Joan.

Half Bernhardt's age when she played Hamlet, Jamois became one of Baty's closest colleagues and took over the Montparnasse company in 1943. However *Hamlet* became associated with his name rather than hers because he accompanied it with a manifesto essay, 'Shakespeare's Face', and because one aim of the project was to attack the star system – which Baty polemically dated back to Burbage and 1604. The year was crucial because Jamois played the 1603 First Quarto *Hamlet*. Poel revived it in 1881 and 1900 and its directness impressed Craig who called it a real 'stage play' which Shakespeare polished excessively into a 'literary play'. Gémier, Lugné-Poe and Desprès read Q1 in 1913 but chose to explore the later texts' lyric complexity; but after the war Baty jettisoned poetry for action. He aimed to recover the 'original conception' and a lost aesthetic. As a propagandist for ensemble theatre, he argued that the

1603 and 1604 texts recorded a cultural shift: the balance of sympathy in Q1 was more even: Laertes was a decent young man 'duped' by Claudius (in Q2 he has already bought poison), and Gertrude conquered her 'semi-barbaric' passion:

> QUEEN: I will conceal, consent, and do my best,
> What stratagems so'ere thou shalt devise.
> HAMLET: It is enough, mother good night.

Baty said Shakespeare cut this long-forgotten resolution to create a star vehicle where 'Burbage-Hamlet was the only sympathetic character'. He argued that there was a power-shift within the King's Men as the players (masters of improvisation and clowning) lost the initiative to the Actor-Manager and Author ('Speak the speech as I pronounced it to you') and Shakespeare's emergence as businessman-playwright announced the *embourgeoisement* of art. Baty's democratic, anti-poetic *Hamlet*, the visual harshness, and Jamois' antirealist casting were all radical. He was one of the first outside Germany to direct Brecht, who also believed *Hamlet* – a study of the 'feudal family's' collapse – was rewritten for Burbage: 'Hamlet's new bourgeois way of thinking is part of Hamlet's sickness.'[56]

The Q1 *Hamlet* Marguerite Jamois played is less eloquent and enigmatic and less outside the action. At the wedding he has no asides and his first brief speech is dignified:

> Him I have lost I must of force forgo,
> These but the ornaments and suits of woe.

Following Baty's reading of Q1, Jamois overheard the plot to spy on Hamlet, which motivated her contempt for Ophelia (Baty: 'She betrays him, she is their accomplice,') and Corambis (the Polonius). Jamois expressed psychology through action, the clear and powerful 'progress of the interior life'. The Q1 Hamlet is only offstage for eight lines from his first appearance after meeting the Ghost through to 'Oh what a rogue and peasant slave' (here 'Why what a dunghill idiot slave am I'), therefore there was really no 'delay' at all. Baty saw the latter speech as a confession, the revelation of *fear*. In this brutally material world of death and commitment, what most Hamlets made a rhetorical question ('Am I a coward?'), Q1 and Jamois made a fact: 'Why sure am I a coward.' Though Hamlet was never insane, 'It is clear that he is afraid.'[57] The speech behind the praying King was an evasion of political responsibility – 'a poor excuse, a defeat', as 'his terrible duty. . . flies before him.'

His experience was the war generation's: 'In the first version Hamlet isn't yet twenty', so 'this child is bent beneath a man's mission and he struggles against his weakness.' Horatio became a father-figure because after bereavement and the re-marriage, the prince 'feels doubly orphaned' and the dead King imposes a duty which is 'too heavy. The strength he lacks is as much physical as moral. He knows it, to his shame.' Young Hamlet turned for help to the little philosophy he had read. The concise Q1 death scene was unfamiliar in its physical pathos:

> Oh my heart sinks, Horatio,
> Mine eyes have lost their sight, my tongue his use.
> Farewell Horatio, heaven receive my soul.

'It is direct, moving, human theatre', Baty wrote.

In Britain it was different; no established actress played Hamlet between 1923 and the late 1970s except for four 'special' matinees by Esmé Berenger in 1938. In 1923, the year Eve Bond took the Soliloquy to radio, the critic Herbert Farjeon attacked the 'horrifying' and 'growing custom of entrusting male Shakespearean parts to female performers'. It reduced Shakespeare to 'Christmas pantomime'; in the current Old Vic *Merchant*, 'just after Portia had been ridiculing the idea of a woman turning "two mincing steps into a manly stride", I found the Venetian Court of Justice packed with feminine magnificoes in moustaches, all doing their best to illustrate the sense of Portia's remark.' This 'regular feature of almost all modern performances of Shakespeare must be reformed altogether'.[58]

The actresses playing male roles during the war were literally under-studies and had to return to conformity; instead, the war generation of British *male* actors now explored the 'feminine' in Hamlet. Shell-shock horrifically established hysteria as a male illness, Freud undermined the myth of masculine 'normality', and in 1930 Gielgud's tearful prince was as distraught as the traumatised soldier-heroes of *Journey's End*. American critics began to sneer at British Hamlets' effeminacy and though performances increasingly involved the exploration of indeterminacy of gender, Hamlet became connected with male 'sensitivity'; for decades London's leading critics James Agate and Kenneth Tynan dropped sly insider hints about the actors' sexuality. Agate compared Robert Helpmann's Hamlet to Bernhardt – 'A most heart-breaking little figure. And how like Sarah! The same tousled mop, the same collarette, the same provocation'– and Tynan compared Michael Redgrave's Hamlet to Miss Berenger and Gielgud's to a tormented public school 'fag'.

He praised Jean-Louis Barrault for 'changing sex' with a curtsey after calling Claudius 'mother', but accused Olivier of 'obstinate' monotony 'in a perverse desire to amputate every trace of fatal effeminacy from the part'.[59] (When they first met, Agate tried to seduce the student Tynan and they called themselves 'Hamlet' and 'Horatio' in their letters.) As one marginal culture became more visible in Elsinore, another withdrew. In 1920 there was a parliamentary attempt to criminalize lesbianism as 'an undercurrent of dreadful degradation' creating 'neurasthenia and insanity' which 'causes our race to decline';[60] Nancy Hewins, whose all-female Osiris Players toured Britain from 1930 to the 1960s and staged *Hamlet* with a cast of six, stressed that 'I never engaged a rough, square, hearty, masculine type of woman.'[61] Englishwomen virtually abandoned Hamlet but in America, as in the early 1800s, a few independent, courageous – and in several cases publicly lesbian – actresses did attempt it. Like Desprès they concentrated on poetry and the protagonist's spiritual journey; like Jamois they explored new stage spaces and reflected the darkening spirit of the times; but above all they looked back to Bernhardt and the idea of independence. And all, in different senses, created studies of tragic isolation.

v

'Now I am alone'

In 1900 the poet and essayist Richard Le Gallienne – the Decadents' so-called 'golden boy' – cycled to Stratford to attend Bernhardt's gala *Hamlet*. At the stage door he offered her flowers but she gave him hers, ushered him into her private train, and for a few days he vanished from the lives of his wife the Danish journalist Julie Norregaard and their baby daughter Eva. Eva Le Gallienne (1899–1991) was deeply affected by her parents' later divorce and Bernhardt became a figure of obsession: 'I am mad about her!'[62] Bernhardt inspired her to be an actress; when *they* met backstage the star gave her flowers too – camellias – which she afterwards wore in a locket for remembrance. At sixteen Eva made a list of the roles she must play before she was forty – Camille and L'Aiglon, Hilde Wangel and Hedda, Juliet, Peter Pan and Hamlet. In 1937 she was struck when a reviewer of her *L'Aiglon* asked, 'And why not a Le Gallienne Hamlet? . . . I think the poet's daughter has the poet's mind for the part, the cerebral graces as well as the physical.'[63]

That summer she played Hamlet in her own production at the Cape Playhouse in Dennis, Massachusetts.

Le Gallienne revived Bernhardt's reading but personalised it. Hamlet's 'melancholy, his thoughts of suicide, his hero-worship of his father, his mercurial changes of mood, and above all his jealous resentment at his mother's second marriage, are touching and understandable in a boy of nineteen, whereas in a man they indicate a weak and vacillating nature in no way admirable or attractive'.[64] Making Hamlet an adolescent clarified the psychology, she said: his 'morbid' suicidal brooding and 'his obsessive affection for his father' became more 'natural'. However, where Bernhardt insisted on Hamlet's bright temperament, Eva played a child idolising a lost father, dragged out of the 'gay boy-world', and she drew parallels with Oswald in *Ghosts*, whose father's hunt for the 'joy of life' was tainted like the alcoholic Richard Le Gallienne's. She made Hamlet's personal significance obvious and dedicated *Hamlet* to her Scandinavian mother's memory by setting it in the Viking period.[65] 'To enhance the crudeness and violence of the North of that period, we limited our colours to every conceivable shade of red, set off by black and varying shades of gray.' In a new democratic spirit the company worked together to make the red tunics, and she told the local press she had cut firmly 'to expedite the telling of the story rather than to build up the character of Hamlet, thereby depriving herself of one or two soliloquies'. The first scene was stripped to what she saw as its essentials – the Father's Ghost – and she cut Fortinbras and 'How all occasions'. Like Charlotte Cushman, she placed great weight on the Hamlet-Gertrude scene and unusually placed it after the first interval (of two) so that Gertrude and Ophelia dominated the middle Act: 'Here Miss Le Gallienne's ideas. . . were most completely justified. . . and the star became Hamlet, a harassed, bitter, distraught, pleading boy.'[66] She saw him as 'proud, revengeful and ambitious', and ashamed of his weaknesses, but though she diagnosed his mind she also celebrated Hamlet's (and women's) athleticism, hiring the US Olympic fencing coach as fight arranger. Craig had called her 'that young warrior', capturing 'fortress after fortress': wounded, her Hamlet struggled up the steps, then with her last reserves of strength reached, collapsed and died on the throne.[67] It was crucial for Le Gallienne finally to reach that goal.

She stressed language and clarity and though some felt it was a cool recitation, what made this an extraordinary event was the fact that four years earlier she had been the centre of sensational newspaper claims that the husband of a young actress, Josephine Hutchison, had cited Eva Le Gallienne as co-respondent. This coincided with a moralistic assault on lesbianism in American theatre, yet she accepted her unwanted role as one of the most visible homosexual women in America and staged Susan Glaspell's *Alison's House* (1930), a coded discussion of Emily Dickinson's sexuality. Playing Hamlet even a few years later was quietly defiant. Le Gallienne wrote, 'I shall never forget it. The theatre was crowded every night. I was aware that many people came out of curiosity, expecting to see a freak performance, a ridiculous sort of stunt, came prepared to scoff.' In 'crude, violent' Elsinore, forced to conform outwardly in a world of sexual hypocrisy and rumour, with every intimate encounter ringed with spies, Eva Le Gallienne-Hamlet wore the same uniform as the others, a scarlet tunic blazoned with three crowns; but beneath it she was in black. After a week in Massachusetts she was offered a New York transfer; however 'the thought of all the fuss and commotion and publicity, the quips of columnists, the storm of controversy, that a "female Hamlet" would in all likelihood provoke, filled me with dismay.'[68] She knew *Hamlet* would invite the yellow press to turn on her again: 'I shall always be ashamed that I had not the courage to accept the offer.'

Yet Le Gallienne's production became legendary within the profession, partly because of the significance she gave it in her autobiography; and she was not the only twentieth-century actress for whom Hamlet was especially significant. When Nance O'Neil (1874–1965) played it in 1924 it was a 'lifelong dream' (she owned Fechter's costume). Esmé Berenger had played Romeo to her sister Vera's Juliet in 1896 (when Clement Scott called her the best he had seen) and in 1938 she was Hamlet in London: 'For years it has been Miss Berenger's ambition to undertake such a very big adventure.'[69] Judith Anderson (1899–1992) spoke of playing Hamlet for twenty years before she did so in her seventies. All had been the subject of homophobic rumours. For them, as for Edith Wynne Matthison (1875–1955), Sybil Ward and Siobhan McKenna (1923–86), *Hamlet* was a significant personal experience – and a gesture of contact with the past.

All were confined to short runs or a few matinees, all looked back to Bernhardt and to the turn-of-the-century aesthetic of visual simplicity. O'Neil, a statuesque actress whose successes ranged from David Belasco dramas to Hedda and silent film, chose to play Hamlet in the epic space of the University of California's Greek amphitheatre, 'the most perfect theatre I can imagine for this play'. At first, she said, 'its immensity rather overpowered me and I felt as though I had to conquer its huge spaces. Since then, however, I have found its largeness and its beauty wonderfully inspiring.'[70] The classical arena pushed the play towards the mythic – critics and psychologists were currently exploring the affinities between Hamlet and what Baty called the 'sacred horror' of the Orestes-Electra myth. Eva Le Gallienne's version was also formalised – she married neo-Elizabethanism to the new stagecraft, with a stark four-level set, an apron stage and white 'modern trick lighting' – and her colour-scheme was quoted years later in McKenna's tunic for the Play scene and Judith Anderson's blood-red set and costumes (men and women all wore a 'Gothic' uniform except for Hamlet in mourning black). For all these actresses the voice was paramount. Poel had prized Matthison's ability to begin poetic arias 'at the highest point of feeling and go on from there', and the press were excited because 'the glorious voice of Nance O'Neil will be perfect in the part. It is deep, husky and very resonant, like a cello.'[71] Yet this style was losing favour. Though O'Neil was praised in her scenes with the Ghost, Ophelia and the Players, 'the Soliloquy' was said to be 'purely recitative, with a woeful absence of light and shade'. Berenger's choice of director was WG Fay, who had shaped the acting style at Yeats' Abbey Theatre – simple, static, emotional realism supporting verbal music – and though the *Observer* thought she spoke Hamlet impeccably 'both as verse and drama' and communicated the 'intolerable conflict', *The Times* dismissed her 'sing-song intonation'. Understandably Berenger paid more attention to her audience ('I am very pleased and proud', she wrote, 'at the wonderful reception my Hamlet has had'[72]) and Matthison gave Hamlet special weight in her *Who's Who in the Theatre* entry – 'a great success' – as did O'Neil. Forced on their own resources, the logical next step for these actresses was monodrama: Sybil Ward's solo 'Dramatic Recitals', incorporating quick-change costume effects, included *Hamlet*, which she advertised in 1941 with photos of herself as Hamlet and Ophelia ('You are gloriously independent', Shaw wrote to her: 'I can only regard you with respectful envy.')[73]

Significantly, Hamlet gave Sybil Ward and Le Gallienne a vocabulary to deal with questions of faith and death. In her poem 'The Readiness is All', Ward, an English actress and writer who moved to America during World War II, described death as a journey 'homeward'. At the end of her life Le Gallienne stated, 'I don't fear anything that may come afterwards. I don't think that there is anything . . . The very best thing is just going to sleep – eternal sleep. Remember, ''tis a consummation/Devoutly to be wished".'[74] In 1957 the Irish actress Siobhan McKenna took this theme and the concept of isolation to the ultimate extreme when she appeared alone on the stage of the Theatre de Lys, New York, in 'an experimental version of *Hamlet*' that began with a religious debate.[75] In a prologue an unseen choir sang a hymn honouring death as a 'consummation good' – 'a dreamlike sleep through all eternity'. But McKenna's Hamlet retorted, 'What is death?':

> There rivers run with flaming floods, and dreadful monsters be
> That poison foam with gaping throats, there places may you see
> Of divers forms, where infants cry ...[76]

McKenna and her director the critic Henry Hawes set Christian quietism against this Hamlet's horror of the afterlife; then the play began, inside the mind: 'The curtain rises to reveal Hamlet sitting alone on the steps at the front of the stage. Behind Hamlet a large screen glows with a painting of the Danish court. . . From behind black drapes at either side of the screen, we hear the voices that Hamlet hears. These voices create the interior world of Hamlet.'[77] The tragedy became a meditation on three funerals; McKenna was alone on the threshold of the afterlife and there would be another hymn over Ophelia – 'All things begun shall have an end; nothing remaineth still,/Death ends all pain' – before Hamlet's own death ended – or began – everything.

McKenna had become known internationally for her work on the Irish classics, especially Shaw's *Saint Joan* which she translated into Gaelic. She and Hawes sidestepped the issue of gender 'illusion' and returned to the spirit of Poel's *Everyman* by circling McKenna with Voices like Joan's and allegorising *Hamlet* into a debate about spiritual crisis and martyrdom: 'I just thought to see Hamlet's mind in action. . . and that the audience saw the other characters through Hamlet's eyes. . . one must see the play through his eyes.'[78] In this theatre of the mind – other images of Elsinore's labyrinth of rooms were projected onto bare 'mind's eye' walls – McKenna played to the voices of an unseen cast, 'sometimes as if the other parties are two inches away from him, and sometimes as if they are miles distant'. When he was sent to England the stage emptied and her voice narrated Hamlet's escape. Later she had reservations about the circumstances ('I only had ten days. . . I really worried about lines') and more importantly about the solipsism: 'There is a political situation in the play and I think it's sometimes drowned. . . I think Hamlet was ambitious, personally ambitious.' She would also reassess the *Saint Joan* connection: 'I don't think spiritual life worried him.'[79]

Pacing, 'soliloquising, agonizing, duelling and feigning madness' alone, Siobhan McKenna's experiment was generally received with respect: 'She handles her strange and demanding assignment with considerable grace and warmth, and with an absence of the grotesque . . . except possibly in the duelling bits.'[80] Some described it as a pretentious stunt, though, and the critic Whitney Bolton was vicious: 'If she believes that no role in English is beyond her compass', as though 'deep, full voice and defiant mien were the sum of Hamlet's character', then 'I must dissent.'[81] 'Very few actresses', Bolton added, 'have had the audacity to believe that they could play this most difficult and demanding of roles . . . In recent years only one, Miss Judith Anderson, has talked of doing it . . . Miss Anderson for years has hesitated to undertake such a crucifying role.' In fact this was prophetic; in 1971 Anderson did play Hamlet, and the experience was crucifying.

Though McKenna was a generation younger she felt rooted in the era of Shaw, Yeats – and Bernhardt, whom she played in one of her last projects, *Memoir* (1978); Judith Anderson however was born the year Bernhardt played Hamlet and was 72 when she followed suit. She was born in Australia, played Gertrude to Gielgud and Olivier, and her harpy-like Lady Macbeth partnered and dominated Maurice Evans on stage, television and film; she matched sinister screen roles (Mrs Danvers in *Rebecca*) with Medea and Clytemnestra on stage and kept the Grand Manner breathing: 'She cannot by temperament play wallflowers', said Le Gallienne.[82] The press reported her physical regimen, her early morning jogging round Santa Barbara in preparation for Hamlet. She opened with a three-week run in San Francisco and climaxed (amidst some jeering) a nationwide tour at Carnegie Hall. The director William Ball had been a Voice in McKenna's version and found a less laborious frame for Anderson, the simple metatheatricality of travelling players who marched in, took their positions, and created sequences of stylised tableaux. It was half theatre, half recital. Ball explained, 'It will be clear, simple and free of distractions. There'll be no swords or rapiers. And when people die, they'll merely turn their backs to the audience.'[83]

The Ghost entered to the sound of a heartbeat and stood behind Hamlet, who seemed to see it in the audience; Ophelia's funeral – a high-point in the Bernhardt tradition – was imaginatively stark: 'Draped completely in black veiling, Ophelia was led to a place on the stage level, understood as her grave, where she knelt. When the ceremony was over, she was gently led off.' Blurring life and death in the opposite way to McKenna – here physical *presence* was everything – the evening flowed towards Hamlet's death, which reworked tradition to suit a performer in her seventies. Judith Anderson's Hamlet died standing, supported by Horatio, relaxing into his arms on a sigh, which Morlin Bell thought 'subtle yet vivid', almost a rite. More cynical commentators including the *New York Times* complained of spasms of inept mime ('An actor holds a book or a paper, then forgets about it, using the hands for other purposes such as pointing or smiting a brow') but reserved the venom for Anderson: 'She quickly – and with obvious boredom – quizzes the grave-digger, not bantering with him, hardly even looking at him, until he picks up Yorick's skull – or rather until he cups his hands as if holding a skull. Then, suddenly, she stops and sobs the Alas Poor Yorick number. Mostly, she plays with a pained expression, fixed gestures (right knee slightly bent, hands firmly behind her back or at her sides), and many sighs and suspirations.'[84] Even Bell judged her Hamlet 'perfunctory' and 'clichéd', 'accented occasionally by a suddenly shouted sentence'. Yet despite her reception, Anderson played on and kept the production in the public eye with, for instance, advertisements for Lucky Strike cigarettes: 'My present role in *Hamlet* is a special strain because of the declamatory style of Shakespearean drama. . . Luckies never irritate my throat.'

William Winter could rest in peace. Finally the female Hamlet was officially absurd. For fifty years, as the English-speaking theatre moved in new directions, the few crossdressed *Hamlets* had involved eminent older women increasingly isolated in a ghetto of matinee intellectualism; to outsiders they seemed increasingly strange, gazing back in nostalgia to a theatre that had been so symbolic of a morning of opportunity for women. In Ken Russell's 1971 film *The Boyfriend* a pompous seaside *grande dame* (played by Joan Hickson) flaunted her press-book, oblivious to her reviewers' sarcasm: '*Hamlet: a tragedy!*' The generation inspired by the suffrage movement and Bernhardt was passing, and Anderson's declamations seemed the last gasp of a half-forgotten eccentricity. And yet Nance O'Neil's words were still resonant: 'I have nearly always interpreted the unloved woman in the theatre, the woman crucified by the unseen, the conventional traditions', she said in 1920: 'Often in women, who live out their destinies in the small places into which they have been driven, there is a storm that broods but never bursts. Few women realise the joy of real liberty, not merely the freedom of time and place, but the greater freedom of supreme faith in their own feeling. They distrust their emotions and so confuse their lives. . . Better an outlaw than not free.'[85] In 1924 as Shakespeare's avenger she broke out of the 'small places' at the Greek amphitheatre, and 'How much better to have a woman play Hamlet', one critic wrote: 'No man could understand and portray the psychology of some of his behaviour.'[86] For O'Neil and her successors, playing Hamlet, irrespective of critical approval, was a statement of 'faith in their own feeling', the expression of a personal truth. But beyond the Anglo-American theatre the female Hamlet in the twentieth century came to assume a less private, less marginalised significance; and in fact Bernhardt's Hamlet had already led others in a different direction, into a new medium.

Notes

1. Sarah Bernhardt, *The Art of the Theatre* (London: Bles, 1924), p. 142. Bernhardt was discussing 'my three Hamlets'.
2. Madam Judith, *My Autobiography* (London: Eveleigh Nash, 1912), pp. 313, 317.
3. See Romy Heylen, *Translation, Poetics and the Stage: Six French Hamlets* (London: Routledge, 1993).
4. Judith, *My Autobiography*, p. 86.
5. *Ibid.*, p. 314.
6. May Agate, *Madame Sarah* (London: Home & Van Thal, 1945), p. 159.
7. Bernhardt, *Art of the Theatre*, p. 137. See also Sarah Bernhardt, 'Men's Roles as Played by Women', *Harper's Bazaar* 15 December 1900.
8. Gregorio Martinez Sierra, *Hamlet y el Cuerpo de Sarah Bernhardt* (Madrid: n.p., 1905); Gerda Taranow, *The Bernhardt Hamlet* (New York: Lang, 1996). On the film, see below, chapter 5. For wider perspectives see Taranow, *Sarah Bernhardt: The Art Within the Legend* (Princeton: Princeton University Press, 1972), John Stokes *et al*, *Bernhardt, Terry, Duse* (Cambridge: Cambridge University Press, 1988), and Elaine Aston, *Sarah Bernhardt: A French Actress on the London Stage* (Oxford: Berg, 1989). Parts of this chapter appeared in 'The Woman in Black: Some Notes on the Actress as Hamlet', *Women and Theatre: Occasional Papers* I (1992), pp. 63–83.
9. Bernhardt, *Art of the Theatre*, pp. 45, 142.
10. Bernhardt in interview, *Daily Chronicle*, and in a letter to *Daily Telegraph*, both 17 June 1899.
11. Reviews of Bernhardt's *Hamlet* (Adelphi Theatre, 12 June 1899) used here: *Morning Leader*; *St James'*; *Daily Telegraph*; *Globe*; *Sunday Times*; *Times*; *Standard*; *Daily Mail*; *Daily Chronicle*; *Star*; *Morning Post*; *Referee*; *Punch*; *Era*. For the Stratford matinee (26 June 1899): *Daily Chronicle*; *Birmingham Gazette*; *Birmingham Post*; *Stratford-upon-Avon Herald*; *Stage*; *Referee*. See also Elizabeth Robins, 'On Seeing Madame Bernhardt's Hamlet, *North American Review* (December 1900), pp. 908–19; JT Grein, *Premieres of*

the Year (London: Eveleigh Nash, 1900), pp. 37–40; Max Beerbohm, *Around Theatres* (London: Rupert Hart-Davis, 1953), pp. 34–7; Clement Scott, *Some Notable Hamlets of the Present Time* (1900, reprinted New York and London: Benjamin Blom, 1969), pp. 156–8; Desmond MacCarthy, *Theatre* (London: MacGibbon and Kee, 1954); Kate Terry Gielgud, *A Victorian Playgoer* (London: Heinemann, 1980), pp. 84–5.

12. Maurice Baring, *Sarah Bernhardt* (London: Nelson, 1933), p. 137.
13. Bernhardt, *Daily Telegraph*. [Italics mine.]
14. *Birmingham Gazette.*
15. Bernhardt, *Daily Telegraph.*
16. *Morning Leader.*
17. Baring, p. 137.
18. Bernhardt, *Daily Telegraph.*
19. See MacCarthy, Robins.
20. *Sunday Times.*
21. *Daily Chronicle, Birmingham Gazette.*
22. Marvin Carlson, *The German Stage in the Nineteenth Century* (Metuchen: Scarecrow Press, 1972), p. 195.
23. Mrs Blinn had played Hamlet at the Windsor Theatre, New York in December 1880.
24. At Coolgardie in the goldfields. John Golder and Richard Madelaine, *Shakespeare in Australia* webpage, http://ise.uvic./Library.Criticism/ Shakespearein/au3.html.
25. Joel Berkowitz, *Shakespeare on the American Yiddish Stage* (Iowa: University of Iowa Press, 2002), pp. 96–106. On Yiddish Shakespeare, race and Bernhardt, also see Alisa Solomon, *Re-dressing the Canon* (London and New York: Routledge, 1997).
26. William Dean Howells, 'A She Hamlet', in Howells, *Literature and Life: Short Stories and Essays* (New York: Harper, 1902).
27. *Referee.*
28. See *Era*, 21 January and 17 June 1899.
29. Laurence Hutton, *Curiosities of the American Stage* (New York: Harper, 1891), p. 322.
30. W T Price, *A Life of Charlotte Cushman* (New York: Brentano's, 1894), p. 141.
31. William Winter, *Shakespeare on the Stage* (New York: Blom, 1911–16,) pp. 427–37.
32. *New York Tribune*, 30 March 1869; *Shakespeare on the Stage*, pp. 429–30.
33. *Athenaeum*, 17.6.1899.
34. Max Beerbohm, *Around Theatres* (London: Rupert Hart-Davis, 1953), p. 37.
35. *More Theatres: 1898–1903* (London: Rupert Hart-Davis, 1969), p. 60.
36. George CD Odell, *Shakespeare from Betterton to Irving*, vol. 2 (London: Constable, 1920). p. 394, quoting *Athenaeum*, 17 June 1899.
37. Bernhardt to Maurice Baring when he took her to Craig's exhibition of *Hamlet* designs. Baring, *Sarah Bernhardt*, p. 117.

38. *The Mask*, July 1913, p. 91. See Edward Gordon Craig, *Index to the Story of My Days*, London: Hulton, 1957). pp. 91–2.

39. Quoted in Laurence Senelick, 'The Craig-Stanislavski *Hamlet* at the Moscow Art Theatre,' *Theatre Quarterly* 6, No. 22 (Summer 1976), p. 74.

40. *The Mask*, July 1913, p. 91.

41. *Daily Chronicle*, 17 June 1899.

42. Lilah McCarthy, *Myself and My Friends* (London: Butterworth, 1933), p. 295. 'Dionysiac man might be said to resemble Hamlet', Nietzsche wrote in *The Birth of Tragedy*: ' Both have looked into the true nature of things; they have *understood*, and they are now loath to act.'

43. See Speaight, *William Poel and the Elizabethan Revival* (London: Heinemann, 1954), p. 121. In 1910 Poel reprimanded the actress he cast as Valentine in *Two Gentlemen of Verona*: 'I am disappointed, very disappointed indeed. Of all Shakespeare's heroes, Valentine is one of the most romantic, one of the most virile. I have chosen you out of all London for this part, but so far you have shown me no virility whatsoever.' Margaret Halston played Calderon's Seigismundo.

44. 'Mme Suzanne Desprès has always been a magnificent actress, and it will always be one of my regrets that Paris sees comparatively so little of her,' said the *Stage Year Book* correspondent, praising her 'marvelous' Hamlet. *Stage Year Book 1914*, p. 79

45. 11 October 1913.

46. Quoted Speaight, *Shakespeare on the Stage* (London: Collins, 1973), p. 183.

47. Quoted Jean Jacquot *Shakespeare en France: mises en scène d'hier et d'aujordh'ui* (Paris: Le Temps, 1964), p. 44. The designer was Jean Variot. The translation was by Georges Duval.

48. Baring, *Sarah Bernhardt*, pp. 117, 136.

49. Sybil Thorndike, letter quoted Elizabeth Sprigge, *Sybil Thorndike Casson* (London: Gollacz, 1972), pp. 57–8.

50. Sybil and Russell Thorndike, *Lilian Baylis* (London: Chapman and Hall, 1938), p. 56.

51. *Hamlet* previously played at Reading, Cambridge, Surbiton and the Tottenham Court Road YMCA.

52. *Merchant, Merry Wives, Henry VIII, Much Ado* and *As You Like It*.

53. Quoted Grigori Kozintsev, *Shakespeare, Time and Conscience* (London: Dobson, 1967), p. 129.

54. Gaston Baty, *Rideau Baissé* (Paris: Bordas, 1949), p. 219. Baty believed *Hamlet* had two authors, the actor Shakespeare and a poet over-fond of metaphor. Baty like Gémier related Shakespeare to Greek and medieval drama (he linked *Macbeth* to the Passion). Arthur Simon described *Hamlet* as one of his most remarkable productions; see his *Gaston Baty, Theorétician du Théâtre* (Paris: Klincksieck, 1972), pp. 68–93.

55. Baty, *Rideau Baissé*, p. 145.

56. Bertolt Brecht, *The Messingkauf Dialogues*, Translated by John Willett (London: Eyre Methuen, 1965), p. 20.

57. Baty, *Rideau Baissé*, p. 140.
58. Herbert Farjeon, *The Shakespearean Scene* (London: Hutchinson, n.d.), pp. 117–18.
59. James Agate, *The Contemporary Theatre, 1944 and 1945* (London: Harrap, 1946), pp. 32–3. Kenneth Tynan, *Tynan on Theatre* (Harmondsworth: Penguin, 1964), p. 125; Tynan, *He That Plays the King* (London: Longmans, 1950), pp. 37, 112, 134. On their Hamlet/Horatio (and Queen) role-play, see Kathleen Tynan, *The Life of Kenneth Tynan* (London: Methuen, 1988), p. 46.
60. House of Commons debates cited Sheila Jeffries, *The Spinster and her Enemies: Feminism and Sexuality 1880–1930* (London: Pandora, 1985), p. 114.
61. Quoted Elizabeth Schafer, *Ms-Directing Shakespeare* (London: Women's Press, 1998). pp. 222–3.
62. Robert A Schanke, *Shattered Applause: The Lives of Eva Le Gallienne* (Carbondale: Southern Illinois University Press, 1992), p. 37. On her father and Bernhardt, see Eva Le Gallienne, '*S B Quand-Meme*', *Forum* 11 (Summer-Fall 1973), pp. 32–42.
63. Review quoted Eva Le Gallienne, *With a Quiet Heart* (New York: Viking, 1953), p. 107.
64. *Ibid.*, p. 105.
65. *Ibid.*, p. 108.
66. *Cape Cod Colonial*, 19 August 1937. See also *New York Times* and *Boston Transcript*, 24 August 1937.
67. 1928 letter from Craig to ELG's lover Mercedes de Acosta, quoted Robert A Schanke, 'Say What You Will About Mercedes de Acosta', Kim Marra and Robert A Schanke, eds., *Staging Desire: Queer Readings of American Theater History* (Ann Arbor: University of Michigan Press, 2002), p. 96.
68. Le Gallienne, *With a Quiet Heart*, p. 114. O'Neil was scandalously linked in 1905 to the 'axe-murderess' Lizzie Borden; Matthisson had a relationship with the poet Edna St Vincent Millay.
69. Unidentified clipping, Theatre Museum. For reviews see *The Times* and *Daily Telegraph*, 22 June 1938, and *Observer* 23 January. She often worked with the British Empire Shakespeare Society. During the Great War she was on the committee of the Actresses' Foil Club: members fenced at the London Salles d'Armes.
70. 23 August 1924.
71. Quoted Tumbleson, p. 97.
72. Letter in Berenger file, Theatre Museum.
73. Letter quoted in publicity. She also performed *Snapshots from Dickens*, *Important Scenes from Modern Drama*, and twenty other condensed Shakespeares. For her poetry see Theatre Museum file.
74. Schanke, *Scattered Applause*, p. 274.
75. 26 and 29 January 1957.
76. Texts printed in programme.
77. ANTA Theatre Matinee Series publicity.

78. Interviewed by Tumbleson (1976), pp. 105–7. See Tumbleson for fine accounts of the Le Gallienne, McKenna and Anderson *Hamlets*.
79. In Holly Hill, *Playing Joan* (New York, Theatre Communications Group, 1987), pp. 5–9. See also McKenna in Des Hickey, *A Paler Shade of Green* (London: Frewin, 1972).
80. *New York World-Telegraph*. Brooks Atkinson (*New York Times*) thought neither her reading nor the abstract staging adequate.
81. Whitney Bolton, *Morning Telegraph*, 29 January 1957.
82. Axel Madsen, *The Sewing Circle* (London: Robson Books, 1988), p. 175. See *Times* obituary, 6 January 1992.
83. *San Francisco Examiner*, 31 August 1970.
84. *New York Times*, 15 January 1971.
85. Quoted Carolyn Gage, 'The Real Mystery Behind the Fall River Murders', www.feminista.com/archives/v4n1/gage.html.
86. *Daily Californian*, Nance O'Neil cuttings book, New York Public Library.

Case studies: Hamlet, the actress and the political stage

CHAPTER 5

'I am whom I play': Asta Nielsen

It is pretty generally accepted that the original Hamlet (the Hamlet
of the Norse saga) was a woman.

Pantomime film magazine, 1921[1]

The female Hamlet appeared on film almost as soon as cinema itself
emerged, as if to celebrate its potential to transform the cultural economy,
redefine distinctions between high and mass art, and invade the
imagination.

I

Observed of all observers

At the Paris Exposition of 1900, spectators crowded into the new Photo-
Cinéma-Thèâtre of Mme Marguerite Chenu. They had come to see an
international bill of star performers via the latest invention – film accompanied by recorded sound. It included Bernhardt in *The Duel Scene from
'Hamlet'.* The lights dimmed in the booth. Two minutes passed . . .

The duel is over. On a small, bright shallow stage, against a faint but
elegantly painted colonnade backdrop, four soldiers with high plumed
Rembrandt helmets cluster together round a slight, dark figure. Dying,
Bernhardt throws out her left arm, reaching for support against one
guard's shoulder, and as she does so she stiffens. Her right hand still
holds a dagger. As the soldiers shuffle round her, something snaps; she
takes a short convulsive step; it is 'the final flicker of life'.[2] Her long cloak
slips to the floor, twisting beneath her like a trickle of black blood. In one
connected movement she sways, arches, her head falls back and her whole
body, frozen into a cross, sinks down, gently lowered by the officiating
soldiers to the floor. The physical images are simple, the staging and
lighting stark; but the costumes are heavily embellished with patterning

and detail – buttons, scarves, chain-mail links, rivets – so that, defying the insubstantiality of the projected image, there is a sense of the dense weight of the body. The absence of speech enhances its power, half-excluding the spectators from a ritual. At the heart of it are Bernhardt's stocky figure, her enraptured face, and the open arms embracing death.

In this brief pioneer film, Bernhardt abbreviated her *Hamlet* into what was for many its essence, a pantomimic death scene where Hamlet experiences extinction so that Bernhardt could defy it: 'I rely upon these films', she said, 'to make me immortal.' Unlike every Hamlet before her, Bernhardt's survived, if only as a fragment, adding to the legend of her 'divinity'. Though it was not the first Shakespeare film – it followed Beerbohm Tree's highlights from *King John* (1899) by a few months – Bernhardt launched Shakespearean cinema on the Continent. The single scene was less a clip than an encapsulation, for she was partly attracted to Hamlet because, like her greatest triumphs Phèdre and the Lady of the Camellias, he is possessed by death and effectively dying from the first entrance and 'O that this too, too solid flesh would melt.' The two-minute glimpse could not do justice to the energy or wit of her stage performance, and of course we have lost the '*voix d'or*', but it matched her myth exactly. Bernhardt's *Hamlet* seized the imagination and whereas Tree's film was soon lost and half-forgotten, hers never was.

The first screen Hamlet, Bernhardt, and the boldest, Asta Nielsen, outdid some of Europe's foremost leading men including Mounet-Sully, Ruggero Ruggeri and Johnston Forbes-Robertson, and produced the two most iconic images of Hamlet on silent film. For most modern film theory, cinema privileges the male gaze, but from the beginning there were women who tried to use it to shape the mass perception of Shakespeare. Mary Pickford would produce and star in the first Shakespearean sound film, reslanting *The Taming of the Shrew* to show women how to control men by flattering their vanity; and Mme Chenu, who presented Bernhardt's film, was one of the originators of screen sound.[3] (The director was Clément Maurice.) The actors could record speech and sound-effects for a wax cylinder, though *Hamlet*'s no longer exist. Mme Chenu put Bernhardt at the top of a bill including clowns, several musical numbers and arias, Little Tich's 'big shoes' routine and – in another duel – Coquelin's *Cyrano de Bergerac*. The programme was carnivalesque, intrigued by physical deviance, but Bernhardt's film was recognised as historic. While *Le Figaro* praised the 'rare perfection' of the marriage of two 'modern marvels', the phonograph and cinematograph, for another journalist the 'marvel of marvels' was that here in a little room was 'Sarah Bernhardt herself'.

On a new frontier between classicism and mass spectacle, the *Hamlet* duel displayed Bernhardt's agility, disseminated her mythology of death, and celebrated an ambiguous eroticism. Maurice Rostand said, 'There were two people in Sarah – an extremely virile one and an extremely feminine one, and she was the sum of the two joined together in a single body.'[4] The Laertes was Pierre Magnier, but there is another significant figure in this short film, who intrigues through immobility: at the rear of the set there is an observer, another cross-dressed woman – a page in a Russian-style white tunic. As Bernhardt is lowered to the floor, the page stands behind her awkwardly, not reacting to the tragedy but returning the camera's stare. This is Bernhardt's 'kind friend' Suzanne Seylor, a young actress who dedicated herself to her and became her secretary and inseparable companion. It was strange that onscreen Hamlet's corpse at the bottom of the frame becomes as uninteresting as a discarded prop and it is Seylor – the nervous onlooker reprising her real-life supporting role in fancy-dress – who is the film's last subject. This is a true naive film: there is as yet no way to control and direct attention, no close-ups or montage, yet perhaps the closing image is not quite accidental. Seylor recalls the Page in Wilde's *Salome* – written for Bernhardt – who watches from the margins in silent yearning. If *Salome* articulated the dangers of the gaze, which mesmerises and drains those who look on what they love, so Bernhardt's *Hamlet* film is a meditation on performance, gender and spectating, on *thanatos*, *eros* and the audience's desires.

Bernhardt created for a moment a transvestite Shakespearean cinema focused on her image; Chenu's invention toured that image round Europe, reaching America in 1908, and Bernhardt was invited to star in a 'full-length' silent *Hamlet* to be filmed on location at Elsinore: it would unite *travesti* with 'authenticity'. Because the French Pathé company balked at the cost, the Elsinore *Hamlet* was produced by Nordisk with the actor Alwin Neuss (1910), but in 1912 there were rumours that the first major American film *Hamlet* would star a woman, the Russian emigré Alla Nazimova, a leading figure in Hollywood's lesbian community who later bankrupted herself producing her Art Deco *Salome* (1923), a film with an entirely homosexual cast and crew. Like the Bernhardt-Elsinore *Hamlet*, Nazimova's remained unmade, though her lover Eva Le Gallienne played Hamlet onstage. What these projects pointed to, however, was women's potential strength within the new industry, and the female Hamlet's appeal – not just as a carnival attraction but as a spectacle touched with complex emotions. In 1921 the actress Julia Arthur wrote passionately in support of a new silent *Hamlet* which had just opened in New York: 'I am telling all my friends to see this truly great picture and I could never tire of seeing it. It is thrillingly intellectual and passionately human, and she is great, GREAT, GREAT.'[5] 'She' was the Danish actress Asta Nielsen.

II

The silent muse: Asta Nielsen's Hamlet

She is an artist of genius, a fascinating and remarkable personality. To my mind there were just two geniuses of the silent film era: Asta and Chaplin. It is very hard for anyone now to conceive the huge scale of Asta's personality in Germany. Wherever we went, even in the smallest towns, crowds immediately gathered round her. In every inn the guests gazed endlessly at our table. Whenever we walked to a waiting car, our path was manned by self-appointed bodyguards. *'Die Asta! Die Asta!'*, they whispered wherever we walked, wherever we stood. (Svend Gade, *The Screenplay of My Life*, 1941[6])

Asta Nielsen (1883–1972) played Hamlet in a film directed by her compatriot Svend Gade in Germany, where she had worked since before the Great War. The most extraordinary aspect of her film was her eager appropriation of Vining's theory that Hamlet is really a woman, brought up as a boy to preserve her family's hold on the Danish succession. Dismissed for decades as an oddity, the film has now come to be accepted as the most brilliant silent screen treatment of Shakespeare thanks to Nielsen's startling performance, and indeed one of the most daring Shakespeare films of any kind. It was mould-breaking even within the tradition of *travesti* Hamlets because whereas earlier actresses were expected to subsume their personality and gender in an act of male impersonation, Nielsen played a woman trapped in a life-long masquerade. This meant she could test the limits of masculinity and femininity and play unprecedented tragi-comic variations on Shakespeare, and could do so in close-up on the big screen, bringing audiences visually and emotionally closer to 'Hamlet' than any other performer in the play's history. Despite the melodramatic absurdity of its plot device, Nielsen's maverick *Hamlet* succeeded both as an historical film (it influenced Fritz Lang's epic Niebelung cycle) and an ironic essay on gender in the Twenties (see Figure 14).

Gade had made a name in Scandinavian theatre, with for example a Symbolist *Dream Play* on a black velvet stage; a young writer

Figure 14 Asta Nielsen as Hamlet, 1920. Director: Svend Gade, Art-Film, Berlin.

Edwin Gepard did the scenario; but in most respects Nielsen was the
auteur. *Hamlet* was the first production of her company Art Film (Asta
Films in America; the logo was her sphinx-like face) and was designed to
be prestigious yet subversive. Her publicity celebrated the line of female
Hamlets, including Bernhardt and Adele Sandrock, but her tactics were
more extreme because Vining let her twist the story in strange directions.
She wrote in her autobiography:

Erwin Gepard put the text together: even now I should like to record my
praise for his work. Based on exhaustive studies. . . and with the help of

a rediscovered old saga, he achieved a new version of the story, according to which Hamlet must have been a woman, and thus the tragic motif is traced back to her enforced dressing as a man. So: it was not in any way a filming of Shakespeare's play. . .[7]

'The leading motive', as *Pantomime* put it, 'is Hamlet's sex, and the lyric motive is her love for Horatio.' Though Gepard researched *Hamlet*'s sources, Nielsen's inspiration was Vining, who she pretended was an authority equal to Goethe. 'The whole film team was against it', Nielsen said, as was much of the German press. One critic pronounced it 'a film for idiots', but she knew the value of scandal: 'This guaranteed a huge reception for the film in advance.' Even Gade called the concept 'a heap of rubbish' and described a lost sequence:

God knows where the man had come upon this bizarre notion, but American professors do discover the most incredible things. For Asta Nielsen, this 'discovery' was manna on the wayside: given this, she was obviously born to play Hamlet. A tale was cooked up. . .A Prologue was written, in which famous philosophers from Voltaire to Georg Brandes made their appearance and delivered themselves on the topic of Hamlet. After them Professor Vining in horn-rimmed spectacles came and declared: 'Hamlet was a woman.' And then the film began.[8]

Nielsen's flouting of tradition was especially bold given the reverent nationalist myth that 'Hamlet is Germany'; but '*Hamlet* was a huge success', she recalled, 'and had the biggest takings of any German film that year.'

A silent Shakespeare film cannot be Shakespeare, but it can aim for 'Shakespearean' range and a mood and logic of its own. Nielsen gave *Hamlet* new social and psychological meanings. Silent Shakespeare fore-grounded narrative, tableaux, locales and stylised acting; Gade's opening sequence, set on the day of Hamlet's birth, created tension through thematic cross-cutting between two brutal medieval worlds: male (public) and female (private). He opened with location shots of warfare, anti-heroic images of massed foot-soldiers and trench-like mud-slopes evoking recent newsreels. There is no chivalry and no epic victory for Hamlet's father, who is suddenly struck down; troops hustle his body away. Meanwhile in the Queen's bedchamber Gertrude is in agony, giving birth. To her bitter disappointment a girl is born, so news of the King's death triggers a conspiracy, *Phèdre* crossed with Dumas. Gertrude's Nurse suggests they announce the baby is a boy, Prince Hamlet, so Gertrude can rule. However the King is not dead. He returns like a ghost (one of many ironic Shakespearean variations) and Gertrude (Mathilde Brandt) persuades him to support her lie. Years later, we see them teach Hamlet to preserve her secret. But Gertrude is now infatuated with Claudius (Eduard von Winterstein), a brutish satyr beside Paul Conrath's ineffectual King. In a neat palace garden – nature contained – a youthful-looking Nielsen hugs her knee pensively. Intertitle: 'Compelled to act the man, but in lonely wistful moments still a woman.' 'Asta Nielsen seems to us the greatest artist on the screen,' one reviewer wrote. 'There is a delicacy, a power, an artistry in her work which makes it a revelation of what acting for the films can be.'[9] Another said, 'You are swayed by the magic of her sad eyes, the doleful tread of her weary feet, the mournful droop of her shoulders as she weeps . . . Miss Nielsen's magnetism is something almost weird. She is frailly majestic.'[10] *Film Daily* understood the attraction of Hamlet in the age of the close-up: she 'carries you along through her many emotions. She has that remarkable gift of making you see what she thinks.' Again, 'Thought reaches straight out from the screen. Complex, distraught, conflicting thought – the thought of a morose, self-searching girl forced to play the man before a bloody background. Surely there is no greater art than that displayed by Miss Nielsen in these eight or nine thousand feet of film.'[11]

Asta Nielsen was the first international screen star and the only early film actress to be ranked with Bernhardt. She was born in Copenhagen, the daughter of a laundress and a coppersmith. Orphaned, she worked in a bakery but dated her determination to be a tragic actress from the age of eight, when she read Ibsen's *Brand*. Shoehorned into character roles and feeling that like so many physically unconventional actresses she would never be 'accepted as a leading lady', in 1910 she accepted the lead role in the novice film director Urban Gad's *The Abyss* to showcase herself to theatre managers – 'only to show that I *was* an actress'. Unpromisingly, she played a repressed schoolteacher who discovers ecstasy, dances with abandon, murders her circus cowboy lover, and in a famous image ends walking straight at the camera, traumatised. Cinema's status was so low that the theatre managers boycotted *The Abyss* yet it became an international sensation, one of several Danish films drawing on Ibsen and Strindberg's psychological intensity, and introduced Nielsen's unique style and range. Apollinaire was rhapsodic in his attempt to convey her multiformity: Nielsen was a Japanese print, she was the élan of Yvette Guilbert singing in the Montmartie night; she was a happy laughing girl, she was Faustian – 'She is everything! She is the drunkard's vision and the hermit's dream.'[12] She became 'the Duse of the Screen' and *The Abyss* gained Nielsen and Gad – now married – an invitation to work in Germany at what grew into UFA, Europe's biggest film company. She made almost thirty of her eighty films before World War I. Cinema made Nielsen the first universally visible tragic actress, an icon from San Francisco to Sidney, Paris to Saigon – all cities with 'ASTA' Cinemas – and in Germany she was exceptionally popular with young working women. Her kohled eyes and blanched face became a screen-within-the-screen onto which women and men projected fantasies.

Hans Richter said she revolutionised acting because she 'could dictate passions from the screen with the precision and economy of a machine'; her smallest movements – even 'one corner of her mouth' – were 'precisely calculated and the audience felt the psychological event'. Nielsen's *Hamlet* is crucial to any study of early cinema and the psychology of the gendered gaze.[13] Blending techniques from melodrama, naturalism and mime, she seemed able to inhabit feelings while commenting on them ironically, nowhere more so than as Hamlet where the challenge was to find physical correlatives to the absent protean text. Nielsen consciously developed what she called 'a silent language' to 'make the spirit visible'. The Hungarian screenwriter and theorist Bela Balasz praised her 'polyphony': 'A rich vocabulary is a mark of poetic greatness. Shakespeare is given credit for having used 15,000 words. It will only be possible to appraise the extent of the "vocabulary" of Asta Nielsen's gestures once the first encyclopaedia of gestures has been compiled with the aid of cinematography.'[14] Her 'silent language' was political in that she systematically exposed the interior life of women robbed of a voice by their world. She showed how actresses could *exploit* silence and called her autobiography *The Silent Muse*. Like her theatre-based predecessors – but for a vast audience – she managed her own career, provoked scandals (as an unmarried mother), ran a production company and created fashions (her androgynous clothes, her dark fringe). Lotte Eisner wrote in 1953, 'People nowadays cannot understand what that pale mask, with its immense blazing eyes, meant for the nineteen-tens and twenties. . . A hypercultivated, unstable, sophisticated period had found its ideal, an intellectual of great refinement.'[15] Asta was the prototype who marked out options for the modern actress. Deconstructing gender, she made *Hamlet* a Weimar fantasia on the nature of sexual identity.

III

Nielsen in Wittenberg

During World War I soldiers on both sides pinned up Nielsen's photos in the trenches; she worked for a company called Neutral Films. Hers is a postwar *Hamlet*. The German Right was obsessed with revenging Versailles; war reparations were taking place round *Hamlet* as they filmed the interiors at a Berlin aerodrome, in a hangar built from iron and glass Germany had seized in Belgium: 'Hundreds of military aeroplanes lay on the fields around us. Several times a week, a French military commission arrived and destroyed as many planes as they could manage to blow up: even the engines were totally demolished. The fields of destroyed aircraft came to look more and more grim.'[16] Nielsen's *Hamlet* was literally built from military destruction, recycling fuselage fabric for the decor and turning drainage pipes from the wrecked airfield into palace pillars. Nielsen made *Hamlet* comment on the German social and psychological upheavals caused by war and defeat – and by women's transformed economic roles, typified by her own power as producer: 'Now', she wrote, 'I felt richly rewarded for all the effort and patience.'[17]

Weimar's imagination was fascinated by the 'modern woman' crossing gender lines and Nielsen avidly showed what George Eliot had found difficult, a female Hamlet at university. This Wittenberg is a finishing school for 'noble youths', with learning and swordplay on the curriculum: she excels the men at both. Nielsen established books and weapons – mind and body – as her signifying props. The self-consciousness of her/his gestures indicates precision, intelligence and *pleasure*. She balances a book on slender spread fingers, relishing its weight; fencing, she flexes like a ballerina in response to every feint. Later she will study piles of books for the answers to her dilemma, or leaf goofily through them at top speed ('Words, words, words'), but whatever she does, her fingers creep to the dagger at her side as if independently alive. Nielsen was already famous for *travesti*. As early as 1912 she kissed girls and shaved in *Youth and Madness*. In *The ABC of Love* (1916) she cross-dressed to show her naive beaux the nightspots, because as in *As You Like It* the woman understands masculinity best. As Patrice Petro writes, Nielsen's 'appropriation of masculine styles' made her 'a figure of sexual mobility – a figure who destabilizes the polarized opposition between masculine and feminine identities . . . It was Nielsen who paved the way for the popular acceptance of female androgyny in the cinema.'[18] Garbo and Dietrich were inspired by her.

Her film tied Hamlet closer to Horatio, Laertes and Fortinbras by making them all fellow-students. Laertes is a man's man who beats his servant and revels with bare-shouldered girls; from a window, excluded but observing, Nielsen studies him carefully. In postwar Germany the empowerment of women went with the perceived feminisation of men. As Petro has shown, popular magazines like *Die Dame* argued that 'the man has lapsed into femininity and nervous exhaustion . . . reflected in fashion with sentimental curls and romantic high collars'.[19] In Nielsen's film the feminised man is almost as important as the androgyny of Hamlet, with three very different examples. First King Hamlet returns from war emasculated. Dominated by Gertrude and blind to the threat of his 'virile' brother (the war profiteer safe behind the lines), he is a benign but catastrophic father. The second such figure is Fortinbras who, humiliated by his father's defeat, spurns Hamlet's friendship (he stares away from her; the dynamics of the gaze are fundamental to the film) but her open-heartedness moves him and ends *'our fathers' strife'*. There is a spontaneous intimacy between them – which would be impossible if Hamlet's gender were known – and Fortinbras discovers a sensitivity which militarism and patriarchy have stifled. The third figure is Horatio (Heinz Stieda), passive, supportive – and Princess Hamlet's object of desire. Horatio's full lips, flowing locks and fey costumes (including a white skirt and large bonnet) plus lingering camerawork make him the film's erotic interest. When they meet accidentally by bumping heads (*'This head will wear Denmark's crown'*), Nielsen eyes him with a knowing appreciation that makes the audience complicit. Her *Hamlet* was a study of young people reinventing gender roles in the aftermath of war and its explosion of patriarchal tradition. Women are the motors of change in her film; but only men will survive.

Hamlet's adolescent idyll is about to end. Gade opposes her easy penetration of Wittenberg's male milieu with a series of archetypal images charting Elsinore's Fall and regression. Gertrude and Claudius embrace passionately, she guides him down steep stairs, and he descends deep beneath the castle, holding a phosphorescent torch. In its lurid glare he heaves open a trapdoor whose Sisyphian weight bends him double. From Claudius' viewpoint we see a pitful of snakes twisting in dark scum: *'A serpent shall crown me king.'* He thrusts his hand into the pit to catch one, protecting himself with his dagger. Winterstein plays Claudius on one note of lowering brutality but his gorilla-like performance, dragging melodrama into Expressionism, balances Nielsen's electricity.

The king is killed, and in a Wittenberg lecture hall Hamlet grows up in a single scene. She starts as a scamp, parodying her professor while the 'noble youths' run riot. Because they are actually heavy middle-aged actors prancing like infants, only Nielsen is physically convincing; she dominates through concentration. But a messenger of death punctures the comedy (cf. *Love's Labour's Lost*) and from this moment the film focuses on Hamlet's anguish. In the first of several close-up sequences – mime soliloquies – which punctuate the film Nielsen employs a limited but expressive vocabulary of tragic gesture, repeating a very few moves with sharpening intensity to create a poetry of the body, slowing and stretching the moment of loss. Hand to head, she sinks back, reaches out to Horatio, gives him the letter, grips his hand. Hand to head, then hand to heart, she half faints. Hand to head (the back of her hand to the top of her head), she reaches out to the Messenger for information, grips his hand. Her eyes open wide then close, on the edge of tears. Her hand goes to her heart (she falls against Horatio's shoulder), then to her head, her fingers splaying wide. She strains against the sympathetic crowd surrounding her. Hamlet runs out.

This is an unusually operatic moment. Normally 'a single tear from Nielsen, a single flicker of her mouth, says more than any superimposed effects of suffering. She was and is the great actress, the canvas that makes dignity visible.' (Leopold Jessner)[20] Her Hamlet is balletic, the slim body looks breakable. She moves with gymnastic energy yet her gestures are minimal, the long hands move like a conjuror's. She acts a great deal with the twist of her neck, which is elongated by a tight high collar; the white face seems suspended in space. Each shift of her eyes and quizzical mouth is premeditated, she can switch instantly from tragedy to farce. Hamlet is Balazs's 'polyphony' in action. 'The externals', Nielsen argued, signified everything 'in an art where the word is silent.' She lived herself into her roles months in advance and filled her home with the props and costumes: 'I am what I play, throughout. I like to build such a detailed notion of my characters that I know them down to the last externals, which precisely consists of little bagatelles like these. They are more revealing than any blatant exaggerations can be.'[21] Critics competed to describe her distinctive visual *signs* – the dark eyes and the slender hands whose 'strange and beautiful gesturing' was 'as delicate and refined as the description of a sundown by a Chinese painter'.[22]

In liberal Wittenberg Hamlet and Fortinbras reject the legacy of violence, but Elsinore, the old world, is built on a pit of serpents. At the wedding revels, Gertrude stares rapt at Claudius as he crowns himself in belligerent ecstasy. In an immensely high hall, for the first time the camera clearly shows Claudius' mindless face as he chews meat and tosses bones to the dogs, and in scenes of cartoon debauchery ('They clepe us drunkards') a drunk swims in beer. Outside, a huddle of poor people greet Hamlet with a warning. They evoke forgotten values of family and labour. In a stunning long-shot Hamlet strides down a broad staircase between torch-bearing guards, 'voluminous black cloak billowing from her shoulders'; years later Oswald Blakeston remembered 'Asta Nielsen's face and the black costume, a white passion flower on a black stalk'.[23] Hamlet finds Gertrude and Claudius wild in each others' arms and condemns them with a taut and horrified gesture. Nielsen reverses Shakespeare's I. ii by making the guilty couple sullen while Hamlet is dynamic, with right publicly on her side. While all the men have shaggy Dark Age locks and the women are buried under wedding-cake head-dresses, Nielsen's short hair makes her a woman of the 1920s, and like Bernhardt's Hamlet she is a modern rationalist, a detective. There is no Ghost. Hamlet dreams of her father and stumbles on the murder herself. An old gardener confides that the King was killed by a snake like those in the castle dungeons, so she investigates. These subterranean descents become ritualistic: Claudius was brute strength; Hamlet is androgynous intelligence and clear sight. Too slight to lift the last trapdoor, she finds his incriminating dagger dropped in the dirt.

IV

Elsinore, sanity and gender

Vining's *Mystery of Hamlet* was based on the assumption that Hamlet's behaviour is 'weak', 'feminine' and 'hysterical' yet must be rationalised as *ideal*. The idea that Hamlet is pathologically feminine was intensified by the War; in 1917, as cases of shell-shock filled the sanatoria, the psychologist Edward Somers diagnosed 'the strange malady of Hamlet' as the 'comparatively rare disease known as Male Hysteria'. Somers described hysteria as a 'complex nervous disease consisting of physical, mental and moral disturbances, and revealing itself by sudden and fierce paroxysms... the will power lacks exercise and the emotions lack discipline... It is primarily a disease of adolescence contemporary with the first stirrings of love, and the beginnings of life's disillusions, *and thus infinitely common in young women, and comparatively rare in young men.*'[24] Somers believed hysteria stemmed from shock, here 'the infidelity of the

Queen Mother'. (Ophelia, he said, suffered from nymphomania.) The film was not inconsistent with such thinking – the war-wounded King's submissiveness is strange – but Asta Nielsen's androgynous Hamlet is the sanest person on view. Her acting style incorporated the sudden 'parox-ysms' that fascinated psychologists, but she made the fraught overlap of male and female selves the source of Hamlet's *strength* because it equips her to reject conventions and live authentically. It trains her to survive by improvising new selves for every situation. In her much-expanded antic disposition scenes Nielsen stressed sly cunning and a fired imagination, and made Hamlet a great comic actress.

Playing the Man: Nielsen had fun demonstrating the gestures of masculinity – she leans on one elbow, folds her arms, waves dismissively, fixes people with a frank 'manly' stare. *Playing the Fool*: she squats, obses-sively sorting through a bag of mushrooms, then sprawls and chops one into a tiny crown. Passers-by laugh, but not Claudius – she shows him the crown and waits for his reaction with pursed, ironic lips. *The Mime*: Claudius crushes the crown, then cowers when he sees she has his dagger; she slithers snakelike towards him on her stomach, turning herself into a writhing black line. *The Innocent*: Polonius, a senile clown, brings Hamlet toys. Charmingly, she demonstrates their proper use: she sticks a peg on his nose and a mouse on his head, and invites him to sit on a skewer (he does). Here Hamlet is a choirboy Mephisto, improvising anarchy. *The Satirist*: Advising the Players, Nielsen whirls her arms and pulls baboon faces to burlesque ham actors. The joke is that the Players are acting in the same melodramatic style as everyone in the film except Nielsen. But she parodied herself too. *Moving Picture World* – already exasperated 'to see a human being whose sex is proclaimed in every line of her figure, go through life without her nearest friends suspecting' – was outraged by a new scene where the truth would not 'penetrate the skull of the court physician even when he puts his ear to her chest'.[25] But her point was to push the gender game to absurdity; when the idiot-phrenologist examines Hamlet's skull, she indicates her problem's lower down. Then Nielsen hunches her shoulders and slow-marches 'insanely' past them, burlesquing the Somnambulist in *Caligari* (1919) and herself in *The Abyss*. Hamlet becomes an acting master-class. Fascinatingly – and in contrast to the reverential performances by Olivier and Branagh decades later – the actress's versatility translates as proof of Hamlet's genius. She conveys mental processes through tableaux (Hamlet fixedly reading), recurring images (a suicide's dagger), or by miming inner conflict: *She'll feign madness. . . shall she tell Horatio?. . . no. . . perhaps. . .* She makes

Figure 15   Asta Nielsen as Hamlet. The father's tomb.

inter-titles redundant. And yet without recourse to Shakespeare's soliloquies, her Hamlet seems more bereft.

Hans Richter stressed that Nielsen always acted in collaboration with her surroundings.[26] She and Gade used the *mise en scène* to make Elsinore her prison. Hamlet looks down from a balcony at the wedding feast, with a dagger at her breast. She alternates between scenes of Hamlet *performing*, where she is all-powerful, and sequences where she is trapped alone by shadows and stone. As Monika Seidel points out, she haunts intermediate spaces – corridors, doorways, stairs and alcoves framed by layers of light and darkness.[27] When soldiers see her here they mock her. Gade isolates Hamlet in intimate locales that bind her to Denmark's heritage but denote oppression; she mourns by a window, caught between worlds, and lies across her father's vast catafalque; pinned beneath a lowering curved ceiling, penned by a swirl of Secessionist wrought iron (see Figure 15). Her body twists. Horatio occasionally finds her but in her version male support sharpens the pain. An intimacy grows between them (cf. *Twelfth Night*) that neither dares confess.

Nielsen's *Hamlet* was in the psychological vanguard. Otto Weiniger had argued early in the century that each human being is both male and female, but women who developed the masculine side were still classed as aberrant. Joan Rivière's 1929 essay 'Womanliness as Masquerade' discussed the anxieties of women unable to resolve 'the bisexuality inherent in us all'. She would argue that masculinity is a strong unconscious presence, often hidden – especially by 'intellectual' women – with a 'womanly masquerade'.[28] Nielsen anticipated Rivière because many of her films probed the Masquerade in this sense – the tragedy of complex women forced to wear masks. Nielsen deliberately presented as vast a film gallery of female types as possible, using her versatility to demonstrate the possibilities offscreen. In *The Suffragette* she was the New Woman; she was often the disruptive Wild Girl (gypsy, bandit, even eskimo); and by playing many artists (a writer, a blind sculptor) and especially performers (ballerina, nightclub diva, drug-addicted opera star, *The First Lady of the Screen*) she placed role-play at the centre of the modern woman's life. The mask became a key image. In *Tragedy of the Street* (1927), she played a prostitute seen blacking her grey hair with boot polish; she examines herself in a cracked mirror that splits her face in two and duplicates it like badly-spliced film. Nielsen's women fought to shape their own identities but many were trapped or torn; her *Hamlet* showed Family and Society affixing an iron mask. Given this interest, it is at first sight surprising that whereas Charlotte Cushman had championed the women in *Hamlet*, Asta Nielsen turned Ophelia and Gertrude into grotesques.

The women
Ophelia becomes a caricature of naivety, and Gertrude a darkening image of voracious desire. Hamlet only meets the girl when Polonius introduces her as a quack cure for lunacy ('*Ah! I have a daughter!*') posed in lumpish embarrassment. Lily Jacobsson had featured billing but the film trivialises her, as critics said, into a silly, flattered, 'ogling' and 'coquetting' blonde. Her identity is so undeveloped that she has no mad-scene, simply wanders into a river when her clown-father dies. Hamlet dismisses her with theatrical yawns, but the twist is that Horatio is attracted. He confesses it as he and Hamlet lie on a sunny bank with her head in his lap like Ganymede and Orlando, and this last shock destroys Hamlet's impossible pastoral/platonic hopes, the attempt to keep wit, tragedy and romance in equilibrium. From now on the film's pretty landscape is poisoned (Hamlet attempts suicide in a black field) and Nielsen holds her head in her hand, 'The Thinker'. At that moment Claudius comes to invade her space, but this Hamlet is always energised by conflict; switching back to the subversive freedom of madness, she *climbs up* Claudius like an ape, then decides to mask her distress by pretending to woo Ophelia. And so Nielsen deconstructs and parodies 'conventional' love: she paws raffishly

at Ophelia's sleeve, mumbles sweet nothings, kisses the girl's fingers (literally tongue-in-cheek), and scrawls love-letters (barking at Polonius, the postman).

Nielsen's variations on desire create dazzling guilty pleasures – at once heterosexual (the heroine loves Horatio), homosexual (Hamlet loves Horatio), heterosexual again (Hamlet woos Ophelia) and lesbian (Asta Nielsen woos Ophelia). The responses – Horatio's unease, Ophelia's infatuation, Polonius's glee and the Queen's rage – increase the instability, but unlike a Shakespearean comedy, here erotic games bring no release. Tragedy returns in accelerating vignettes: Hamlet dreams of her father and wakes clutching at air; she clings to his catafalque, arms spread in martyred despair; and in Nielsen's silent précis of 'To be or not to be', she makes for the dark field and tries to slash her wrist. Stumbling into Ophelia, she damns all women, including herself, and unexpectedly the Ophelia sub-plot leads Hamlet towards the tragic/melodramatic heart of the gender maze.

When Gertrude reads Hamlet's love-letters she summons her to account for herself in what becomes a kind of coming-out scene. Losing control, Nielsen clasps her breasts and collapses: *'I am not a man! And must not be a woman!'* She sees through her mother's frantic lies: *'I wanted to save your father's crown for you.'* Mathilde Brandt's Queen is outrageous. The film is ultimately about a dark mother-daughter relationship where a passionate woman arbitrarily reconstructs her child out of self-interest. Gertrude begins sympathetically as a totally powerless figure, a woman in childbirth, then systematically discards her roles as wife, mother and consort, replacing them with other stock identities – adulteress, abuser, murderess – until she blossoms perversely into a Medea, a child-killer/witch. (Joan Rivière: 'Always with girls, the mother is the more hated, and consequently the more feared.') Gertrude and Ophelia's common factor is that they giddily embrace erotic domination by male power-figures, however ludicrous (Polonius) or primeval (Claudius) these are. Nielsen made Hamlet a poly-morphic woman in a stereotyped world; her film condemns everyone, female or male, who collaborates with reactionary structures of gender and power. Two Hamlet-Gertrude scenes frame and diminish The Mouse-trap (played outdoors in daylight, it's just a tableau of a murderer dangling a snake in his victim's ear). Nielsen gives the traditional images some moral complexity, however, by her demonic grin as she crawls towards her mother and uncle; they huddle in terrified guilt, which suggests a pitiful side to Gertrude's monstrosity. When the King drags himself to the altar Hamlet wields a huge executioner's sword behind him, poised to cleave him in two, but reels back ('*No! I will strike deeper!*'), dismisses him with gloating contempt, and moves on to the real climax, her confrontation with her mother. But they already know all each other's secrets. They have nothing to say. Scarcely able to meet each other's eyes or move their lips, Gertrude sits and Hamlet, bolt upright, wearily lifts, then drops, her mother's hand. When she kills Polonius, Hamlet shrugs and sadly wanders out, trailing the sword, the maternal bond severed. In this poignant but pivotal moment, Hamlet discards the residues of childhood. She must choose her final roles for herself.

In Hamlet's bedroom, she and Horatio slump on either side of the screen, she in black, he in white; but when Claudius sends Hamlet on a fatal mission (to Norway) he dooms himself. Followed by the King's cronies, Hamlet rides a white horse across a new panoramic landscape of lakes and hills. Fences block the view, suggesting Elsinore's influence, but action comes naturally here and at last her intelligence is not frustrated. In a rude border inn – bars and shadows – Hamlet finds the death-warrant and at last mind and action achieve symbolic balance as she writes new letters, then seals them with a royal seal in the hilt of her sword. When at Fortinbras's palace the letters order him to kill the messengers, Nielsen affects ignorance with a hilariously black-comic 'beats me' shrug. A liberating army assembles ('*To Denmark!*') and Hamlet rides ahead. 'She is as vibrant as a Damascus sabre, the Danish Saint Joan' (Lotte Eisner[29]), as Gade cross-cuts between the troops, Ophelia's death, and '*AN ORGY OF THE KING*'. In a hut, Claudius carouses with his gang and mockingly wears black: '*A toast to Hamlet's health!*' He is appalled when she walks jauntily in on the revels with her helmet (not her head – more games with the supernatural) under her arm: '*Is it Hamlet or his ghost?*' She bewilders him by playing the back-slapping nephew, unwinding after a diplomatic trip, and he is soon too drunk to notice when she pours her wine down his throat: '*It is not every King who can drink his own funeral wine.*' Two years after the 'war to end wars' Nielsen showed her audience Saxo-Grammaticus' stark world: Hamlet takes a torch and burns her sleeping enemies to death. Asta Nielsen's Hamlet was more remorseless than any man's. She easily repels Claudius when he staggers awake and seizes her throat; she seals the door, leaving him to choke in the smoke of a personal hell with Expressionist zig-zag lightning on the walls. Thus Nielsen dismantles Shakespeare's ending: Hamlet has revenged her father's death on Claudius easily; now she must face her mother and take revenge for her own life.

But Hamlet's identity is in crisis. In early morning mist she finds Horatio awaiting Ophelia's funeral, but Nielsen is transformed, exhausted, like a victim of an unseen assault. Hamlet's hair is wild, her legs show through ripped tights and her half-undone tunic reveals her breasts. Yet despite the exposure of her body, Horatio sees the male Hamlet he is conditioned to see. Nielsen stretches sexual schizophrenia to breaking point: after killing with 'manly' savagery, her 'femininity' becomes stereotypical and out of control; she snatches Ophelia's veil from Horatio in a jealous fit, and as they fight for it the front of her tunic tears open; she recovers herself in panic, grasping at black shreds. Nielsen's climactic centre-staging of her own body for the first time draws the spectator's gaze into the film problematically. Till this point it is as visually chaste as a fairy tale; male and female spectators are united in complicity with Hamlet's dilemmas and charades. But in the last minutes Nielsen/ Hamlet's actions and the camera's observation of her become 'adult' and unpredictable, we cannot tell what to make of Hamlet or be sure what kind of film experience this is. Meanwhile her gender turmoil is framed by two extreme stock images of the Female – a drowned virgin and a witch-queen. Gertrude now wears a high black wimple and controls the plot's last twists like a Borgia; she watches Claudius' charred corpse dragged from the ashes and incites Laertes: '*Take double vengeance for thy wrongs and mine!*' In the Chapel – stronger than Claudius, more determined than Hamlet – Gertrude turns her back on the Cross and anoints Laertes' sword. She pours liquid in a cup like poisonous milk.

Nielsen's mercurial shifts and 'paroxysms' accelerate. She tests the weapons but picks one wearily, without trying it. She gestures – there's some foreboding, about her heart – then laughs and waves it away. The film's opening 'male'/'female' dialectic returns as formal fencing is inter-cut with Gertrude's darting movements. A servant moves two cups and the Queen drinks the poison: poetic justice kills her, and the last in a tale of substitutions. A scream distracts Hamlet and Laertes' rapier pierces her tunic at the breast. Hamlet dies almost at once in Horatio's arms, fighting to keep her secret, forcing his hand away. Her mouth is half-open, the intimacy creates a flood of almost grotesque sexual images. Horatio embraces her. . . '*Hamlet, my beloved Hamlet*'. . . his hand slides from her face to her breast and at last he discovers. . . '*Death reveals thy tragic secret. Now I understand what bound me to that matchless form and feature – Your true heart was a woman's. Too late – beloved – 'tis too late.*' He kisses her. Frozen in her last pose, Nielsen lies rigid on the stairs, half-way between throne and earth, her back arched, her hands half-open at her side. This sequence turns them into lovers and reinstates the conventional relationship of grieving hero and sacrificial heroine. When screened in modern cinemas Horatio's manual discovery of the secret usually triggers astonished laughter. There is no evidence that audiences found it funny in the 1920s ('powerful and touching' was one US verdict), but in the very banality of the moment Nielsen and Gade, like conjurers exposing an illusion, confront us with the bizarre nature of the fantasy we have participated in and ask: Is that all? Are the sexual organs all a person is? Immediately, Horatio reimposes the military funeral imagery that ends all conventional *Hamlets*. He covers the body with a black cloak with the sword beside it. Shakespeare's male myth will survive. Fortinbras reaches the throne: '*On its steps your wings did break.*' A caption card shows a swallow, yet it is not the story of a swallow's fall, but of one person's struggle to be free. Machine-like soldiers carry her through an arch of spears. The camera looks down as they cross Elsinore's chequerboard stone floor, black and white segregated geometrically. There is a last long close-up of Asta Nielsen, the ironic eyes finally closed, and an iris in on her stilled lips.

After-image

In Nielsen's film gross gender stereotypes represent the conservative rearground against which Hamlet stands out as modern and complex, mapping debates film theorists would explore half a century later. For Andrew Britton, crossdressing in film 'testifies to our anxious fascination – half fear and half longing – with the idea of a world in which the iron laws of gender have been relaxed or even abolished'.[30] Anette Kuhn argued that it 'denaturalises' gender roles and offers 'a utopian prospect of release from the ties of sexual difference that bind us into meaning, discourse, culture' – a 'visionary multiplicity'.[31] Shakespearean *travesti* is less clear-cut, however, and Nielsen respects this. Although Rosalind and Portia are empowered when they don men's clothes and hold 'a gallant curtle-axe' or book, for three other heroines – Viola, Julia and Imogen – cross-dressing entails misunderstanding, *painful* knowledge, sad isolation, and metaphorical death. Like Hamlet, each loses a male who gave her old life meaning – brother, lover or husband – and while a boy's identity brings new relationships, they are uneasy and incomplete. *Travesti* frees Rosalind and Portia to speak and manipulate; the others become trapped spectators. Nielsen's Hamlet borrows and pinpoints these contradictions; she is both the androgyne as complete hero/ine and a victim locked in pretence. Cross-dressing in Shakespeare can be comic because the revels are merely transitional, a preparation for the married world and socially-limited power. After Hamlet's adolescence – and despite many interludes of satire and farce – Nielsen makes *travesti* tragic. All the Shakespearean heroines choose their sexual charade; she cannot. Nielsen shows first the arbitrary construction of gender – Hamlet is 'male' because she is trained to be – and then its instability. Princess Hamlet masters 'male' disciplines perfectly (the book, the sword) but 'femininity' intrudes in the disruptive form of mute desire. Yet if Hamlet's masquerade both liberates and destroys her, the film is framed by our knowledge that what we are watching is Asta Nielsen rewriting the canon to break 'the iron laws of gender'. She disrupts genres too, switching constantly between statuesque tragedy and farce, expressionism and melodrama, realism and mime. She is more 'Shakespearean' in her range than any other film Hamlet but unifies her effects through dance-like discipline and burning watchfulness, the power of the critical gaze.

Joan Rivière offered a psychological reading of the 'sacred' medieval building as a metaphor for the mind ('the thinker' and his/her 'highest aspirations and capacities – love, truth, nobility') and for an inescapable preoccupation with 'the inside of the idealised mother's body'. A 'bloody outrage' takes place – 'desecration, ruin and corruption . . . the murder of the father' – and it's accomplished below, in the depths of the building.[32] After Claudius' descent into Elsinore, death becomes archetypal – by fire and water – or sexual: murder by serpent, mother's 'milk', and a sword-point in the breast. In the last scenes the camera draws our gaze to Hamlet's body, and *seems* to say that underneath the disguises lies an 'essential', objectified and suffering female self. Certainly Hamlet is not acting when she jealously snatches Ophelia's veil; but nor is she acting when she becomes Saxo-Grammaticus' stark avenger. Horatio cannot read her body correctly, even though the black costume literally dissolves, until she dies because Asta Nielsen's Hamlet is polymorphous, beyond definition. So she earns contradictory epitaphs: loved by Horatio, honoured by Fortinbras as a king. That last close-up of her lips is the necessary coda for a great life lived without intimacy, beyond speech.

As cinema's foremost 'intellectual' actress, Nielsen went on to film three of the great modern female roles: Miss Julie (1921), Lulu (1923) and Hedda (1925). She made Hedda a repressed Dresden figurine; her Lulu, in geometrical jazz-age costumes, was Expressionist and angular, snapping between arch seduction and *ennui*. In many of her later films she showed Weimar women struggling with poverty and prostitution, and their destruction by patriarchy; even the predator-victims Hedda, Julie and Lulu can only forge an identity in death. Hamlet had freed her to explore gender and entrapment from unprecedented angles. Art Film announced a second Shakespeare for 1922–3 which might have been equally provocative, Nielsen's *Taming of the Shrew*, but it was never made. She gradually lost artistic control of her output and after one sound film (1932), she stopped. In 1928 she co-founded (with Käthe Kollwitz, Piscator, Pabst and Heinrich Mann) the People's Association for Film Art, a leftist group promoting progressive cinema, but when Hitler came to power he and Goebbels personally tried to woo her by offering Nielsen her own studio. In her account, Hitler said he needed a thousand words to say what she could express in one gesture. She replied, 'You mean this one?', made a Nazi salute, and left Germany forever. In Denmark she returned to the stage occasionally and painfully reinvented herself again, as a writer on film and as a painter and sculptor, one of her most striking canvases being a jagged self-portrait as Hamlet. Meanwhile in Germany, *Hamlet* became one of the most performed plays of the Third Reich, the glorification of Aryan Man.

Nielsen's deconstructions and analyses of identity, her kaleidoscopic exploration of the relationship between for example tragedy and irony, formalism and social reportage, so matched *Hamlet* that while her film could be said to bear very little resemblance to Shakespeare's text, she registered its multiplicities exactly. Moreover Nielsen demonstrated the inseparability of gender politics from the political upheavals of her time. She offered images of human diversity that could not coexist with the rigidities of totalitarian ideology that now began to dominate European life, and that in Germany allocated women their place defined by *kirche, küche* and *kinder* while giving sexual 'deviants' a pink star. The following chapters will examine the work of a number of other twentieth-century activist actresses in close-up, locating them in their - sometimes extreme - historical situations in order to see how their own explorations of Hamlet, imagined as the embodiment of active consciousness and conscience, led them to step outside social stereotypes and onto the political stage. From the early 1930s onward the phrase 'Denmark's a prison' resonated as never before. The female Hamlet, the embodiment of questioning and self-redefinition, took on extraordinary symbolic meanings in an age of repression and of warring, incompatible 'truths'.

Notes

1. Unless stated, reviews of Asta Nielsen and Sven Gade's *Hamlet* are quoted from Asta Film's American pressbook (1921). An early version of this chapter was published as 'The Rest is Silence: Asta Nielsen as Hamlet', *Women and Theatre: Occasional Papers* 2 (1994), pp. 28–72. The reputation of Nielsen's *Hamlet* has been transformed since then; the many excellent studies include Lawrence Danson, 'Gazing at Hamlet, or the Danish Cabaret,' *Shakespeare Survey* 45 (1993), pp. 37–51; Ann Thompson, 'Asta Nielsen and the Mystery of Hamlet.' *Shakespeare the Movie: Popularizing the Plays on Film, TV, and Video*, eds. Lynda E Boose and Richard Burt (New York: Routledge, 1997), pp. 215–24; Monika Seidel, 'Room for Asta: Gender Roles and Melodrama in Asta Nielsen's Filmic Version of *Hamlet* (1920)', *Film / Literature Quarterly* (2002); Lisa S Starkes, ' "Remember Me": Psychoanalysis, Cinema and the Crisis of Modernity', *Shakespeare Quarterly* vol.53, no. 2 (Summer 2002). Film credits: *Hamlet* (Germany 1920). Art-Film GmbH. Writer: Erwin Gepard. Directors: Svend Gade, Heinz Schall. Producer: Asta Nielsen.

2. William Archer on Bernhardt's *Lady of the Camellias* death scene, *The Theatrical 'World' of 1894* (London: Walter Scott, 1895), p. 194. There were resemblances; as Marguerite she fell back, embraced by Armand, who lowered her onto the bed.

3. See Robert Hamilton Ball, *Shakespeare on Silent Film: A Strange Eventful History* (London: Allen and Unwin, 1968), pp. 23–8; 304–5. The Paris Exposition ran from April to October 1900. For more information on Bernhadt's film see Gerda Taranow, *The Bernhardt Hamlet: Culture and Context* (New York 1996). See also *Le Figaro*, 8 June and 8 September 1900. According to some accounts the noise of the foils was provided live.

4. Rostand, quoted Ruth Brandon, *Being Divine* (London: Secker and Warburg, 1991), p. 347.

5. In a letter to Asta Films, used in publicity. Julia Arthur had been an eminent Imogen and Rosalind. A year before she retired, she played Hamlet in the Closet scene with Mona Morgan as the Queen (week of 2 April, 1923 at Keith's Theatre, New York).

6. Gade, *The Screenplay of My Life*, quoted in Renate Seydel and Allan Hagedorff, *Asta Nielsen: Ihr Leben in Fotodokumenten, Selbstzeugnissen und Zeitgenossischen Betrachtungen* (Berlin: Henschelverlag, 1981), p. 158.

7. Asta Nielsen, *Den Tiende Muse* (Copenhagen: Gyldendal, 1966). Translation supplemented from Robert C Allen, 'The Silent Muse', *Sight and Sound* (Autumn 1973), pp. 205–9.

8. Gade quoted in Seydel and Hagedorff, *Asta Nielsen*, p. 158.

9. *New York Commercial* 12 November 1921.

10. *New York World* 13 November 1921.

11. *Film Daily* 13 November 1921.

12. Apollinaire quoted in Pablo Diaz, *Asta Nielsen* (Berlin: n.p., 1920), p. 69. This was not the first book about her; see Adolf Langsted, *Asta Nielsen* (Copenhagen 1917).

13. Nielsen was the first actress to achieve such *visibility*; 'Nielsen frenzy' often drove male critics to ramble about the nature of attraction: 'There will be discussion as to her physical charms. Some undoubtedly will call her beautiful, while others, preferring a different type of wife or sweetheart or sister, will say she is merely striking. . . Her mouth is not simply something to paint a cupid's bow on, (*New York Times* 9 November 1921). Some admirers of her 'mature art' used her to attack less androgynous screen women: 'She does not show off her things, unlike Anita Berber', that 'dancing harlot' (Bela Balazs, see note 18 below) or Hollywood's 'curly-headed girls and painted hussies' (*US National Board of Review*).

14. Bela Balazs, 'Asta Nielsen's Eroticism', *Hungarofilm Bulletin*, no.3 (1984), pp. 14–16.

15. Lotte H Eisner, *The Haunted Screen* (London: Thames and Hudson, 1973), p. 261.

16. Gade, quoted Seydell and Hagerdorff, *Asta Nielsen*, p. 160. The Hamlet-like slogan of the Weimar Chancellor Joseph Wirth was 'patience, more patience, and still more patience'.

17. Nielsen, quoted Seydell and Hagerdorff, *Asta Nielsen*, p. 158.

18. Patrice Petro, *Joyless Streets: Women and Melodramatic Representation in Weimar Germany* (Princeton: Princeton University Press, 1989), p. 153.

19. *Ibid.*, p. 111.

20. Jessner, quoted Seydal and Hagedorff, p. 221.

21. Nielsen, quoted Diaz, *Asta Nielsen*, p. 6.

22. John W Winge, 'Asta Nielsen', *Sight and Sound* (Winter 1960–1961), pp. 58–9.

23. Oswald Blakeston, 'Asta Nielsen in *Hamlet*', *Close-up* (March 1929), pp. 91–2.

24. Edward Somers, *An Address on Hamlet's Ecstasy: Hysteria the True Cause*, (Manchester 1917), p. 2. [Italics mine].

25. *Moving Picture World* 19 November 1921.

26. See Hans Richter, *The Struggle for Film* (Aldershot: Scolar, 1986), pp. 70–2.

27. Monika Seidel, 'Room for Asta', *passim*.

28. Joan Rivière, 'Womanliness as Masquerade', reprinted in Athol Hughes (ed.), *The Inner World and Joan Rivière: Collected Papers 1920–1958* (London and New York: Karnak, 1991), p. 91.

29. Eisner, *Haunted Screen*, p. 262.

30. Andrew Britton in National Film Theatre season brochure, 'Crossdressing in the Cinema', 1990.

31. See Anette Kuhn, 'Sexual Disguise and Cinema', in *The Power of the Image* (London and New York: Routledge, 1985), pp. 48–73.

32. 'The Inner World in Literature' (1952), in Hughes, *The Inner World and Joan Rivière*, pp. 325–6.

CHAPTER 6

'Why are you looking at me like that?': Zinaida Raikh

What is most theatrically effective in drama is the process by which the hero makes a decision. That is . . . precisely why Hamlet is the most popular play of all ages and all countries.

Meyerhold, 1935[1]

In order to change the conditions of life, we must learn to see them through the eyes of women.

Trotsky, 1924[2]

In 1931 the controversial Soviet actress Yelena Goncharova was murdered.

She had been playing Hamlet with her own Moscow company and was given official leave to visit Paris, partly to defuse the political criticism she received – and which she seemed deliberately to provoke. *Hamlet* would soon effectively be banned by Stalin; Goncharova's choice of play, her interpretation, and her decision to act the Prince herself were all controversial, and at post-performance discussions she made her hostility to contemporary Soviet art, and her sense of alienation, dangerously clear: Soviet plays were, she said, 'Schematic, false, devoid of imagination and obvious'. Visiting Paris in the Depression, when she tried to perform extracts from *Hamlet* at a variety theatre, the manager suggested that she improve the recorders speech by playing the instrument with her buttocks: 'The fact that you're a woman makes it even more piquant.' The émigré press printed outspoken extracts from Goncharova's stolen private journal, which listed what she saw as the blessings and crimes of Soviet rule. Warring ideologies fought over her, pressuring her either to defect or return to Moscow immediately. KGB agents in Paris called her a traitor and she suffered a breakdown. She was shot dead in the street during a march of the unemployed, saving a labour leader from an assassin's bullet. Her public presentation of herself as Hamlet reflected the struggle of the artist under Stalin, torn between commitment and doubt. But no one understood her tragedy and the man she saved was unaware of her death. Moments before she died, a woman in the street screamed at her: 'Why are you looking at me like that? Scratch out her eyes!' Goncharova begged for her body to be covered with the red flag, but the request was refused and she was left unmourned in the street.

In 1939 the controversial Soviet actress Zinaida Raikh was murdered.

She was the wife and leading actress of the great director Vsevelod Meyerhold, who planned for her to play Hamlet. In 1928 they visited Paris, partly to defuse artistic and ideological criticisms, which Meyerhold seemed deliberately to provoke; in 1930 Raikh and the company acted in a suburban Paris variety theatre and met Michael Chekhov, the playwright's nephew, whose own Moscow *Hamlet* (1924) had caused ideological outrage. His choice of play, his interpretation, and his decision to play the Prince himself as a lonely soul in a society ruled by the spiritually dead were all controversial. When Chekhov tried to play Hamlet in Germany, a manager asked him 'Do you dance? We'll start a cabaret act. I'll make another Grok out of you. Do you play any instruments?'[3] Yet Chekhov refused to return and stage Soviet plays. He tried to persuade Raikh and Meyerhold – who was offered work in America – to do the same. She called him a traitor. Despite their continued commitment to the blessings of the Revolution, Raikh and Meyerhold increasingly came under fire. At first, because of his pre-eminence, it was her alleged lack of talent that was the target – he was said to be besottedly promoting his wife – but in 1938 the group was liquidated as anti-Soviet. Raikh, who was playing the Lady of the Camellias, suffered a breakdown onstage. She wrote Stalin an outspoken defence of her husband and it was later implied that her letter led to his death. He was arrested and their flat was broken into by agents of the KGB (or, it was claimed, thieves attracted by her decadent wealth). Neighbours ignored the screams as she was savagely stabbed to death. Her eyes were mutilated. Meyerhold was shot in 1940, unaware of her death. Raikh was refused an official burial and, almost unmourned, was interred wearing the Lady of the Camellia's black dress. Her life, her interest in *Hamlet*, and many of the iconic roles she played reflected the struggles of committed artists under Stalin.

Two actresses drawn to Hamlet, two violent political tragedies. The difference is that Yelena Goncharova was a fictional character, played by Zinaida Raikh.

Goncharova was the heroine of Yuri Olesha's *A List of Blessings* (1931), one of the last new works directed by Meyerhold and – though it was absolutely hostile to the decadent West on the verge of Fascism – one of the most overt in its criticisms of Soviet realities. It was one of

Figure 16   Auditioning Hamlet. Zinaida Raikh as Goncharova: *A List of Blessings*, Moscow
1931; director: Vsevelod Meyerhold.

Meyerhold's attempts to develop a new genre, Marxist tragedy, to succeed
the propagandist theatre he pioneered during the Revolution. Olesha
based Yelena Goncharova on a host of real models, including Michael
Chekhov and Raikh herself (see Figure 16). His play, and the career of
Zinaida Raikh – who was systematically denigrated for decades – illuminate the complex significance that a Soviet woman playing Hamlet gained
at a time when it seemed the world could be changed forever and the
theatre was the place to show how.[4]

I

New worlds

Writing after the Revolution, Yuri Olesha defined the Old as Emotion
and the New as Rationality, and for him *Hamlet* demonstrated the historical victory of the mechanistic. 'Remember how *Hamlet* ends?' asks
a character in his *Conspiracy of Feelings*, 'Corpses, dire passion, misery, and
suddenly enter Fortinbras. Enter the conqueror. And all passions come to

an end. Enough is enough. Enter Fortinbras – who doesn't give a damn for passions . . . All soliloquies are over.'[5] But *A List of Blessings* asked what happens afterwards and showed that past and present inhabit the same space. It opens metatheatrically in Moscow at a question-and-answer session after a performance of Goncharova's *Hamlet*. 'She was permitted a great deal', sneers an anti-Communist exile, 'She put on *Hamlet*. Just think of it, *Hamlet* in a country where art has been lowered to propaganda for the breeding of pigs, for the digging of silo pits.'[6] But from the first minute she is in a three-way conflict; a dashing Van Dyke Hamlet with rapier, cloak and riding boots, she fights an intellectual duel with the State while parrying the audience's hostile questions. The stage image is simple: a few Renaissance characters and, at 'an ordinary little table covered with a red cloth', the bureaucrat Comrade Orlovsky who 'presides', frantically ringing a bell whenever Goncharova's embarrassingly frank answers (she praises Chaplin, not *Battleship Potemkin*) step completely out of line. Orlovsky – an undistinguished object wrapped like his table in the red flag of authority – is the Soviet Polonius. He nervously reassures the public there's 'no offence' in the play while censoring the player:

GONCHAROVA: [*Reading*] 'The play that we have seen, *Hamlet*, is obviously written for the intelligentsia. The workers can't understand it, it's foreign and belongs to ancient history. Why show it anyway?' *Hamlet* is the finest work created by the art of the past. That's my opinion. In all probability, Russian audiences will never see *Hamlet* again, so I decided to show it here for the last time. (*Orlovsky rings his bell.*[7])

Goncharova, the last Soviet romantic, dreams of redistributing cultural wealth to the proletariat but yearns equally intensely for Paris in the rain. 'Proud to be an actress in the land of the Soviets' (p. 78), she puts her skills at the service of 'the new man'; but her intense vision of *Hamlet* is at odds with such real-life Soviet directors as Akimov and Okhlopkov who made the Prince a proto-Marxist, anti-feudal rebel. Like Michael Chekhov, Goncharova is denounced as a reactionary elitist for playing Hamlet as a troubled critic of modern times. One spectator complains, 'In this era of reconstruction, when everyone is gripped by the furious tempo of national development, it's revolting to hear the tedious drivelling of your Hamlet.' But this female Hamlet is a cultural provocateur who praises introspection –

Comrade Orlovsky, grab your bell. I will now say something terribly seditious. [*To the audience*] Honoured comrades! It seems to me that in an era of quick tempos the artist must think slowly, (p. 72)

– and she condemns Party-line dramas as 'schematic, false, devoid of imagination and obvious. Acting in them means to lose one's skill.'

Skill, not genius, was the key concept in Meyerhold's radical theatre, where worker-actors trained to demonstrate how people and historical processes operate, and Olesha shaped this first scene to provide a bravura opening display of Zinaida Raikh's talents (he called her performance brilliant), and to legitimise an anti-authoritarian voice. *Hamlet* frees Goncharova – and Olesha, Meyerhold and Raikh – to speak her thoughts publicly in a world where we learn it is unsafe to write them in secret. The speech which means most to her is the 'recorders' sequence which, according to the stage historian Konstantin Rudnitsky, Raikh played 'sarcastically, acidly':

'Why do you go about to recover the wind of me, as if you would drive me into a toil?' The question to Guildenstern sounded sharply challenging. Even more abrupt was the command to play the pipe. But the phrase: *'Tis as easy as lying'* was pronounced calmly, with insidious goodwill. Then followed a real explosion of rage: *'Why, look you now, how unworthy a thing you make of me. You would play upon me; you would seem to know my steps; you would pluck out the heart of my mystery; you would sound me from my lowest note to the top of my compass . . . 'Sblood, do you think I am easier to be played on than a pipe?'*[8]

Blessings established this speech as a demand for intellectual freedom and as the heart of *Hamlet* in the USSR. Immediately after Stalin's death Grigori Kozintsev rushed to direct *Hamlet* and told his leading actor 'it seems to me the most important passage in the tragedy'[9], and his composer Shostakovich morosely agreed: 'It's easy for him, he's a prince after all. If he weren't they'd play him so hard he wouldn't know what hit him.'[10] Similarly Goncharova's 'terribly seditious' words made her an instant symbol for dissidents. In November 1931 Evgeny Zamyatin, author of the dystopian *We*, left the USSR and quoted her in an essay that provoked international debates: yes, in a time of rapid revolution the artists must be free to think at their own pace. Just as Goncharova speaks out through Hamlet, Meyerhold 'used Raikh's lips to answer many people'.[11]

Zinaida Raikh was born in 1894, twenty-one years after Meyerhold. Her mother was from an aristocratic family but had been orphaned, her father worked as an engineer; both had some Jewish blood. Her high school tried to bar her from further education (she was in trouble for reading Darwin) but she qualified to teach and studied sculpture and architecture. During the Great War she joined the Social Revolutionary Party and in 1917 she was a secretary with the radical Petrograd paper *The People's Cause*. That year she met and married the peasant-poet Esenin and they joined the crowds outside the Winter Palace during the October Revolution. The relationship was violent and Esenin summarised it tersely: 'In 1917 my first marriage took place, to ZN Raikh. In 1918 I parted from her.' In fact she left him, but his circle began a defamation process that was to recur throughout Raikh's life – for them she was 'the jewess', 'this woman with a face as white and round as a plate'.[12] Physical insults revived at the height of her career and persisted long after her death as if it were essential to scar her image forever. Shostakovich's *Testimony* (1979) called her 'a typical Odessa fishwife', 'an obnoxious pushy woman', 'voluptuous': 'God will forgive her.' In contrast Esenin's second marriage to Isadora Duncan and his suicide in 1925 fed romantic myths; in Olesha's words, 'He departed young, golden, with strands of hair drifting in the air.'[13] During the revolutionary months, Raikh constantly attended Meyerhold's theatre. In 1919 she ran an agit-prop theatre group and when they met she was working at the People's Commissariat of Education.

Raikh enrolled in his directing class and Meyerhold was struck by what he called 'her characteristic frankness'.[14] They married in 1922 and became inseparable. She was soon a major member of his team, training students like Eisenstein in the extreme physical demands of Biomechanics. She and Eisenstein were in the design team for the sensational 'impromptu' production of *A Doll's House* which Meyerhold and the students staged in under a week. Given one day and no money to create Nora Helmer's world, they used old reversed flats with the timbers exposed, mismatched furniture, grid-irons and bars, and showed bourgeois structures disintegrating round the characters. Constructivism revealed the mechanics of emotional, intellectual and economic systems, and created stage mechanisms within which worker-actors accelerated the dynamics of change. By the late 1920s she was the leading actress in the company and though many complained that she was far from the most talented, her role extended beyond performance. When Lenin died in 1924 the Meyerholds made their support for Trotsky clear in *DE*, a political fantasy-cabaret celebrating his doctrine of world revolution, with his texts and Lenin's projected onto the set. Raikh proposed a plot in which Soviet workers should burrow under the Atlantic so the Red Army could join forces with revolutionaries in New York. 'It was she who made him stay close to . . . Trotsky, Zinoviev, et al', *Testimony* claimed, 'And it backfired'.[15] Raikh was involved in many experiments in rhythmic, de-psychologised theatre (including the technique of 'pre-performance', where actors prefixed each speech with a gesture, destroying the apparent fluency of 'natural' acting) and above all she pressured him to explore the experiences of women. In 1928 Meyerhold revived one of his most famous productions, *The Magnificent Cuckold*, with Raikh as the heroine; he dedicated it to her and reshaped the farce into an attack on violence against women: Raikh had been the victim of domestic violence in her first marriage and Meyerhold said her 'mind and talent helped me discover the tragic source of this wonderful play'.[16] In 1930, as Meyerhold told Olesha in a letter, they welcomed his tragi-comic variation on *Hamlet* putting a woman at the heart of the post-revolutionary experience: 'When we got home we said simultaneously (Zinaida Nikolaevna and I) "What a wonderful play!"'[17]

II

Roads to Hamlet

The old and the new struggle in the souls of women, in permanent enmity. (Alexandra Kollontai[18])

There are two worlds, the old and the new!. . . [But there is a third world:] It's the world of the artist. (Yuri Olesha[19])

Meyerhold was obsessed with *Hamlet* throughout his career (he had been the first Moscow Arts Konstantin, a modern Hamlet, in *The Seagull*) and always thought of it dialectically. In 1915 he rehearsed a version with students and used Craig's Symbolist *Hamlet* as the model they must reject. Craig saw it as pure poem, a matter of 'vision' and 'ecstasy' with Hamlet as a saint who kills, and to catch that paradox he used an archetypal feminine image: 'Remember Gioconda's smile. . . Hamlet has that smile.' Meyerhold's *Hamlet* would be the opposite, 'impulsive, dynamic, musical and buoyant', sometimes grotesquely comic.[20] He told his Ophelia to reject Craig's 'pretentious staging and sugary gestures' for the directness of the Elizabethan popular stage. The disastrous course of the war killed the project, and reviving this symbol of individualism and passivity at all was already controversial on the Left, particularly given the Russian tendency to see Hamlet as the 'superfluous man'. Meyerhold however insisted that creativity and ideology could annex Shakespeare for the Revolution, and later argued that Shakespearean technique is the tragic face of Marxist thought, the dialectical 'conflict of contradictions.'[21] In *Hamlet* especially 'the elements of high drama and low comedy alternate not only in the play as a whole but within individual characters (particularly in the title role).'[22] This equation not only allowed

Meyerhold to correlate politics with the inner lives of individuals, it rapidly led him to explore and politicise the *dialectics of masculinity and femininity* in *Hamlet*.

During the Civil War he planned a Bolshevik *Hamlet* to include prose passages, including the Gravediggers, rewritten and updated by Vladimir Mayakovsky, who would insert news, satire and polemics. But while Agit-prop carnival led by worker-clowns would invade the sacred text, Meyerhold also invited the poet Marina Tsvetaeva to translate the rest of *Hamlet*, the 'poetry': two voices, two genders, comedy and tragedy, prose against verse. Tsvetaeva refused and publicly denounced the project because of her hostility to the Reds, but since Meyerhold (who said of her, 'poets are proud people') must have known of her anti-Bolshevism, he clearly calculated that her distinctive voice and her anger would intensify *Hamlet*'s internal dissent. This was the essence of Meyerhold's 'October in the Theatre', the conviction that political commitment and formal innovation must assimilate debate. Certainly, Tsvetaeva was fascinated by *Hamlet* and in an equally radical spirit, but it was the women who preoccupied her, and the Prince's misogyny. Her brilliant *Hamlet* variations include the poem 'Ophelia in Defence of the Queen' (1923) where Ophelia compares Gertrude to Phaedra and dismisses the 'hero' with contempt: 'Who do you think you are/to pass judgement on blood that burns?' 'Blood' versus 'judgement': Elsinore's gendered conflicts fascinated the revolutionary generation.[23]

Meyerhold aimed to deconstruct *Hamlet* and Hamlet. There were at least two later projected versions involving Zinaida Raikh, in which she would either play the title role, or explode it. According to Shostakovich, Meyerhold envisaged a male comic Hamlet who would 'bother' a female tragic one: 'I think Raikh would have read the tragic monologues.'[24] Meyerhold told Alexander Gladkov (1935), 'I dreamed of a production where Hamlet would be played by two actors: one vacillating, the other resolute':

They would constantly replace each other, but while one was working, the other would not leave the stage, but sit at his feet, and thus underline the tragic situation of two opposed temperaments. Sometimes the second one would even express his relation to the first and vice versa. He might even jump up at a certain point, knock the other out of the way, and take his place.[25]

'Meyerhold had already tried her as Hamlet'[26] – *A List of Blessings* was widely seen as Raikh's public rehearsal for Shakespeare's play. In the USSR the female Hamlet suggested contradictory meanings. S/he was an image of female empowerment and of androgynous equality in a communist world, but the tragedy also indicated internal crisis, the war between 'passion' and 'thought'. The female Hamlet offered both heroism and destabilisation. Goncharova is a feminist; eloquent about the new rational sexual ethos and women's social progress, she sees herself liberated from the roles of mother, wife and lover – 'The revolution has freed us from petty sentiments. There's one of the revolution's blessings for you' (p. 75) – and yet Party men are mystified:

FEDOTOV: What part are you performing now?
GONCHAROVA: Hamlet.
LAKHTIN: You mean Ophelia?
GONCHAROVA: No, Hamlet himself.
LAKHTIN: Really, a woman playing a man's role?
GONCHAROVA: Well, yes.
LAKHTIN: But you only have to look at your legs to know you're a woman.
GONCHAROVA: Women must think like men now. The Revolution. Men's accounts are being settled.
LAKHTIN: I'll pour you some tea.

Even Kozintsev attacked all feminisations of the Prince as decadent.

The Soviet propaganda conflict between 'old' and 'new' was often represented in the arts through a militant woman bringing Marx to a backwards group, like the heroines of Gorki's *Mother* or Vishnevski's *Optimistic Tragedy*. But in 1929 the Moscow Central Art Workers' Club put Yuri Olesha and two other dramatists on trial: they were accused of writing too few good female roles. This was a glorified literary debate – a 'show' trial in the gentlest sense – though sadly prophetic given the fates of some of those involved during the coming purges. A group of actresses organised it in protest against playwrights' 'underestimation of the role of women in the building of socialist society'. Zinaida Raikh was a counsel for the defence but Meyerhold led the prosecution, accusing the dramatists of downgrading women's achievements during the Revolution, the Civil War and the new phase of industrialisation: they had ignored 'the complexity and variety' of Soviet women's 'modern' lives and minds.[27] Olesha's self-defence was sardonic, calculated to win neither feminist nor Party friends: 'The revolution is men's business – a time when men get even with each other.' But Meyerhold unexpectedly used the event to propose an anti-realist gender manifesto for Russian theatre in the 1930s: 'Women should take over "men's roles" on stage as well as in real life, by acting parts written for male actors.' 'Give me the actresses', he said, 'and I'll make a Khlestakov and Hamlet of them, a Don Juan or Chatsky!'

Meyerhold had explored theatrical cross-dressing long before in his assault on Naturalism, and indeed the first time Olesha saw him act was in his film of *Dorian Gray* (1915) where the actress Varvara Yanova played Dorian. Also in 1915, a year after the Bolsheviks first espoused the feminist argument in what Alexandra Kollontai called 'an earnest and practical way', Meyerhold directed Nina Kovalenskava as Calderon's martyred *Constant Prince*. A more recent, overtly revolutionary example of cross-gender casting was Maria Babanova's heroic Chinese Boy in *Roar, China!*, and Zinaida Raikh herself had just played the Phosphorescent Woman, a flying-suited time-traveller in Mayakovsky's *The Bathhouse*, where she was the ambassador from a Marxist future that would be apparatchik-free and evidently androgynous. However their new focus on sexual politics put them in a subversive relationship with the social direction of Stalinism. For in 1930 it was declared that the 'Woman Question' was solved.

In 1930 Stalin closed down the Party's Women's Sections; since all were equal under Socialism, women's rights were no longer an issue. The role of the Socialist nuclear family was stressed and in 1936 abortion was recriminalised: Trotsky condemned 'Thermidor in the family', the renewed 'household slavery of women', and the Meyerholds refused to bury gender issues. Goncharova in *A List of Blessings* is still a woman at odds with a patriarchal world; it is, however, evolving rapidly because of Stalinism, Capitalism and Fascism into unimagined new repressive forms. She is also, like the Hamlet she insists on playing, trapped in a nightmare: 'I'm carrying on a long agonizing argument with myself, an argument that's drying up my brain.'[28] She enacts her – and her audience's – inner debates in public, because by 1930 no private space for subjectivity remains. Alexandra Kollontai spoke of a peculiarly female inner war: 'Contemporary heroines. . . must wage a struggle on two fronts: with the external world and with the inclinations of their grandmothers dwelling in the recesses of their beings.' Reason must crush Emotion: 'Dominance of feeling was the most typical trait peculiar to the woman of the past', Kollontai said in 1920; now it was 'imperative that she conquer her feelings [and]. . . strengthen, through the exercise of her will, her eminently passive, easily guided spirit.'[29] Kollontai saw George Sand's life, for example, as a struggle between an active androgynous self and an 'atavistic' femininity. The female Soviet Hamlet focused these contradictions, while asking what role in the Communist future awaited the culture of the past.

Meyerhold's group tried to address the *volatility* of gender in the twentieth century. In Olesha's *Conspiracy of Feelings* and its source novel *Envy*, a dissident invents a feelings-machine to undermine the new technocratic order. It has subversive emotions; it loves, cries, picks flowers, sings, and is called 'Ophelia'. But this Ophelia has a phallus, in the novel she impales her maker on a needle-like extension, and Olesha's phantasmagoric slippages intrigued the Meyerholds. His female-artist-Hamlet, like his male-machine-Ophelia, destabilised gender and showed individuals and regimes caught in an unprecedented internal struggle. Soviet writers and theatre practitioners – if they were permitted to deal with such conflicts at all – were required to demonstrate their resolution in the synthesis of Marxist action. Whether or not this could viably resolve Hamlet's questions is the central tension of the play.[30]

III

Red, white and black: tragic dialectics

Olesha intensified Hamlet's choice between duty at home and intellectual exile. Goncharova goes abroad, but she cannot escape the tragic decisions of her time; she asks whether individual consciousness can figure at all in theatre now, and is unsatisfied with the official answer:

GONCHAROVA: I am an actress, and my essence must be humanity. . . An actress will only become great when she embodies a democratic, generally comprehensible idea that moves everyone. . .
FEDOTOV: That idea is socialism.
GONCHAROVA: Not true.[31]

In Moscow Yelena Goncharova can – at least for the moment – play Hamlet, but in a world of warring (and for Olesha, male) ideologies she is profoundly divided. Echoing Hamlet ('My tables. Meet it is I set it down') she keeps a secret double-entry diary in which she records the regime's 'blessings' and 'crimes'. And she is the sum of what she sees: 'We'll put the two halves together. That's me. Do you understand? Those are my fears, my anxieties. Two halves of a single conscience, a muddle that's driving me out of my mind.' The journal is stolen and the 'crimes' are published by White exiles as propaganda:

Secret of the Soviet Intelligentsia. . . Every line of this document is washed in tears. This is the confession of an unfortunate being, of a highly gifted nature which has been worn out by the yoke of Bolshevik enslavement. This is the shining truth about how the dictatorship of the proletariat deals with what we consider to be the most precious treasure in the world, free human thought.[32]

There was indeed a Western audience for texts of female protest, like *We Soviet Women* (New York 1930) by Tatiana Tchernavin ('Author of *Escape from the Soviets*') who was in prison when *Blessings* was written: 'When the giant tidal wave of the Russian Revolution had spent its force, the world saw many of the lowest people in Russian life appearing on the top, and many that were fine, especially women, submerged into the depths.'[33] However, though Left and Right see her as anti-Soviet, Goncharova is actually heir to the non-Party but supportive 'fellow travellers' (originally Trotsky's term) and to literary groups of the early twenties who 'wanted to take a deeper look into life around them and to show in their work not only the "pluses" but also the "minuses" of revolutionary life'.[34] Unfortunately the Association of Proletarian Writers denounced the Fellow Travellers as anti-Soviet in 1925, and in *Blessings* the last word as drama critic goes to Fedotov the KGB spy who sees playing Hamlet as reactionary self-indulgence:

Go and shoot at the unemployed. . . . Anybody who complains about the Soviet regime sympathises with the police shooting the unemployed in Europe. There's no point in pretending, no point in wrapping yourself up in a philosophy; your exquisite philosophy is simply that of the . . . policeman. (p. 85)

A List of Blessings re-examined the myth of the Actress, and Hamlet's costume was a key symbol in this. When Goncharova garbs herself androgynously in his doublet and hose, the working clothes of the Thinker, her angry public (who all see her as Other, whether a political tool, a desirable body, or a threat) want her re-clothed. Asta Nielsen's Hamlet repeatedly used her black bell-like cloak to reinvent herself: she could wrap herself tight in it like a toga, or let it float round her, occupying screen space; it could signify sensitivity or power. Zinaida Raikh's cloak was some eight feet long and trailed her like a shadow; she fell ill during rehearsals so Meyerhold coached her understudy Remisova in its use during a bravura matador sequence in which Goncharova's movement and costume physicalised her experience of force, concealment and defeat. Meyerhold, playing Raikh playing Goncharova playing Hamlet, 'drew himself up, stood erect and with a quick movement of his right hand threw the right hand edge of the cloak over his left shoulder and, proudly, with his head held high, looked sternly into the auditorium.'

Then with his right hand he folded back the edge over his right arm and, slightly bending his head, he went quickly out into the wings . . . He ran out again onto the stage, extending his right hand and holding the edge of the cloak in it. His whole figure was in profile, hidden from the spectator by the cloak, but the left edge was quivering from the rapid running and was dragged along the floor. The impression was of a bird with dark wings flying past. Finally, he turned his face into the audience and, falling on one knee, but leaving his right hand holding the cloak up, he covered his bowed head.[35]

Blessings established a visual conflict between the intellectual's black cloak and a clinging silver gown which the Right want Goncharova to wear at a ball organised by Fascists. For whereas Asta Nielsen flourished because audiences projected dreams on her mask-like face, everyone fights to *control* Goncharova; they demand that her body enacts their incompatible desires. Many want to rip her clothes or expose her nakedness, and the Soviet Actress is still labelled 'slut', 'streetwalker' and 'whore'. The female Hamlet finds herself surrounded by hectoring men in an overheated world heavy with sexual threat; her only Horatio is a fellow-actress left behind after Scene Two, almost every other woman in *Blessings* is envious, browbeaten, and shrill. They turn on her in frustration, scapegoating her for the theft of whatever they have lost – whether a lover or five rationed apples in a block of drab flats – and even she is unstable, which makes the play's diagrammatic structure skew out of control disturbingly as Olesha plays out a philosophical debate through characters close to psychosis. Goncharova, who begins with such bold poise on the stage, slips minutes later – 'hysterically' – into shrieking near-madness: 'Get out of here . . . I spit on you.' (pp. 77–8) Despite her pledge that she only lists serious crimes against freedom in her journal, petty squabbles inflame her: 'I'll note that down right away . . . The actress who played Hamlet for the new man lived next to a scrounger in a dirty hovel.' The hysteria is almost universal: men, women, rich, poor, Whites and Reds all succumb, and though Goncharova's refusal to be 'played on' enrages politicians, it is the insecure majority that she most disturbs: Hamlet's doubt undermines their crumbling faith in themselves, her searching unease appals them: 'What else do you need? Why do photographs show you with such a worried look in your eyes?' 'Because I find it very difficult to be a citizen of the new world.' (p. 71)

Goncharova's eyes obsess everyone. Onstage and off she is the focus of the masses' gaze, yet what disturbs them is that they are caught in hers. Moscow audiences are outraged by what they see in Hamlet's eyes: 'What are you? What? An aristocrat of the spirit, is that it? . . . But you, you're an actress. I spit on that!' In Paris a sad émigré longs to see whether her eyes 'smoulder or sparkle' but soon screams, 'I'll scratch them out. Whore! Whore!', and lashes her face with flowers. Her eyes are mirrors: she releases people's irrationality and after *Hamlet* at a collective farm, a Young Communist 'leaps onto the stage with a circus bound. He yells like a carnival Petrushka, repeats mechanically, with false feeling, the words of greeting that Goncharova asks him to transmit to the workers. Then he begins to behave like a cad, grabs the actress' diary from the table and begins to dig through it.'[36] In this abusive energy Meyerhold travestied the gymnastic propaganda of his own old Red Guard theatres; radical 'feeling' is repressed and perverted into a warped new individualism in scenes of rat-like backbiting and paranoia. 'He jumps about in front of me', Goncharova says of a ranting neighbour, 'grimaces, strikes poses. And it's a matter of complete indifference to me. I see you through the mist of a journey, and already I can't make out your gestures or hear your voice . . .' (pp. 77–8) *Blessings* suggested that the System was deforming bodies and minds; she yearns to escape to Europe's sophistication, sense of history, and light. Paris however is worse.

'The theme of the play', Olesha stated, was the nature of 'the Intellectual' and 'the European spirit'. Meyerhold dropped Hamlet into a Cubist Paris, centred on a ten-foot high screen with a collage of fragmented texts – a roundel, the number five at an angle, 'OLYMPIA' in capitals, and the name of a circus act: the '*Fratellini*' clowns displaced '*fraternité*'. *Blessings* was designed on a diagonal so that the audience spied on Goncharova from an angle, trying to 'penetrate her mystery' in a skewed world (Meyerhold: 'An actor performing full-face toward the audience always tends to pose a little, as if he were performing a solo act.') This created visual insecurity and matched a script inspired by *Hamlet's* traps and eavesdropping. At one point gendarmes chase a Leftist into Goncharova's boarding house and, '*weak with horror*', she witnesses his beating through glass: '*He crumples to the floor. He doesn't shout, doesn't groan. The entire scene takes place in complete silence . . . [She] is almost in hysterics behind the glass door. She shouts almost inaudibly behind the door.*' The play becomes a silent film about oppression, impotence and the death of language. The actress is marginalised everywhere and the theatre manager M. Margaret turns Hamlet's tragic anger into pornography. When Goncharova reprises the recorder speech for an audition, he classifies her as a novelty flute act ('But I can't play';[37] 'But you said yourself . . . it was as easy as lying') and suggests commercial improvements:

Swallow the flute. The public gasps in amazement. A reversal of mood – surprise, alarm. Then you turn your back to the public and it turns out that the flute is protruding from you, from a place from which flutes are not known to protrude. The fact that you're a woman makes it even more piquant. You see. Listen, it's a great idea. Then you begin to blow the flute . . .[38]

Margaret-Claudius has usurped the Globe, which also has a new deity –
a crooner called Ulalum. Ulalum is Nietzschian, the seedy Dionysus of a
Fascist dawn: 'For men he is a man, for women he is a woman. Perhaps he is
a god? . . . It's ecstasy.' Ulalum and Goncharova are both multi-gendered
but the singer is bewildered by the actress' *intellectual* androgyny ('Why are
you wearing pants?') and offers her escape into mindlessness, sex and submission: 'Please take off your blouse.' Like the rest he tries to deconstruct
and fit her into his fantasy: 'But what are you?' he asks, 'Today I dreamed of
my childhood. A garden, wooden banisters . . . You have young arms like
banisters . . . You've come from my childhood . . . Come here . . . Come to
me . . .' They kiss, in 'general rapt silence', and she admits that 'For a while
now life has seemed to me like a dream . . . I thought that the theatre . . . but
this is a torture chamber.' Torn between totalitarianism and the frenzy of
the Market, she is driven from what she believed was her subjective space,
her 'third world', theatre. The fusion of thought and feeling, conscience
and action that she tried to achieve as Hamlet is impossible in a West that
worships the Self and is unleashing unreason.

Olesha suggested that progress had created a generation of Hamlets:
'The Revolution deprived me of my past and didn't show me a future',
Goncharova says, 'And so my thoughts became my present. To think . . . I
thought, only thought – by means of thought I wanted to attain what
I couldn't attain by feeling.'(p. 82) She believes 'life is natural when
thought and feeling form a harmony', and Paris is her search for lost
childhood and the security of seeing her shadow on ancient stones:
'In the new world I lay about like a fragment of broken glass. Now I
have returned', she says in a moment of hope, 'and the two halves have
united.' (p. 83) But her innocence ended in October 1917 – she graduated
the day the Winter Palace fell and her schizophrenia cannot be healed by
ignoring history. Meyerhold expressed her crisis visually: he elongated
Raikh's body and split her in two. Hamlet's long cloak trailed down
steps like the tail of a black peacock while her shadow climbed above
her on the wall.

IV

Remember me

I can always distinguish a genuine from a poor actor by his eyes. The good actor
knows the value of his gaze. (Meyerhold[39])

I was dazzled by her large shining chestnut eyes. (Mikhail Sadowsky, actor[40])

There was a lot of gossip about Raikh. When Lee Strasberg visited Moscow in 1934 a sceptical assistant told him *The Lady of the Camellias* was built round her inadequacy: 'When I told him that I thought the 5th Act poor, he suggested that it was because M. was aware of Raikh's limitations and had simply not built the scene too difficult for her – but had tried to use her limitations.' Yet when Strasberg watched her *rehearse* he was surprised: 'There was an actual psychological ease and therefore spontaneity that was lost the moment they knew they were acting. Zinaida Raikh looked a much better actress and more interesting personality than she did on stage.'[41] Was Raikh, so often accused of vanity, actually most confident when she was not on display? In this respect Olesha's meta-drama about a modern woman's struggle to establish her role was tailored for her: we never see Goncharova play Hamlet onstage, she only speaks his lines in the audition and the audience debate, because the play reflects Meyerhold's fascination with the actor's process of discovery, the median state: 'Most of all I love to watch a good actor when he's half-way to the character he's going to portray, still Ivan Ivanovich and a little bit Othello.' And again, 'What is most theatrically effective in drama is the process by which the hero makes a decision . . .'[42] So *A List of Blessings* climaxed like *Hamlet* with Goncharova finally committing herself to a cause.

Meyerhold listed the portents of Western collapse to the cast: 'unemployment, depression, competition for markets . . .' Like *Hamlet, Blessings* is a revenge play and Goncharova imagines herself watching Chaplin's films in Paris, 'thinking of the fate of the little man, of the sweetness of finding vengeance for past humiliations'. (p. 76) But like Hamlet she becomes enmeshed in both personal and global counter-plots, especially the Right's yearning for a European war of vengeance. As others rave around her, her articulacy gives way to spasms of speechlessness, 'silent as a mirror', and unlike Hamlet she has almost no soliloquies. She must play so many roles – outfacing Stalinists like a dissident, confronting anti-communists like a commissar – that her alienation becomes total: '*Humiliated and alone, she hears the sound of a party behind shuttered windows. And, listening to it, she thinks about her own life.*'[43] In this numbed state she drifts from the theatre and meets not two gravediggers but a lamplighter and a hungry musician (sacked by Margaret for his politics) living off jokes from *commedia* and *The Gold Rush*: 'I'll eat some fence. See it? Very tasty. Reminds you of waffles.' (p. 105) He offers to eat a tree, and a policeman. She leaves before the lamp is lit and '*a strong resemblance is revealed between the man and Chaplin*'. Perhaps Hamlet has been superseded by a new figure of universal humanity – the Little Man, starving on the streets but still laughing and committed. And unlike Goncharova he knows how to play the flute.

Superficially, Yuri Olesha compromised his play by turning the end into propaganda. The heroine decides to return to Moscow, takes a gun, joins a demonstration and dies a martyr. However the *tone* of these last scenes is nightmarish. There is no Shakespearean duel between right and wrong: the Reds interrogate her, the Whites make her a sexual toy; her killer is her Dostoievskian stalker, and hunger-marchers and industrialists unite to call her a whore. Her bloody end bewildered Meyerhold's critics. Some praised the choreographic power of the climax, others found it grotesquely stylised – 'daubed colours, doll-like capitalists and unnatural unemployed'. Rudnitsky, writing in Russia during the Thaw, felt free to condemn the whole play as 'purely geometrical', denying 'the painful complexity of life', and called her self-sacrifice a sell-out to Stalin; but Vyachesla Zavalishin, an emigré journalist in America, called the end 'hopelessly pessimistic'.[44] Olesha himself insisted, 'Both sides execute Goncharova.' The street becomes the ultimate theatre where she regains her voice and joins the people, but like Olesha's Fortinbras they 'don't give a damn'. Rudnitsky described her death:

Shot. Hit: Goncharova stretches to her full height, tense, still. Run: Goncharova runs up to the fountain, bends her head under the water. . . comes out onto the proscenium. Shakes her wet head, staggers. The unemployed workers catch her up. She tenses again, straightens up, frees herself from their hands, staggers again. Almost falls. She is caught up again and carefully, quietly laid down on the floor. Raikh lay on her side, facing the audience. Then dropped her head back and onto the floor.[45]

In death Goncharova accepts Fortinbras – 'The Soviet armies are coming. . .' – and even finds a new Horatio, a weaver's wife who bends over her to hear her last words. But she will never report them: 'I can't hear. I can't make out a word.' The wife does catch her last request – 'She wants me to cover her body with a Red flag' – but the crowd damn Goncharova ('She's a traitor! The whore!') and march off, leaving her in the dirt; there is no funeral exit. Olesha asked for a march offstage; Meyerhold refused to revive old revolutionary gestures; the ambivalence remained to the last. It was equally possible to see the tragedy of the 'female Hamlet', the feeling intellectual, as historically irrelevant or as proof that something essential to humanity was under threat. When history obliterates the individual, Olesha said, the result is not 'a corpse, but a zero'. Meyerhold called Goncharova 'a flower that will be crushed by a boot', yet for him she represented a force that was not completely destroyed. Raikh and her understudy wanted to play failing strength at the end: 'It seemed to us that when dying you should show you are weakening, but he shouted at us' and ran on stage, acting it out himself. Shot, Meyerhold hurled himself at the crowd. He showed the body die inch by inch, from the right hand to the head, but demanded 'lightness, grace and vitality': 'Life! You have to play life!'

'Everything that is written down', said Meyerhold, 'becomes a lie.' In the darkening atmosphere of the Purges, the balancing act of the critical Marxist became increasingly impossible. In 1934 the doctrine of Socialist Realism was imposed at the Soviet Writers' Conference, where Olesha publicly and this time with deadly seriousness confessed his 'errors'. With this clampdown Raikh and Meyerhold's *avant-garde Hamlet* became inconceivable and so *A List of Blessings* was the closest to playing Hamlet she ever came. Ignoring the 'resolution' of the Woman Question, Meyerhold planned a trilogy on women's history, dealing with the pre-revolutionary, Bolshevik and Stalinist periods ('We, too, in the Soviet Union, have had a wrong conception of love and of women') and starring with Zinaida Raikh as *The Lady of the Camellias* (1937).[46] Raikh's women had always been disruptive, now she rehabilitated a courtesan as the one worthwhile consciousness in a predatory society.[47] She made her 'poetic, chaste', yet conveyed 'restlessness, gaiety, eagerness, energy' instead of sentimental sickness.[48] It was Raikh's greatest success; ceramic figurines were made of her in Marguerite's black dress, and for a moment their interest in gender seemed safe. Engels had stated, 'The modern individual family is founded on the open and unconcealed domestic slavery of the wife', and this production condemned the sexual politics of Capital: 'I am interested in the bad attitude of the bourgeoisie to women. Marguerite is treated like a slave or servant. Men bargain over her, throw money in her face, insult her – all because they say they love her.'[49] But grave clashes followed over Tretyakov's *I Want a Child*, dealing with abortion, which was banned. Meyerhold had imagined a sexually egalitarian theatre where *travesti*, the transcendence of biological determinism, was a symbol of revolutionary rights; Olesha however created a female Hamlet whose attempt to reinvent herself was traumatic. Goncharova not only played but *was* Europe's new Hamlet, the bewildered conscience of twentieth century men and women on the edge of an abyss.

Boris Pasternak was translating *Hamlet* for Raikh and Meyerhold when news came of her murder and his arrest. He put it aside. He once joked that the couple's relationship was like Eve and God's; several rehearsal photographs of *A List of Blessings* survive, including one where Meyerhold holds Raikh's head with his right hand, adjusting the angle of her gaze, and almost moulding her expression with his left. She stands, he stares, like Hamlet with the skull. 'There is an opinion', her understudy Remisova said, 'that he did something with the actor's will'; but she believed he could reach the performer's creativity – 'awakening it, freeing it' – and she was especially struck by his direction of women in ways that seemed partly based on observation, partly intuitive.[50] Remisova recalled the way he showed how Goncharova should don the silver dress, studying his own direction in a mirror. Where, in any relationship, do partnership and manipulation begin and end? Goncharova's greatness stems from her power of observation and her outspokenness, and the latter, absolutely, was Raikh. She passionately defended Nikolai Erdman's satire *The Suicide* – another *Hamlet* variation – and prepared a private preview for Stalin after turning on Erdman's enemies: 'It is everything despicable in a man and a jealousy towards fame that are speaking in you!. . . You, with your struggle, will increase the thunder of Erdman's fame.'[51] *The Suicide* however was banned. Whereas it had once been necessary to attack Meyerhold vicariously through sneers about Raikh or his advancement of her, the attacks were direct now. From the day she suggested Eisenstein should leave Meyerhold's class, to the night she asked Stanislavsky why he put on rubbish, to the moment she wrote to Stalin to condemn her husband's persecution, Zinaida Raikh broke rules. She was what the system had to suppress – emotionalism, self-expression, confrontation. In a culture based on self-censorship, Raikh refused and was written out of history until *glasnost* in the late 1980s, when the magazine *Teatr* reviewed her career and state documents relating to the Meyerholds' murders began to emerge.[52]

At the Globe music hall, a Constructivist parody of Shakespeare's stage, her Hamlet met the undead of Western culture. Meyerhold packed in a kaleidoscope of acts, a human chain including showgirls, black-face tap-dancers, a Njinski and a Valkyrie. Dressed as Hamlet in this chaos, Raikh's constant quality in surviving photographs is *stillness*. In some shots, with her white open collar and white cuffs she looks a child, in others she seems middle-aged, heavy and tired – retouching may explain this – but the dominant image is of strength in sorrow. M Margaret – a squat, slick-haired ringmaster who growled, pounced, and thwacked himself with a whip, then lapsed into torpor[53] – hunches on his chair as Raikh reprises the recorder scene; she makes Hamlet statuesque and challenging and in spite of the situation wields her sword proudly. She 'looked sternly into the auditorium'.[54] In other photos, away from the theatre's 'third space', Goncharova is interrogated by the KGB Rosencrantz and Guildenstern in a boulevard cafe or trapped in a madman's flat, and stares out in anguish. Time and again what we see is Raikh-Goncharova-Hamlet open-eyed, demanding with history's victims to be remembered.

Notes

1. See Michael Glenny, ed., *Novy Mir: A Selection, 1925–1967* (London: Cape, 1972), p. 176.
2. See Leon Trotsky, *The Revolution Betrayed* (London: Faber and Faber, 1937), p. 144.
3. Quoted in Eleanor Rowe, *Hamlet: A Window on Russia* (New York: New York University Press, 1976), p. 140.
4. Meyerhold asked Olesha to heighten several details from Chekhov's life and clarify the ideological significance. As this book was preparing for the press, the post-Soviet reassessment of 1930s theatre produced a monumental work on this project: Violetta Gudkova, *Yurii Olesha i Vsevolod Meyerhold'd v rabote nad spektaklem 'Spisok Blagodeyanii'. Opyt teatral'noi arkeologii [Yuri Olesha and Vsevolod Meyerhold at Work on the Production of 'A List of Blessings': An Essay in Theatrical Archaeology]* (Moscow: Novoye Literurnoye Obozrenie, 2002). For an earlier version of the present chapter see Tony Howard, '"Why are You Looking at Me Like That?": Raikh and Goncharova, Two Actresses After the Revolution,' *Women and Theatre: Occasional Papers* 3 (1996), pp. 118–54.
5. Yuri Olesha, *A Conspiracy of Feelings*, in Bernard F Dukore *et al., Avant Garde Drama* (New York: Crowell, 1976), p. 255.
6. *A List of Blessings*, Yuri Olesha, *Complete Plays*, edited and translated by Michael Green and Jerome Katsell (Ann Arbor, Ardis, 1983), p. 90. Page references in the text are to this edition. Green and Katsell's title for Olesha's play is used here in preference to the less pointed earlier translation, *A List of Assets*: see Andrew R MacAndrew (ed.), *Twentieth-Century Russian Drama* (New York: Bantam, 1963).
7. *A List of Blessings*, p. 71.
8. Konstantin Rudnitsky, *Meyerhold the Director* (Ann Arbor: Ardis, 1981), p. 394. The book was published in Moscow in 1969. For Zamyatin, see his 'The Modern Russian Theatre', in Ellendea and Carl R Proffer, (eds.) *The Ardis Anthology of Russian Futurism* (Ann Arbor: Ardis, 1980), p. 206. Zamyatin explained that during this 1930–1 season Moscow theatre was briefly liberalised from above in an internal campaign against 'red nonsense'. It is in this atmosphere that Goncharova is given leave to play Hamlet and (like Raikh, Meyerhold and Laertes) visit France.

9. Grigori Kozintsev, *Shakespeare, Time and Conscience* (London: Dobson, 1967), p. 217.

10. See *Testimony: The Memoirs of Dmitri Shostakovich Related to and Edited by Solomon Volkov* (London: Hamish Hamilton, 1979). The authenticity of these memoirs remains controversial but their hostility to Raikh was common in Moscow cultural circles.

11. Rudnitsky, pp. 494–5.

12. See Jessie Davies, *Isadora Duncan's Russian Husband* (n.p., n.d.), pp. 133–44; Gordon McVay, *Esenin: A Life* (London: Hodder and Stoughton, 1976), pp. 84–9; p. 179.

13. See McVay, p. 94 and *Testimony*, pp. 19, 207.

14. See Alexander Gladkov, 'Meyerhold Speaks', *Drama Review* 43.3 (1974), p. 12.

15. *Testimony*, p. 90.

16. *Contemporary Theatre* claimed she 'moves ponderously over the construction and speaks her lines lifelessly; she lacks Stella's fire, her spiritual infectiousness, her youth. She is a woman of experience simulating naiveté and innocence, but no matter how much she rolls her eyes, nobody is likely to believe her.' Cited Edward Braun, *The Theatre of Meyerhold* (London: Eyre Methuen, 1979), p. 226.

17. Meyerhold to Olesha, Paul Schmidt, *Meyerhold at Work* (Manchester: Carcanet, 1981), pp. 79–80.

18. See Alexandra Kollontai, *The Autobiography of a Sexually Emancipated Communist Woman* (London: Orbach and Chambers, 1972), pp. 66, 102.

19. Olesha in 'The Cherry Stone', 1929. See George Reavey and Marc Slonim, *Soviet Literature* (London: Wishart, 1933).

20. Craig quoted in Laurence Senelick, *Gordon Craig's Moscow Hamlet* (Westport and London: Greenwood, 1982), p. 186; Meyerhold quoted in Braun, *Theatre of Meyerhold*, pp. 151–2.

21. Rudnitsky, p. 495.

22. Braun, p. 152.

23. Tsvetaeva admired George Sand and translated *L'Aiglon* after seeing Bernhardt's performance. Pasternak, who called her a 'woman with a practical, masculine mind . . . decisive, militant and indomitable', believed she was almost alone in her generation in using a classical style while speaking 'like a human being'. Like Olesha's Yelena Goncharova, Tsvetaeva emigrated to Paris, where she was close to Natalya Goncharova, the scene designer and painter whose 'Cyclist' was an archetypal image of early Futurism. As in the play, the White press made use of Tsvetaeva (a 1928 meeting with Mayakovsky was maliciously misreported). Her husband was prominent in attempts to persuade Russian émigrés to return; he was executed when the family did so, their daughter went to the Gulag, and Tsvetaeva committed suicide in 1941.

24. *Testimony*, p. 85.

25. Gladkov, 'Meyerhold Speaks', p. 17. 'Of course', Meyerhold added, 'it's easier to imagine than to accomplish physically, since it would be hard to find two actors of equal physical gifts, and that's the whole point.'

26. *Testimony*, p. 85.
27. See Boris Filipov, *Actors Without Make-up* (Moscow: Progress Publishers, 1977), pp. 40–42.
28. *List of Blessings*, p. 83.
29. Kollontai, *Autobiography*, pp. 102, 66.
30. See Yuri Olesha, *Envy*, published with Valentin Kataev, *Embezzlers* (Ann Arbor: Ardis, 1975). Esfir Shabs, who had been Meyerhold's secretary, compared life in Russia and the West in her film *Today* (also 1930). Despite her leftism she was accused of a 'relish and admiration for life in foreign countries' and her project *Woman*, which like Meyerhold's trilogy would have contrasted pre-revolutionary stereotypes with Soviet women, was never made.
31. *List of Blessings*, p. 83.
32. *Ibid.*, p. 109.
33. American publisher's notes.
34. Vera Alexandrova, *A History of Soviet Literature: 1917–1964* (New York: Doubleday, 1964), p. 25. Olesha wrote a story, 'From the Notebooks of Zand the Fellow-Traveller'.
35. Remisova in MA Valenti *et al* (eds), *Ustrechis Meierkhol'dom* (Moscow 1967), pp. 436–7. Here cited from Robert Leach, *Vsevolod Meyerhold* (Cambridge: Cambridge University Press, 1989), pp. 71–2.
36. Rudnitsky, p. 493.
37. *A List of Assets*, MacAndrew translation, p. 354.
38. *List of Blessings*, p. 100.
39. Quoted Gladkov, 'Meyerhold Speaks', p. 111.
40. Quoted Schmidt, p. 201.
41. Lee Strasberg, 'Russian Notebook (1934)', *Drama Review* 42.1 (1973), pp. 118–21.
42. Quoted Gladkov, 'Meyerhold Speaks', p. 110; *Novy Mir*, p. 175.
43. Rudnitsky, p. 104.
44. Vyachesla Zavalishin, *Early Soviet Writers* (New York: Praeger, 1958), p. 304.
45. Rudnitsky, pp. 494–5.
46. Quoted Harold Clurman, 'Conversation with Two Masters', *Theatre Arts Monthly*, November 1935, p. 874.
47. Precisely because of their commitment, the Meyerholds could not supply simplistic images, which less alligned directors like Tairov were prepared to do (eg the heroic female commissar in Vishnevsky's *Optimistic Tragedy*).
48. Marc Slonim, *Russian Theatre: From the Empire to the Soviets* (London 1963), p. 328.
49. Friedrich Engels, *The Origin of the Family, Private Property and the State* (London: Lawrence and Wishart, 1942), pp. 61–73; Meyerhold quoted in Clurman, 'Conversations with Two Masters'.
50. Remisova in Valenti, *Ustrechis Meierkhol'dom*, pp. 436–7.
51. Letter to Vsevolod Vishnevsky, 1932. Quoted John Freedman, *Silence's Roar: The Life and Drama of Nikolai Erdman* (Oakville: Mosaic, 1992), p. 151. Stalin did not attend and the play was banned.

52. At the height of *glasnost* Lyubov Rudneva's 'Zinaida Raikh', appeared in *Teatr* 1: 1989, pp. 110–29. Later *Teatr* published a second long piece, memoirs by Raikh's daughter Tatiana. KGB documents emerged and were published in, for example, Edward Braun, *Meyerhold, a Revolution in Theatre* (Second ed., London: Eyre Methuen, 1995). On older, hostile attitudes to Raikh – perpetrated by both Meyerhold's opponents and defenders – see Spencer Golub, 'Revolutionising Women: Iconic Women in Early Soviet Russia' in Laurence Senelick, ed., *Gender in Performance* (New Haven: University Press of New England, 1992), p. 174.

53. Rudnitsky, p. 492. Margaret was played by Straukh, recently seen as his mirror-image Pobedonosikov, the Stalinist bureaucrat and would-be censor in Mayakovky's *The Bathhouse*.

54. Remisova on Meyerhold with the cloak.

CHAPTER 7

Behind the arras, through the Wall: Poland 1989

> I kept reading, surreptitiously plotting. . . I was afraid to think concretely. . . I desperately wanted to do something with my self. Not necessarily in the theatre. It wasn't that I felt professionally unfulfilled, but there came a moment in my life when I wanted to pause. I'd always run so fast, and it seemed, reading it in silence, that *Hamlet* would help me pause. What matters there isn't the narrative but the way of thinking. One day I plucked up courage, I wanted to use the play for my own ends. . .[1]

This time her name was Teresa Budzisz-Krzyżanowska. One of Poland's leading actresses, she played Hamlet in Andrzej Wajda's production in 1989 at the Stary Theatre, Kraków (see Figure 17). She entered, took off her street coat to reveal the black doublet, sat at her mirrored dressing table, and prepared. Slim gaunt face, sad smile, pale hair – aged forty-seven. The small audience was crammed with her behind the stage. They had been ushered inside the actress's private space of thought and withdrawal where, privileged but uncomfortable, they could see their own faces in Hamlet's mirror. A wide scene-door opened onto the stage, the footlights, and beyond that the historic Stary auditorium – rows and rows of empty grey plush seats. Onstage – their backs to Hamlet – Claudius and his Court acted their scenes in a posturing, two-dimensional style to a public who had not come.

I

The woman's room

Hamlet (IV) was rehearsed in the last days of Polish Communism, just as General Jaruzelski's regime gave way to the first Solidarity-led democratic government. In Poland the production heralded the fall of a system; abroad (it toured widely) it stood for the falsity of all despotisms

Figure 17   Hamlet's mirror. Teresa Budzisz-Krzyżanowska in *Hamlet (IV)*, Kraków 1989;
director: Andrzej Wajda. (*Photo:* Wojciech Plewinski).

and the official histories that push conscience into the wings. Half a
century after Raikh's death the actress-Hamlet was again, and less ambiva-
lently, a symbol of the individual conscience in the upheavals of Eastern
Europe. The Kraków audience shared Hamlet's marginalised perspective

from this bare corner s/he would hardly ever leave. They witnessed Hamlet's reactions to others' scenes; and they spied on an isolated, exposed actress locked in a task of self-transformation that paralleled Hamlet's. The audience were privileged eavesdroppers, watching at an unfamiliar angle – as in Meyerhold's theatre – as a woman became Hamlet. This time however the director was a leading opponent of a dying regime, the spectators gathered at a side door as if at a clandestine event, and Teresa Budzisz-Krzyżanowska was one of the finest Hamlets of modern times.

The concept was Wajda's, she explains: 'We were at Berlin airport, and I was very tired that day. It wasn't a great time in my life, and he looked at me from a distance and said, "You know, you should play Hamlet." And I said, "OK, but hurry up. I'm getting old."' In fact she was sceptical: 'I didn't see any reason for it. I told him I definitely didn't want to play Hamlet, because it seemed inappropriate just to show off my acting skills, just to prove I could do it.' So for three years the idea was left suspended but gradually the possibility gained importance for Budzisz-Krzyżanowska as a step in her self-development. Her *Hamlet* became an exploration of truth, lies, and the meaning of acting: 'It's not at all difficult to play a man', she said, 'But the whole production came into being out of love for theatre and actors.' This production was a paradoxical ensemble exercise – paradoxical because Poland's greatest classical company, 'every one of whom could, would like to, and should play Hamlet', had to be persuaded by the actress herself to accept a heavily edited text. Few *Hamlet*s have so honoured the protagonist's subjectivity; external events and characters were little more than Budzisz-Krzyżanowska's cues, and 'the rehearsals turned out to be very heated'.

Everything was subordinated to the concept. The scenes with the Queen, the King, Polonius and Ophelia were very severely cut. It demanded great modesty, understanding and love of the theatre from everyone, it meant discarding one's vanity and it involved very special skills, playing the synthesis of a role rather than developing it in detail. It was difficult to persuade my colleagues (and I took a very active role because I'd become very eager for the production to happen) to play crumbs of parts.

Her performance was animated, sensitive, remorselessly open. Rather than play the character, she nakedly presented herself moving towards identification with it, and the sense of privileged intimacy was astonishing and confrontational; it would have been unimaginable before Grotowski.

Here the stock reception problems of earlier actress-Hamlets did not apply. She never mimicked masculinity. This was never 'he' (Hamlet), always 'she' – Teresa Budzisz-Krzyżanowska exploring the limits of her art. The audience saw her 'make herself' Hamlet while he 'makes himself' the time's scourge. Any gap between her and Hamlet – she was not quite plausible in the backslapping *camaraderie* with Rosencrantz and Guildenstern – only reinforced the parallel between her quest and his. This was Hamlet in the making, an enquiry into the act of self-transformation. What follows are notes, made immediately after the performance.

Ghost Scene: A blackout and an ear-splitting roar, a terrifying close encounter with another reality. No 'Swear!' from the Ghost, only that electric noise. In the aftermath, the room was in total darkness – except for the square of bright bulbs around the actress's mirror.

The Regime: On the public stage – rich Renaissance costumes plus a mix of stock groupings and vivid images – Claudius was crass and bullish, Gertrude was inert, and Rosencrantz and Guildenstern crawled from sacks. Polonius, though, was gentle, breathless and worried – charming in his donnish regret at Hamlet's bad poetic style, thoughtful recalling his own love-madness – because Poles knew first-hand that service to an autocratic regime didn't necessarily destroy all one's humanity. Political truth was uncomfortably complex. Polonius crept in like a kindly but intrusive doctor while TBK/Hamlet lay drawn and exhausted on a couch. She was nervous, didn't play with him at all: there was a moment of lighter energy at 'Words, words, words' (spoken leafing through her *Hamlet* script) but the description of old age and degeneration disturbed her. She hugged smug Rosencrantz and Guildenstern with unselfconscious warmth, sharing her inmost thoughts even when she realised they were spies. They dressed like her, but had nothing else in common. She exposed her pain with total frankness.

Theatre: TBK's Hamlet was physically generous in ways male perform-ers might have found difficult. She was ecstatic to hear of the Players, perched on the dressing table, parodied actors she'd seen. The actors were a tiny group in modern dress; their leader was her close friend and fellow-spirit. Their world was tactile, benign and self-mocking, alert to all forms of falsity, not least their own: the First Player had heard 'Speak the speech' so often that he sent Hamlet up and she laughed at her own pomposity. She leant on his shoulder and praised actors, the chroniclers of *our* time. Alone, she ventured onto Claudius' stage and shouted 'Oh what a rogue and peasant slave' into the empty house, but recognised her own self-pity.

She ran desperately back, struck her reflection, hammered at the table, then clamped her hand over her mouth, forced herself to stop and to think. Gradually, she saw that she must make the world she lived in – this echoing cavern, this theatre – a political weapon, her medium for truth, as theatre in Poland had been for two centuries.

Hamlet retreated into another private room even the audience couldn't enter, then re-emerged for 'To be or not to be'. It was beautifully spoken; she began as she watched Ophelia, then sat head in hand like countless sacred statues of the Man of Sorrows – the 'Polish Christ', the sacrificial tragic thinker. In this space behind the Stary stage a real blacked-out window opens onto the city. Hamlet gazed out: could s/he escape? No: the script of *Hamlet* was in her hand. Paralleling this, Ophelia (Dorota Segda) stood in the mirrored entrance to Claudius' stage, then reluctantly entered Hamlet's, straying from the regulated theatre of paternal power for the first time in her life. It was only in the two intimate scenes with other women that TBK's gender seemed foregrounded: she tried to bring them both alive.

Hamlet, arms crossed, was enraged by this young woman's lisping and ambling. Yet their intimacy was extraordinary: they seemed aspects of one person as TBK, an older self, lashed passive Ophelia with bitter wisdom till Hamlet lost control, hacked the air. Ophelia seemed uncomprehending and left, but suddenly she returned and yelled 'O what a noble mind is here o'erthrown' *at* her persecutor. TBK's Hamlet, maybe uniquely, was delighted as Ophelia's suppressed fury burst out. Ophelia could not break free – she retreated from Hamlet's space and her speech regressed into a stock soliloquy – but the staging stayed radical: Hamlet listened to her and to Polonius and Claudius plotting by the footlights, and Ophelia began to rip the pages from the Bible that the politicians made her hold.

Media: Hamlet drew a curtain to reveal a video monitor – Horatio and the audience would watch Claudius in close-up. Hamlet's praise for Horatio's calm was heartfelt – *her* skin was excruciatingly thin – and TBK sat Ophelia in the mirrored doorframe, the no-man's-land between truth and lies. Hamlet paced everywhere and the bawdry seemed to startle the actress herself as out-of-character lines burst from somewhere deep down. No dumb show. Hamlet closed in on Claudius, talking of poison, anxious for a sign. The sign was minimal, but the video camera caught it: the King's hand clenched behind his back. He rose, cueing a welter of reactions, including farcical embarrassment as he and Gertrude collided with their Player doppelgangers. Gertrude, bewildered, stared at her child who – happy, not hysterical – crooned the rhymes like pop songs.

Mirrors: the core of Teresa Budzisz-Krzyżanowska's performance was a series of moments where Hamlet confronted the others face to face, only for them to retreat, incapable or terrified of matching her honesty. Now Wajda showed why: remorse is savage. Claudius was onstage kneeling by a lifesize crucified Christ, bellowing his guilt and thrashing his naked back. Sword in hand, Hamlet studied the ruler's face in the monitor, shouting her own lines ('Now might I do it pat') across his. The scene was not about Hamlet's 'failure' to kill but the monstrosity of totalitarian guilt: she looked into his masochistic, posturing mind, and stepped back, reluctant to emulate it with murder.

Claustrophobia: Hamlet covered the monitor; opulent tapestries blocked out the stage. The Queen entered Hamlet's space freely for, at long last, confrontation. But there was a sudden roar from behind the curtain, like Claudius' minutes earlier; TBK registered the awful stupidity of what she must now do even as she drove her sword two-handed through the curtain. Hamlet believed that this act of violence, this violation of her own respect for life, was the climax to which everything had been moving – the tyrant's assassination. She held on, mouth open and eyes clamped shut. She imagined her victim's agony – and when she discovered Polonius she collapsed. There was more horror as the Ghost's noise returned. Gertrude tried to caress and comfort her child but Hamlet stared in her eyes, forcing Gertrude to share her knowledge.

Polonius' death was catastrophic. At last Hamlet had committed the unnatural act, but with obscene consequences, achieving nothing. From this point on, life slowly drained from Hamlet. There was no manic chase. She reached down for the sword, but Claudius entered. The regime's force was overwhelming. TBK ran a hand through her hair, her voice congested with sobs and spasms of mirthless laughter. For the only time, Claudius and Hamlet were alone together: the actress seemed physically defenceless, expecting an attack, but Claudius gestured gently. Tyranny could wear benign masks. So Hamlet kissed his hand: 'My mother'.

Martial music. Male choir. The actress watched as armoured men filled the stage to create a canvas of European militarism. Fortinbras was a black-plumed warmonger, ranting in stage smoke. Hamlet was enraged by the war and gestured at the stage/battlefield/graveyard. As Rosencrantz and Guildenstern summoned TBK onto it, Ophelia entered the abandoned dressing room. Her song mingled with the war's.

For three Acts, Hamlet's conscience had been the brake on history. In the Prince's absence, Wajda hacked cinematically through the text. Darkness: the uproar of a *coup*. Lights: Laertes' sword was at the King's throat.

Claudius forced Laertes against the mirrored door-frame of rudimentary self-consciousness, where he dropped his sword . . .

Ophelia tugged her wild hair, her thumb in her mouth. She sat at Hamlet's mirror, half-listening and half-reading letters which she screwed up, chewed and spat. Hamlet's words were her flowers. She inherited Hamlet's confrontational role; she literally spewed and hurled accusing gobbets of text, and before she left for the last time she too stared through the window into the street. She rubbed the glass . . .

Laertes and the hectoring King attacked Hamlet's room. Claudius waved a prop sword, fantasising Hamlet's murder. But it was Ophelia's body that her brother brought in. The Queen remained alone with Claudius. She stood inert. He dragged her off by the hand . . .

A hand poked from a trapdoor, waving a leafy twig. A graveyard pastoral. But no Ophelia had a starker burial than this, carried in Laertes' arms. And few Hamlets have been more moving here than Budzisz-Krzyżanowska, who was shattered, gasping for air, by this latest revelation of the consequence of her actions. The small room split: Horatio and Gertrude helped Hamlet to the window; Claudius bellowed to his wife to follow him. As Hamlet told how Rosencrantz and Guildenstern died, TBK kept drifting towards unconsciousness. Horatio held her up, tender as a nurse, made shushing sounds, cooled Hamlet's neck with a damp cloth, tried to keep her calm, tried to keep her talking because to speak was to live. Hamlet could hardly stand, but must meet Laertes' challenge . . .

To appreciate *Hamlet (IV)* fully, it is necessary to consider the nature of the theatrical collaboration that produced it, and also *Hamlet*'s specific significance in Poland.

II

Hamlet: some part of Poland

What kind of evil is presented by King Claudius? . . . What is the need of this play in our present time? . . . Is it a play which will drug the audience, make it indifferent to the events of contemporary life with all its conflicts, or will it arouse in the audience a protest against negative powers? (Michael Chekhov, 1942[2])

Hamlet was first staged professionally in Poland in 1797, two years after the liquidation of the Polish state. Its leading actor Wojciech Bogusławski had been involved in the Kościuszko Insurrection whose defeat led to the division of Polish territory between Russia and the Austro-Hungarian Empire, and the suppression of the Polish language. Hamlet became a symbol of the Polish struggle for identity and was remodelled by the Romantic poet Adam Mickiewicz as Konrad, the protagonist of his patriotic dramatic epic *Dziady*.[3] Both characters were then reworked by Polish playwrights from the turn of the century to the 1980s in a continuing self-conscious debate about the nature of subjectivity and freedom in a repressive state. In 1904 the Symbolist Wyspiański – admired by Craig – argued that *Hamlet* was so relevant to Poland's tragedy that it should be staged in the crypts and chambers of Wawel, Kraków's royal castle. This was a founding statement for modern Polish theatre because it demonstrated how classical culture could be made 'contemporary' and local, and because it established the idea of the site-specific environmental production, where the history of the performance space would itself be part of the meaning of the event.[4] The relevance to *Hamlet (IV)* is obvious. In 1956, Krushchev's denunciation of the crimes of Stalin triggered a renaissance in Polish theatre, including the Stary Theatre production of *Hamlet* starring Leszek Herdegen which Jan Kott discussed in 'Hamlet After the Twentieth Congress', later a key chapter in *Shakespeare our Contemporary*. In 1956 Hamlet was the modern intellectual, brooding on political and existential freedom in a world controlled by self-perpetuating power structures. Kott welcomed that Stary *Hamlet*'s 'terrifying clarity': 'This interpretation was so suggestive that when I reached for the text after the performance, I saw in it only a drama of political crime... Hamlet is mad, because politics is itself madness, when it destroys all feeling and affection.'[5]

Hamlet was a template as Polish theatre showed how Shakespeare's plots commented on the traumas of the twentieth century. In a totalitarian context, Hamlet's death as he overthrows tyranny made the play's flash of hope both inspirational and oppressive; the concepts of freedom and tragic determinism ruled each other out, and philosophical paradoxes mirrored political ones: Khrushchev proclaimed the thaw and crushed the Hungarian uprising in the same year. After Auschwitz and the Stalinist decade that followed, Polish theatre inevitably made Claudius's regime a tyranny and Fortinbras an ambiguous liberator: 'What matters', Kott wrote,' is that through Shakespeare's text we ought to get at our modern experience, anxiety and sensibility.' In Poland, 'Shakespeare our contemporary' meant Shakespeare as collective self-examination, and the obvious relevance of the Histories and Tragedies was a cultural lifeline that offered scope for coded commentary on the present situation: *Hamlet*,

Measure for Measure, Richard III and *Macbeth*, all studies of the emergence of state repression, were used to confront Eastern Europe's cycles of autocracy and terror.

Polish women writers kept some distance from this national myth-making but there was a strong tradition behind the foregrounding of female consciousness in *Hamlet (IV)*.[6] Budzisz-Krzyżanowska's Hamlet became a 'male' national icon when she assumed the pensive attitude of the Polish Christ, but she was a 'female' icon in an opening image of bereavement: before the play began, she sat still and remote under a black veil – 'It was a sign of mourning', she said, and 'the feminine element.' Before her transition into Hamlet, she was Grief – evoking the deaths and exile of fathers and sons through Polish history that demanded strength and leadership from the women left behind. The national symbol Polonia denotes a feminine concept of nationhood, and during *Hamlet (IV)*'s rehearsals Wajda actually rushed to Warsaw because of a political crisis, saying 'The Motherland's in danger.' The woman in mourning black and the female freedom fighter (like Emilia Plater, honoured in Mickiewicz's poetry for her part in the 1831 Rising) were common cultural images: Budzisz-Krzyżanowska's Hamlet evolved from one to the other. The dressing room became the Private Sphere, opposed to the stark actuality outside the window and the martial fantasies of Claudius' arena.

Such allusions were important in 1980s Poland. A secret Party memo criticised Wajda as someone who imagined 'he has the right and the possibilities to apply the standards of humanism and morality to the problems of the world without having to resort to Marxism'.[7] He was increasingly at odds with the censors and 'the real problem', he wrote, 'is how to conceive of a work that will render them inoperative.' Now. The historic role of women in the Polish intelligentsia was signified here too. Wajda was drawn to classical theatre where political comment could be encoded and, equally important, complexity explored: 'I never touch those texts; I don't try to "improve" the scenes; I do not change a word of dialogue; I never adapt. For weeks on end I read and reread the text with the actors, firmly believing I will find an answer. . . These analytical rehearsals, carried out in peaceful surroundings, give us a better chance of understanding the mysteries of *Hamlet*.'[8] Theatre 'taught me to tell the difference between what is natural and what is true. Theatre is the art of form. The imitation of life, which is essential for the cinema, did not suit its purposes. Theatre takes place both on the stage and in the auditorium; the two indispensable elements are the actors and the audience.'⁹ In the case of *Hamlet (IV)* we are in a position to study the process of collaboration between director and actress.

Wajda's Hamlets

Wajda first directed *Hamlet* at Gdańsk in 1960. He partly drew his interpretation from Wyspiański's study, believing the allusion would connote contemporaneity, but coolly. On a conventional proscenium stage, elegant scaffolding broke up the space: sometimes characters drew curtains to hide in solipsistic boxes, sometimes the action was simultaneous with all Society on display. Then in 1980 Solidarity made symbols redundant. Wajda's film *Man of Iron*, with Jerzy Radziwiłowicz as a Gdańsk shipyard activist and Krystyna Janda as a dissident filmmaker, fused fiction and *cine verité*: Lech Wałęsa appeared at their imaginary wedding. But Wajda also chose this moment to stage two new versions of *Hamlet* for the Stary Theatre. First they performed 'Scenes and Soliloquies' at Wawel Castle to honour Wyspiański's vision of it as a play for a free Poland, then the same cast opened a full version at the Stary in November 1981. Two weeks later, Martial Law was imposed. When *Hamlet* re-opened four months later, Fortinbras's soldiers patrolled the stage, coldly eyeing the audience like the militia on the streets.¹⁰ Despite the clampdown, in June 1989 democratic elections produced a Solidarity-led government under Tadeusz Mazowiecki; Wajda became a Senator, and in July the Kraków premiere of his fourth *Hamlet* closed the Martial Law era just as his third unwittingly began it.

Wajda has said that the key to both film-making and innovative theatre is '*the idea*', which the director must provide and which ensures 'the general becomes specific, the abstract concrete, and the idea incarnate as human drama.' *Hamlet (IV)* was unusually rich in simple and brilliant 'ideas'. The title itself evoked Pirandello (*Enrico IV*), drew attention to Wajda's avowedly inadequate attempts on the play over thirty years, and suggested ideas of theatrical succession and continuity. *Hamlet (IV)* originated in Wajda's personal responses to four outstanding artists – a Russian balladeer, an emigré poet in Harvard, a Japanese female impersonator, and a Polish actress – all brought into collision through an English Renaissance text.

As the Cold War world died, the Stary Theatre offered glimpses of a new postnationalist Shakespeare, intensely local yet cosmopolitan, which scrutinised the phenomena of theatre and the creative process. Firstly the production was a response to the Russian singer and poet Vladimir Vysotsky. He played Hamlet for the Moscow Taganka

Theatre in the 1970s and his verse gave discontented Russian youth a voice in a stagnant period; in a 'hard epoch', as his director Yuri Lyubimov said, Vysotsky 'managed to sing freely': 'Moscow buried him like a national hero.' The critic Elżbieta Baniewicz, reviewing an evening of Vysotsky's poems and songs in Warsaw (1989) and revelling in the growing freedom of speech, praised him as 'an artist brave enough to speak – some years before the *perestroika* – about the great tragedy of his nation'.[11] But Wajda's response to Vysotsky was personal. In 1980 Wajda 'saw Vysotsky play Hamlet for the last time in his life. . . He was dying from the effort. I hugged him after the performance and cold, deathly sweat was pouring off him. He died a few weeks later.'[12] For Wajda, Vysotsky's death gave the play and 'To be or not to be' new meanings: it meant 'to last to the end, to bear the part's pressure. To play it to the end. To survive.' Wajda became fascinated by the courage and self-exposure involved in playing Hamlet – 'coming out onto the stage, coming out to the audience'– and this became both a metaphor for personal commitment and an act of endurance in itself: *Hamlet (IV)* would be about the high cost of integrity both within and beyond a theatre's walls.

Wajda planned it as a collective laboratory experiment: 'I have never seen a *Hamlet* that worked completely', he wrote. 'Why? Because art is about limitation, elimination, choice and *Hamlet* is a picture of life itself. I can't direct it, just as I can't direct my own fate. I can only confront it.' It followed a series of brilliant Dostoevsky adaptations where Wajda increasingly stripped the novels down to a series of claustrophobic emotional duels. *Nastasja Filipovna*, his version of *The Idiot*, retained only two characters, Mishkin and Rogozin, who confronted each other while the corpse of Nastasja lay in another room. It was an event in 'real time': performances began in private before the audience were admitted and the actors were free to improvise. Having tried to synthesize the spirit of a novel into one eavesdropped incident, Wajda wished to re-examine *Hamlet* using similar Poor Theatre techniques of focus and elimination: how much text is necessary? He contacted the emigré poet and former activist Stanisław Barańczak to translate. His poetry had exposed the distortion of language under totalitarianism and he left for America after Martial Law. Originally Wajda asked him to translate only fragments of *Hamlet*, five soliloquies, so that in the most private moments Hamlet would speak with Barańczak's modern voice (cf Meyerhold's planned clash of Tsetayeva and Mayakovsky). The other characters would use an antiquated translation that seemed as false as the State discourse

Barańczak deconstructed.[13] Gradually, however, Barańczak wrote more and more; Wajda told him, 'I'll be juggling the fragments I got from you. I like surprises, difficulties, unexpected things.' He felt the play was a collage – 'Hamlet's greatness lies in a mystery that's hard to solve. It's an awkward work with huge gaps'– and the only way to stage it was to reconstruct it from its heart: 'Any consistent and uniform concept fits this play, which is life itself, like a saddle fits a cow.' He told Barańczak, 'The whole thing will only come into being with the actors', and indeed in rehearsal the text reasserted itself: the production became less mono-logal and Barańczak translated everything. In fact he went on, despite illness, to translate all Shakespeare's plays. For commercial and diplomatic reasons Hamlet (IV) was first seen widely in America after a single Polish performance.

After Vysotsky and Barańczak, the third influence on Wajda was the Japanese Kabuki actor Tamasaburo Bando. In March 1989 Wajda directed the Dostoievsky in Tokyo, but this time Nastasja appeared alive – doubled with the 'idiot' Mishkin.[14] Wajda found it instructive to work with an actor trained in onnagata; it strengthened his wish to use Hamlet to inves-tigate difference and the acting process – 'Hamlet is an actor', he said, 'a human being in disguise.' To quote Budzisz-Krzyżanowska, 'He was fascinated by Tamasaburo Bando: "What a phenomenon, how great!" He showed me photographs and said, "If it's possible for a man to play a woman, why can't a woman play a man?" ' For the fourth factor behind Hamlet (IV) was Teresa Budzisz-Krzyżanowska herself.

III

Hamlet in the mirror: Budzisz-Krzyżanowska

She was born in 1942. She made her debut in 1964 and was soon cast as Juliet. She joined the Stary Theatre in 1972 and was equally powerful in the Romantics, Chekhov and Kurt Weill. Wajda told Barańczak, 'I think she's the most gifted actor in Poland,'[15] and though he was not at first especially interested in cross-gender in itself, he wanted to work with her. Budzisz-Krzyżanowska, however, believing that playing Hamlet would be pointless in a 'conventional, classical production', established her creative independence. She knew Wajda was 'fascinated' by Vysotsky but she had not seen his Hamlet and 'I didn't relate to it particularly. To tell the truth and though it sounds immodest, I didn't want to know about other Hamlets.' Again, after Tokyo Wajda wanted her to concentrate on trans-sexuality, to 'play a man', but she responded much more to his idea that *Hamlet* should be a chamber-piece where the audience would watch her taking on the role, spy on her preparations and consider the gaps between the character and herself. Acting – her acting – became in effect the subject of *Hamlet (IV)*. Wajda: 'In front of the dressing-room mirror, the soliloquies are confessions of doubt. . . not just Hamlet's, but the Actor's playing the role.' What was that role through her eyes?

The audience of about a hundred crammed backstage; Budzisz-Krzyżanowska joined them unexpectedly:

Sometimes I entered across the empty stage, sometimes I came in with the spectators, mingling as if I were one of them. The production's structure allowed for improvisation and generally depended on the psychophysical condition of the evening, on one's imagination, one's ideas, the pitch of thought. It was just alive.

She wore her own hat and fawn coat: 'I fought to be able to come in wearing my own ordinary clothes. I wanted to defend my privacy and my thinking about the role. I didn't want to enter as a character but as myself.' She sat at the mirror: 'Changing into Hamlet, the attempt even to fit my body into the role, was a separate *étude* in itself before the performance began.' 'In a word, it will all be to do with Theatre. . . The actor is the body through which the lifestream of the dramatic character flows', Wajda said: 'The gender doesn't matter'. But it did matter to the extent that an actress in her forties was reinventing herself as the most famous male role in all drama – in Kraków the female Hamlet became the quintessence of Theatre. Budzisz-Krzyżanowska covered her head with the mourning veil; then 'A gong announcing the start took me by surprise, emotionally naked, because it was as if I'd crept in secretly, testing whether I could play Hamlet, and suddenly I was caught. And I had to do it.' She was almost never allowed to rest because the spectators saw Hamlet between Shakespeare's scenes: it was an encounter with the committed actor, caught in the nightly offstage drama for which Shakespeare supplied no guidance. 'They breathed with me. It was simply impossible to lie.'

In total contrast to the brute King (Jerzy Gralek), Budzisz-Krzyżanowska's Hamlet was astonishingly sensitive and responsive, and when other characters entered her space they were forced to play more intimately and reveal their secret selves. The production respected cinematic acting in close-up and mocked stage histrionics. Cinema became a metaphor, and more – watching Claudius on the monitor, the audience saw *exactly* what Hamlet saw, as if through his/her eyes. Budzisz-Krzyżanowska:

This approach not only demanded that I act but also that I observe everything and sometimes even direct it, because everyone's behaviour depended on me. I couldn't afford one moment of psychological laziness. It was fantastic but at the same time exhausting - sometimes it slipped out of my hands terrifyingly as though someone else's hands were on the rudder. It was very personal, though I hope it wasn't exhibitionistic.

For many spectators the unrelenting intensity made *Hamlet (IV)* a psychodrama; yet while it remorselessly explored the creative isolation of acting, for Budzisz-Krzyżanowska it also explored theatre *as community*. Because theatre had been the symbolic mouthpiece for Polish identity for so long, especially under Martial Law, the Players' arrival was crucial – they demonstrated how authentic communities can survive within a false society. Their leader (Jan Peszek) was a balding intellectual with a carpetbag – and a fawn coat like Budzisz-Krzyżanowska's. He was presented as a great tragi-comic actor (which Peszek was) and (unlike Shakespeare's) a master of cinematic understatement. The 'Hecuba' speech was close to his heart; he and Hamlet knew each other intimately so he teasingly downplayed his admiration for her acting till they fell laughing into each other's arms. After this warmth, he whispered the harrowing climax in Hamlet's ear.

Peszek was also the Gravedigger. This was not conventional doubling, it alluded to Martial Law when protesting actors boycotted the mass media: 'The First Player later becomes a gravedigger, just as Krzysztof Kolberger became a waiter and others taxi drivers', she explained. It 'had a special meaning at that specific moment. We tried not to make these contemporary allusions too blatant. . . but it seemed necessary then.'[16] *Hamlet (IV)* drew on the audience's immediate memories in its exploration of authenticity and conscience. 'The whole production', Budzisz-Krzyżanowska said, 'came into being out of love for theatre and for actors. There were moments we invented ourselves that were only possible in this company where we'd performed together for decades.'[17] The Polish audience were aware of the actor as well as the role, so that for instance, Krzysztof Globisz was not only Hamlet's ally Horatio but also the actress's 'young, talented' friend – supportive (he was the assistant director) and 'eager to help an older female colleague', as she modestly described herself, 'playing a role I can't really carry. Here he comes to help me, with a great deal of tolerance and understanding.' But the production could also joke about the company's internal politics: Hamlet caught Globisz/Horatio reading Budzisz-Kryżanowska's lines, dreaming of being the Prince. And the Stary building became part of the play for if Denmark's a prison, Poland was a theatre. The key images were the dressing-room mirror, the video screen and the familiar architecture, from the echoing auditorium to the blacked-out window that Budzisz-Krzyżanowska opened: 'You could hear the noise of the traffic, singing, drunks, arguments, footsteps. It was impossible to pretend that something separate was happening in here, it had to correspond to the reality outside. Of course I could close the window if it became too obtrusive, and I tried to enter my own world, to cut off, but it was a clear sign that everything was happening here and now.'

Pirandello-like, she played herself playing Hamlet but with such emotional intensity that the boundaries of truth and acting blurred. She made Hamlet profoundly compassionate and criticised the usual treatment of Rosencrantz and Guildenstern: 'The boys playing Hamlet expose these fellows so unpleasantly, with all their superior knowledge. I've always thought the scene is about true friendship. Hamlet should try everything to preserve this friendship, to protect them from degradation. Only a woman could do that.' Gender was not an issue for most Polish critics, whereas when she toured in the West she met a general assumption that her motives for playing Hamlet lay in feminist or gay sexual politics: 'Everyone was concerned with the fact that a woman was playing a man – not with *what* she was playing.'[18] Organised feminism was distrusted in '80s Poland because of the role of women's organisations within the Communist system. For Budzisz-Krzyżanowska, playing Hamlet was a private exploration of the Actress' life-experience, and a response to her own sense of time passing.

Yet for her the fact that three women were playing the key roles in *Hamlet* became the heart of the event. During rehearsals a complex relationship developed between Budzisz-Krzyżanowska, Dorota Segda (making her debut as Ophelia) and Ewa Lassek (Gertrude) who was one of the Stary's most respected older actresses but was very ill. Three generations of actresses, three approaches to theatre: 'Ewa Lassek played wonderfully but – intentionally – in an old-fashioned way, defending her dignity. I took my own wild, intractable route, and the youngster acted with her eyes wide open, wanting to learn.' If the basic concept, reversing *A List of Blessings*, set Old (Communism) against New (dissent), the three actresses developed a meditation about age and knowledge. When

Gertrude entered Hamlet's dressing room (reversing Shakespeare's dynamic) the Queen and the febrile figure in black moved in and out of each other's trust; the scene movingly reprised earlier key motifs and emotions. At the premiere, the shocked recriminations became an overwhelming 'fight for life'. 'Ewa acted beautifully but as it were too truthfully. I virtually had to hold her up. She was apologising to me on stage, with tears in her eyes, for being unable to carry on.' Ewa Lassek was only able to play that one fraught performance and died soon after, but her painful contribution echoed the Vysotsky story and indeed Teresa Budzisz-Krzyżanowska's own commitment. She herself had to fight physical problems to play the part and found that key scenes, like Ophelia's burial, strained her heart.

The Queen was recast. The younger Dorota Pomykała took the part on without notice and the joint self-exploration so crucial in rehearsal was lost. But even watching *Hamlet (IV)* with Pomykała, it seemed that this Hamlet was the guardian of Gertrude's conscience and of Ophelia's potential – both of them semi-comatose and swathed in layers of clothing. Hamlet awoke them but at unknown cost: the girl ripped apart her father's book; Gertrude tottered slowly out, supporting herself with a white stick. And though this triptych deepened the drama, Budzisz-Krzyżanowska remained cut off.

I tried not to see the audience. The mirror helped me enormously, the very ability to look into your own face as you speak opens amazing possibilities: 'What do I think? What do I do?' So the mirror had multiple meanings. I rarely looked at myself as a woman in it, but this had great significance for me in the scene with the skull and Hamlet's 'Let her paint an inch thick; to this end she shall come.' That was me in the mirror.

Hamlet placed the skull on the dressing-room table as a *momento mori*, having finally found eyes that did not flinch from hers.

Her response to *Hamlet* focused on a 'stark, contemporary' phrase in Barańczak's version of 'To be or not to be', which she paraphrased as: '*We halt for a moment and lose purpose, and the moment grows into a long, meek life of sufferance.*' 'I revolted against this one verse body and soul. Yet so often you must do something so ugly that the price may be too great.' She underlined consequences. When her attempt at assassination killed Polonius and Ophelia, Hamlet was destroyed: 'You commit an act for the good of others – "Cleansing wars! Make it better for the next generation!" they say, "So let's slaughter each other now!" It's all futile. The moment Hamlet commits the act – which is *horrific* to him – he puts himself at risk. Psychologically and philosophically speaking and in the best of faith, he commits an act against himself.' From the moment of Polonius' murder, her appalled Hamlet began to die, fighting like Vysotsky to the end: 'The emotional explosion over Ophelia's grave took me to the verge of a heart attack. Hamlet's death isn't caused by a poisoned sword – that's all histrionics, out on the stage. It's a true death, simply from exhaustion, from the terrible effort which living is, which each performance is. One should play every performance as though it were one's last.' In Wajda's film *Danton*, another Martial Law allegory, Gerard Depardieu pushes his voice till it becomes hoarse and cracks as Danton shouts for his life; similarly Teresa Budzisz-Krzyżanowska showed the physical price of integrity, and life and art plagiarised each other: the company were shocked when, just before the premiere, Mazowiecki took office as democratic Prime Minister and collapsed in front of the television cameras.

The duel was fought on the regime's terms – on the main stage. The combatants moved in and out of the spectators' limited vision. Breathless, half-confused, Hamlet somehow sensed something was wrong with the pearl . . . But then Laertes, contemptuous of subtlety, stabbed her in full view. In this version Hamlet's real enemy was time, and finally the body almost failed the will. As Hamlet stabbed, Horatio held the King fast, and it was Horatio who despatched him: solidarity. Hamlet stumbled to the seat by the window and Horatio slid the great iron fire-door shut. In the sealed room the sound quality changed; their quiet voices almost drowned the noise of Fortinbras' army: death brought privacy. As Horatio prepared to leave and bear witness, clutching Shakespeare's text, Fortinbras entered and the Stary offered one last *coup de théâtre*. Fortinbras was Jerzy Radziwiłowicz, the hero of *Man of Iron;* in Act IV he had been a ranting warmonger, but now Radziwiłowicz was himself – another modern actor in a fawn coat, stepped in from a Kraków street. Unrecognisably thoughtful, Fortinbras seemed re-tempered by Hamlet's suffering. He crouched and talked to the body just as Hamlet confided in the skull.

And Hamlet stood up.

Budzisz-Krzyżanowska walked briskly out. Suddenly, on the main stage Claudius was alive again celebrating his coronation. This cyclic vision seemed Absurdist but was not: Radziwiłowicz took off his coat, and revealed a black doublet; he sat at the mirror and spoke Hamlet's opening lines. As the Cold War world disintegrated outside, the Stary Theatre argued that though all victories against the lie are provisional, each man and woman must at some point be prepared to be Hamlet, to marry action with conscience and attempt a role that draws them to the brink. Whereas the actress-Hamlet lay forgotten at the end of *A List of Blessings*, in Poland in 1989 Fortinbras learnt from her integrity, and at the so-called 'End of History' a line of ethical succession carried on.

IV

Sable revolutions

Budzisz-Krzyżanowska was not the Communist bloc's only female Hamlet of 1989. However, Siegfried Höchst's production with Cornelia Schmaus at the East Berlin Volksbühne that February spoke from *within* the official discourse, and with some bewilderment. Höchst's *Hamlet* drew on local traditions (Schmaus' Prince had a Berlin accent) exploring the sociological realities of East Germany, where gender equality was enshrined in the founding constitution but women, expected to join the labour market, were also still tied to the domestic sphere. This was known as the 'double burden', prompting the saying 'Our mummy is also a man': thus Marianne Wünscher played Polonius, smoked cigars, and cooked meals in a pan. S/he was a uniformed Goering-figure: Höchst evoked a genre of East German drama from *The Good Person of Setzuan* to Manfred Karge's *Man to Man* which insisted that gender was inseparable from economic and political factors. In Karge's monodrama a woman assumes the identity of her dead crane-driver husband in the Depression and 'is' him for the rest of her life, but in the process commits war-crimes for the Nazis. Brecht and Karge historicised the concept of men and women's interchangeability – they celebrated their heroines' resource but demonstrated the brutalisation that 'being a man' in the twentieth century entailed. Gender was socially defined and therefore packed with contradictions. In the Schmaus *Hamlet*, when the Ghost appeared – also played by an actress – revolutionary figures marched past: 'Marx and Engels, Rosa Luxemburg, Marianne, Christ, a nude (womankind as revolutionary potential?). The Ghost is placed among the public figures of world history, who posthumously remind their sons of their duty.'[19] In a nostalgic flashback, the Prince was a child walking hand-in-hand with Old Hamlet, both in heroic armour; but the present-day Ghost was a pathetic figure in a suit – and whereas the everyday reality of the street promised progress in the Polish *Hamlet*, it signified decay here. In the last months of the GDR, *Hamlet* was a Marxist memory-play where the framework still looked intact but 'from world history to psychoanalysis, everything is topsy-turvy'.[20] 'Some things' *Shakespeare Jarhbuch* commented, 'are emotional, some aggressive, some satirical, but there is no unity.'[21] Laertes' weapons were rapiers and petrol-cans. Elsinore was in decline, disfigured by cages and withered trees.

In this over-determined framework reviewers found it hard to read Cornelia Schmaus' Hamlet. She sat in a hole in the armour-plated floor wagging her feet in the air, and 'cheekily' rattled through 'O that this too solid flesh would melt.' Schmaus played a 'high-spirited' non-conformist in a fedora: 'Sometimes calm, sometimes hysterical, always rebelling, someone who knows how to draw a pistol or pull a bottle of schnapps from a rucksack'. Yet elsewhere she seemed 'forced into the conventional Hamlet figure . . . whom we have not seen for a long time: the aristocratic youth swathed in black, slim, noble, melancholy' – 'ideal' but incapable 'of seizing the wheel of power with his small hands'.[22] Whereas Budzisz-Krzyżanowska's personality was central to *Hamlet (IV)* Schmaus's casting seemed accidental. One German critic complained because the concept was not explained in the programme and put it down to the failures of a hierarchical theatre structure: 'The theatre couldn't produce a male actor equal to it.' It was 'as if the theatre wanted to say, "It's true we don't have a Hamlet, but Schmaus imitates one so well you won't see the difference." This is a terrible pity; of course one wants to see the difference.' In 1989 the female Hamlet suggested transformation in Poland; in the GDR his/her ambiguous gender embodied slippage and crisis. Hocht hinted at sexual anarchy (Hamlet seemed to have slept with Horatio, Rosencrantz, Guildenstern, Ophelia, Gertrude and maybe the Ghost) and in his postmodern staging ('Much is hinted at without being confirmed in the course of the evening or leading to consequences. Central issues are left obscure, we remember what's peripheral') a female Hamlet was merely one of a gallery of alienated figures and inconsistencies.

In contrast to East Germany's highly conceptualised directorial theatre, the Stary tradition was actor-driven. Only the last scene of *Hamlet (IV)*, when Budzisz-Krzyżanowska left the stage, invited allegorical readings, and then the result was contentious. The fact that responsibility for change passed to a man, Fortinbras/Jerzy Radziwiłowicz, exactly recalled Wajda's cinema, for the same actor fulfilled the same function in *Man of Iron*, taking over from the radical filmmaker played by Krystyna Janda whose work has exposed the regime. In *Hamlet (IV)* Budzisz-Krzyżanowska's video screen turned television (a Party propaganda tool in Poland) into an inquisitorial eye and made the audience share the woman's gaze. Yet she disappeared, just as Janda's character became secondary in *Man of Iron*, going to prison and bearing the hero's child. This gendered transfer of agency unwittingly foreshadowed complaints that despite the key role of feminist groups in the Velvet Revolutions, the post-communist systems actually marginalised women in Germany ('You can't make a state without women'), Czechoslovakia ('When we were dissidents, the men needed us') and Poland ('Polish democracy is masculine democracy').[23] For example, in 1991 Poland's Under-Secretary for Women was forced from office because she opposed the Church over reproductive rights, and the post was abolished; next year it was claimed that Hanna Suchocka only became the country's first female Prime Minister because of her opposition to abortion. New gender battles would be fought.[24] Yet it was typical of this complex moment that in *Hamlet (IV)* the final appearance of Radziwiłowicz/Fortinbras/Hamlet also carried personal meanings that had nothing to do with politics and everything to do with the exploration of theatre, fate and time. In 1975 the great Stary director Konrad Swinarski was rehearsing *Hamlet* when he died in a plane crash. 'The Hamlet was Radziwiłowicz', Budzisz-Krzyżanowska explained, 'It looked as if it would be a revelation. He was perfectly prepared but he never had the chance to play it. Never. The fact that *he* comes on at the end to take on that role, in Kraków, in the Stary, was a code the audience might find unreadable, but it moved us all.' When Wajda first offered her Hamlet they were based in Warsaw, but she was only interested in playing it with the Kraków ensemble – 'All the director's ideas were filtered through our own vision.'

'I remember Wajda's fantastic remark at one point: "Don't show me what I know."' But in a theatre accustomed to months of rehearsal, *Hamlet (IV)* was put together in only five weeks because it was 'presold', as she put it, to America and the festival circuit: 'I was convinced that we'd take ages to work on it, and in fact it was sad that it happened so quickly. To tell the truth, the first performances in New York weren't good, because we were terribly under-confident, I felt too shy to act. I hadn't yet found myself in there. I was a little afraid it would be shallow, absurd, that no-one would understand my intentions, that I'd be accused of exhibitionism.' And *Hamlet (IV)*, rapidly mounted, soon disappeared from the repertory because it could not survive in the market economy it heralded. With its tiny audience it was a deficit production, only possible in the old system of total subsidy. The last performance was at the Festival of European Culture in Kraków, advertising Poland's fitness to join the West. The cast were disappointed, but despite the ambiguities Teresa Budzisz-Krzyżanowska felt *Hamlet* had taught her many lessons, especially concerning the relationship between thought and feeling: 'Emotion comes through reason and not only through the skin.' Alone and unseen at the end of the performance, she often looked into a mirror before applause intruded:

It's an appalling sight when actors take off their make-up facing the dressing-room mirror. It's like death. And that's how I wanted my Hamlet – in a theatre, playing for my life. I can't specify the moment when I felt it made sense. The meanings are so rich that every night you can discover new things. And that's how it grew with me. Until I decided I could try it forever.[25]

Notes

1. Teresa Budzisz-Krzyżanowska in interview. Translated by Barbara Bogoczek. All quotations from the actress are taken from this conversation at the Dramatyczny Theatre, Warsaw.
2. See Alma H Law, 'Chekhov's Russian (1924) Hamlet', *Drama Review* vol. 27 no. 3 (Autumn 1983), pp. 34–45. See Zdenek Stribrny, *Shakespeare and Eastern Europe* (Oxford: Oxford University Press, 2000). *Hamlet (IV)* was greeted coolly in Poland, partly because political events seized the attention, but the journal *Dialog* (no. 6, 1990) published an extensive analysis.
3. In 1968 a Warsaw production of *Dziady* was banned as anti-Russian and students took to the streets. The protests grew and for a time the Government was shaken in the Polish version of the events in Paris and Prague.
4. See Josephine Calina, *Shakespeare in Poland* (Oxford: Oxford University Press, 1923).
5. Jan Kott, *Shakespeare Our Contemporary* (London: Methuen, 1964), p. 51.
6. Poland's finest female playwrights included Maria Dąbrowska, Gabriela Zapolska, and Maria Pawlikowska-Jasnorzewska whose satire on Hitler, *Baba Dziwo* (which turned him into a woman) was attacked by the German embassy. The Nazis invaded the day it was due to open in Warsaw. In the 1950s the director Izabella Cywińska pioneered the development of innovative theatre forms within a socialist agenda.
7. Secret files published in Andrzej Wajda, *Double Vision: My Life in Film* (London: Faber and Faber, 1990), p. 120.
8. Wajda, *Double Vision*, p. 115. From the Stary programme for *Hamlet (IV)*, which printed extracts from his correspondence with Barańczak. Translated by Barbara Bogoczek.
9. *Ibid.*, p. 117. Poland's three great quasi-Absurdist dramatists all reworked the Hamlet motif in their most influential plays, all of them reducing the women on the whole to sex objects or symbols of lost idealism. Tadeusz Różewicz's

The Card-Index (1960) focuses on a bedridden Everyman-Hamlet bound and confused by the postwar welter of doubts and loyalties. In both Witold Gombrowicz's *Marriage* (1953) and Sławomir Mrożek's *Tango* (1964) the new Hamlet overthrows his parents but graduates into despotism. Gombrowicz makes him a soldier returning home in 1945 while Mrożek's is a sullen student who never leaves home at all but in both, Freudian fantasies become Stalinist terror: Gombrowicz's new Hamlet mutates into Richard III and Mrożek's intellectual dances the tango in a murderer's arms. Fortinbras – who sacrifices thousands to seize 'some part of Poland' – became menacing, from Zbigniew Herbert's poem 'Fortinbras' Elegy' to Janusz Głowacki's 1980's black comedy *Fortinbras Got Drunk*, where Norwegian agents devise the Ghost.

10. Two years later Wajda's Stary *Antigone* was an allegory of Polish history since 1944. The Chorus became returning partisans, Party bureaucrats, student protesters and finally the shipyard strikers of Gdansk. See Maciej Karpiński, *The Theatre of Andrzej Wajda* (Cambridge: Cambridge University Press, 1989).

11. *Le Théâtre en Pologne/Theatre in Poland* (September 1989), p. 6.

12. Wajda in a letter to Stanisław Barańczak, printed in the Stary *Hamlet (IV)* programme. Translated by Barbara Bogoczek.

13. This experiment built on the fact that when Wajda's 1981 *Hamlet* visited Rome, Jerzy Stuhr spoke the soliloquies in fluent Italian.

14. Wajda had used cross-gender playing before; he cast an actress as a male theatre manager in Wyspiański's *November Night*, and the climax of *Marriage Blanc* by Tadeusz Różewicz (Yale 1977) is an act of sexual self-transformation: an adolescent girl takes control of her identity by shearing off her hair and declaring she is her own brother. The first used drag as comic disguise; the second, confrontational nudity.

15. Letter, Stary programme.

16. It was not the first *Hamlet* to refer to the actors' boycott and Solidarity. In Janusz Warmiński's 1983 version (Warsaw Ateneum), Denmark was a paranoid modern dictatorship and the dignified Players were led by Jan Świderski, one of Poland's greatest stars.

17. She insisted on playing it at the Stary – even though she and Wajda were both based in Warsaw – because of its ensemble spirit.

18. Some Polish reviewers, reluctant to discuss the politics, complained that Wajda's secular emphasis belittled 'the tragic', but Urszula Bielous, for example, praised the actress's, achievement ('light, effortless' and 'without a shadow of falseness') as she exposed 'the pain of self-knowledge': Urszula Bielous, *Le Théâtre en Pologne/Theatre in Poland* (March-April 1990), p. 6.

19. Maik Hamburger, review in *Shakespeare Jarhbuch* 126 (1990), pp. 191–3. Translation by Kirsten Ludwig. See Michael Hattaway *et al*, *Shakespeare in the New Europe* (Sheffield: Sheffield Academic Press, 1994). Then George

Tabori directed his wife Ursula Höpfner as Hamlet in Vienna, where s/he was seen by *Theater Heute* (August 1990) as a crushed but declamatory 'mother's boy' manipulated by Rosa Krantz and Gilda Stern.

20. Cf. the East German playwright Heiner Müller's *Hamletmachine* where Stalin became an irremovable character in the postmodern *Hamlet*. Höchst used Müller's translation of *Hamlet*.

21. *Shakespeare Jarhbuch.*

22. *Ibid.*

23. Quoted Barbara Einhorn, *Cinderella Goes to Market: Citizenship, Gender and Women's Movements in East Central Europe* (London and New York: Verso, 1993), p. 148. See also Nanette Funk and Magda Mueller (ed) *Gender Politics and Post-Communism* (NY and London: Routledge, 1993) – especially Małgorzata Fuszara, 'Abortion and the Formation of the Public Sphere in Poland' (pp. 241–52) and Ewa Hauser *et al*, 'Feminism in the Interstices of Politics and Culture: Poland in Transition' (pp. 257–73). In 1989, a new East German feminist movement led by the Independent Women's Association questioned both totalitarianism and patriarchy's role in it. The Association was instrumental in devising the new post-communist Social Chapter.

24. Women formed 23 per cent of the Polish parliament in the early 1960s; the percentage fell to 13 per cent in 1989 and 9 per cent in 1991. However the first post-communist cultural minister was a woman, the director Izabella Cywińska: in 1990 she made a keynote speech on Anglo-Polish relations, 'A Little Patch of Ground', invoking Wajda, Brook and *Hamlet*.

25. *Hamlet (IV)* was recorded, broadcast and sold as a videotape. The moment was not lost.

CHAPTER 8

Hamlet from the margins: Spain, Turkey, Ireland

Shakespeare is not an English writer – he's a confrontational writer.
Fiona Shaw 1993[1]

Have you heard the argument? Is there no offence in it?
Hamlet III. ii. 212

Hamlet (IV) was unique because of the alliance of Catholicism and radicalism in 1980s Poland. The distortion of religious images by Claudius emerged as both blasphemous and totalitarian while Hamlet's dressing-room soliloquies took on qualities of the confessional and a Solidarity enclave. It was interesting to see what happened to the female Hamlet when the Church was inseparable from the power of patriarchy and the State. Or where the country was not Christian at all. In Spain, Turkey and Ireland over nearly fifty-five years, several iconic modern actresses played the Prince.

I

Spain 1960: the image of a murder

In spring 1960 Nuria Espert, aged 25, played Hamlet in Barcelona, directed by her husband the writer and actor Armando Moreno. One of the first productions of their independent company, which would be the most famous in Spain within a decade, this *Hamlet* was a civic event, staged in the open in the Teatro Griego amphitheatre at Montjuic Park. Nuria Espert was the first major female Hamlet of the postwar era. The fact that a young working-class actress with Leftist connections was appearing cross-dressed as Hamlet in the repressive climate of Franco's Spain was inflammatory, and Espert's performance was greeted as an outrage by groups of right-wingers. 'It created a massive scandal', she recalls, 'because it was not acceptable for a woman to take this male role':

They were barracking from the very start. In fact as soon as I appeared on stage. I remember the exact moment. Ramon Duran playing Claudius said, 'And now, my cousin Hamlet and my son', and as I (Hamlet) replied, 'A little more than kin and less than kind', the audience began to shout. Only a section were yelling, but from the stage it seemed the entire theatre was against me . . . I thought to myself, 'Now when the audience stop shouting I'll have to start speaking and I'll have no voice.' But of course I did, what else can you do.[2]

At the first interval the crowd split between jeers and support and 'at the final curtain there was tremendous applause mixed with frantic abuse from a section of the audience, each side trying to drown and silence the other.' Afterwards Espert's *Hamlet* toured with growing success; 'The best performance', she felt, 'was in Oropesa, in the palace of the Papa Luna on a moonlit and windy evening.'[3] It continued to challenge the play's safe status as a canonical Renaissance classic: while Espert defamiliarised Hamlet's gender, Moreno's *mise en scène* mixed historical periods and in Spain, as in Stalin's Russia when classicism was disrupted, *Hamlet* came into focus as a study of contemporary dictatorship and dissent. Fratricide had deep political resonance in Spain.

'Haply a great man's memory may outlive his life half a year': *Hamlet* in the old Republican stronghold of Barcelona could wake memories of conflict: in 1940 Franco had the Catalan president Lluís Companys killed in Montjuic Castle close by the amphitheatre. After the Civil War, Spanish theatre 'acquired an important place in the social life of the country,' as a guide published under Franco said. It was required to project a condition of well-being 'as a counter-balance of simple escapism and fun to the miseries of the fratricidal struggle'.[4] To guarantee 'escapism', the regime policed rehearsals and performances while censors suppressed criticism of the government, army and Church (over forty scripts Espert submitted were banned). Catalan-language theatre was made illegal till 1946 and playing-spaces were politicised: before the Civil War, open-air performances for the people by groups like Lorca's La Barraca had spearheaded the Left's educational agenda; under Franco, amphitheatres and civic spaces were programmed with festivals and monumental revivals of classics honouring conservative traditions and 'spiritual need'. Nuria Espert made Hamlet abrasive, 'a stubborn adolescent, wilfully amazed by his mother's impending nuptials, sullenly seeking amusement by teasing those around him'.[5] In the context of Franco's long dictatorship her Prince was triply deviant – the individual conscience fighting collective amnesia, the impatient spirit of 'sixties youth, and an actress, Nuria Espert, rejecting gender roles that – as her later brilliant Lorca productions insisted – tried to shackle Spanish women to motherhood, domesticity, and Christ. Espert's cross-dressing offended against propriety – she knew there had been a scandal when Ana Mariscal recently played Don Juan – and injected tragedy with carnival. When Espert played Hamlet she estranged Shakespeare, reminding audiences of its themes' enduring relevance: surveillance, the suppression of democracy, the poisoning of relationships, and the gulf between the disarmed liberal conscience and a revelling, complacent nationalist elite.

   Hamlet served notice that Espert's career would be confrontational and in her words 'swim against the tide'. She was unhappy with the production and her own performance and the attacks so demoralised her husband that he gave up directing: she went on to introduce plays which were polemical, morally outrageous in the Spanish context, and shattered the spectacle of 'normality'. She played many passionate transgressive women forced by family and a prison-society into prostitution (Sartre's *The Respectable Prostitute*, O'Neill's *Anna Christie*) or self-consuming violence (including *Medea, Mourning Becomes Electra, Yerma, The Maids*). As Shen Teh/Shui Tah, the prostitute/businessman in *The Good Person of Setzuan* (1967 – one of the first Spanish productions of Brecht), she indicted the manufacture of gender norms and the price of survival. Espert also had a provocative sense of history: by playing Hamlet she revived memories of Margarita Xirgu (1888–1969), the great Republican actress for whom Lorca wrote many of his plays, including *Yerma* (whose premiere was disrupted by fascist violence). Xirgu was in exile from the outbreak of civil war in 1936 until she died six years before Franco; in 1938 she played Hamlet in South America, after investigating the role for years. Xirgu had worked on Shakespeare with Spanish students at Stratford-on-Avon in 1933 – she was an inspired teacher – and her Hamlet especially drew young people. Maria M Delgado describes it as 'a mercurial feminisation of the agonised prince' that gave 'the angry rivalry with his dead father. . . an Oedipal dimension' – as radical as Bernhardt's because of 'the ambiguously sexual nature of the Hamlet/Ophelia encounter' and 'the repositioning of the Gertrude/Hamlet relationship away from a simplistic male reverence and fear of the maternal body'.[6] When Xirgu played Hamlet, the Civil War was still raging, Lorca (whom she called the hope of the theatre) was murdered, and Guernica was a graveyard: Shakespeare became a front-line report from Europe. The fifty-year-old star made Hamlet the voice of articulate resolution, just as she made Cervantes' *Siege of Numantia* an epitaph for the Republic; she was called 'a symbol of Spain in exile and the purest tradition of its theatre'.[7] A generation later Nuria Espert in turn became 'the emblematic opposition artist of the Franco era for the international theatre community'.[8]

Espert consciously emulated 'the Xirgu myth' and worked to uphold her memory, substantially erased from official histories. Both were working class, trained in the amateur theatre, and made sensational debuts aged eighteen. Espert played many parts associated with her predecessor including Hamlet, both embraced surrealism, and both were ardent leftists: in the mid-1930s Xirgu campaigned for political prisoners, in 1970 Espert demonstrated on behalf of suspected ETA terrorists. Above all both were actresses of rich intensity. For Lorca Xirgu embodied theatre's contradictions, a 'cool and rational' actress who 'hurls fistfuls of flame': 'I see her always at the crossroads.' Espert called herself 'an extreme actress', using 'the strongest edges of my character', yet as Delgado notes, 'a steely intelligence has infused all her roles.'[9] Their appearances as Hamlet took on sharp political meanings and the fundamental difference was historical: Xirgu played a mature Hamlet in exile as the Falange triumphed, Espert's prince mocked a geriatric regime that had ruled for a lifetime. *The House of Barnada Alba*, Lorca's study of Spanish women's choices when the authoritarian shutters slammed down, also connected their careers: Lorca wrote it for Xirgu shortly before his murder and Espert chose it as her first directing project. Its first and last word, 'Silence!' is of course the last word on Hamlet's lips: when Xirgu spoke it in 1938 it was a protest against the onset of fascism; in 1960 silence was entrenched, but not forever.

Having politicised gender as Hamlet, Espert played many women who defied oppressive definitions of themselves, and the body became her subject. In her theatre psychological intensity pushed the voice towards tormented music and movement towards dance, and *Hamlet*'s structure, progressing through numbness to bloody catharsis, anticipated her most famous peformances, where she drove towards climactic scenes of physical frenzy and ambiguous release. Yerma and her fellow-victims thrashed in a vast womb-like membrane; as a sexual outlaw in *Divine Words*, she rose skywards on a phallic organ-pipe; and in both Espert used her own nakedness to express the torment of denial and the ecstasy of revolt. It was the extreme but logical development of her first re-evaluation of the hidden female body as Hamlet's.[10] With Franco's death, Espert became an influential cultural presence and she challenged Shakespearean tradition again in 1983 by doubling Prospero and Ariel, patriarch and androgyne. She took the study of regulated identity and revolt into new postcolonial areas and tried, she said, to examine her own 'feminine tics without adopting masculine ones'.[11] The cast performed two versions, in Castilian and Catalan, the language Franco banned from the stage, and Espert's *Tempest* showed again that Shakespeare's conflicts, ontological and social, are written on the body and shape language itself. 'These our actors' are bounded not just by 'sleep', but by history.

Most female Hamlets emerged in contexts of intertextuality, where *Hamlet* is part of a common but disputed culture and haunts the intelligentsia's imagination. S/he registers tectonic shifts in the politics of gender and culture, but in this chapter we are looking at artists with a more distant or equivocal relationship with Anglo-Saxon theatre. On Shakespeare's map Spain is alien territory and South America a testing ground for utopias, peopled by monsters; Ireland is a pit of civil violence which English kings fail to tame and which exports chaos, from York's armies in *Henry VI* to Macbeth's mercenaries; and for Othello, Turkey is 'malignant' Negation: 'Are we turned Turk?' In some societies the plays are 'Other' yet as Shakespeare became a global twentieth-century presence, women played Hamlet in countries where the texts were relatively unfamiliar. Exploring the 'female' in Hamlet does not always mean what it meant in Victorian England, and the qualities released in Hamlet's vendetta by a diva known for Medea or *Blood Wedding* could be quite different from those where 'the actress's Hamlet' is Hedda, the essence of self-repressive waste. Like Espert and Xirgu though with different agendas, actresses in Turkey and Ireland for example used free adaptations of *Hamlet* to interrogate gender assumptions and probe the facade of the patriarchal State.

II

Turkey 1976: Hamlet's dance

Metin Erksan's Turkish film *Angel of Vengeance* or *Lady Hamlet* (*Intikam Malegi/Kadin Hamlet*, 1976) broke every rule of Shakespearean cinema. To European (and many Turkish) eyes it is a bewildering cross of Shakespeare, the avant-garde, and low-budget exploitation cinema; it adopted *Hamlet*'s plot but modernized it as freely as Turkish cinema remade many English-language hits from Audrey Hepburn comedies to James Bond. Some major directors investigated rural poverty or the problems of the urban working classes but more made action thrillers, musicals or – increasingly in the mid-seventies – softcore sex comedies, and *Lady Hamlet* has elements of them all. It is a modern-dress melodrama of blood, corruption and broken hearts, starring the popular actress Fatma Girik (b. 1942) as Hamlet – a strong woman seizing revenge.

One hundred and seventy-three Turkish films appeared in 1976 and directors were hungry for plots. The open form of English Renaissance drama was often compared to Turkish folk theatre, and because of the strength of the Family the Elizabethan revenge ethic could translate with a directness and even relish inconceivable in modern Britain. There was another striking affinity with Shakespeare's world: until 1923 Turkish theatre was all-male. It had been a place of Islamic segregation, women and men could not attend together, and when the first trainee actresses entered drama school in 1918 – the school itself was only four years old – there was public outrage. They were forced from Istanbul. Actresses were only accepted in 1923 when the modern Turkish state was created and Atatürk, the Republic's founder, prioritised women's rights: 'The weakness in our society lies in our indifference towards the status of women', he said: 'A society one half of which is incapacitated is a half-paralysed society.'[12] He insisted (1923) 'We have to believe that everything in the world is the result, directly or indirectly, of the work of women,' and in a country with 90 per cent illiteracy this depended on education: 'Turkish women must become the most enlightened, virtuous and dignified in the world.'[13] Atatürk demanded changes in legal rights, manners and dress to combat what he called Islamic 'bigotry' because the seclusion of women made Turkey a 'laughing stock': they 'ought to show their faces to the world, and they ought to look on the world with their own eyes.' Monogamy, divorce and equal inheritance rights were introduced and in 1934 women gained the vote. In 1976, when *Lady Hamlet* was released, Tezer Taskiran celebrated the fact that the current ministers of health and culture and the vice-president of the National Assembly were all women: 'Turkish women', she claimed, 'feel a debt of gratitude to Atatürk.'[14] Maureen Freely wrote twenty years later, 'Feminism in Turkey isn't anti-men, it's anti-tradition.'[15] It was unexpected but understandable that the least inhibited of all transgender *Hamlets* should be Turkish.

Shakespeare was introduced into Turkish culture within Atatürk's programme to create a secular literature. In the 1930s Shakespeare appeared on Turkish popular stages in such versions as *The Mad Prince* (*Hamlet*) and *Revenge of the Arab* (*Othello*); within 25 years Shakespeare was called Turkey's leading playwright.[16] There were arguments – was this the colonisation of Turkish culture, or did the appropriation of Shakespeare demonstrate the Revolution's cultural strength? – but Laurence Raw notes the official tendency to speak of Shakespeare as 'universal', and in *Angel of Vengeance* 'Universe' is Hamlet's family name. Fatma Girik's dynamic Hamlet relates to a long line of strong, often cross-dressing, folk heroines. They turned *Hamlet* into a low-budget melodrama punctuated with songs, a dance, and scraps of Fellini; it was a bravura celebration of female strength and began and ended like a spaghetti western. In 1961 in Ankara, *Hamlet* was staged respectfully in English Renaissance dress but by 1976 it was the tale of a Turkish daughter battling local corruption. Filmed mostly in bright sunlight with bold acting from everyone, especially the flashing anger of Girik herself, it had nothing to do with canonical North European conceptions of *Hamlet*, but it returned revenge to its roots and was much more considered than it sounds.

Shakespeare's *Hamlet* begins with unease, *Lady Hamlet* opts for action. There is no mystery. We watch the assassination as bulky, grey-bearded Kasim Bey shoots down his astonished brother Ahmet in a forest; guitars twang, Ahmet resembles Lee van Cleef. A folk lament resounds as his coffin is carried though the trees, followed by Kasim Bey's thugs in cheap suits and by Fatma Girik's Hamlet. She moves like a sleepwalker, her face impassive but puffy with grief. Her hands hang limp. Far from every Hamlet stereotype, she is an amply-built woman, no neurasthenic, in a black trouser suit and with long loose black hair. There is a grave's-eye-view of the descending coffin, then Kasim Bey (played by Reha Yurdakul) gives a politician's speech, his husky voice modulated and calming: 'The most difficult speech is in front of a grave . . . The murderer will be caught. That day will be a terrible day.' The camera picks out Hamlet and her mother: 'I'll try to lessen their unbearable grief.' Suddenly there is a shock-cut to Kasim roaring with laughter in distorted close-up. It's an *al fresco* wedding party, all flags, drink, and disco. Like the unpredictable camera angles this is one of Erksan's basic devices – abrupt mood switches, usually launching new scenes with a disorienting close-up, to suggest something of *Hamlet*'s range and Girik's alienation.

The nostalgia for a lost Herculean Father which saturates *Hamlet* made the play resonant. Mustafa Kemal, who founded the modern Turkish state by military force and took the name of Atatürk – 'Father of Turkey' – was systematically mythicised after his death so that later leaders lived in his shadow or tried to wrap themselves in his name: 'There was a sense of anti-climax when ordinary and lesser men took over the reigns of power.'[17] *Lady Hamlet* is set in 1975, on an estate in an undeveloped part of Eastern Turkey where within living memory there was a tradition that widows marry their husband's brother. Claudius becomes a *derebey* ('valley lord') a landowner with no legal authority but quasi-feudal and hereditary powers. In total contrast Fatma Girik's Hamlet is an educated modern woman who has been studying theatre in America (where her uncle has his own contacts, in organised crime) and everything about her bespeaks personal liberation, from her clothes – a different outfit in every scene; she only twice wears a dress instead of trousers – to her demeanour. Outdoing Shakespeare's prince, she lounges, smokes cigars and walks on tables, yet always with total authority: she seems middle-aged, no younger than her mother. Girik, moreover, was the first star to play Hamlet in a substantially gender-*reversed* version: that is, Ophelia becomes a man who drowns himself for love. He is Orhan, a sensitive boy bewildered by Hamlet's sense of purpose; already isolated from each other before the Ghost scene, they are first seen by the broken jetty of a deserted lake:

ORHAN: I can't live without your love. If you leave me I will die.
HAMLET: I can't give you love but only sorrow.
ORHAN: Let me help you.
HAMLET: No-one can help me.
ORHAN: Accept life as it is.

– which is what Girik's Hamlet will not do.

She is dynamic, bitter, but never detained by self-doubt. The Freudian tradition does not exist in this film. She refuses to marry, even for love, and is devoted less to family honour (as Orhan's brother is) than to her private bond of memory with her Atatürk-like father. She commands the plot: scenes are shuffled to empower her, so whereas Shakespeare's Claudius and his spies constantly lay traps for Hamlet, here the reverse is true. Little surprises her. But she is an alien in a backwoods fiefdom, she has the freedom to wear trousers, but not to be heard – summed up in the surreal image of her in men's evening dress, orating 'To be or not to be' into an empty field. 'Changes in clothing styles and social behaviour are only secondary issues in women's liberation', Atatürk said, 'The main struggle must be the search to acquire knowledge' and this is Girik's quest.[18] At the wedding party Hamlet wears a man's white suit with a red tie and red pocket handkerchief (red is a political symbol throughout, though it also denotes death and sex). She leans against a tree, studying the party from a contemptuous distance and smoking a cigar. She idolises her father and despises her mother, though she seems to identify with them both and feels tainted: 'My father loved my mother as I love you', she tells Orhan: 'She acted as a beast in heat.'

'If women are debased/The whole of humanity is degraded', wrote the poet Tevfik Fikret in one of Atatürk's favourite verses, and Girik-Hamlet echoes Atatürk's ambivalence towards the Turkish Mother: 'The highest duty of women is motherhood', he said: 'We have been educated by our mothers and they have done the best they could. But our present standards are not adequate.' Hamlet's mother, however, is *self*-degraded, she is not the victim of poverty or prejudice. She – and Rezzan and Gul, the female Rosencrantz and Guildenstern – are corrupted by Westernisation or have corrupted it (a central unresolved question) by embracing materialism at any cost, becoming hedonists and sex-objects. Hamlet scorns her mother's Dior glamour. Most of the film's performances work within the frame of realism, except for the two fathers – Hamlet's is operatic, Ohran's is revolting – and Girik herself. Hamlet is strangely stylised; she snaps between extremes of rage, hauteur and taunting whimsy; her lips purse or snarl, and her wide, staring eyes never blink. Hamlet makes herself artificial, weaving slow rhetorical gestures and speaking in an over-enunciated voice which proclaims she is always acting, will not 'accept life as it is'.

The effect of *Lady Hamlet* was inseparable from Fatma Girik's public identity and the political climate. Girik was born in Istanbul in 1942, and made her breakthrough with *The Stain* (1958). During the sixties she became one of Turkey's most popular actresses, typically as an indomitable rural bride or young mother fighting poverty and domestic slavery. By *Lady Hamlet* she had over 160 film credits. Girik won best actress awards in Turkey and abroad for such films as *The Whore's Daughter*, *Hot Land*, and *Pain* (1971) which she made with Yimaz Güney just before he was imprisoned for his communist sympathies.[19] The director of *Lady Hamlet* was equally eminent: Metin Erksan, a former film critic, directed his first feature in 1952. *Dark World*, an exposé of rural conditions, was harassed by the censors but established Erksan as one of the first distinctive voices of Turkey's emergent cinema. *Hamlet* had particular point in Turkey because of its history of coups and the frequent failure of democracy; but the arts' attitude to military power was not clear-cut. When in 1960 the army deposed a 'corrupt' government to restore Kemalist principles, it had wide support, introduced a reformist constitution, and liberalised the arts. Erksan's place as a national figure was consolidated when his *Waterless Summer* (1964) won the Berlin Golden Bear. It was Turkish cinema's first international recognition. He explored realism and personal symbols; his ability to reach diverse audiences and to offer social criticism while winning Government approval defined his prolific, controversial achievements through the 1960s.

However, increasing social turbulence and frustration made serious film work difficult. In 1971 the military imposed martial law in many provinces: strikes were banned, human rights suspended, and hundreds of intellectuals were jailed. In 1973 a coalition government under Bülent Ecevit (a journalist, poet and translator of TS Eliot) offered hope for reform, though Ecevit had to assume the militaristic image of a Turkish leader by invading Cyprus. He was out-manoeuvred by the Right and, in a period of spiralling crisis and minority governments, fascistic groups began a terror campaign, and civil unrest broke out. An extreme National Front government imposed draconian censorship (while pornography grew to over half Turkish film output in 1977) and the campaigning realism that made Erksan's name was curbed. Thus Girik's Hamlet comes home to a world which has regressed into parochial violence; power is in the hands of a parody of her father, and she alone keeps the past alive in her heart.

The film is as secular as Atatürk would wish. The Horatio figure points out that spirits are 'symbols' and the 'supernatural' only intrudes in response to Hamlet's angry protest, 'We don't even know who killed my father.' By a stockade at midnight, the Ghost appears in a scarlet-lined cloak and a cloud of smoke pierced by spotlights. Swept by a shrill wind and stabbing her fist at the camera, Hamlet embraces her 'destiny' in a forest watchtower: 'I knew it. . .I'll follow him to hell.' With the Ghost she for the first time shows her capacity for love – 'My dear father. . .Poor father. . .I'll always listen to you . . .I'll never forget you' – but she is implacable: 'I promise your revenge will be great!. . .Your blood will be paid in blood.' A sudden zoom and we are back in bright sunlight as Hamlet, in cream and crimson, returns to the graveyard with her Horatio and the worker-guards. They swear an oath, linking hands on the headstone: 'Ahmet Evren: 1920–75'. There were muffled echoes here: it was in 1919–20 that Atatürk achieved the military successes that led to the Turkish state; *Angel* mourned the gulf between contemporary politicians and the founding generation, but not so overtly as to interest the censors. This is popular narrative, clear and unambiguous: 'Know only that his murderer is among us.'

'It is necessary', Bülent Ecevit said, 'for us to give up claiming that only intellectuals know what is best.' If people rejected reform, he claimed, it was not because of their backwardness but because they saw 'the reformists were alienated from them'.[20] This is reflected in the film's style. Erksan tried to build bridges by making a populist film from sophisticated material. The gulf between intellectuals and the people is also a key theme. Just before taking a bus, apparently to be a guest-worker in Europe, Orhan's older brother Osman tells him he and Hamlet are incompatible because of class: 'She is rich and from a different world.' The brothers are dignified country people but Osman is wrong; Girik's Hamlet puts her privileges to use: mixing with the people, she is an intellectual who acts instinctively, an artist fighting lies. She is an advertisement for Westernisation whereas her enemies embody its decadence. This leads to Erksan's central invention, a running debate about the purpose and strategies of art; in 1970s Turkey the 'antic disposition' became a series of weird charades.

Girik's Hamlet uses performance to disconcert. Orhan is a painter and in her first 'mad' scene she interrupts him painting a landscape. She signals 'lunacy' with pop eyes, splayed-out hands, a dancing step, stage whispers, and an air of confiding secrets to idiots. She comes to Orhan in a scarlet uniform, dressed as a nineteenth-century bugler. He assumes she's going to a costume ball and asks to paint her, so Girik gives him guidelines for Turkish art: 'Seek the truth: people have an outer and an inner face. Try to see what is hidden. . . Research the meaning of words you think true. Don't be afraid for your mind, you won't lose it.' Orhan's landscape is bad: 'You painted what you saw.' She throws red paint over it. After the Artist, Hamlet lectures the Spectator. Now disguised in ancient armour with plumed helmet, gold breastplate and sword, she finds her mother and uncle asleep; she wakes them with a banshee shriek, whirls her sword and darts between them wielding a shield-like mirror: 'Mirrors show the outer face of people but they have an inner face.' The mind contains angels and devils, she tells them: 'Can you see your inner face? Don't be afraid, that kind of mirror has not been invented. If it were the world would be a different place.' She smashes the glass and bows. Her terrified mother (played by Sevda Ferdağ) is convinced of her insanity, but not Kasim.

He and Hamlet inhabit opposed locales. Her space is the watchtower with an Olympian view of the woods. The air is free there yet she is trapped, always seen in extreme close-up, pacing so restlessly the camera cannot keep up. She hugs the timber in anguish. Meanwhile Kasim Bey calls councils of war in a white vaulted room, sterile but expensively furnished. In the first, everyone debates Hamlet's condition: she is having a breakdown (Orhan), needs her educated friends (her mother), or is plotting (Kasim). Orhan's father dismisses her as 'crazy!' but changes tack to suit his boss. Though the brothers are played naturalistically, their father is a cartoon creep, the modern politician bending his opinions to get promotion. He volunteers to find Hamlet's secret and stumbles into a piece of surreal theatre: in her third 'mad' scene Girik mocks her mother's sexuality. She plays a vamp in a tangerine nightgown, lounging on a bed and smoking as she reads ('words, words') poems and listens to an old Turkish song, 'The Grave', on a psychedelically painted horn gramophone. The bed is in a field. She tells the politician honest men are so rare today that she looks forward to the grave: 'You're a pimp.' Typically, he applauds. Hamlet laughs, having trailed the red herring that she is infatuated with 'handsome' Orhan. Erksan reverses Shakespeare's narrative to give her the initiative, so now in the white room the clique hear her love letter, which seems more sincere than in Shakespeare: 'Words cannot explain my feelings. I love you. Remember this.' They send Orhan to her but he has no idea what awaits him.

Erksan cuts to Hamlet's frenzied face. She is conducting Shostakovich's dissonant score for the end of Kozintsev's *Hamlet*. She unleashes her rage in a fantasy catharsis. First we see Girik, in a tailcoat, trousers and bow tie, then unmanned instruments, then a tape recorder: the crescendos come from a scratchy pirate tape. The film's music is self-conscious. Her uncle and his cronies are linked to American pop, fragments of indigenous Turkish tunes evoke her lost father, but Hamlet turns to the USSR. Girik convulses, her arms flail and her hands are claws. Orhan arrives as she accepts a storm of applause from an invisible audience and yells 'To be or not to be' into the camera, turning it into a passionate political tirade aimed at the cinema spectators of 1976: 'Should man's mind accept tyranny or revolt against it?' She mimes killing herself and dismisses Orhan ('If you marry take a stupid wife. . . Intelligent wives know that their husbands will make them into monsters') and she sums up the liberal tragedy – which is *not* hers: 'It's intelligence that makes man a coward' – but admits the cost of her commitment:

ORHAN: I had such dreams.
HAMLET: I also lost my dreams.

She sheds one tear. Girik's is a Hamlet with passions but no interiority; not only is 'To be or not to be' turned into a political harangue, it's the only Shakespearean soliloquy kept in the film. Just once she speaks her secret thoughts as a voice-over when her mother's and uncle's freedom from conscience amazes her ('How they sleep, their conscience is clear. . . I'll make life hell for them') but otherwise her face is blank. This is not to say she lacks complexity; she is tormented by the need to know the truth, and Kasim Bey's triumph makes her despair: 'I should never have been born.' But Girik never plays vulnerability or draws the spectator in, for who is entitled to identify with an Angel of Vengeance? Hamlet ignores her anxious mother when she asks, 'Have your bad dreams stopped?'

When her two jet-setting girlfriends – one blonde, one dark – meet Hamlet she turns 'Denmark's a prison' into lampoon performance art: wearing a baggy striped convict's uniform in a cage, she pushes comedy to the edge. Now her endless pacing is tiger-like and she eyes her visitors hungrily. She is caged, she says, 'to make a lie a truth. But *I* can come out.' She does, but after artificial hugs and kisses ('You're the prettiest girl', they tell her) she catches them lying, wags her finger, and re-enters her cage: 'I lost my will to live.' When Rezzan and Gul nervously suggest they put on a play and hire some professionals, Hamlet jumps at it: 'I need two men and a woman.' The casting of women as Rosencrantz and Guildenstern is revealing; Hamlet's friendships are with men, Horatio and the guards, (Turkish women and men should work together 'without misunderstanding or embarrassment' said Atatürk[21]) and she has nothing in common with Rezzan and Gul except gender. She says the body is only 'the envelope'. Though her mother assumes the same upbringing and education must have made them soul-mates, R and G have opted for luxury without ethics or (unlike the older woman) even embarrassment. In Erksan's *Hamlet* male beauty connotes innocence, female beauty corruptibility – Rezzan and Gul accept the plot to murder Hamlet.

Hamlet's fifth piece of guerrilla theatre is by far the most elaborate, because in the Play scene Girik takes centre-stage. Hamlet begins as chorus, in a black robe printed with a pile of skulls; but suddenly Erksan jettisons continuity to Brechtian effect and Hamlet is wearing a bowler hat, trousers and braces – and dancing. She replaces the dumb-show with cabaret. Hamlet's endless pacing becomes a skip, with hunched shoulders, hands in her braces, and a disapproving pout. Rezzan and Gul gyrate behind her in top hats and red, white and blue striped body-stockings like *Playboy* Uncle Sams and on disk a man sings to a plunking piano. The clique are enraged because, starting with a 'strange riddle' about man – '*No-one can solve it./There's a mouth, a nose, an ear,/ But they're all in an odd shape*' – the song becomes satire:

> *How long will the system carry on like this,*
> *Where the fleas swallow the elephants?*
> *A system where a family of seven feeds*
> *On three and a half sesame seeds?*
> *The matter is very complicated,*
> *The writer writes a lot, but it's all gibberish.*
> *Some people believe in prophets*
> *And some wear a watch and chain,*
> *Some people become clerks and write,*
> *And some beg in the street. . .*
> *How long will the system carry on like this,*
> *Where the fleas swallow the elephants?. . .* [22]

The lyric is by Orhan Veli Kanik, a leading modernist who called for 'poems in civilian dress' for the masses: 'New roads, new means'.[23] It was often sung at leftist meetings, and this is the moment when Kasim knows Hamlet is dangerous. Girik mimes walking poshly, stuffing herself, writing, and mindless happiness. She winks and silently brays. And then she is back in the skull robe, formal Chorus to a traditional Ottoman court drama, as if the song were edited in by mistake or indeed never happened. Hamlet's mother clearly knows nothing of the murder but she squirms under the accusing stare of the Player Queen (the leading stage actress Nevra Serezli), the Player King dies screaming with a dagger in his chest, and Kasim Bey walks out. Ironically, though, his conscience has not been caught; the final shot shows *Orhan*'s despair: 'I think we lost Hamlet. . .' Hamlet is tragic because her dedication to her father destroys her ties with normal life; Orhan's tragedy as artist and lover is his blindness.

There is no prayer scene. In the watchtower Hamlet and Horatio share a litany: 'The Ghost was right', 'My idea was right', 'The theatre was a mirror, the killer saw himself.' In black and scarlet, with a Lenin cap, she states her hatred: she could drink his blood and 'Even my dead body will kill him' – which in fact it will. Meanwhile in a round white bedroom with a red bed, men call Hamlet 'A monster!' but her mother defends her and insists they talk. This cues Girik's fifth and last performance, a mirror scene: again Hamlet dresses like her mother and sprawls on the bed. Believing Kasim is in hiding, and much cooler than in Shakespeare, Hamlet demonstrates what murder means: 'I'll show you your inner face.' Forcing her to watch, Hamlet drives a paper-knife through the curtain. When the spy falls into the room with the knife in his stomach (the image of the dying Player King) Hamlet is enraged to be cheated of revenge. She advances on Gertrude with the knife and as they trade accusations there is no ghost, no breakthrough: so Hamlet, hungry for the finale, orders her mother to tell Kasim everything.

This leads to Hamlet's exile to America for her 'safety' and to Erksan's most outrageous sequence. In a white limousine, en route to the airport, the three young women face a five-hour drive and a five-hour wait; so Hamlet proposes a swim. As Rezzan and Gul stroll along a beach in bikinis to the blare of 'Get Up and Boogie!', Hamlet (in bikini plus enigmatic dark glasses) finds the murder letter in a handbag, addressed to a New York Godfather: 'The bearers know the contents of this letter – please give them money.' Hamlet throws their clothes out and drives, leaving them helplessly scampering. There's another shock cut: Orhan lies drowned in the reeds. His brother lifts his body and the action accelerates. Hamlet prepares herself at a rifle range: 'It's time.' Girik's intensity is framed by surreal images – cut-out men, targets and a giant fairground globe. Hamlet learns of the suicide: 'Poor Orhan. Even our love was a dream. Something not real. Like smoke.' Back in the white room Hamlet's murder is plotted. Osman wants to avenge his family's honour publicly but Kasim persuades him to kill her 'Like her father'. Osman's corruption is imaged in distorted shots from below. At Orhan's funeral the gravedigger has no jokes but sings of the shroud awaiting everyone, and when Osman confronts her Hamlet leaps in and cascades dirt over herself: 'Do you dare to die? Go on, bury me with him!' The grave's-eye-view shot from scene two is repeated, but it is Hamlet's perspective now.

Shostakovich returns to announce the final bloodbath. In the forest Osman ambushes Hamlet as he did her father and Erksan stresses physical horror. She staggers away and Kasim, hunting her in dense woodland, mistakenly guns down his wife. He falls on her body in unexpected grief. Hamlet finds him and after a Leone-like slow face-off – she refuses to shoot an unarmed man – she is avenged. Though it has been a private conflict, the end is an open attack on a culture of violence. In jagged slow motion, her white suit bathed in blood, Girik beats her gun to pieces in the rifle range, smashing it with her dying reserves of strength. Atatürk: 'Women . . . ought to look on the world with their own eyes.' The frame freezes on Hamlet's agonised stare.

Westerners did not know what to make of *Angel of Vengeance* and many Turkish viewers thought Erksan had lost his grip. In 1971, when Yimaz Güney's *Hope* pointed towards a new era of political cinema, Erksan had contributed a 'trite' musical, *Undying Love*, followed by a fairy tale. Ostensibly, *Angel of Vengeance* was equally detached from reality and some suspected an attempt to trade on Girik's domestic popularity and Shakespeare's international prestige. But their *Hamlet* was a veiled yet bold response to a period of democratic impotence and authoritarian violence. In most quarters, Shakespeare seemed irrelevant given Turkey's problems and there were no major productions in Istanbul from 1970 to 1981 (*Hamlet*), yet *Lady Hamlet* was given meaning by its time, when women had achieved very visible freedoms but when the liberal intelligentsia, who had played a clear leading role in the early sixties, were under attack and paternalistic militarism was looked back on, even by the Left, with nostalgia. The film expressed profound frustration – Hamlet's six plays-within-the-film awake no-one's conscience – but the final frames demanded a future unshackled from violence.[24] In 1977 an election rally was fired on in 'the May Day Massacre', and Fatma Girik was one of the leaders of a marathon march against censorship which took her from Istanbul to the capital, Ankara. In 1980 the Army seized control again in a coup which Yimaz Güney said 'institutionalised fascism in Turkey', and acknowledged deaths from political violence rose to 1500 a year in the 1980s. When Turkey began to move towards democracy and its unpredictabilities again, Fatma Girik like her Hamlet went from art to action and then fused them. She was elected mayor of the Istanbul district of Sisli for the Republican People's Party. In the 1990s she launched the reality television programme *Soz Fato'da*, where she tracked down perpetrators of violence against women and sexual abuse, including doctors, teachers, husbands, and confronted them on camera. Actresses worked as her *agents provocateurs*. Meanwhile another female Hamlet confronted abuse differently.

III

Dublin 1993: Hamlet's nightmare

Have your bad dreams stopped? (Hamlet's Mother, *Angel of Vengeance*)

Imagine a world peopled by shadows and dark figures where nightmares are real and reality even more frightening. Hamlet inhabits such a world . . . (Dublin press release)

In 1984 the playwright Frank McGuinness wrote, 'The major undertaking of confronting Shakespeare's plays in unique and native forms has consistently intimidated the Irish theatre, betraying post-colonial insecurities.'[25] McGuinness believed directors and actors were hobbled by an ambivalent relationship to English culture but that Ireland must 'evolve independent readings of these most essential texts'. 'There is a massive anti-Shakespearean feeling in Ireland', the Irish actress Fiona Shaw said in 1993: 'Irish actors seem to have a block, an understandable block.'[26] At the time, she was directing *The Hamlet Project*, a low-budget version (design: £140) performed in a disused munitions factory, involving young Abbey Theatre players whom she encouraged to draw on their own families' experiences. John Lynch's Hamlet linked the tragedy to internment in the North and like an H-Block hunger striker smeared himself with excrement. What Ireland needed, Fiona Shaw said, was to 'explode the polite relationship to Shakespeare' the 'quintessential Englishman' because Shakespeare 'is not an English writer' but 'a confrontational writer'. Simultaneously, at the Project Arts Centre Dublin, Michael Sheridan was directing another experiment meant to 'unlock the darker elements' and 'rattle the senses' – *Hamlet's Nightmare*. In this hallucinatory two-hour condensation, Hamlet was the actress Olwen Fouere (see Figure 18).

Hamlet is 'a sacred cow in England', Fiona Shaw said, 'but here not so'. JM Synge argued the Abbey Theatre, the home of Irish cultural nationalism, should only stage classics if they could directly 'illuminate our work', and that 'giving one day Shakespeare, one day Calderon' damaged a national theatre's identity.[27] The Abbey only staged Shakespeare in 1928, twelve years after the Easter Rising, with a Futurist *Lear* directed by the playwright Denis Johnston, followed by *Macbeth* (1934) and *Coriolanus* (1936). The Abbey directors argued heatedly over this: one condemned 'museum theatre' whereas Yeats turned to Shakespeare to snub 'slacking' Irish playwrights. The three plays were studies of political masculinity and it was left to Dublin's cosmopolitan Gate Theatre run by the gay couple Micheál Macliammóir and Hilton Edwardes, to explore Shakespeare's other aspects. Macliammóir played Hamlet in eight revivals from 1931 to 1957 and toured from America to Elsinore; however when playing in London (1935) Macliammóir, the most self-confident of actors, hit 'a block': 'I was obsessed by terror of the only effective weapon the English have against the Irish, that bantering, indulgent smile as of a kindly doctor for a fractious child.' He felt infantilised, colonised: 'If only, I thought, our wretched country had never been invaded, had never lost a language . . . [T]o bring him there in his own tongue was to handicap me from the start: it was not in the main a linguistic

Figure 18 Hamlet's gaze. Poster for Olwen Fouere in *Hamlet's Nightmare*,
Dublin 1993; director: Michael Sheridan.

impossibility, it was a racial one.'²⁸ The postwar Abbey avoided
Shakespeare till the 1970s and *Hamlet* until 1983, when it chose Michael
Bogdanov (based in England but trained in Dublin) to direct. Bogdanov
was then a symbol of opposition to the British Establishment because

of his prosecution for directing the homosexual rape scene in Brenton's *The Romans in Britain*, which allegorised the violation of Ireland. Bogdanov's Abbey *Hamlet* was prefaced by half an hour of army drill: Claudius ruled a military regime touched with the belligerence of post-Falklands England.

This was the first *Hamlet* Olwen Fouere saw and she felt uninvolved, except by Ophelia. Bogdanov was reworking his own earlier British productions, but as we have seen there was an alternative Irish tradition he might have drawn on, beginning with Fanny Furnival in Dublin, 1742. Her protégé Roger Kemble married the Irish actress Sarah Ward and their daughter Sarah Siddons triumphed as Hamlet there; Millicent Bandmann-Palmer was immortalised by *Ulysses* ('I hear that an actress played Hamlet for the fourhundredandeighth time last night in Dublin. Vining held that the prince was a woman. Has no-one made him out to be an Irishman?'[29]); Siobhan McKenna kept *travesti* alive in the 1950s and Fiona Shaw was frequently asked to play Hamlet – though she declined (saying there was nothing in her relationship with her father she wished to investigate) and instead opted for the powerful, less exposed, role of director. The director of *Hamlet's Nightmare* called the cross-gender aspect 'accidental' – 'There is no symbolic significance whatsoever' – and it happened because the *actress* took the initiative: 'I was approached by Michael Sheridan who wanted me to be involved', recalls Olwen Fouere: 'He proposed to focus on the "adolescent" Hamlet as the product of a wealthy, powerful and dysfunctional family. Michael was still searching for his Hamlet. I suggested myself.'[30]

Olwen Fouere established her reputation as one of Ireland's most brilliant actors with several portraits of women *in extremis* (*Antigone, Agnes of God*) and radically different female archetypes, from the Queen in *Snow White* (in a play by Tom Hickey) to a slaughterhouse worker to Salome. Critics were struck by her 'unsettling' intensity and precision and the 'rich metallic quality' of her 'strange, harsh, cawing voice'.[31] 'The creative choices within one's sexual identity has been one of my pet subjects for years', she comments, 'so my choice of acting roles reflects that. I have played a number of cross-gendered roles since the early '80s. My first solo show called *The Diamond Body* (1984) was about a man reconstructing himself to a hermaphroditic state.' She played Salome for Steven Berkoff while rehearsing Hamlet and she wanted 'to explore the similarities of both roles – Hamlet and Salome – as products, and sometimes victims, of a dysfunctional family in a position of power'. Moreover, 'I had just played Ariel as an extra-terrestrial boy-girl, in any case gender indeterminate; Hamlet felt like a link between the experience of playing Ariel and Salome – the avenging angel Ariel and the spoilt rich kid who kills what she loves because she can't have it.' 'I hadn't had any particular ambition to play it', she admits, but 'I was interested in further developing and exploiting my abilities to play across gender.' Fouere was less tied to 'impersonation' than many of her predecessors: 'I concentrated less on developing an externally convincing masculinity (which I have done when playing men before – timbre of voice, etc.). As there is an accepted tradition of women playing Hamlet, I approached it as I would any other role. Playing a man was simply part of the character.'

Sheridan spoke of 'a mystery at the heart' of *Hamlet*, which he saw as a case study of 'a dysfunctional family' – 'The mother is sleeping with the uncle who murdered the father. . . incest as it was conceived at the time. All the psychology was there long before Freud came along, and I wanted to examine much more closely, in close focus, the effect of this family dysfunction on a person, and my feeling was that it would be no different in 1601 to what it is in 1993.'[32] Fouere called this her 'brief': 'The concept was fairly persuasive and helpful in terms of the choices I was then left with in order to play the role. Limitations are often liberating – to explore within a given framework rather than to be faced with a limitless ocean of possibilities when dealing with such a massive play and subject.' Though Sheridan said gender was irrelevant, it was important for Fouere: 'I'm playing *him* as a male character, but I do feel that Hamlet has a lot of "femininity", for want of a better word, very feminine "sensitivities"' and this exposed disturbing areas:

In my explorations, before and during rehearsals, I began to experience the Claudius character almost invading Hamlet's body, which I think is a very female feeling. I think part of Hamlet's confusion about what way to wreak his revenge comes from that confusion of the sexual and the moral. It's a sexual revenge that he experiences. . . similar to a sense of rape.

She re-gendered the Oedipal analysis: 'I felt that the legitimising of Claudius as Hamlet's mother's lover was experienced by Hamlet as a kind of sexual violation against which he felt impotent. Hamlet's self-disgust, his uncontrollable but guilty rage, his impotence, was a response to Claudius' penetration of his mother, with whom Hamlet continued to have a symbiotic relationship. In penetrating Gertrude, Claudius was penetrating and violating Hamlet.' 'It's quite interesting as an actress to discover this within Hamlet', she commented, 'but I think it's very much part of the *male* character.'

The *Nightmare* began with Hamlet trapped in the Ghost scene.[33] Reviewers found the inescapable sound-score by Pol Brennan of Clannad, the folk-and-synthesiser group, 'deeply, disturbingly atmospheric, with its percussive throbs, howls and wails'. 'Haunting music and recorded voices reverberate through the play.' 'The initial tragedy. . . is obscene. . . It is this grotesque scenario which proves a living nightmare for the prince and. . . destroys him.'[34] In the darkness a spotlight caught Fouere's eyes; she stared out as hard and unblinking as Girik had, but this Hamlet had to fight for control. Every critic was struck by her intensity, a sense of range and fury: 'In one scene she quakes the stage with desperate wails and in the next she wields a fearsome placidity.' 'She sets out to disturb and challenge, and succeeds' – 'pulsingly passionate', 'outstandingly intelligent and perceptive.'[35] 'In her quietest moments, the raging soul of the character is still bare', and she spoke 'O what a rogue' as if possessed. 'Near-madness' and the 'frailty of sanity' were suggested visually, like Hamlet's slippery mental position between past and present. Ophelia wore Elizabethan dress, the Queen a 1950s ball gown, and Fouere offered a 'nineties street-image: peroxide hair, Doc Martens, and a business suit with turned-up cuffs: 'My hair seemed right as it was. . . I felt I should be seen in contemporary clothes.' Cold and detached, Fouere examined Ophelia's face, caressing it thoughtfully with the backs of her hands; she gripped Gertrude's arm harshly, spurning her 'crumbling', 'tremulous' gentleness; pinned from behind by sharp-suited Claudius, Hamlet grimaced in angry pain.[36] She spoke 'To be or not to be' on a tightrope, physicalising 'the unbalanced nature of Hamlet's mind and the indecision that is rife in his body, as he steps back and forth along the thin line'.[37] Some disliked this 'arbitrary' direction and symbolism but the image emerged organically 'by chance' (Fouere): 'I had a practice wire in the rehearsal room for my own amusement and Michael then wanted to use it.' Even those who disliked her performance ('vocal stridency. . . contorted features. . . antisocial. . . verging on the ga-ga') blamed the director for imposing a reductive concept ('Sheridan has saddled her with one of the least subtle Hamlets imaginable. . . raving from the word go') on a brilliant actress.[38] Others were thrilled: 'Fouere is not the first woman to play Hamlet, but I'm willing to lay odds that hers is the finest interpretation.' (*Sunday Independent*)

For Fouere, 'The particular aspect of the role which resonated most powerfully for me was the inevitability of Hamlet's fate – the playing out of a pattern written in his bones – however he tries to fight or control it by refusing to act/not act on his impulses. In our production, Hamlet's relationship with his dead father as his inner voice and mirror image of himself – Hamlet's double in other words – was physically represented as a chess game with Death, who was also his father's ghost.' This was Sheridan's idea – 'I liked it.' She felt 'my Hamlet probably followed the path of most male Hamlets in his relationship to Gertrude and Ophelia – playing rage, neurosis and a sense of betrayal.' But she exploited the fact that the cross-gender performer inhabits the unmarked space between definitions – the whole production blurred the distinction between fact and fantasy and the *Sunday Independent* felt her Hamlet was a schizophrenic – a divided self driven 'to interpret the gentler side of his nature as womanish folly, and therefore as a darkness in nature'.

By comparison with Nuria Espert and Fatma Girik, the focus in Dublin was relentlessly psychological and Fouere herself said 'I personally missed the political dimension of Hamlet's conflict – as the son of a ruler with inherited responsibilities for the state of Denmark.' However *Hamlet's Nightmare* did not take place in a social vacuum. Fouere's work was especially interesting given the romantic myths of Irish femininity, which had dominated political and artistic discourse for centuries, that were being challenged by feminism. Historical revisionism was questioning the gender assumptions written into standard histories of Ireland, from Tudor accounts of colonisation as legitimate ravishment to the suffering beauty of Yeats' Mother Ireland. Films and plays were questioning the stereotypes, yet Field Day, the most ambitious Irish cultural project of the eighties, could still publish a three-volume historical collection of Irish writing which included no women.[39] Fouere was one of many artists opening up new understandings of gender in Irish theatre, indeed her distinctive cutting voice was like a reproof to Yeats' lament over the 'unfeminine' activism of Constance Markewicz who 'spent her nights in argument until her voice grew shrill'. *Hamlet's Nightmare* also opened up areas that plays like Connor McPherson's *The Weir* would soon confront – a vision of people haunted and distorted by memories of abuse. 'In the psychological arena', Sheridan said, the family is always 'a metaphor for what is happening in the rest of the world'; therefore in Ireland *Hamlet* had to refocus: 'I see Hamlet to a certain extent as an abused child.'

In this country recently there's been a . . . lid lifted off the psychological aspect of sex and sexual abuse. There is an interest now, greater than at any time in Ireland, I think, in the effects of this . . . because Ireland was a country in which . . . the sexual and psychological abuse was kept well under the lid because of the Church and society's attitudes.[40]

The uncovering of child abuse in Ireland in the 1990s was collectively traumatic, because so many accusations were directed against members of the Catholic Church, which replied with an equivocal 1996 report calling for compassion for the penitent and warning of the dangers of loss of faith and loss of respect for the priesthood. The government called for a 'national debate'.

In this context the reception of *Hamlet's Nightmare* was revealing. 'I said, "What would you like to play?" and she said "Hamlet"', Sheridan explained casually, and 'afterwards it was on the basis that she was the best possible person for the part, male or female, in this country.' He said the same of Laertes, played by Andrea Irvine: 'Both women simply expressed a desire to play the roles.' The press was fairly flip beforehand – 'Women. Of course. Both are women. Very good, and about time too. Why not? Why shouldn't women be given the opportunity. At long last.' (Patsy McGarry, *Irish Press*) – but then Fouere was accepted without question. Dublin's gay press called it a totally persuasive 'diagnosis of Hamlet', and 'a theatre-goer's dream'.[41] This said something for Dublin's sophistication in the nineties (Ireland's first woman President, Mary Robinson, was one of the most respected political figures in Europe) and there were successful recent precedents like Marie Mullen's Oedipus (Druid Theatre, 1988).[42] However that was not the whole story.

Hamlet's Nightmare had a strong profile. A film was planned and there was great interest because of Sheridan's involvement of Irish rock culture – Pol Brennan's sound score and especially the casting of the singer Sinéad O'Connor. There were press rumours that O'Connor would play Hamlet. Then it was announced that she was Ophelia, and journalists heard that she might also play Death, Hamlet's 'double'. In a British television interview screened shortly before rehearsals, O'Connor talked about the Family with characteristic frankness:[43] 'My mother was a very violent woman. . . physically and verbally and psychologically, spiritually and emotionally abusive to all of us. . . I was a battered child – well I am still.' In 1993 O'Connor signed up as a student at the Parnell School of Music, Dublin, and she began to work in films. According to Fouere, 'Her desire to be involved was based on her wish to develop an acting career – the child abuse agenda was secondary' but was perhaps 'the inspiration for Michael Sheridan's "angle" on the play'.

O'Connor historicised it: 'I hold the Church entirely responsible for the circumstances of my childhood and for the circumstances under which a lot of Irish children are growing up – Ireland being the country which has the highest statistic in Europe of child abuse.' The Church, she said, 'produced my mother through her own family, through the generations of her family. . . who were of course affected by what the British did in this country – which they couldn't have done without . . . permission from the Roman Catholic Church. . . The Church used the English to do their dirty work. . . They took away our right to speak our own language . . . to educate ourselves . . . I would compare Ireland to an abused child.'[44]

The publicity image of Olwen Fouere's Hamlet with a snake round her shoulders was a challenging post-punk/post-feminist image of Eve, but also an echo of O'Connor's first album, *The Lion and the Cobra*, where the lion and the serpent (Psalm 91) 'were the facts of my abuse'. The casting of women as three children lacerating each other at the heart of the nightmare could not be neutral. Crucially, there was no Horatio; Fouere/Hamlet was solitary, robbed of the confidant whom, as the Church now said, every victim of abuse most needs. With 'sinister, detached kindness', dropping in 'cryptic' fragments of text, shaven-headed Death became Hamlet's only companion. In the 1993 interview O'Connor discussed her own impulse towards suicide 'because of the frustration of not knowing who we were. . . There's silence about it, a wall of silence.' Fouere believed 'Sinéad O'Connor's appearance/presence would have been a positive contribution – she is a very talented woman – however, the personal traumas she was experiencing at the time made it too difficult for her to continue.' Two weeks before the opening, she withdrew. The press sniggered and the confused hostility so often directed against a woman playing Hamlet was diverted onto her: 'She was intimidated by the role. Very shy girl, low self esteem, insecure, very, very talented, would've been a brilliant Ophelia. I see. What a pity. But didn't she have another non-speaking role, sort of "Death" or something like that? She had. She gave up Death too. Dear, oh dear. Alas and alack.'[45] It typified O'Connor's treatment by sections of the Irish media – the *Sunday Independent* ran a cartoon of her with 'Pain' scrawled across her abdomen, alluding to her earlier withdrawal from a music tour because of pregnancy. 'She's performing her usual role instead.' (*Irish Press*)

'Any role involves a degree of self-investigation', Olwen Fouere comments, though the 'ability to connect and play a role not only varies from actor to actor but also from role to role.' For her – unlike O'Connor confronted with Ophelia and Death – 'Hamlet, for me, was a fairly direct experience – no great mystery or trauma about it – specifically with particular focus on the dysfunctional family, which is an experience which is emotionally or imaginatively accessible to most people.'

It was a very flawed production with some sublime moments. Playing Hamlet was not a particularly profound experience for me but then I have had the opportunity to play a number of powerful roles. Perhaps I just wasn't a particularly good Hamlet or more likely not in the right production to really shake me around. I wonder how many men would be invited to play Hedda Gabler or Lady Macbeth except in the most marginalised theatrical context? Why aren't they and why shouldn't they?

'Mr Sheridan's main thesis', said the *Irish Press*, was that 'It is not Hamlet who is "out of joint", but the "world" he lives in. It is mad, corrupt, and rotten.' In different times and places, under different faiths and ideologies, subject to different forms and degrees of repression and abuse, the modern female Hamlet, by deconstructing gender identity, exploded other sureties and opened the anxieties of personal and national identity for inspection. The actress – assuming disguises as Hamlet does and exposing the contradictions involved in any compromise with pressures that are 'mad, corrupt and rotten' *and limiting* – became a medium for uncomfortable truths. In 2000 the Abbey Theatre proposed that Fiona Shaw play Hamlet. She decided not to – instead she chose Medea – but was still thinking about Hamlet two years later when the BBC commissioned her to make a prime-time documentary about Shakespeare for the breezy patriotic series *Great Britons*. The Irish actress's strategy to encourage Britain's masses to vote for Shakespeare was populist, evoking rock concerts and soaps: '*Hamlet* is the ultimate domestic drama' – it 'distils an enormous range of human experience into one character' through whom 'Shakespeare is allowing us to experience nothing less than the contradiction and tragedy of existence. He lets us see ourselves, even our worst selves.' But she also stressed Shakespeare's 'universality' – the issue of translation, the appeal to foreign film-makers, the way the plays assumed coded meanings under repressive regimes: 'Hamlet is all of us. He's Everyman. He's lost, shocked by the world. . . He's equipped to think but he can't quite act. . . He's a sort of car-crash between aspiration and self-hatred, and no character represents the twentieth century and its anxieties so completely.'[46]

Notes

1. In *Front Row*, BBC Radio 4, July 1993.
2. Nuria Espert and Marcos Ordóñez, *De Aire y Fuego* (Madrid: Aguilar, 2002), p. 66. See *Premier Acto*, July–August 1960, p. 60. For a fine study of the careers of Espert and Margarita Xirgu, see Maria Delgado, *'Other' Spanish Theatres: Erasure and Inscription on the Twentieth-century Spanish Stage* (Manchester: Manchester University Press, 2003).
3. Espert: 'There was room for improvement in all aspects: the lighting, the decor, our own acting. From this I learned a fundamental lesson: never have an opening night during a long tour.' Moreno felt responsible for a lack of preparation – 'to the point of his thinking of giving up directing altogether'.
4. *Panoramica del Teatro en Espana* (Madrid: Editora Nacional, 1973), p. 241.
5. Delgado, *'Other' Spanish Theatres*, p. 136.
6. Delgado, *'Other' Spanish Theatres*, p. 61. I am indebted to Maria Delgado for many details here.
7. Review of *Siege of Numantia* in Uruguay (Antonina Rodrigo, *Margarita Xirgu* (Madrid: Aguilar, 1988), p. 262). In Latin America her productions helped sustain Lorca's reputation; she ran theatres and theatre schools in Uruguay and Chile, employed other exiles, staged anti-fascist drama, and imported controversy. Argentinian Peronists banned her production of a Camus play in 1949.
8. Delgado, *'Other' Spanish Theatres*, p. 132.
9. Federico Garcia Lorca, *Obras Completas: 3 Prosa* (Barcelona: Galaxia Gutenberg, 1996), p. 196; Delgado, *'Other' Spanish Theatres*, p. 135.
10. In *The Maids*, she played a bandaged servant on *cothurni*, enraptured by rituals of power – play-acting, poison and revenge – in a metallic mirrored arena on a dangerously raked stage.
11. *El Pais*, 27 August 1983, quoted Delgado, p. 160.
12. Feroz Ahmad, *The Making of Modern Turkey* (London and New York: Routledge, 1993), pp. 55–6.
13. *Ibid.*, pp. 61–3.
14. Tezer Taskiran, *Women in Turkey* (Istanbul: Redhouse Yayinevi, 1973), p. 78.
15. See Maureen Freely, 'True or False', on the first Turkish woman premier, *Guardian* 23 July 1996.
16. OJ Campbell, *A Shakespeare Encyclopaedia* (London: Methuen, 1966), p. 900. See Saliha Paker, '*Hamlet* in Turkey', *New Comparison* no.2 (Autumn 1986), pp. 89–105. I am indebted to Lawrence Raw for information on Shakespeare in Turkey and for facilitating contacts in Ankara and Istanbul. Dilek Inan's advice was indispensible.

17. Ahmad, *Making of Modern Turkey*, p. 122.

18. *Ibid.*, pp. 60–63.

19. He was accused of harbouring dissidents and imprisoned on a false murder charge. He continued to direct by proxy in prison. Girik's other films at this time included *The Legend of Ali from Kesan*, Erksan's *The Uncouth Ones*, *Legend of Ararat*, and *The Fugitive* (1981). She had won awards in 1967, 1969, 1974 and 1975.

20. Ahmad, *Making of Modern Turkey*, p. 157.

21. *Ibid.*, p. 78.

22. Translation by Dilek Inan, adapted to suggest the song's rhythm.

23. Nermin Menemencioglu (ed.), *The Penguin Book of Turkish Verse* (Harmondsworth: Penguin, 1978), p. 53.

24. Erksan seemed disillusioned afterwards. He retreated into teaching and television, with literary adaptations and such non-contentious projects as a history of Turkish music. Like a bleak appendix to *Lady Hamlet*, his last cinema film, *I Can't Live Without You*, concerned a girl with terminal cancer who hires a man to kill her.

25. *Theatre Ireland*, Winter 1984, p. 81. In his play *Mutabilitie*, McGuiness showed Shakespeare in Ireland, caught between colonial politics and a matriarchal Celtic world of the imagination.

26. *Front Row*, BBC Radio 4, July 1993.

27. Letter to Lady Gregory, 1906, *The Collected Letters of John Millington Synge*, Vol.I., ed. Ann Saddlemeyer (Oxford: Clarendon Press, 1983), p. 251.

28. Micheál Macliammóir, *All for Hecuba: An Irish Theatrical Autobiography* (London: Methuen, 1947), pp. 162–5.

29. James Joyce, *Ulysses* (New York: Random House 1934), p. 196.

30. Unless stated, quotations from Olwen Fouere are from personal correspondence.

31. *Evening Standard*, 8 October 1984; *Time Out*, 11 October 1984.

32. Sheridan in *Irish Press*.

33. Whereas Macliammóir spoke of 'that pale interminable afternoon in which the first part of the play is steeped before the dreadful night of action begins'.

34. Quotations from daily (16 July 1993) and Sunday (18 July) reviews: *Evening Press; Irish Press; Sunday Press; Evening Herald*.

35. *Sunday Independent; Irish Independent; Express; Sunday Independent*.

36. *Sunday Independent, Irish Press*.

37. *Express*.

38. *Irish Times; In Dublin*.

39. *The Field Day Anthology of Irish Writing* (Derry: Field Day, 1991). In response to protests, a volume of women's writing was added in 2002.

40. *Irish Times*.

41. *Gay Community News*.

42. Rosaleen Lineham was Feste in the Gate's *12th Night* (1989).

43. *Faith and Music*, ITV, May 1993.

44. She discussed her own impulse towards suicide 'because of the frustration of not knowing who we were . . . There's silence about it, a wall of silence . . . All the evil of the world is committed by those of us who have been abused as children and not dealt with it.'
45. *Irish Press*, 15 July 1993.
46. Fiona Shaw, *Great Britons: Shakespeare*, BBC1, November 2002.

3
Repression and resurgence

CHAPTER 9

Films and fictions: Hamlet,
ages of won

'I know that I'm ignorant, and I can't deny that I'm you...
I do not identify myself with Ophelia!'

'Of course not. You identify yourself with Hamlet. Everyone does.'
Iris Murdoch, *The Black Prince*, 1973[1]

In 1863 Mary Braddon's *Eleanor's Victory* was an unusual attempt to assimilate a female Hamlet into the Victorian novel. In the twentieth century however this androgynous figure took on fascinating life in the teeming worlds of fiction and popular cinema, and gradually became part – a sharply contested fragment – of our collective imagination.

I

Hamlet versus Hollywood

When Asta Nielsen's *Hamlet* opened in New York in 1921 its critical success in Germany was outdone: 'Extraordinary', 'romantic', 'fascinating', 'One of the finest things ever done on the screen.'[2] America's fledgling film reviewers ignored her irony but praised her emotional power. A *Movie Weekly* editorial said *Hamlet* proved 'Motion pictures have reached an aesthetic height that permits invasion of master works', and *Motion Picture Classic* agreed: Nielsen had legitimised silent Shakespeare and proved, by 'frequently slipping far away from the story', that creative freedom was the key: it was a breakthrough for 'Shakespeare on the silver sheet'.

Nielsen was a 'revelation' and, a few months after American women won the vote, the idea of a female Hamlet fascinated the New York press. Gertrude Chase called it 'most plausible', permitting 'a very clever and whimsical madness', and the *New York Journal of Commerce* thought Nielsen's version of the Hamlet myth as 'masterly' as Shakespeare's.[3]

237

tereotypical claims that it became more 'plausible' when
d by feminine scruples and motives' and jealousy, but the
hought Nielsen's strange pansexual love scenes involved 'some
est acting that has ever been done anywhere'. Two women journal-
Alison Smith and Harriette Underhill said she transformed their
derstanding of *travesti*.[4] Smith had been hostile: 'It seemed exactly
ike seeing Juliet played by a leading man, as in the topsy-turvy old
days of Queen Elizabeth. But after the opening of the first reel I saw
I was wrong' – Nielsen's 'intense, smouldering' face 'would convince you
of anything.' Underhill 'went to scoff but remained to pray' – it was 'the
most fascinating picture I have ever seen'. Nielsen's cross-dressing was
welcomed as an extension of the tragedy's appeal – both for newcomers
('A Hamlet that everyone can understand and love') and experts:
'Inasmuch as the tale differs in places from Shakespeare's version we
were hoping against hope that Hamlet would not have to die.'[5] S Jay
Kauffman thought it would turn Shakespeare into true popular cinema –
'It will not allow you not to care. That's why it is a great picture' – and the
trade journals predicted, 'It will prove more fascinating to the general
public than would *Hamlet* according to Shakespeare.'[6] 'Your big talking
point is the star, Asta Nielsen . . . You can safely play up her acting to the
limit. At this no one will be disappointed.' Asta Films avidly summed
up the response: 'The Most Remarkable Criticisms Ever Received by Any
Motion Picture.' But it was deceptive.

Though *Hamlet* premiered lavishly in New York – an orchestra played
Tchaikovsky and a live acted prologue included Shakespeare's Ghost
scenes – the *Tribune* complained because Nielsen was forced to open
off-Broadway: 'Surely the picture magnates are never going to overlook
the greatest foreign film that has ever come to our shores?' A month later
the *Times* protested because this 'extraordinary' work had still not reached
a major venue. The reasons partly explain why Nielsen's *Hamlet* was soon
almost forgotten in the English-speaking world, and why her bold
approach to Shakespearean film was abandoned: it landed in the
middle of a cultural panic. In 1921 there were 'film menace' fears of a
'German invasion'.[7] Cinema was already the fifth biggest industry in the
USA but the arrival of a wave of European works provoked paranoia:
Equity campaigned to exclude them, German films were condemned as
morbid, and in Los Angeles *The Cabinet of Doctor Caligari* was banned.
To quote David Robinson, in 1920–1 fears of European competition
'launched the American cinema on a policy of conquest and annexation,
which was to maintain the domination of the American film whilst

effectively destroying the industries of smaller countries'.[8] Nielsen's publicity pretended *Hamlet* was a Danish film made in Elsinore, not Germany, and stressed her debt to the American Edward Vining, but it was seen as 'another milestone in the foreign invasion' and fell victim to the trade war.[9]

Louella Parsons thought *Hamlet* 'as fine as anything America has produced' and complained, 'To praise a picture made abroad is nothing short of treason and should be punished by instant death . . . If we shut our doors and our hearts against any outside films we are only starting serious trouble . . . We cannot imitate the ostrich by hiding our heads in the sand.'[10] East Coast reviewers used *Hamlet* to condemn Hollywood's standards: the *Tribune* asked 'wherein our own pictures fall down', others praised Nielsen's 'European' refusal to 'sugar-coat' unpleasantness, and the sophistication of European actor-training.[11] This last point contradicted D W Griffiths' formula for film stardom (and his belief in the supremacy of the director). He called on Hollywood to use actresses who were 'beginners . . . untrammelled by so-called techniques . . . I prefer the young woman who has to support herself and possibly her mother. Of necessity, she will work hard. Again I prefer the nervous type . . . If she is calm she has no imagination.'[12] What kinds of women should quivering semi-amateurs play? Nielsen challenged the partition of actresses' work into two erotic types – waifs and sinners, Ophelias and Gertrudes – and this was ultimately why she and her *Hamlet* would never fit into the world Hollywood was creating: 'For here is a woman whose like we have not seen on our own screen. Asta Nielsen's art is a mature art that makes the curly-headed girlies and painted hussies and tear-drenched mothers of most of our native film dramas seem as fantastic for adult consumption as a reading diet restricted to the Elsie Books and Mother Goose.'[13]

Valentino's *The Sheikh* had just arrived and Kauffman was appalled by the contrast: 'One has an IDEA. An IDEA. [The] *Hamlet* of Shakespeare plus a theory that Hamlet was a woman. The other? Sheer theatrical nonsense.' 'A girl is abducted by a sheikh and finally loves him. Who cares? What does it mean? What does it say? Does it mean that being abducted by a sheikh is delightful and that girls should try it?' The public that preferred *The Sheikh* to Nielsen's 'magnificent' work 'is to be pitied'.[14] Like Nazimova ('I rebel against the eternal love theme in drama', Nazimova complained, 'Always woman represents love') Nielsen was drawn to radical material.[15] She controlled her own means of production, and against the yielding escapism of Agnes Ayres helpless in Valentino's arms, the childlike Lilian Gish, or Theda Bara's vamping, she offered intellect and emotional danger. After writing passionately in her support, Julia Arthur was inspired to defer her retirement to play extracts from *Hamlet* herself; Le Gallienne would remember the film fondly; but as Hollywood geared up and produced its stock of fantasy images and role models, Asta Nielsen's *Hamlet* did not become the symbol of a women's cinema that its first reviews promised. An era of experiment ended, and soon sound imposed prescriptive notions of what was 'realistic', 'plausible', 'Shakespearean' – and feminine. Yet many actresses still declined to be pigeonholed and Hamlet remained a challenge. So there emerged a small but fascinating sub-genre of fiction films, chinese-box dramas about women who wished to play the Prince, or became him.

Hamlet between the wars: 'She's a nut.'
As early as 1919 in the Italian melodrama *Amlete e il suo Clown* (English title: *On with the Motley*), the idea of a modern woman identifying herself with Hamlet was presented as unhealthy. Alexandra Tranda finds her father murdered and her mother remarries: 'Alexandra broods over this in a morbid way, seeing in the events of her own home a parallel to the story of *Hamlet*.' She hires some circus clowns to perform a show based on *Hamlet* and, convinced that her stepfather's reaction proves his guilt, she stabs him. In fact he is innocent: she suffers a breakdown and attempts suicide. According to *Bioscope*, the director Carmino Gallone cast his wife (Soave Gallone) as 'a weak, irresolute creature. . . so inclined to morbid reflection that the mind becomes unbalanced and a tragic end is the only solution'.[16] Gallone linked Hamlet to the 'feminine' in terms of impressionability and obsession. At the same time however *Amlete e il suo Clown* set a precedent by associating the female Hamlet with popular culture and carnival spaces: Alexandra herself abandons privilege for the circus, only to fall to her death in the ring. Her Hamlet fantasy is fatal, then, but in the early US sound film *Morning Glory* (1933) – for which Katharine Hepburn won her first Oscar – the character Eva Lovelace's obsession is more subtle.

Morning Glory was based on a play by Zoë Akins, a key figure in Hollywood's half-hidden gay community who created strong roles and bravura scenes for women (e.g. Garbo in *Camille*), and here she drew in *Hamlet* for an iconic moment. Hepburn's performance mapped conflicting options available to young women in the Depression. Eva, a strange insect-thin young actress, finds herself at the first-night Broadway party for a play from which she was sacked – 'I was very sure of myself in those days.' Starved, drunk and out of control, she lurches into 'To be or not to be' to prove her talent – and for a few moments she is the first female Hamlet on sound film.[17]

A low-angled close-up transforms her: her working-girl dark dress seems like a doublet; Eva-Hamlet creates a tense circle of concentration and arrogantly stares us down. Hepburn provides just one physical token of 'masculinity' – her right hand stabs into a fist – but sitting with her head cradled in her left hand, casting deep shadows, her voice bitterly roughens. This Hamlet sequence is unsettling because it is unmediated: we are given no indication of how to respond here to Eva ('Monotone of voice and observing everything around her,' as Hepburn put it[18]) whom the other characters have dismissed as charming, irritating, or insane: 'She's a nut, you'll probably never hear of her again.' There are no reaction shots: behind her stand a line of frozen party guests but their faces are chopped from the frame. So Eva provokes the same questions as Hamlet – is she shockingly truthful, posing, or mentally disturbed? Is her Hamlet monologue brilliant or embarrassing? But it does convey her essence – 'The feeling of being great and lonely'.[19] A sozzled writer breaks the tension ('I saw Charlie Chaplin do this in California, and he was never as funny as this kid') but releases Eva's furies. Yelling 'I'm the greatest young actress in the world!' she throws a shawl round her shoulders, lunges up a staircase and becomes Juliet. This time there is no ambiguity: Juliet is bathed in twinkling light, the camera caresses her, and a young playwright Joseph Sheridan (Douglas Fairbanks Jr) is hypnotised into replying to her, reciting Romeo. A veteran sums her up: 'Beautiful! Childishly beautiful. Impossibly beautiful.'

Eva's two Shakespearean speeches were cut in clumsily with different lighting, like screen tests for life. They pictured contrasted selves, potentially 'mannish' or 'feminine', and mapped out emotional possibilities for young women in the thirties. Her Hamlet side is destabilising, ambitious and intellectual (like Eva Le Gallienne, Eva Lovelace translates European plays). Juliet is more orthodox, and desirable – the sentimental stereotype of a rapturous ingénue ringed by excited older men. Eva-Hamlet repels men but Eva-Juliet is their fantasy and victim, and as soon as she reveals her 'childishly beautiful' aspect, a stock plotline takes over. The producer seduces then discards her, and 'the little Lovelace girl' becomes a figure of fragile pathos. Flesh on display now, she models underwear, pawed by drunks – until a fairy-tale climax when Sheridan the playwright, hitherto a strange weak figure, helps her stand in for a star and become an overnight sensation.[20]

The Hamlet/Juliet split personality helped define the unique screen persona of Katharine Hepburn. She was fascinated by this script and insisted on playing Eva Lovelace. Her mother Katharine Houghton was a leading Suffragist close to Mrs Pankhurst and Emma Goldman, and even as a student at Bryn Mawr, Hepburn was drawn to the challenge of playing complex nonconformity. In John Lyly's *Woman in the Moon*, for example, she was Pandora: 'A great part. She played in different moods under the influence of different planets. I was warlike under Mars. Loving under Venus.'[21] In 1932 the *Hollywood Reporter* had stressed her sexual indeterminacy: 'She has a rugged sincerity that is momentarily masculine in its graceful strength, yet in the passing of a few tiny celluloid frames she becomes as soft, as appealing as a lovely woman can be.'[22] *Morning Glory*'s Shakespeare sequence explored this exactly, yet the script itself never prepares for the sudden *harshness* Hepburn gave Eva's Hamlet – she fractured the role here and announced her refusal to follow Hollywood rules. Soon after, Hepburn notoriously played a girl disguised as a boy in *Sylvia Scarlett*; she confused publicists by dressing mannishly off-screen; and in her autobiography she stressed her pleasure working with Lowell Sherman and Dorothy Asner, the homosexual directors of *Morning Glory* and Akins' *Christopher Strong* (where she was a leather-suited aviatrix, an idol for young women, who flies to her death rather than accept the dependent life of a politician's mistress). Douglas Fairbanks Jr let it be known that when she was Juliet in *Morning Glory* Hepburn was 'musical and poetic. She was feminine and frail, her voice soft, frightened, and yet exquisitely passionate.'[23] He fell in love with her – but at other points he 'was repelled by her preoccupation with self, her masculine mind'.[24] 'When I was beginning', Hepburn commented, 'they thought I was a freak.' She went on to play several Shakespeare heroines, who were predictably emancipated (Kate, Cleopatra) and androgynous (Viola, Portia, Rosalind). She avoided victims.

The producers of *Morning Glory* originally had different ideas. They too wanted a Juliet, not a female Hamlet, and filmed an elaborate (unusable) Balcony scene with Fairbanks and Hepburn in Renaissance dress. Posters invented a passionate affair for their characters ('The screen's newest and most sensational starring combination in a tempestuous drama of burning desire') and though Hepburn's electric complexity made the film an unexpected triumph, the industry chose not to repeat it.[25] In 1957 *Morning Glory* was remade as *Stage Struck* – redefining Eva (Susan Strasberg) as immature – and this time she spoke only Juliet's lines, not Hamlet's. Strasberg seemed to have been instructed to imitate Hepburn's feyest mannerisms (with painful results – press attacks were brutally personal[26]) and in keeping with the domestic values of the Eisenhower era, Eva shrank to a naive child, a weak copy of Nina in *The Seagull*. Indeed the Shakespeare parallels were reslanted to make *Sheridan* the Hamlet figure. He was played by Christopher Plummer (fresh from Hamlet at Stratford, Ontario) while Eva's rival Rita Vernon, originally a mouthy platinum blonde, became a faded Gertrude. Hepburn's Eva triumphed in a European play she herself discovered; Strasberg appeared in Plummer's masterpiece, and her dreams challenged no-one – she longed to play Ophelia. Worst of all, the men, so tainted in *Morning Glory*, became saints led by Henry Fonda as a very caring seducer. In fact, *Stage Struck*'s erasure of Akins' female Hamlet was a mild example of a postwar tendency in gender politics, a patriarchal hijack, that was actually more marked and serious in current British fiction. There however the neurosis being probed through Shakespeare was male.

II

Sent to England: the rape of Hamlet

No English actress played Hamlet professionally between 1937 and 1979. Yet during this period the female Hamlet was not absent, s/he became the property of writers, mostly men, creating a private symbol – fluid, metatextual, arcane and always darkly erotic. In a strange recurrent psychodrama s/he became a fantasy figure, an object of hate and desire acting out psycho-political tensions.

Harold Pinter's *The Dwarfs* and John Fowles' *The Magus* (both begun in the early 1950s) and Iris Murdoch's *The Black Prince* (1973) included passages in which men (all would-be authors) and women (all teachers) in sexual situations talked of *Hamlet*. In Pinter's novel, his first major work, the protagonist Pete verbally assails his girlfriend Virginia because she has undermined him in front of his mates – by expressing her opinion of Hamlet in a London pub. She is half-naked after a bath:

'It made me look very foolish. Did you realize that? You don't know anything about Hamlet, Ginny. Don't you understand that? And yet you come in with the book under your arm. Why did you do that in the first place? Was it to make an impression? Are you mad?. . . I've told you to leave him alone. . . Do you realize that that statement was an abortion?. . . In other less charitable company you would have had your balls chopped off. . . Did you think you would be excused because you were a woman?'[27]

And so on for three pages. It is the prototype of all the grotesque brow-beatings in Pinter and all the verbal misogyny. But she is more abjectly defeated than any later Pinter woman: ' "I'm sorry," Virginia said, her head in her hands, "I'm sorry. I won't do it again." ' Sexually and intellectually threatened, Pete takes instant revenge.

In John Fowles' *The Magus*, Nicholas Urfe escapes fifties London for a Greek island and is alone at night in the sea with another half-nude young woman, called (so she claims) Julie. She confides she played Ophelia at school, 'Against a ghastly repressed lesbian girl who revelled in every minute of being in male drag.' This image excites him – 'Right down to the codpiece?' – and the girl-Hamlet becomes a masturbatory fantasy: 'She pulled away a little and a hand slipped down through the water between us. She brought me gently up, curled her fingers round me . . .'[28] In Iris Murdoch's *The Black Prince*, the violence and eroticism fuse; the narrator Bradley Pearson, a fifty-eight-year-old tax inspector and self-proclaimed literary genius, takes Julian Baffin, his friends' student daughter, to the sea but he is impotent, until –

She was dressed in black tights, black shoes, she wore a black velvet jerkin and a white shirt and a gold chain with a cross about her neck. She had posed herself in the doorway of the kitchen, holding a sheep's skull in one hand.
'I thought I'd surprise you! I bought them in Oxford Street with your money, the cross is a sort of hippy cross, I got it from one of those men, it cost fifty pence. All I needed was a skull, and then we found this lovely one. Don't you think it suits me? Alas poor Yorick. . . Don't I look princely?'. . .
I strode to her and took her wrist and pulled her into the bedroom and tumbled her on the bed. The sheep's skull fell to the floor. I put one knee on the bed and began to drag at her white shirt. 'Wait, wait, you're tearing it!'. . . For a moment, still fully dressed, I surveyed her naked. Then I began to tear my clothes off.
'Oh Bradley, please, don't be so rough, please, Bradley, you're hurting me.'. . .
Later on, she was crying. There had been no doubt about this love-making. I lay exhausted and let her cry. . . I held her in a kind of horrified trance of triumph and felt between my hands the adorable racked sobbing of her body. . .
'What made you like that, Bradley?'
'The Prince of Denmark, I suppose.'[29]

Thus the female Hamlet was drawn into a peculiarly English stew of role-play, stifled homoeroticism, pornography, and pretension. In these postwar novels s/he became the Forbidden, a mysterious protean presence who excited and frightened the men – hinting at intellectual equality and new sexual formations, triggering insecurity. Peter, Urfe and Pearson gave a voice to intellectual misogyny and fantasies of male power, expressed through abusive games.

Via *Hamlet*, Fowles, Pinter and Iris Murdoch presented eroticised fights for the right to consider oneself a Subject. Pete and Urfe are titillated by thoughts of lesbian conspiracies – Pete imagines Virginia seduced into talking about Shakespeare by a girl in a 'masturbatory rut', and like Bradley Pearson he reduces the woman to a body: 'Keep that robe done up! I don't want to see the hair on your crutch.' In all these stories the men enforce an absolute distinction between body, which is abhorred and desired, and mind, which is male; and all embrace the Lawrentian tradition which offered a crude way to reassert male prerogatives: penetration. Humiliated by the idea of a woman usurping Hamlet – articulate consciousness – their counter-tactic is to strip, de-androgynise, and possess her. For them, ironically, identity is corporeal, a matter of phallic difference: there can be no *Hamlet* without the Prince and no Prince without a penis. And in all three novels the 'hero', by finding a skull, asserts himself as the true modern Hamlet, the Man who Understands Death. Pete sees an animal's remains by the Thames, Urfe discovers a skull and a hanging ritualistic black doll: 'The doll was Julie, and said that she was evil, she was black, under the white innocence she wore. I twisted the skull and made it spin. . . Alas, poor Yorick.'[30] Aroused and alarmed by female independence, they resurrect old myths.

There were tensions in the Fowles and Pinter novels due to a blurred distinction between the writers' voices and their surrogates'. Fowles admitted he was attempting a difficult double game in *The Magus* by allowing free play to male fantasies before exposing the narrator as 'a typical inauthentic man of the 1945–50 period'.[31] He wished to show that despite 'the now general political emancipation of women', there was 'sickness' in male-female relations due to 'the selfish tyranny of the male' – 'Adam is stasis, conservatism; Eve is kinesis, or progress.'[32] Urfe compulsively forces reductive even pornographic roles on his lovers, often plucked from Shakespeare's basket (Ophelia, Desdemona) and 'My monstrous crime was Adam's, the oldest and most vicious of all male selfishnesses: to have imposed the role I needed . . . on her real self.'[33] So in a punitive scene that shifts from Lawrence to Kafka, Julie-Ophelia, a 'childlike' 'geisha', gives way to June, a torturer-psychologist in black trousers. Fowles later conceded that *The Magus* might be 'adolescent'; but though he praised women's liberation he lamented the loss of feminine 'mystery', attacked 'the aggressive advocation of lesbianism', and often recycled the phallic power trips he condemned.[34] 'See and feel my defencelessness,' his naked Muse in *Mantissa* tells him, 'How small and weak I am, compared to you – how rapable.'[sic][35] Fowles, Bruce Woodcock commented, 'promotes a realigned version of the very myths of masculinity he lays bare'.[36] As it happened, Pinter and Fowles' *Hamlet* sequences were not published until the late 1970s; Pinter suppressed *The Dwarfs* and Fowles kept the 'lesbian Hamlet' masturbation scene and some other sexual episodes out of *The Magus* through what he called a failure of nerve. By that time Iris Murdoch had covered similar ground in *The Black Prince*; she showed much greater objectivity towards her obsessional narrator – part-Nabokovian, part-Prufrock – whose account of his rape of the female Hamlet exposes more about him than he knows. Bradley Pearson, like Fowles, philosophises about role-play. 'The unconscious mind . . . has only a few characters to play with', he explains: 'Being is acting. We are tissues and tissues of different personae and yet we are nothing at all.' *The Black Prince* showed how a new figure, a meditating woman in black, had become a modern archetype.[37]

'Society has conspired unfairly to make women seem inferior',[38] Murdoch said in 1962, and in these three novels Shakespeare was the focus for male claims to intellectual monopoly. These women all have a down-to-earth view of Hamlet ('Maudlin, spiteful, and sensitive to nothing but his own headaches'[39]) whereas the men continue the debate in *Ulysses* provoked by Mrs Bandmann-Palmer's Hamlet and deliver lectures. Pete proclaims Shakespeare an existentialist – 'He laid bare, that's all'[40] – whereas Pearson waxes transcendental:

'Hamlet is speech. He is the tormented empty sinful consciousness of man seared by the bright light of art, the god's flayed victim dancing the dance of creation . . . Shakespeare here makes the crisis of his own identity into the very central stuff of his art. He transmutes his private obsessions into a rhetoric so public that it can be mumbled by any child . . . What redeems us is that speech is ultimately divine. What part does every actor want to play? Hamlet.'
'I played Hamlet once,' said Julian.
'What?'[41]

He is obsessed with her from that instant.

For all three male protagonists, women are the undiscovered country. Bradley Pearson is nauseated by mature sexuality, especially when Julian's mother, the novel's Gertrude, tries to seduce him. He despises Julian and her 'awkward sulky aggressive attitude' from the moment she reaches puberty and is 'appalled and embarrassed' by her wish to write: 'Julian's fate was to be typist, teacher, housewife, without starring in any role.'[42] But when she adopts the androgynous fashions of the day, he mistakes her for a boy and distaste becomes fixation. He endlessly describes her clothes ('Slim, dressed in dark narrow trousers, a sort of dark velvet or corduroy jacket and a white shirt. . .') which edge her into homoerotic territories where he feels on more familiar though dangerous ground: 'I found her older. . . with more of a brooding expression, suggestive of the concurrence of thought. . . she still slightly resembled a boy.' Now 'I did not mind the dourness.'[43] Pearson knows *he* embodies Hamlet's genius; therefore he confines Julian's Hamletness to fetishistic externals:

'Describe your costume.'
'Oh the usual. All Hamlets dress the same, don't they. Unless they're in modern dress. And we weren't.'
'Do what I ask please.'
'What?'
'Describe your costume.'
'Well, I wore black tights and black velvet shoes and a sort of black slinky jerkin with a low opening and a white silk shirt underneath that and a big gold chain round my neck and – what's the matter, Bradley?'[44]

He tries to enfold her in his airless world ('I think I'll close the window again') but ultimately Iris Murdoch identifies Julian with Hamlet on a more creative level. *Hamlet* becomes Julian's way of negotiating the Freudian family romances happening surreptitiously around her in odd corners of literary London, grotesquely dominated by a priapic Post Office Tower. Though she asks set-text questions, they bite: 'Do you think she was having an affair with Claudius before her husband died?. . . I think some women have a nervous urge to commit adultery, especially when they reach a certain age.'[45] Hamlet frees her emotions (she writes 'Feeble' next to Ophelia's 'noble mind' speech, 'Hypocrite!' by Claudius' prayer) and though 'I wasn't very good,' playing him was her first taste of empowerment: 'I enjoyed it ever so much. Especially the fight at the end.'[46]

Edward Gordon Craig turned the female Hamlet into his hero's *anima*, embodying death and desire; similarly Bradley Pearson incorporates the figure into his secret hermetic musings on 'the dark powers of imagination', 'the black Eros whom I loved and feared'. He persuades himself that the roots of lust and art are identical as the girl Hamlet uncovers hidden appetites and chimeras. S/he becomes a disturbing erotic presence and a complicated arcane symbol to be set beside Apollo (nude and androgynous in the Perugino painting which was one of Murdoch's starting-points) and Death. In Pearson's repressed mythmaking s/he is 'the black glass of the future', a manifestation of a dark angel haunting a black star that lights this planet 'where cancer reigns'.[47] S/he is also a version of himself: garbed as Hamlet, Julian offers the self-loathing narcissist a cure for impotence, the chance to rape his own image: 'Is Shakespeare a masochist? Of course. He transmutes his private obsessions.' In postwar British fiction, in a tight literary culture struggling to redefine itself and come to terms with new notions of identity (and a lost grip on greatness), the female Hamlet became Eros-Thanatos. But Iris Murdoch in *The Black Prince* was also experimenting with a fluid postmodernism where familiar constructs, literary and psychological, broke apart: 'I am not a very convincing character', Julian Baffin objects in a metafictional appendix. Pearson always describes her as pure Object, yet we learn she is now a major writer and she reclassifies the would-be genius as a monomaniac in a female text. He is found guilty, perhaps wrongly, of murdering her father; so to the world he will always be Claudius – or, he fears, a Caliban. When male intellectual prerogatives are threatened in these novels, stock personae unravel and men imagine themselves evolving backwards, while in *The Black Prince* the woman in Hamlet's costume finally becomes the master-mistress of the words.[48]

In all three novels the men represented theory, the women practice. When in 1981 Ian McEwan's novel *The Comfort of Strangers* also referenced the actress-Hamlet, the meanings had evolved. Holidaying in Venice, Mary – an actress – and Colin see modern feminism literally changing the cityscapes of Europe. 'A crude stencil in red paint. . .showed a clenched fist enclosed within the sign used by ornithologists to denote the female of the species.' Mary is delighted: 'The women are more radical here. . .and better organised.'[49] Unexpectedly however they meet Robert and his crippled wife Caroline, unaware that Robert broke her spine testing the borderline between sex and death: 'I liked it . . . being reduced to nothing.' On a balcony, Caroline and the actress make conversation:

'I was working for a women's theatre group. We did quite well for three years, and now we've broken up. Too many arguments.'
Caroline was frowning, 'Women's theatre? . . . . Only actresses?'

'Some of us wanted to bring in men, at least from time to time. The others wanted to keep it the way it was, pure. That's what broke us up in the end.'
'A play with only women? I don't understand how that could work. I mean, what could happen? . . .'
'Well, you could have a play about two women who have only just met sitting on a balcony talking.'
Caroline brightened, 'Oh yes. But they're probably waiting for a man.' She glanced at her wrist-watch. 'When he arrives they'll stop talking and go indoors . . .'
'You're right in a way, of course. Most of the best parts are written for men, on stage and off. We played men when we needed to. It worked best in cabaret, when we were sending them up. We even did an all-woman *Hamlet* once. It was quite a success.'
'*Hamlet?*' Caroline said the word as if it were new to her.[50]

Caroline luxuriates in her husband's cruelty ('It wasn't theatre') and they will drag Mary and Colin into their world, murdering him for his 'beauty'.

McEwan used the feminist *Hamlet* to suggest a gulf between the rationality of political gender debate and the labyrinth of private desire.[51] He balanced both pressures, but in 1990 Harold Pinter adapted *The Comfort of Strangers* for the screen and returned the female Hamlet to the realm of erotic conspiracy and male rage. Pinter made Caroline more clearly a masochist Ophelia and Robert became a monstrous Blackshirt Hamlet. Pinter also gave the women's conversation overtones of seduction: Caroline gets Mary to massage her, the contact disturbs the Englishwoman, who tries to retreat to her own world:

MARY: (*Uneasily*) We did an all-woman *Hamlet* once.
CAROLINE: *Hamlet?* I've never read it. I haven't seen a play since I was at school.
  Isn't it the one with the ghost?
Lights go *up behind them. Footsteps.*
And someone locked up in a convent?
Footsteps stop, start. A chair scrapes. Sound of glass. Robert comes out onto the terrace. . . Caroline limps across the terrace into the apartment. Robert does not look at her. . . He is wearing black.[52]

The man in black returns, wearing a razor-blade instead of a locket on a chain; he will slash Colin's wrists. Heightening the sex war, Pinter made the Italian feminists gynaecologically confrontational ('a clenched fist within the female organ') and Mary shallow: It's great. . . They want convicted rapists castrated.' Pinter's Robert hates feminists: 'All these – are women who cannot find a man. They want to destroy everything that is good between men and women. They are very ugly.'[53] His is the revenge of the recently repressed. Thus in some postwar British writing the regendering of Hamlet dramatised fears of collective emasculation, a cultural castration fantasy.

Fowles and Murdoch both affirmed the androgyny of the creative process. 'I have a feminine mind', he claimed, and Murdoch said all her characters were androgynous, because women's and men's minds were not *spiritually* different.[54] *The Black Prince*'s readers were challenged to disentangle Pearson's bizarre mind from Murdoch's. 'Being is acting': but for him hope dwells in the dream of rising from *mere* actor to writer-philosopher; by casting himself as Hamlet-Shakespeare he might address 'the redemptive role of words in the lives of those without identity'. Instead it is ultimately Julian who achieves identity through language. 'Everything I write', Murdoch said, 'is *Hamlet*.' Her novel was far more intricate philosophically than the others, yet in each case echoes of *Hamlet* were morbidly distorted by the male character's paranoid belligerence and prurience. Julie hooks Urfe with hints of her 'years in a convent dormitory. Where nothing was left to the imagination'.[55]

In the novels, gender tensions were projected on the body of the female Hamlet; but meanwhile in what seemed a totally different England, popular cinema provided a burlesque footnote to these obsessions – at the St Trinian's school play. In *Pure Hell at St Trinian's* (UK 1960; directors Frank Launder and Sidney Gilliatt) the riotous girls' school became 'progressive' and presented a 'Slap-up Festival of Culture – bags of Shakespeare'. After a fashion show for shocking uniforms and a paint-hurling Happening, they do *Hamlet*, and their programme cover shows Hamlet sticking her tongue out at the skull. The St Trinian's Hamlet was a middle-class blonde teenager who gracefully elocuted 'To be or not to be. . .' and at 'To take arms against a sea of troubles' carefully discarded her belt. At 'by opposing', she peeled her sleeves off. At 'end the heartache', she unzipped and dropped her black tunic. Hamlet now wore tights, silk underwear and a ruff ('Perchance to dream. . .') and two middle-aged men in the audience, Ministry of Education inspectors, stared astonished – one goggle-eyed in suspense, the other apoplectic: 'This is the final outrage. The Soliloquy to striptease!!'[56] *Pure Hell*, like all St Trinian's films, celebrated the anarchy of childhood and adolescence while exposing/exploiting the lure of the forbidden in postwar middle England. In *Pure Hell*, the Establishment from the Law Courts and Cabinet downwards are mesmerised by this temple of wildness and almost-underage sensuality. The St Trinian's Hamlet was a sophisticated provocateur; she put herself on show on her terms and her genteel articulation of Shakespeare defined her unattainability – intellectually, socially and sexually superior to the inhibited voyeurs at her feet, a nation of Poloniuses and Bradley Pearsons caught out.

While *Pure Hell* was sharp about shamefaced male desire, it was in some ways prehistoric. The actress playing the girl playing Hamlet was left from the credits and was indistinguishable from all the other teenage hopefuls directed to pose, flashing smiles and a promise. Nonetheless, *Pure Hell* was less neurotic than the contemporary English novels because of *the force of performance*; this anonymous actress' onscreen presence registers as power, and her scene still delights audiences. *Pure Hell* had a half-conservative message, Britain was changing too fast, and so slick politicians praise the striptease *Hamlet* to the skies: 'You fellows aren't moving with the times,' they warn 'mischievous . . . reactionary' civil servants. But Miss Hamlet's precise play on bourgeois fantasies ('a consummation devoutly to be wished') paralyses them all; soon the entire British Army are helpless in a travesty Suez Crisis involving Arab seizure of English erotic property (the Sixth Form, who progress from *Hamlet* to a harem). The anarchic girls save the day, not the massed ranks of neutered Englishmen remembering better days, and they sell the rights to their striptease *Hamlet* to Stratford, where it doubtless becomes the authorised version for the Swinging Sixties.

Bizarre though the conjunction seems, on different levels – lowbrow and high – both *Pure Hell* and *The Black Prince* dramatised the war generation's envy of its liberated daughters. In 1989 Murdoch – whose contribution to the feminist movement had been much debated – adapted her novel for the stage with Annabel Cruttendon as Julian. Murdoch argued that times had changed and she made the new Julian-Hamlet far more manipulative. With a jogging suit and a Walkman s/he now represented what Murdoch saw as a solipsistic generation, and the play promoted Pearson into a kind of tragi-comic Prospero. Ironically, however, critics were now less mesmerised by his rhetoric and Cruttendon's Hamlet scenes seemed a 'dirty old man's fantasy'. It was one thing to read, 'quite another to see it enacted in a theatre'.[57] But this critique was foreseeable; for by 1989 desire was under the microscope and female Hamlets were everywhere.[58]

III

The doors are broke

In 1992, a press release announced that Madonna and the gay comic Sandra Bernhard would play Ophelia and Hamlet – it was unclear who would be which – in a movie. That same summer Sinéad O'Connor was engaged for the stage and film versions of *Hamlet's Nightmare*. In 1996 in a BBC documentary, Ruby Wax asked the *Baywatch* star Pamela Anderson if she wanted to do serious acting. She replied curtly, 'This is serious' and delivered The Soliloquy in fast-forward as she tracked across the sand in her swimsuit: '*Tobeornottobethatisthequestion* . . .' Wax made Anderson an offer: 'I can get you the gig – but you'll have to cover those up in a bodkin.'(*sic.*) A discussion of codpieces and penis sizes followed. In 1997 after Kurt Cobain committed suicide, his widow the grunge rocker and actress Courtney Love confided, 'Too bad I'm not a guy because all I really want to do is play Hamlet. . . all the guys I go out with have to be . . . Hamlet.'[59] None of those performances materialised but the multimedia threat was there – and the threat, the guerrilla assault on hierarchy via pop culture, bawdry, Girl Power and Hamlet, was the point. Geri Halliwell compared herself to Hamlet after splitting from the Spice Girls ('I have Hamlet's disease of introspection'[60]), in 1997 the Estonian punk poetess Merle Jaage played Hamlet, and that year a Soho-based all-woman-*Hamlet* invoked Madonna's image for 'The Blonde Ambition Tour'. The prospect of an unrespectable woman playing the Prince became the modern equivalent of the moustache on the Mona Lisa, and there were many volunteers. 'Gender is just the soul's pyjamas', said the American confrontationalist performance artist Lydia Lunch in 1995, adding, 'Everyone is male – a prefix meaning evil.'[61] She was in London that year, like the 'gendertainer' Diane Torr who staged *King for a Night* workshops at the ICA, the first of her many British events 'for women who want to extend their experience of cross-dressing . . . The newly-transformed power-dressed executives, dandyesque clubbers and clean cut college boys are invited to join Torr for a night on the town putting their new personae to the test.'[62] As it had been a century earlier, playing Hamlet was power-dressing for the nineties but with post-modern twists.

On film, more women played women playing Hamlet, and moreover in the process they deconstructed several stages in the Actresses' life.

The subversive school *Hamlet* returned in *The Addams Family* (USA 1991). Against a storm cloud backdrop, Wednesday (Christina Ricci), a pale and unsmiling little girl with a big hat, fought a pirate. Rapiers and daggers scythed the air while she honed the play to its gothic essence: 'How all occasions do inform against me/And stir my dull revenge!/O from this time forth/My thoughts be bloody or be nothing worth!/If I must strike thee dead I will!' Wounded, she chopped off her opponent's arm; he severed an artery in her neck; pulsing showers of blood drenched two rows of paralysed parents, teachers, lawyers and a judge. 'Sweet oblivion, open your arms!': Hamlet died choking, her family bravoed, Tudor music played, and the blood sprayed on.[63] *The Addams Family* derided New Right values, and Wednesday's *grand guignol* Hamlet was only the first strike in her generational guerrilla theatre campaign, that would lead in the sequel to a summer-camp *Pocahontas* where she and a rainbow alliance of fat, short-sighted, Black, Jewish and generally unacceptable children roasted their WASP persecutors on a spit. Mel Brooks had devised *Springtime for Hitler* to reduce Society to gaping dummies; St Trinian's and Wednesday Addams showed it only required Hamlet plus a schoolgirl with attitude. *Outrageous Fortune* (USA 1987) took the rebellion into acting class.[64]

This was an odd-couple vehicle for Shelley Long and Bette Midler, a comedy-thriller about friendships and aspirations. In a New York fencing class, the pompous Lauren Ames (Long) nearly kills her partner ('Isn't that the point?'):

LAUREN: It's my ambition to play Hamlet.
ACTRESS: That'll have them in the aisles!
LAUREN (MATTER-OF-FACTLY): Yes.

At the Russian actor Korzenovski's class she meets trashy Sally (Midler), who appeared in *Ninja Vixens* and thinks 'Actors are just bullshitters who get paid.' *Hamlet* maps their contrasts: Sally cannot mime The Soliloquy as an exercise because she has never heard of the play, whereas Lauren has no access to emotion and ruins their *Hamlet* 'death workshop'. They share the same lover, and when he's apparently killed they meet at the morgue and agree the mutilated corpse is not him (Male Identity = Penis). He is alive and a traitor and used them to carry secrets to Korzenovski (Russian = Spy). *Outrageous Fortune* plays with Middler's 'bullshitters' question: is an actor any more than a liar? The women put their acting lessons into practice and solve the case by applying cross-dressing theory. Visiting a brothel disguised as boy virgins disguised as macho cowhands, Middler remains a literalist about acting: 'Now tell me how we're gonna get it up.' Again the female Hamlet forges an alternative alliance, leading hippies and Native Americans against the villains ('SALLY: Aren't you dead yet? LAUREN: Not until I play Hamlet') and since this is Disney, the finale is pure wish-fulfilment. At the rapturous curtain-call of her *Hamlet*, Long is beaming, Middler – much more incongruously – is Ophelia, and the joyful audience assimilates all the male characters left alive – cowboys, indians, CIA men and penitent spies: KORZENOVSKI: 'That was the best Hamlet ever, except for mine.' Hamlet and Ophelia punch the air in a victory salute borrowed from Madonna in *Desperately Seeking Susan*.

After training, of course, most performers face unemployment especially older women. In Alyse Rosenberg's short *The Voice-Over Queen* (USA 1990) an actress in trousers and black tee-shirt, Naomi Strutski (played by Joan La Barbara), begins her audition piece:

NAOMI: To be or not to be –
DIRECTOR: Thank you.

Mocking laughter drives her off and in the next shot this female Hamlet is sprawled on the floor, having apparently killed herself. Rosenberg's film confronted women's frustrations in the entertainment industry, with 'industry' as the operative word – the commercial complicity between spectacle, sexism and consumerism. 'Like every serious actress I've always wanted to play the classics', Naomi says, but she works in commercials: 'I do appliance voices. They say I have a talent for it, personifying the products.' She is the voice of massage chairs, irons, mowers and microwaves in a cut-throat trade dominated by abusive male directors: 'How about giving me a massage?' 'Suck it up! Swallow that sucker!' Never uttering words, just amiable noises, Naomi is literally a corporate tool. She is the Voice-over Ms Eastern America, with a press-book full of photos of famous products she has played, but 'I'm ready to do Shakespeare, to go deeper, to transcend my own limits.' She is a low-caste actress in a double bind: advertisers patronise her and Shakespearians think her absurd: 'Stick to self-cleaning ovens . . . I hear they're looking for someone who can do "Out damned spot!" Hahahah!' Hence her apparent suicide. However, 'dead' Naomi gets up laughing, and recites 'To be or not to be' to a store-room of appliances, who join in:

TV: That is the question!
ELECTRIC FAN: 'Tis nobler!

Rosenberg's film magically reconfigures Shakespeare for the worker's and housewife's world. Naomi-Hamlet chats to the gadgets in a new vocabulary of blank verse and bleeps. She takes arms against a toaster's loose connections and by opposing mends them; she cradles an ailing juice extractor and discovers joy in 'perchance to dream!' The Domestic Actress triumphs as Hamlet on her terms and the products cheer.

However the true carnival apotheosis of this feminist/post-feminist *Hamlet* – intriguingly, considering the precedents – came in English fiction. Angela Carter's extravaganza *Wise Children* (1991) confronted 'the idea of Shakespeare as cultural ideology'.[65] Commenting that intellectuals were 'still reluctant to treat Him [Shakespeare] as popular culture', Carter derided the splitting of art into 'high' and 'low' – 'The English pretend that such an absolute division exists between them, between the bawdy and the remote.' Within an analysis of a protean culture, *Wise Children* offered an inspirational non-sectarian feminism and, unique as her style was, Carter's novel summarised a century of actresses' work.

Hamlet dances again: the Shakespeare circus

Carter imagined a World War II revue called *What You Will* (or *What! You Will!* or *'What? You Will?'*) in which the sisters Nora and Dora Chance become the first singing-and-dancing identical-twin female Hamlets on record: 'We were eighteen years old, hair like patent leather, legs up to our ears. We sported bellhop costumes for our Hamlet skit; should, we pondered in unison and song, the package be delivered to, I kid you not, "2b or not 2b."' 'Tragedy, eternally more class than comedy. How could mere song-and-dance girls aspire so high? We were destined, from birth, to be the lowly ephemera of the theatre.'[66] The nearest Nora and Dora (later in *Nude Follies* '52) can come to 'legit' High Art is parody, because they were born poor and illegitimate and are proud of it. They find solemnity ludicrous. At the opposite extreme from Fowles and Murdoch, Nora, now in her seventies, is the rambling, lewd narrator and one of her many mottos is 'Life's a carnival', but *Hamlet*'s in their genes. They are linked to the Shakespearean acting dynasties the Hazards and the Chances; and their grandmother Estella 'A Star Danced' Hazard, like the real Shakespeare prodigies the Bateman sisters, worked for Barnum: 'PT Barnum, Barnum of Barnum and Bailey, that Barnum, struck by her legs in *As You Like It*, made her an offer. Hamlet in a tent in Central Park. A tent because, he prophesied, no theatre on Broadway would be big enough to hold the crowds' (p. 16).

Wise Children takes place in an alternative universe writhing like a Richard Dadd canvas with densely-populated reshaped highlights from the history of entertainment; performance became Carter's comic/erotic metaphor for the twentieth century's dreams and miscalculations. Estella is her reinvention of Ellen Terry: like the real Terry she made her debut as Mamillus in Charles Kean's *Winter's Tale*, was photographed by Lewis Carroll (who 'got her to slip off her frock after the crumpets,' [p. 13]), and triumphed as Juliet, Portia and Beatrice. But then their stories diverge and anything becomes possible. Though Terry recited 'To be or not to be' to Welsh miners, she never played Hamlet. Estella Hazard does, and thereby exits 'legitimate' history. She demotes her husband ('the most melancholy Dane of his generation') to the role of Ghost and takes up with her Horatio, an invented brother of Edwin Booth. And so Carter let Hamlet sleep with Horatio at last. The result is a pair of Shakespearean twins, Melchior and Peregrine – actors.

'Hamlet under canvas, a smash': abandoning the Haymarket for the circus tent (cf *Amletto e il suo Clown*) Estella enters disrespectability and myth. 'Here she is in drag as, famously, Hamlet. Black tights. Tremendous legs. Wasted on a classical actress. We've got the legs from her. She's emoting with the dagger: "To be or not to be . . ." '(p. 12) 'It ran and ran and would have run ad infinitum except the twins announced they were on the way and a female Hamlet is one thing but a pregnant prince is quite another.' (p. 16) Like many real Victorian *travesti* stars she tours the Wild West and Australia (with a town and an ice cream named after her); Nora and Dora were reared on tales of Estella and like them and the novel 'she was a marvel and she was a mess'. But her Hamlet haunts her sons. One, 'our greatest living Shakespearean', was afraid to play Hamlet, 'nervous the critics might think he wasn't half the man his mother had been.' Meanwhile her cuckolded husband snapped, and murdered her during *Othello*: 'Perhaps, by then, Old Ranulph couldn't tell the difference between Shakespeare and living.'[67]

Angela Carter parodied the process of writing theatrical history: 'Here she is as Juliet, as Portia, as Beatrice. See that "Come hither!" smile. As Lady Macbeth, she manages to summon up a stern frown, quite the Miss Whiplash.'[68] Nora complains because 'I never rate more than a footnote in the biographies; they get my date of birth wrong, they mix me up with Dora.'[69] But Carter offered the old lady's buttonholings as a healthier, shrewder cultural history than any authorised 'facts'. In their youth the twins were doppelgangers for Ibsen's Nora and Freud's Dora – but anti-neurotic versions, with a different sense of the problems of the twentieth century. They believed Hamlet was wrong – the great existential dilemma was not to be or not to be, but whether or not to *dye*: 'The future lay with blondes. Should we? Shouldn't we?'[70] Carter, a magical-realist cultural materialist, told how Britain turned Shakespeare 'into actual currency, not just any old bank note but a high denomination one, to boot. Though not so high as Florence Nightingale, which gives me satisfaction as a woman.'[71] Carter had a dazzling ability to fuse extreme intellectual rigour with funfair vulgarity; so in her book Hamlet and the gameshow host are literally kin, whereas Highbrow and Lowbrow are distinctions invented by bourgeois neo-puritans and by England's temperamental inability to cope with excess. There were affinities with *Eleanor's Victory*, which defended proletarian taste against the Academy, but *Wise Children* was the polar opposite of recent *Hamlet* fictions preoccupied with neurosis.

So there is no difference between Carter's tragic Hazards and comic Chances. Young Estella's old granddaughters live in a double world, drab and magical. They wait on grey streets for buses that never come, on the wrong side of the river in South London, 'bastard side of Father Thames', where Woolf's Shakespeare's Sister died. In this split city, Carter's maze of relationships ('Romantic illegitimacy, always a seller') offers wild ways to pose universal questions: "Whence came we? Whither goeth we?" I know the answer to the second question, of course. Bound for oblivion, nor leave a wrack behind.'[72] But Carter was less interested in Hamlet's fears for the after-life than in the comic mystery 'Whence?', our search for sources. *Wise Children* is an anti-*Hamlet* novel, or rather anti-Freudian, because in her overcrowded world where almost everyone is connected and no-one unique, the tragic Self is an anachronism. She mocks the very idea of male anxiety because these men never had any potency to lose and for Carter, Estella Hazard, who made Hamlet a sexy woman, was a *better* Hamlet than any of the lugubrious men. When at the end Dora learns that the centenarian Peregrine Hazard is not her father as she always supposed, but her uncle, she has sex with him immediately, exorcising Hamlet's brooding on incest and ignoring all the structures of theory Freud imposed on *his* Dora before she walked out on him.

In the Bakhtinian *Wise Children*, the pregnant prince is the apotheosis of anarchy. Estella is the absence of trauma; the female Hamlet unleashes Carter's revels – disreputable, populist, kitsch. His/her bequest is the anti-intellectual but *not* unintelligent theatre of gossip, legs, and instant gratification, yet it is Shakespeare democratised too: *Wise Children* celebrates life's refusal to correspond to form. So though Estella was murdered long ago, her pregnant Hamlet is the point of departure, the mother/father of two households both alike in lack of dignity. To quote Kate Chedgzoy, 'Carter's challenge to the hegemonic accounts of cultural and familial legitimacy serves to clear a space for new voices, new visions of the family, which may offer the Chances a happier alternative to the tragi-comic histories of Hamlet's family romances.'[73] As the novel ends, Nora and Dora inherit Estella's role. Resilient survivors – 'Two funny old girls, paint an inch thick, clothes sixty years too young,' – they have new twins to care for. Their long lives both recap a century of subversive performance and are a snapshot of the 1990s. Nora's farewell is 'What a joy it is to dance and sing!' and, strolling through Brixton singing 'songs from the show that nobody remembers', she and Dora – now the world's only singing-and-dancing identical-twin geriatric female Hamlets – reprise their bellboy ditty, '2b or not 2b'. (p. 227)

Speaking bodies

The *Hamlet* psychodramas discussed above were not unique to English fiction, nor were Angela Carter's tales simply fancy. For example the Misogynist and the Dancer had clashed in Paris in 1925 when Aicha, a black artist's model and circus rider, became Hamlet in *La Cavalière Elsa* at the Studio des Champs-Elysées. This was Paul Damasay's adaptation of a novel by the surrealist Pierre Mac Orlan; like Olesha's *A List of Blessings* it dealt with Russian agents and exiles in Paris and in it, Aicha recalled, 'To please a Bolshevik, I danced Hamlet – a queer Hamlet, for I was nearly nude.'[74] 'True', she said, 'they had given me a kind of loincloth, but my breasts were undisguised,' and in fact (we can begin to credit Angela Carter with a gift for understatement) what this nude circus rider did was dance Hamlet's *subconscious mind*. The play's asexual heroine was Elsa, a Soviet cavalry officer whose army waited at the Rhine while she penetrated French Society and in Damasay's opinion two kinds of decadence collided. Elsa's Red gang included a malcontent who called himself Hamlet and even wore doublet and hose. A self-obsessed theorist devising an ideal future predicated on slaughter, he embodied the worst contradictions of modernity: 'It is I, Hamlet the neurasthenic.' One surreal night, Comrade Hamlet forces the near-naked showgirl La Déva (Aicha) to act out his fantasy image of himself. The revolutionary rants, free-associating images of negritude and apocalypse which she must turn into orgiastic movements like 'the panthers' or 'the demon of the night' – 'See that woman there, she is my thought.' In a delirium fuelled by Primitivism, Lenin and champagne, he imagines himself as Hamlet the Heart of Darkness – pansexual, savage, liberated, nude – dancing on Europe's grave. Inevitably, for his fantasy to work the dancer must be objectified, silenced and blind, he orders her not to speak or open her eyes and the climax predictably is rape: though, emboldened by dreams, it is not La Déva he assaults but Elsa herself, his androgynous commander. (He fails and dies.) Damasay was not interested in the effect that 'becoming' Hamlet might have on La Déva, and Aicha herself saw it as a lark; but it is significant that the play's: star (Marguerite Jamois as Elsa) and director (Gaston Baty) went on to explore the androgyny of Hamlet more coolly in their First Quarto *Hamlet* (1928). Not only that, in 1934 one of the most brilliant of all the Russian émigrés in Paris did dance Hamlet there – Bronislava Njinska. She created a ballet of the play to Liszt's music at her own Théâtre de la Dance. Combining heavy medieval costumes with expressive movement, Njinska's 'choreopoem' insisted the silent androgynous body can articulate the most abstract truths.

Even the grimmest of these *Hamlet* variations had a degree of authority. They replayed dichotomies in Shakespeare, where Gertrude's body, to quote Janet Adelman, is 'the site of fantasies[75] and Hamlet is obsessed by female sexuality, female speech, and 'the woman' in himself. The intricacy of fiction encouraged novelists to identify with Hamlet's brooding and to darken it. The realm of *performance* however is more objective, democratic, and arguably therapeutic; and so as the century closed the female prince took over Fortinbras' function, becoming an icon of a radical future to be constructed from ourselves. Not that approval was universal.

In Kenneth Branagh's *In the Bleak Midwinter* (1995) a bunch of eccentrics stage *Hamlet* one Christmas to save a threatened church. When the leading man suddenly deserts to go to Hollywood, the panicking cast accept his sister's offer to step in. Since she, another schoolteacher (played by Hetta Charnley), is the neglected spirit behind the save-the-church campaign, the logical ending would be for this to be her apotheosis. Branagh however made the female Hamlet his crowning joke: she has no talent whatever. Terrified, she dries, the woman stays silent, and cinema audiences generally cheer when she is grabbed and literally thrown in the wings by the true prince, who has returned. Branagh set up parallels with countless overnight-star scenarios including *Morning Glory*, only to reassert the status of the male lead.

(He was about to star in his own four-hour film *Hamlet*.) The same year however, a rather different updating of *Hamlet* motifs featured in Wayne Wang and Paul Auster's *Blue in the Face*. This also showed a shambling micro-community, this time hanging round a New York cigar store whose amiable owner Auggie (Harvey Keitel) chats with the ghost of a baseball star, and never listens to what women say. 'Listen. . . Listen. . .' becomes a litany and his Latino girlfriend Vi (Mel Gorham) is reduced to secret soliloquies: 'I talk myself blue in the face. But still it don't do no good.' She is a dancer, and in desperation she strips, snarls and sings 'Fever' in a mirror, rehearsing tactics to jolt some response. But in this film, a semi-improvised ensemble piece, the company created a quirky multi-ethnic world where an Afro-American says he is Italian, Lily Tomlin plays a man, and attitudes evolve. So Vi and Auggie finally commit, and conceive a child, and as they undress he ushers his Ghost out and she begins. . . the Soliloquy. If in Branagh's tight middle England, Hamlet's Sister still could not access Hamlet's language, a Latino dancer on a Bronx street corner could.[76]

Some last examples. In the year of *The Black Prince* (1973), Caroline Johnson played Hamlet in René Bonniére's version filmed in a Toronto chapel; she shared the role with Rick McKenna and was also the Ghost. Linda Certain was one of two Ophelias, the other being male. A cheap 16mm version of a stage production by the Trog Experimental Theatre, it ran nearly three hours and received little attention, but it anticipated gender deconstructions in many later productions.[77] In 1983, Canada provided another take with *Strange Brew*, a *Hamlet* thriller-farce set in a Toronto brewery. This starred the comedy team Rick Moranis and Dave Thomas as dazed Rosencrantz-and-Guildenstern heroes who left 'Pamela Elsinore' (Lynne Griffin) little to do – her uncle drugged and nearly drowned her. But by 1997 the actress heroine of *In the Wings*, a novel by the Toronto journalist Carole Corbeil, could become Hamlet to universal acclaim. When an overwrought actor vanishes, his lover, the older woman playing Gertrude, is his obvious and superior replacement. She brings the role experience, compassion, and the capacity to harness her self-doubt: 'Alice Rivers stood up in the dark, cramped and unsteady from her death, amazed that the applause had already started.'[78] By 1999 an avenging superheroine (Janeane Garofalo) was wielding her father's skull in a bowling ball (*Mystery Men*: US, dir. Kinka Usher), and in 2001 Hamlet became the schoolgirl heroine of *The Glass House*

(US, dir. Daniel Sackheim). Leelee Sobieski plays an orphan fostered by her parents' murderers; she discovers they are abusing her and plotting her death. To destroy her credibility at school ('Forget your lurid adolescent female fantasies') they neatly frame her for plagiarising Harold Bloom on *Hamlet*. But she wins. *The Glass House* was an unpretentious but chilling teen melodrama; eighty years after Asta Nielsen it marked the final, surprisingly easy, re-assimilation of the female Hamlet into the film marketplace of America. Hollywood changed, of course, because the world already had.

Notes

1. Iris Murdoch, *The Black Prince* (Harmondsworth: Penguin, 1975), p. 196.
2. *New York Times.* All reviews (November 1921) taken from the Asta Films US pressbook.
3. *New York Morning Telegraph.*
4. Smith in *Picture Play Magazine* and Underhill in *New York Tribune.*
5. *New York Tribune.* Even though the New York *Evening Post* was sardonic about the use of 'erudite' Edward P Vining to achieve 'a considerable dose of what movie magnates call sex interest', it found the film thrilling and reported that the audience gave it an ovation.
6. *Dramatic Mirror; Screen Opinions.*
7. *Photoplay,* July 1921.
8. David Robinson, *World Cinema: A Short History* (London: Methuen, 1973), p. 99.
9. *New York Journal of Commerce.*
10. *New York Morning Telegraph.*
11. *Motion Picture Magazine; New York Call: Hamlet* 'gives to those who see it a heart throb and a sense of beholding a thing that lives and breathes in every turn of its reel. Less laboratory twaddle and more genuine acting ability before the camera is essential for the welfare of this art in America. Let us hope the De Milles and the Laskys will realize this before the Broadway cinema palaces begin booking their feature photoplays direct from Copenhagen or Berlin.'
12. *Photoplay,* August 1923, quoted Kevin Brownlow, *The Parade's Gone By* (London: Secker and Warburg, 1968), p. 97.
13. See *National Board of Review of Motion Pictures, Exceptional Photoplays.*
14. S Jay Kaufmann in *New York Globe* and *Dramatic Mirror.*
15. Nazimova (1907) cited Schanke, *Scattered Applause: The Lives of Eva Le Gallienne* (Carbondale: Southern Illinois University Press), p. 47.
16. 13 May 1920. This account of *Amleto e il suo Clown* derives from Robert Hamilton Ball, *Shakespeare on Silent Film*, p. 266. The five-reel film was distributed in the UK by the London Independent Film Company.

17. *Morning Glory*: Directed by Lowell Sherman, screenplay by Howard J Green from the play by (1886–1958). See Jennifer Bradley, 'Zoë Akins and the Age of Excess', in June Schlueter (ed.), *Modern American Drama: The Female Canon* (Rutherford: Fairleigh Dickinson University Press, 1990), p. 94.

18. Katharine Hepburn, *Me: Stories of My Life* (London: Viking, 1991), p. 114.

19. This debate continues. While the Lovelace/Hepburn Hamlet has been described as 'averagely adequate', it was shown at the 1997 Oscars as a highpoint of Shakespearean cinema.

20. *Morning Glory* begins with Eva encountering a portrait of Bernhardt in a deserted theatre foyer, and ends with her forging a new relationship with an older actress in the dressing room – images of affinity spanning generations, but also of marginalisation because we never see Eva onstage. Eva's dresser was once a star herself but long ago went into eclipse and this, Zoë Akins implied, was the fate of every actress and by implication all women. In a bittersweet last scene, they cling together and Eva accepts the heartbreaking brevity of the life she has chosen. Knowing it is a dream from which she must wake (and the whole film has the languorous rhythm, muted sound and sudden ellipses of a dream) Eva cries out in desperate defiance: 'I'm not afraid of being just a morning glory! Why should I be afraid?' In *Christopher Strong* (1933) Akins decided that the only resolution for this gender schizophrenia, the conflict between 'male' and 'female' identities, was suicide: Hepburn returns to her leather flying suit and breaks the altitude record without oxygen, flying literally into the undiscovered country. Hepburn found this 'old fashioned'; her own extraordinary nonconformist career would prove Akins' pessimism wrong.

21. Hepburn, *Me*, p. 48.

22. Quoted Glenda Leaming, *Katharine Hepburn* (London: Weidenfeld and Nicolson, 1995), p. 274.

23. Douglas Fairbanks Jr, *The Salad Days* (London: Collins, 1988), p. 283.

24. *Films in Review*, December 1957.

25. '149,854 people pay over £20,000 in one week to see film at Radio City Music Hall. Fervent publicity department compares her with Ellen Terry, Duse and Bernhardt,' *Picturegoer*, quoted Andrew Britton, *Katharine Hepburn: Star as Feminist* (London: Studio Vista, 1995), pp. 12–13.

26. 'A shy, irritating smile, an overwhelming sense of self-assurance (which, under the circumstances, is highly unwarranted) and a terribly affected delivery,' (*Films and Filming*, July 1958). In Britain some of the hostility stemmed from the fact that her father was Lee Strasberg, the father of the Method.

27. Harold Pinter, *The Dwarfs* (London: Faber and Faber, 1990), pp. 86–8.

28. John Fowles, *The Magus: A Revised Version* (London: Grafton Books, 1978) pp. 367–9.

29. Murdoch, *The Black Prince*, p. 328.

30. Fowles, *The Magus*, pp. 459–60. Cf. Pinter, *The Dwarfs*, p. 107. In Murdoch the skull is discovered before the sex, and accompanies it.

31. In J Campbell, 'An Interview with John Fowles', *Contemporary Literature*, 17, 4 (1976), p. 466. Like Ophelia, Urfe's former girl-friend apparently commits suicide two-thirds of the way through.

32. See Bruce Woodcock, *Male Mythologies: John Fowles and Masculinity* (Brighton: Harvester, 1984), pp. 13, 80.

33. Fowles, *The Magus*, p. 400.

34. Woodcock, *Male Mythologies*, p. 72.

35. John Fowles, *Mantissa* (London: Cape, 1982), p. 42.

36. Woodcock, *Male Mythologies*, p. 80.

37. Murdoch, *The Black Prince*, pp. 195, 200.

38. *Observer*, 17 June 1962.

39. Pinter, *The Dwarfs*, p. 81.

40. *Ibid.*, p. 134.

41. Murdoch, *The Black Prince*, p. 200.

42. *Ibid.*, pp. 55, 59.

43. *Ibid.*, p. 56.

44. *Ibid.*, p. 201. Pearson's Hamlet exists only on the page and in his consciousness: ' "I thought I looked a lot like a picture I saw of John Gielgud."/"Who is he?" '

45. *Ibid.*, p. 160.

46. *Ibid.*, p. 201. As Julian's mother says and as Pearson tries to prove, 'Men are physically stronger. That's what it comes to, that's what's behind it all' (p. 40).

47. *Ibid.*, p. 348.

48. The plot shrinks him to Laertes before the rape: his sister kills herself.

49. Ian McEwan, *The Comfort of Strangers* (London: Picador, 1981) pp. 23–4.

50. *Ibid.*, pp. 67–8.

51. Mary watching Colin's murder reverses the climax of *The Magus*, where Urfe, drugged, is forced to spectate as Julie and her lover act out fantasies from *Othello*. Continuing the Shakespearan variations, McEwan includes an 'Ophelia' episode where Colin thinks Mary is drowning.

52. Harold Pinter, *The Comfort of Strangers and Other Screenplays* (London: Faber and Faber, 1990), p. 28. McEwan implies that Colin and Mary's fate somehow satisfies their own yearnings – they have imagined mutilating and imprisoning each other, 'a lifetime of subjection and humiliation' (p. 81).

53. *Ibid.*, p. 13.

54. Fowles (1980) quoted Woodcock, *Male Mythologies*, p. 16.

55. Fowles, *The Magus*, p. 486.

56. *The Pure Hell at St Trinian's*, directed and written by Frank Launder and Sidney Gilliatt.

57. *Daily Telegraph* 26 April 1989.

58. Within a few days David Henry Hwang's *M. Butterfly* also opened in the West End, and at the Almeida Pushkin's *Mozart and Salieri* featured English and German actresses in the title roles.

59. *Time Out*, February 1997 (undated clipping).

60. 'I had Hamlet's disease of introspection. I was always looking for the integrity of it. I believed in Girl Power so much.' *Observer* 6 June 1999. She left the Spice Girls during a Scandinavian tour.

61. *Time Out*, 29 November 1995.

62. ICA publicity, April-May 1995.

63. Directed by Barry Sonenfield, screenplay by Caroline Thompson and Larry Wilson.

64. Directed by Arthur Hiller, screenplay by Leslie Dickson.

65. Angela Carter, in Malcolm Bradbury and Judy Cooke, *New Writing* (London: Minerva, 1992), pp. 185–6.

66. Angela Carter, *Wise Children* (London: Vintage, 1992) pp. 90, 58.

67. *Ibid.*, pp. 89, 21.

68. *Ibid.*, p. 12.

69. *Ibid.*, p. 119.

70. *Ibid.*, p. 77.

71. *Ibid.*, p. 191.

72. *Ibid.*, p. 11.

73. 'The (Pregnant) Prince and the Showgirl: Cultural Legitimacy and the Reproduction of *Hamlet*', in Mark Thornton Burnett and John Manning, *New Essays on Hamlet* (New York: AMS Press, 1994), p. 266.

74. Aicha in Douglas Goldring, *Artist's Quarter* (London: Faber, 1941), p. l66. I owe this reference to John Stokes. See Paul Damasay, *La Cavalière Elsa* in *La Petite Illustration*, *Théâtre* 49 (1925).

75. Janet Adelman, *Suffocating Mothers: Fantasies of Maternal Origin in Shakespeare's Plays, 'Hamlet' to 'The Tempest'* (London: Routledge, 1992), p. 30.

76. In the published text: Wayne Wang and Paul Auster, *Smoke* and *Blue in the Face: Two Films* (London: Faber 1995).

77. Celestino Coronado (UK 1976) cast twins as Hamlet, the Ghost and Laertes, doubled Ophelia and Gertrude (both Helen Mirren) and made Polonius (Quentin Crisp) and the Player King camp icons. On Bonniére's film see *New Canadian Film* 21 (August 1973), p. 22.

78. Carole Corbeil, *In the Wings* (Toronto: Stoddart, 1997), p. 270. Thanks to Ann Thompson for this reference.

CHAPTER 10

Women's voices in the cathedral of culture

In London and New York, the rise of the Women's Movement coincided with two important productions marking the return of the woman's Hamlet. However these proved transitional stagings whose relationship to feminism was complex. Both appeared as the New Right began its project of reshaping British and American society and both involved attempts to create innovative theatrical spaces. Both raised questions about theatrical authorship and power. The actresses were Frances de la Tour and Diane Venora, the directors Robert Walker and Joseph Papp.

I

London 1979: Carnival of oppression

The . . . first production at the New Half Moon will take place this October before conversion begins, and it will be a walk-about show, taking the audience through the building and out onto the grass and paved areas outside . . . The play we have chosen to show the potential of the New Half Moon is HAMLET. HAMLET with its courtyards and graveyards, HAMLET with its players and its murderers, HAMLET with Frances de la Tour as HAMLET. (Press release)

In October 1979 in a disused chapel on the Mile End Road, Frances de la Tour at the age of 34 played Hamlet (see Figure 19).[1] The draughty hall was the new home of the Half Moon Theatre, which made its name with left-wing community drama and under Robert Walker also explored *avant-garde* acting and design traditions from Expressionism to performance art. It staged experimental dramatists virtually unknown in Britain, and was known for Left plays driven by women, like Brecht's *The Mother*. It established the British reputation of Franca Rame and Dario Fo whose *Can't Pay? Won't Pay!* (with de la Tour) celebrated working-class feminism within the frames of international and grass-roots socialism.

Figure 19   The father's throne. Poster for Frances de la Tour in *Hamlet*, London 1979;
director: Robert Walker.

Now the Half Moon was expanding to create a 'people's palace' for the
East End, including a young people's theatre and community resources.
'In a sense no play is a "period" play', Walker said, 'You have to end
up . . . with an English play for an English audience, *now.*' And '*now*'

was a significant moment: Margaret Thatcher's first government had been elected in May 1979. Walker responded with plans for a cross-gender parody *Hamlet*, with Thatcher inspired by ghosts to wreak revenge on the Welfare State; Frances de la Tour's *Hamlet* was a separate but parallel project. The Half Moon sought to 'reclaim' classical drama for working class audiences: de la Tour had a massive following through the television sitcom *Rising Damp*, *Hamlet*'s programme celebrated the East End's tradition of female Hamlets, and children from its Youth Theatre played the Players. De la Tour suspected a gimmick when Walker suggested she play Hamlet; he explained it was not about gender but collaboration and told her, ' "You are the only actor who is ready and who I want to do it with." I thought that sounded OK.'[2] Theatre is pragmatic: 'He simply wanted certain qualities in his Hamlet and I happened to have them; and if he'd found them in a man, doubtless he'd have given the part to him.'[3] 'While my gender may add a certain perspective, my. . . abilities are what matter', she told the press: 'It's not a feminist casting.'[4]

Frances de la Tour was active in the Workers' Revolutionary Party and her analysis of Hamlet reflected her political framework. 'Dialectical materialism is all about change and contradiction', she said before rehearsals, 'and if there ever was a part that is about contradiction, it's Hamlet. It's all about the five hundred separate qualities that can exist separately in one mind.'[5] Twenty years later she felt 'I did not play my Hamlet with any *specific* view, either political or feminist. . . If it made a political or ideological statement it was because of the times it was part of', and 'Marxist ideas would be present in anything and everything I do.' She played 'Hamlet – a young person gripped in the tension of the moment – at the highest point of contradiction.'[6]

The promenade *Hamlet* was a democratic concept: 'You, the audience, can make your own decisions in relation to the action, whether you want to see it in "close-up" or in "long-shot" . . . we want to offer *editing* decisions to the on-looker and participant. Also, we have no chairs.' Though 'it was done on a shoestring' (de la Tour), reviewers admired the way production, venue and actress blended in 'bruising intimacy' as '150 of us crowded into a darkened room'.[7] Walker's team created an 'evocative maelstrom' of drapes, props, trashily opulent costumes, scratchy sound effects, and a welter of small stages. The action overlapped between them in a technique pioneered by Ariane Mnouchkine's carnival recreation of the French Revolution, *1789*, but in the Thatcher year 1979, after Claudius' 'democratic' *coup*, Elsinore became a circus of reactionary grotesques.

Design was meaning. Caught in a spotlight, the Ghost stalked a high platform in the roof of the chapel. A second stage became Polonius' house, the Players' stage, the Queen's bedroom and Ophelia's grave. A gross painting of Claudius was on display as well as mock-innocent cupids. Faces were caked with white make-up, costumes were decayed fairground-Elizabethan and 'ooze bits of stuff – as though the corruption of the court has been repressed, but will still out'.[8] The most startling image was the third stage, which was dominated by an enormous slatted wooden throne shaped like a devouring skeleton king. Claudius sat there uneasily, Hamlet sank into it for 'O that this too too solid flesh would melt', as if retreating foetally into a monstrous paternal womb. It was a disturbing psychological image, but not the controlling metaphor it would have been in a proscenium staging; de la Tour had to manoeuvre through the whole junkyard.

The performance was claustrophobic. The first scene was cut: grotesque rulers and sycophants suddenly swarmed through the audience. Polonius was a shaven-skulled 'great baby', Ophelia a *pierette*; both wore giant ruffs like salvers for decapitated heads. The new regime was greeted 'with a mime of a handclap and an almost rattlesnake sound from the throat'.[9] Promenade theatre in the seventies was normally celebratory, but in this *Hamlet* the sense of New Right unconcern suggested actual physical danger; spectators perched on scenic chunks that might be repossessed immediately. They became voyeurs, crowding for a better view like skulking Polonius; they were accused by Ophelia ('You tumbled me'); duellists with giant swords hacked through them; and poison sprayed the crowd: 'You suddenly realise what it must be like to be cooped up in this court where fever and madness infect the air.'[10] Despite the pre-publicity, the action never left the building: nothing – including Fortinbras – existed beyond the prison. Walker quoted Michael Long's *The Unnatural Scene*: 'Elsinore is a Waste Land of dulled responses, lowered expectations, blindness, stupidity and indifference. The play can leave one in no doubt that socialization at this level, a culture of this kind, is a crime against the possibilities of life.' Many cross-dressed Hamlets over the next few years would find themselves in similarly sham worlds – masked, circus-like, Kabuki-inspired – where Hamlet's androgyny represented human values under threat.

Frances de la Tour's brother Andy played the Ghost and a leering, earringed Rosencrantz; Elsinore looked inbred. Ophelia was the next step in its dehumanisation – a pink and white automaton. In the Nunnery scene she was petrified and cowered at a distance, staring into her book;

Hamlet's furious 'Where's your father?' was an explosion. Only in madness could Ophelia become alive and touching – 'Her springs are busted.'[11] No flowers grew here so she tore up Hamlet's poetry and broke off a cupid's head; when Gertrude described her death she too became mechanical, her voice grinding down to 'Drown'd, drown'd'. When the Players arrived pulling a Mother Courage cart the contrast was astonishing, because they were East End children and their mimed show unnerved Claudius, innocence meeting corruption eye to eye. Sex was distorted and exhibitionist: 'insatiate' Claudius was naked to the waist and Gertrude was bare-breasted with gilded nipples. Yet she hugged the trappings of snobbery; Maggie Steed (soon Berkoff's Thatcher) sneered at Ophelia and flashed disdainful but frightened sharp-toothed smiles. Her relationship with Hamlet, all mutual contempt, was tactile; in their first scene Hamlet caught hold of her and she hit out to escape. Steed and Andy de la Tour were leaders of the emerging Alternative Comedy movement and *Hamlet* was a savage satire – a Left-puritan protest – except for Hamlet.

De la Tour's Hamlet was tall, stooped, unglamorous, and from the streets. Greased dark hair fell in lank tangles; her sleeveless jacket was like a Hell's Angel's, leaving arms and upper chest bare. Her costume never concealed her body, yet it was not flaunted like the others': the actress and Hamlet were unselfconsciously themselves. She was mobile, with strong gestures – she could slap Rosencrantz and Guildenstern heartily, loom over Ophelia and Polonius, and chill them with a glare – and in this stylised decadence her emotional range was dazzling. After years of training at the RSC (where 'I found after six years that I'd done only five proper speaking parts'[12] – Peter Hall told her she had not the looks for Juliet) she had a unique vocal range. Hamlet's voice could be nasal or liquid, sarcastically sharp or a deep sob of contained grief. 'She is a supremely intelligent artist', Michael Coveney wrote, and 'strikes straight to the heart of each scene.' From her first appearance, 'shrouded in black, insolent and outspoken', to the 'consummate swagger and authority' with which she disposed of the spies, 'she decimates the opposition by sheer intellectual force'.[13] The child's anger at Gertrude's paraded sexuality came close to madness. De la Tour crawled over Steed's skirts, scrabbled inside them and forced her to the ground; Hamlet's frenzied 'sex-obsession . . . sends the Queen screaming into the night'.[14] But there were moving moments; Gertrude broke down and de la Tour cradled Steed's head to her breast. Those who had sold their souls were already in torment.

Where did the production stand in relation to current sexual politics? 'It's not a feminist casting', she told the press – her gender was 'irrelevant.' 'The sex of Hamlet did not come into it. I didn't play it "like a man" nor did I play it "as a woman" either.'[15] 'It can't be an accident that throughout history Hamlet has been played by women . . . I think it is because it is such a *universal*, expressing all the emotions of youth – and life – and there isn't another part to match it.'[16] De la Tour did not deny the prince's gender or her own; rather Hamlet was the one body of integrity in a market where flesh was the currency of corruption: masculinity and femininity were redundant terms when Hamlet was the only surviving member of the human race. She emphasised action ('Doing a play is like going on a journey,') and stressed that after the pain of private conflicts, Hamlet in exile gains objectivity, 'finds he's in a world of wars'.[17] She returned in white, detached and transfigured. She spun Yorick's skull on her finger and quizzed Osric with 'the amused weariness of one who can now afford to delight in human eccentricity'.[18] Her strength never flagged. Michael Billington said de la Tour's Hamlet – more 'tough, abrasive, virile and impassioned' than many men – was 'compact with every male virtue except femininity'.[19] For others, 'her greatest successes are in the area of vulnerability', especially her 'trapped' 'O what a rogue and peasant slave am I' ('Venomous self-disgust', disagreed Billington).[20] It was a study in contradiction.

Frances de la Tour's Hamlet transformed her reputation, opening up possibilities in Shaw, O'Neill and Strindberg, even in due course Cleopatra. But the production was attacked both by the Right ('There seems to be no point in a woman playing Hamlet, except to get it on the record like another failed attempt to climb Everest'[21]) *and* by the leading British writer on feminism and theatre, Micheline Wandor. She thought de la Tour was absorbed into the 'kitsch' of a 'generalised freak-show'; she disliked the 'obvious Freudianism'; and called her 'mannered': she 'mirrors the surrounding nihilism'.[22] British feminist theatre was only then developing a history and theory. Wandor was about to produce her influential study of gender and postwar British drama, *Understudies* (1981) where she distinguished between bourgeois feminism, radical (separatist) feminism and the socialist feminism she endorsed. Wandor believed the Half Moon had not thought its gender line through and she later posited a 'Hamlette, Princess of Denmark' to demonstrate that however 'adequately' an actress might play Hamlet, Shakespeare's writing was fundamentally patriarchal, shaped by 'the imperative of gender'.[23] For 1979 was a pivotal date in a British dialogue between feminism and socialism. Many believed the best hope for the defeated Left – whose ideas, wrote Sheila Rowbotham in the influential *Beyond the Fragments*, were 'male dominated and handed down from above' – lay in developing feminist analysis and structures: 'A Marxism which does not base itself on feminism . . . is not what we call "socialist".' The election of a *reactionary* woman prime minister posed ideological problems and de la Tour's Hamlet embodied the Left's shocked debates.

Rowbotham: 'Did socialists believe that women's liberation meant women should become like men, did they argue that women had specific qualities as a sex which men might acquire or develop; or did they imagine men and women contributing towards making a culture in which notions of "masculinity" and "femininity" would dissolve?'[24] There were affinities between the Half Moon *Hamlet* and Caryl Churchill's *Cloud Nine* (also 1979) which used cross-casting to present gender identities as imposed fictions which theatre is uniquely equipped to deconstruct.[25] But Walker's imagistic war between the 'good' woman (marginal, denying gender) and the 'bad' woman (powerful, erotic) seemed confused.[26] Playing Gertrude, Steed felt depressingly isolated within the company, and the inadequacy of current vocabularies was clear when de la Tour was pressed to talk about cross-casting: 'Now I consider it, it *is* rather true that Hamlet is a rather feminine character . . . he prevaricates, he manipulates, he wants to know all the angles before he commits himself.' In 1997 she commented, 'I prefer not to talk or discuss my work for fear of (the *misuse* of) contradiction!'[27] But in her *Hamlet* finally truth resided not in the stereotypes Walker theatricalised vividly (rulers = brutes, women = dolls or whores) but in the power of *playing* – as an actress probed masculinity, and London children toppled kings.

Hamlet fractured the mould for her and she was sufficiently intrigued by the paradoxes of cross-dressing to return to it in 1993 with Hisashi Inoue's *Greasepaint*, a solo piece with similarities to Wajda's *Hamlet (IV)*. She played a Japanese Kabuki actress preparing for a male role (while teaching a man how to act men's Ideal Woman: 'Put a sheet of paper between [your legs] . . . and try to walk without letting it fall.') De la Tour described the 'subtle' 'secret' contradictions of the 'doll-like' *onnagata*: 'It touches something all of us would like – to be perfect', and yet 'it's very feudal. There is something there that has not freed itself.'[28] Hisashi Inoue makes the woman who breaks gender boundaries insane – sacrificing her child for her profession, she forgets biology defines her. But de la Tour has often commented on the mishandling of women by British theatrical power structures: 'So much does depend on whether directors like you. On whether in fact you correspond to their ideas of sexuality'[29] – 'I was always being talked of in terms of gaunt men.' She has spoken of the plight of many brilliant unconventional actresses driven into self-parody ('They suffered the most limited casting and had to constantly repeat themselves' – 'If you're not careful you find you end up becoming what you've been told you are') and she blamed a denigration of actresses' work as instinctual. 'I deal with it through rage', she said, 'to cover up the pain.'[30] Lynne Segal wrote in *Beyond the Fragments*, 'There is no easy solution to the problem of creating new political structures which overcome rather than reproduce existing hierarchies of sex, class and race', and de la Tour comments: 'We are not ourselves unless we make it so.'[31] Even in New York three years later the sexual politics of the female Hamlet were still evolving.

II

New York 1982: love is the hook

The Public Theater has been for over three decades, the flagship in this country for non-traditional casting. . . We try to put on our stage images that people who ride the subways would recognize. They'll see themselves reflected in the productions that we produce. (Heidi Griffiths, casting director[32])

In 1982 Joseph Papp directed *Hamlet* for the New York Public Theater, inaugurating – like Walker – a remodelled playhouse, the Anspacher. But whereas Walker evoked the history of proletarian performance, Papp opted – uncharacteristically – for classicism. There was a bright white marble stage, half stateroom, half mausoleum, and – as if reflecting Ronald Reagan's invention of pseudo-historic ceremonials to dignify his new Presidency – Papp opened with an honour guard laying flags on the King's tomb. It was a Ruritanian regime of fanfares, hussars, ostentatious uniforms, and cold hearts – a Heritage space – though a forestage jutted out for the soliloquies so 'Hamlet', said Papp, 'can move right in among the People.' Hamlet was summoned and emerged cap in hand, defenceless as the boy in 'When Did You Last See Your Father?' Papp emphasised the slightness, pallor and isolation of 'young Hamlet'. Evoking the Delacroix image of aching innocence, Papp wanted Venora to play a lost child – 'tiny' and 'pre-pubescent', critics said – and he wanted the cross-gender casting to introduce troubling undertones to the Hamlet-Claudius relationship, foreshadowing the Dublin 'abuse' scenario. In their first scene he put them tight together: 'He's very close to you', he told Venora, 'You can smell him.' The reviewers were united about her strengths: her 'beauty', 'lithesomeness' and 'passion'; her 'playfulness and her wit'; her 'well-pitched contralto' and 'lithe, athletic' figure' – 'balletic in its grace'.[33] Beyond that, though, Venora's reviews (mainly from men) were appalling: 'a series of increasingly repetitive and inter-changeable rantings'; 'strained, affected'; 'nasty, not at all gentlemanly'; 'painful to watch'. 'So why', the *New York Times* asked, 'did Joseph Papp choose a young, virtually unknown actress named Diane Venora?' It was 'seeming madness'.[34]

Papp and the Public Theater had been at the forefront of radical American drama since the early sixties, integrating Shakespeare – espe-cially free Shakespeare in Central Park – into contemporary experience and developing a theatre of multi-ethnicity. Papp presented a Puerto Rican Hamlet, James Earl Jones' Lear, and a host of new writers, though he faced such intransigence that an academic could still condemn him both for casting Diane Venora and for letting a black actress play Titania.[35] *Hamlet* ('poor. . . slow-paced') and Venora were buried. However, the production itself was less significant than a documentary that was made about it and reached a far vaster audience than the show's short run could ever do. ABC TV broadcast a fifty-minute film, *Joseph Papp Presents: Rehearsing 'Hamlet': The Work Process of the Public Theater Stage Production Directed by Joseph Papp*. It was independently important because of the story it told, through its selection from hours of rehearsal footage for this female *Hamlet*. A counter-statement to *Kiss Me Petruchio!* (1981), a lauded documentary examining a Public Theater *Shrew* in the context of Women's Lib, *Rehearsing 'Hamlet'* constructed a portrait – a 'true-life' *Morning Glory* – of an actress' troubled creativity and the benign paternalism of her director.[36]

Carl Charlson's documentary included a hostile journalist who scoffed, 'It's ridiculous doing *Hamlet* with a woman.' Papp told him Venora was 'capable of playing Hamlet' and he paid his respect to the star tradition: 'Do you know how many women have played Hamlet?' Papp named Le Gallienne, McKenna and Anderson (and Venora added, 'At least she knew about life'). However he had picked 'a young, virtually unknown actress' whose work he too did not know. Diane Venora was thirty and married with a daughter, but 'He'd never seen me act or do anything.' She caught Papp's attention when she joined the company as Hippolyta. 'He approached me during a rehearsal and he said, "I've a project which

I've been trying to cast for a long time, and I think you might be right for it" . . . He wanted a woman to play it.' She read for him (in the Ghost scene 'she made me cry') and 'He said "It's a big risk but let's go for it."' Asked by the press 'Why a woman?' Venora replied, 'I have nothing to say.' She saw Hamlet as a personal challenge:

I can sit and, say, do a poetry reading that costs nothing, or I can dig deeply inside myself and it will cost everything – which is, to challenge my own life, my own fears, my own spirituality, my own inner shadow and blackness.

The story the documentary told – and of course no 'factual' film is neutral – was one of profound conflicts between actress and director.

Papp's concept ignored feminism. He told Venora the boy prince should feel strangely 'soothed' by Claudius. She disagreed ('I feel sullied') but he wanted her to explore a bereaved, masochistic dependency – 'You're weak'– like a concentration camp victim drawn to a guard:

PAPP: There's some human strength there, and that's what you're lacking at the moment. . . Whoever has life and death over you. . .
VENORA: I don't know.

She wanted to play hostility. In rehearsal she made 'Seems, I know not seems: IT IS,' confrontational, accusing Gertrude, and she felt Hamlet's mind was racing, juggling with words and ideas. In the event Venora managed to integrate Papp's 'soothed' reading into Hamlet's anger (she smiled until the Court left, then the raw emotion burst out); but elsewhere the film shows her dealing with directions she disliked by *internalising* them. Her unhappiness with some of Papp's decisions became part of Hamlet. As he talked of Hamlet's attraction to Claudius' strength, Venora stood head bowed, listening deeply; later her Hamlet stood in just the same numbed submission while Claudius lectured and hugged him. But the film privileged Papp's very gendered sense of his protective – avuncular – role in straight-to-camera confidences and long voice-overs:

People are just waiting to rip her to shreds if they could. A lot of people, they want to see her fail. If she fails it'll not be because she's not giving a brilliant performance. . . I'll protect her like I protect my own life. . . The fact that she's a woman does enter into the situation . . . Emotionally, I can't help but see her as a woman. I feel for her as a woman when she's Hamlet. I think of her as a woman when she sits and talks to me. I cannot think of her as a boy, she's not a boy however boyish she might be. She's very female to me.

Venora however was self-analytical and sharp:

I'm an androgynous female. I embody both things. I'm very feminist and at the same time very – if I can use the word – palsied. . . I have guts in my life. . . I didn't reach out to study boys, to study how they walk or how they are. I just happen on my own.

The costumes evoked Delacroix, Manet, and *L'Aiglon* (Papp: 'I want her to be *proper*. I want her to be a noble Hamlet, a classical Hamlet, with all the emotions that she has put in the proper place') whereas Venora was drawn to exactly the qualities Kozintsev accused Delacroix of censoring: 'passion, sarcasm, coarseness and . . . wit'. 'The thing about my Hamlet is that he's much more raw. He's giving in to his passion, his rage, his disillusionment, his fear of not being able to stand up, to do.' She told colleagues, 'What Joe wanted originally was something grand. But it's not right for me.' She wore a leather jacket rehearsing the Ghost scene, and there was a street-fighting rush as she slashed at her companions with a knife; Papp substituted a sword for her to hold like a cross. He defined the rehearsal ground-rules: Venora could do whatever '*feels* right' so long as she then accepted what he decided *was* right. In a voice-over he conceded that all men play Hamlet differently ('more robustly, more effetely, more effeminately') so he must accept Venora's right to play Hamlet her own 'particular way'; but he admitted later that he found it hard to 'let go'. Charlson's film was built round scenes of awkward disagreement.

Venora's crucial qualities were a fluid emotional energy and a determination to immerse herself in Hamlet. Working on the book for the 'rogue and peasant slave' soliloquy, she switched instantly from sobbing agony ('O vengeance!') to laughter ('What an ass am I!') and found it a revelation to play this flow. This delighted Papp, who rushed in to talk about Hamlet (whom for once he instinctively called '*her*'): 'There's something that keeps changing in her, constantly. Her changes in mood are so fantastic.'

PAPP: And to be able to do that, to shift the Mind so drastically, so rapidly sometimes that it sounds like crazy. . . But you have the capacity to do that . . . I'm absolutely certain you can play this role.
VENORA [DRY]: Oh good.

Papp's affable last sentence implied a doubt that focused the documentary. The fact that she was a 'young, virtually unknown actress' was the point of Charlson's film, and perhaps of the production. Charlson called his programme *Joseph Papp Presents* . . . not *Diane Venora Plays*. . . He presented Papp as an absolute authority on Shakespeare and, in his working relationship with the young woman, on life: 'I had to find out the way she functions . . . how she comes to certain decisions. I had to understand her whole psyche.' This Pygmalion/Trilby factor was the film's thread. Charlson's presentation of Venora as a volatile, anorexic ingénue living on her nerves – Eva Lovelace III – reflected Papp's creation of a *conservatoire* situation with her defined as an 'unknown' trainee. Though Papp believed a *Hamlet* director and lead should spend up to a year working together (the performer must 'absorb' the play), there was no such collaboration ('He'd never seen me act') and 'Time is short!' became Papp's refrain. He told Venora that her quarrying the wordplay (e.g. '*I/eye/ see/seem*') was a distraction; she told the filmmakers, as though confessing a crime, 'There's always something in me, this vicious mole of nature in me, that struggles to find the reason, a meaning – *why*.'

Venora and Papp in rehearsal

Some examples. Meeting Rosencrantz and Guildenstern, Venora's instinct is to play hostility and the 'shift of Mind'. Her greeting is falsely fulsome, with a manic smile. She uses gestures to punctuate, and to illustrate rhythm. Wildly animated, Hamlet suddenly realises that 'Thinking makes it so', and touches 'R&G' mock-wooingly, keeps them apart so she can control the conversation by dancing between them. Papp insists she be vulnerable: 'They're going to hurt you, again and again.' But Venora is disconcertingly in character – clowning like a rebellious teenager and refusing to listen except to bounce off his words, just as her Hamlet uses people to feed manic irony. She feels Hamlet is driven by a painful, freewheeling, egocentricity – which bleeds into the actor-director relationship. Papp tells her to stress plot points, says the Players' arrival sets Hamlet planning traps; she thinks it triggers solipsistic fancies:

VENORA: But *I'm* the King. I am the Lover, I'm the Adventurous Knight, I'm –
PAPP [IMPATIENT]: I know, but you're doing all that.

Conversely Venora wanted to make 'To be or not to be' Hamlet's moment of total self-withdrawal, speaking with eyes closed as she lay reduced to exhaustion. Papp told her this was 'bourgeois'. ('We all need rest . . . You're not going to kill yourself just because you need rest.') The speech is active, he insisted, the struggle with suicide. Venora's head sank – and Papp told her she should use that 'interesting', 'Hamlet-like' pose. ('We talk about physique and the nature of being . . . [Hamlet] collapses this way') Venora thought the 'interesting' pose – sitting with one leg curled beneath her, her head on one knee – was 'girlish', but in all these cases she grudgingly, even bleakly, submitted and Charlson always gave Papp the last word:

There were days a few weeks ago when . . . she was impossible to reach. And I had to take her by the hand, and sit down with her and say. . . 'No matter what you try, I'm not going to let you be bad in it.'. . . I know what people will attack in her. I will never let her get up there to be exposed to it. First of all she's a woman playing this role: that's enough, she's going to be under a certain kind of attack for that. But I want her to be good. I don't want any criticism of her for doing something really excessive and out of the way.

Instructed to be dependent on the men, Venora's most 'out of the way' choices concerned Ophelia and the sexual politics of the venture.

Papp wanted her to be dismissive of Ophelia, but in one rehearsal Venora made Hamlet shy and at a loss with her, smiling and nervous. Ophelia, the stronger, thrust her gifts to the floor for him to pick up. He was confused, hands behind his back, head bowed in simple sad sincerity ('I did love you once'); tried to cover up with a pretended, bullying, manliness; but could not. Hamlet's voice broke, he waved helplessly ('Get thee to a nunnery'), hid his eyes. . . Venora was exhilarated, Papp impatient.

VENORA: This woman was very wonderful to me. She was beautiful to me – I mean, almost the hope that we could be together again, even though she did the terrible thing of giving me back these things. Inside her, the intention that Pippa was playing, Ophelia was playing, was so strong that suddenly I wanted to embrace her.
PAPP: You know why you didn't and you shouldn't?
VENORA: Because you'd say 'It's not a *Love Scene*!. . .
PAPP: You're not interested in Ophelia any more. Really. You're just angry there because again she's betraying you. You can even see what she's doing: she's giggling, she's ambling, she's lisping, she's carrying on the same old crap. That gets you MAD when you see that.
VENORA: [DEPRESSED] I must interpret anything she does as something that is absolutely conspiratorial, manipulative, seduction-wise, not . . . not . . . honest.
PAPP: Totally dishonest. From the moment, I believe, that you see her.
VENORA: It's too soon. I'm giving her another chance . . . And this girl, she's this vision of loveliness. I mean, the *eye*: what appears, what seems and what *is*?? She *seems* to be beautiful and lovely and innocent. I must at least play *those* moments, until I *see* what she really is. . . Well we'll play it once your way, once my way.
PAPP: It's not my way. I don't have any way. . . It is a scene that has to erupt. Be savage. Unrelenting.

Venora suddenly fixed Ophelia with a stare and interrogated her: 'Well? — *Well?* — *WELL*???' Papp joined in:

VENORA [IMPROVISING]: What the hell –
VENORA AND PAPP: – are you DOING here?
PAPP: 'I did love you once.'
VENORA [SUDDENLY DEFLATED]: I think that's a fact. I think that's true.
PAPP: 'I DID love you once. I don't love you any more.'
VENORA [STARING AT THE TEXT]: It's a part of me . . . I don't know.

In due course critics found Venora's scenes with the other women 'unusually violent'. Hamlet ripped letters and tossed keepsakes in Ophelia's face; he threw her to the back of the stage, menaced her like a stalker, choked her and limped off sobbing. In the 'particularly ugly' Closet scene Hamlet punched Gertrude in the ribs and dragged her down. Years later when she become a director herself (her first production was Chekhov's *Hamlet* variation, *The Seagull*) Venora's explanation of her working method put the clash over Ophelia in context: 'Every scene I'm in is a love scene; the absence of love, the search for love, the discarding of it, and always the need. Love is basic. Love is the hook.'[37]

In the film, one day Venora grimly reports that her daughter and mother-in-law have gone down with bronchitis, as now she has too. She has no appetite: 'I didn't feel like eating as much, playing this character.' Struggling with the first soliloquy, she ends it in tears, gagging on 'Hold my tongue.' She coughs and sinks withdrawn against a pillar, grinding her hand through her hair – is she in character? Papp is worried, but it is a shock to be reminded that she is a mother with responsibilities in the real world, not the child the film presents her as with Papp. For Venora, playing Hamlet was a two-way struggle – to prise open the text and herself:

Shakespeare says to you, 'So you've given all you've got. Great. Good. Now you have to give more. Now more. Now more. Now more . . . Until your heart and your brains and your guts are pulp, and the part feeds on you, eating you.' And that's exactly what the play does to me. It consumes me, it wastes me.

'I don't sleep at night', says Papp. 'I think about her and I see her face and I see what she's going through.'

No documentary is innocent. Was there really a power struggle? Was she 'unreachable'? Was he proscriptive? In Charlson's edit, Venora painfully but self-indulgently submerges herself in a volatile, attention-seeking Hamlet, and disrupts company work. Her behaviour is presented as aberrant, as illness, like *Hamlet* from Claudius' angle, and vignettes of women in the production imply that the normal, functioning sexual politics of the Public Theater are quite different: the designer Theonie Aldridge expresses her admiration for Papp, Gertrude enthuses about Aldridge, and Ophelia in repeated cutaways watches – disapprovingly, the editing suggests – as Venora argues yet again. And yet Charlson included some sequences of an unrecognisable, professional, Venora discussing training with the fight director or chatting at a costume fitting. Thoughtful, with no trace of the adolescent rehearsal aura, she explains 'I made the choice that I am dishevelled' (she needs tattered trousers for her 'mad' scenes) and is struggling to inhabit Hamlet on her own terms: 'I've found out where I wanted to go.' Yet even here Charlson contrasts Gertrude, thrilled by her costume ('My work is done!') with Venora, who wants her very full shirt-sleeves taken in because she looks 'too Juliet'. The significant, unexplored, detail here was that her dresser agreed but nothing was done: onstage in the duel Hamlet stayed prettified – Juliet with a rapier.

It must be said that much of Charlson's footage justified the critics' harsher comments: Venora elocutes in an artificial 'English' accent and overwhelms several scenes with gestures and cadenzas. But Papp chose an actress who seemed to have 'raw' talent he could shape, and he repeatedly suppresses the quality he cast her for, emotional frankness: 'She's so deep in her feelings.' Charlson offered images of 'male wisdom' versus 'female hysteria' – compassionate directing versus self-destructive acting – which were surprising in 1982 and would soon look suspect.

Late in rehearsals, Venora produced deep new tones and resonance, a vocal coming-of-age. Before the duel her Hamlet was commanding – 'Tis but *foolery*. . . We *defy* augury'– and, confronting death, tried to pass that courage to the balding, crushed, Horatio: 'And in this harsh world draw thy breath, *in pain.*' Reversing the opening image of Hamlet with Claudius, Venora held and consoled Horatio, who sank his head on her chest. Hearing shots outside, Hamlet stood tall despite the 'pain' to proclaim Fortinbras' election. The audience heard advancing drums of war but Hamlet heard something new: '— *Silence.*' Papp saw the play as a study of the emotional effects of encountering death, but for Diane Venora *Hamlet* was about the living. She was fascinated by the breakdown of emotional boundaries and watched 'The Mousetrap' intently: 'The Players. . . for all the pretension and make-up and costume, are honest. They dare to touch passion, which people in everyday life can't handle.'

Venora has argued that acting is not exhibitionistic but does demand emotional 'nakedness':

By the very nature of his work, if he's good, [the actor] has a temperament . . . And he has to live in an open mood all day. . . Now, in normal life, you'd do that and be killed. But . . . he's going to let you into his heart. And that takes transparency of soul . . . Anybody can take off their clothes.[38]

Acting, she has said, is 'hyperactive' education, achieved through 'immersing yourself'.

In 1982 Venora's Hamlet was dismissed as a footnote. However she went on to be the first modern American actress to play Hamlet, Ophelia and Gertrude. Papp invited her back to play Ophelia opposite Kevin Kline (1990) and she gave the role unusual intellectual command, treating Gertrude like a sister and visibly understanding Hamlet's torment. This time the Nunnery scene indeed became a love scene as they hunted for peace and strength in each other's bodies; and in madness Venora's Ophelia *became* Hamlet, wiping and slapping at her 'painted' face as he had done. She gave Ophelia the full depth of her voice – throaty, guttural, moaning out the pain of the play. Then in 1999 she played Gertrude for both Andrei Serban (Public Theater) and Michael Almereyda's film, where the cast regarded her as their authority on *Hamlet*. She has said:

You can never 'do' a Shakespearean play and think you are finished with it. As you grow older, new things come into your life. It's always going to be about something more in your life.[39]

In 1999 *Hamlet* for her touched on motherhood but would always be about exploration. In 1988 she had left the profession to look after her daughter, who suffered from a degenerative condition. Venora worked as a teacher. Returning to Hollywood six years later was 'difficult': 'I have not had the [film] role to show my talent', she said, 'And I may not be pretty enough or whatever they think it is, or it just hasn't come down the pike or someone is just more marketable at that point than I am . . . That's just the rules of the game. I don't fight that because I believe that every dog has its day. . . But one day, if I just be patient, Hamlet will come.'[40]

III

London 1992: Hamlet's roar

A secret stage. London 1605. Moll Cutpurse is the Roaring Girl. Dressed as a man, brawling and breaking the rules, she's the toast of the Elizabethan underworld. Renegades like her spice the crowded taverns and infiltrate the playhouses. Tonight, Moll has gathered a motley troupe of these rogues and those women who work, marry and mother. Together they will perform for you an outlawed act – an all-woman performance of *Hamlet*. (Press release.)

By 1992 the female Hamlet was politically iconic and in female hands. That year the Women's Theatre Group (founded 1974) relaunched itself as The Sphinx with an all-female version. Anne Mitchell played the lead, it was directed by Sue Parrish and included a prologue written by Clare Luckham, the author of the women-wrestlers comedy *Trafford Tanzi*. *The Roaring Girl's Hamlet* attempted to blend and celebrate the work of both feminist theatre practitioners and the feminist academic community.[41] It was a conscious intervention in the sexual politics of British Shakespeare.

In the 1960s the slogan 'Shakespeare our contemporary' had inspired the Oxbridge-educated male directors who dominated subsidised British theatre to subject the male protagonists to unsentimental analysis: Scofield's Lear was a Stalinist tyrant, for example, and the RSC's *Wars of the Roses* cycle redefined 'villains' and 'heroes' as merely products of their time. On the margins some new perspective on Shakespeare's women emerged: Irene Worth rationalised Goneril, showed her deformed by her father's brutality; and Peggy Ashcroft revealed Queen Margaret as the most monumental character in Shakespeare. Yet the re-thinking did not proceed consistently and those directors often borrowed the trappings of sixties sexual liberation in sensationalist, even misogynist terms: a naked RSC Helen lured Faustus to damnation, a naked Desdemona was murdered at the Mermaid Theatre, and in John Barton's 1968 *Troilus and Cressida* nudity proclaimed Cressida's faithlessness. (The very year Gay Liberation was born at Stonewall, Barton also 'explained' Achilles' brutality by making him a transvestite.) Charles Marowitz's influential Shakespearean collages added his insights into Desdemona ('Riding his cock like a bronco into a wilderness of thorns' – 'Well, wouldn't you have, if you'd had the chance?'[42]), a naked-witch Lady Macbeth, the rape of Isabella in *Measure for Measure*, and the sodomisation of Kate in the *Shrew*. In the 1960s Cleopatra was scarcely seen in British theatres – it was argued that no woman could adequately play her – while the comedies dominated by women were often trivialised. Stratford repeatedly staged the *Shrew* as a slapstick romp. *As You Like It* offered pale Carnaby Street utopianism, with pastiche pop. The most publicised version (National Theatre 1967) had an all-male cast and was originally inspired by Jan Kott's

'Shakespeare's Bitter Arcadia', on Renaissance homoeroticism; but the (replacement) director Clifford Williams disowned the concept. The actors were afraid in rehearsal of being thought 'queer' and Williams explained: 'Underlying all the love scenes between Orlando and Rosalind there is an incredible iridescent purity. Men are somehow better at this than women.'[43]

In 1969 Jane Arden's *Vagina Rex and the Gas Oven* at the London Arts Lab launched a new wave of British feminist drama. Her attack on gender myths included an angry chorus of Furies and Shakespearean Witches, and 'as one of the outcomes of the production', Arden wrote, 'the *Observer* carried a piece called "Are Women Oppressed?" as though there was still some doubt about the matter.'[44] Arden's Holocaust group pioneered feminist street theatre, and out of a ferment of workshops, scripts, publications like the news-sheet *Shrew*, and guerrilla demonstrations, the Women's Theatre Group emerged. The RSC's only female director Buz Goodbody was involved in much of this, and in 1973 she tried to engage Rosalind with the women's movement. Her Stratford programme notes ('A Woman's Place') included Sheila Rowbotham on Renaissance education and 'the crucial demands of feminism'; a celebration of Mary Fytton (who would 'take a large white cloak and march as though she had been a man'); and the fate of Woolf's Shakespeare's Sister, who 'killed herself some winter's night and lies buried at some cross-roads, where the omnibuses now stop outside the Elephant and Castle . . .'[45] In 1975 Buzz Goodbody committed suicide. Days later her production of *Hamlet* opened at Stratford's Other Place, which she had founded as a space for experimental and community projects (including her shortened *King Lear* focused on deprivation and Lear's daughters). No woman directed another main stage Shakespeare at Stratford until the late 1980s.

Elsewhere however the feminist group Monstrous Regiment staged *Shakespeare's Sister* (1982) and in 1987 the Women's Theatre Group confronted patriarchal Shakespeare in *Lear's Daughters*, exploring the psychological legacy of the Father and the Mother's absence from the text. Feminist reinvestigations of *Hamlet* included Briony Lavery's *Ophelia*, but productions of Shakespeare's play with women in the lead seemed unwelcome.[46] Mainstream critics were alienated by Madeline Bellamy's Hamlet (1986 Young Vic Studio, London) – 'A most unpleasant boy. He's an aggressive adolescent, more priggish than princely. His actions don't seem motivated by grief, rather by an arrogant assumption that he can stomp on others for his own satisfaction. He/she rather provokes irritation, rather than sympathy'; Bellamy 'gives no reading of Hamlet's sensitive, "feminine" inner self.' Her 'gutsy', 'earnest', 'openly hostile' Hamlet was dismissed as a vanity project or camp nonsense: 'Miss Bellamy with her cropped spiky hair – by Lawrence of Crimpers the programme says – and her mannish attire, looks nothing so much as a handsome French lesbian who runs something sinister in Paris.'[47] Two years later Helen Schlesinger's performance in Jenny Neville's touring Compass Theatre version received little attention and in America in 1991, the director Eric Hill said he did not wish to make a 'sexual state-ment' when he cast Kelly Maurer – 'By turns masculine, feminine and androgynous' – for Stage West (Springfield, Mass.).[48]

But there was a new audience avid for such experiments: 'I rushed to the Young Vic on a wave of great expectation', said Carol Woddis in the left-wing *City Limits*: 'A woman playing Hamlet suggested so much . . . '[49] In her book *Sheer Bloody Magic* (1991) Woddis asked eminent actresses if they wanted to play Hamlet, an issue already raised in Holly Hill's 1987 Shaw study, *Playing Joan*. Eileen Atkins told both that her favourite Shakespeare roles were Viola and Rosalind (in Goodbody's production) but said a woman playing Hamlet – 'the part to end all parts' – was 'rubbish': 'How can you find it in you to play a man? Why should anyone want to go and see it except out of some strange curiosity? I think a woman in the same position would be quite different. I'd rather see a schoolboy in it than a brilliant actress.' Boys, she said, gave Shakespeare that 'quality of purity'.[50] Fiona Shaw had also demurred: 'I was asked to play Hamlet recently. I'd love to play it if it released anything . . . he's some sort of Western European consciousness. Whether a woman could bring anything to it, I don't know.'[51] The Canadian actress Roberta Maxwell rejected offers from John Hirsch (Seattle) and Nikos Psacharopoulos (Williamstown): 'I was so astounded and thrilled and honoured. But I think for me to play Hamlet would be a distortion . . . Hamlet is the greatest role ever written, because of the dimensions, the size, and the language,' but 'I don't think that Shakespeare meant Hamlet to be played by a woman. Simple, bottom line.'[52] Each had a strong sense of the part's magnitude yet felt excluded. It was revealing that even Madeline Bellamy's version opened with a prologue linking the feminised Hamlet to psychological depen-dency: s/he dreamt the first soliloquy while the shrouded Ghost (who was also Claudius) lay on the throne, then swept her up and envel-oped her. The feminist debates about Shakespeare in the 1980s were complex. How far were the plays works of genius which understood 'the Nature of Woman' (Juliet Dusinberre) and promoted female interests? Or enquiries into psychological duality and the 'Division of Experience' (Marilyn French)? Or chunks of patriarchal obsession, 'Still Harping on Daughters' (Lisa Jardine)? It was into these arguments that *The Roaring Girl's* Hamlet stepped.

'More than anything else', said Sue Parrish, 'it is a psychic, a cultural "otherness" which is the power behind women's secondary status. The secondary status is embedded in the plays of Shakespeare.' Her production had two targets. First came the basic question of access to the protagonist and 'inner life': 'Everyone in the world knows Hamlet. Women have no equivalent character. The famous . . . quotation "It is we who are Hamlet" makes me think "hang on, we women don't get a go at doing this creature." '[53] Secondly Parrish asked a group of actresses to interrogate the whole play – offering not 'women who will pretend they are men', but *Hamlet* in 'a woman's voice'.

Sphinx co-opted three 'Shakespeareans' onto the board – Marilyn French and the actresses Dorothy Tutin and Janet Suzman – and Harriet Walter joined in preliminary *Hamlet* workshops. Sphinx promoted their version and its educational support work as 'the coming-of-age of national women's theatre'. After centuries of isolated performances, this *Hamlet* celebrated collectivity:

Scandalising society by dressing as men, and behaving as they pleased, Moll and women like her publicly overturned conventions of masculinity and femininity, and lived a dangerous life as a consequence. Women of her day were forbidden to perform on the public stages. But it may be that if on a cold winter's day in 1605, you had left The Globe and ducked into the back room of an inn on the unruly streets nearby, a furtive crowd would be gathering to see Moll and her Motley troupe. They are preparing a theatrical invasion . . .

Clare Luckham's prologue replaced the Ghost of the Father with the invasion of stage space by forgotten women. It premiered at the Warehouse Theatre, Croydon, a cramped dark room reached up winding stairs; in burst Moll Frith in man's clothes with her friends (nuns, cross-dressers and prostitutes), laying claim to a play ('so close to the hearts of men', she said) which proclaims 'the male and female in each of us'.

Luckham's new material surprisingly stopped there. After three minutes the insurgents disappeared and Moll introduced a candle-lit funeral: the pall was whipped off to reveal a wedding banquet and a stuffed pig's head. 'Heaps of meat, crackling and pastry crusts foreshadowed poisoned bodies "with tetter barked about" and physicalised

Hamlet's disgust with solid flesh.'[54] The Mother Courage-like Gravedigger ate lunch amidst the skulls – 'We fat ourselves for worms' – and this stress on the corporal resonated, given the audience's inevitable preoccupation with the performers' bodies. Sally Greenwood (the engaging Moll) reappeared as Claudius and, relishing male power, played with the most confidence and humour. Sphinx made no more use of the meta-theatrical frame, though. Some actresses stood around as guards in ill-fitting helmets in joking acknowledgement of the history of girls' school Shakespeare (Parrish: 'Peggy Ashcroft learned to be an actor through going to an all-girls' school and playing nothing but men's parts' – she was offered Hamlet to persuade her not to leave at sixteen) but Parrish did not belabour mainstream Shakespeare's marginalisation of women: 'This is not agit-prop.'[55] Her agenda, which drew on Marilyn French, was exploratory: 'Denied the participation of women, Shakespeare created a galaxy of male protagonists with a unique combination of "masculine" and "feminine" qualities, and Hamlet especially.'[56] While the production proclaimed women's right to seize the canon, on the analytical level it looked at the psychological co-existence of 'masculinity' and 'femininity' – and especially at Hamlet's, Claudius' and Laertes' attempts to repress 'unmanliness'.

Parrish: 'There was a tremendous social ferment in the Elizabethan Age which we don't recognise. From the 1580s, it is documented that women wore men's dress . . .'[57] More than that, after Moll's carnival prologue, Sphinx used unfamiliar Renaissance fashions to suggest a male Court playing with sexual amorphousness – acknowledging but containing it. The King – an actress (Greenwood) playing a cross-dresser (Moll) playing a man (Claudius) denouncing 'unmanly grief' – wore a doublet and a black gathered half-skirt which exaggerated the hips. Rather than disguising the actresses' gender, Sphinx emphasised it visually: several courtiers wore dress-length coats and ballooning trunk hose: here on historical authority was an unfamiliar late-Elizabethan androgyny, where men aped the physique of mature women. Like Cheek by Jowl's 1991 *Hamlet* (which made Gertrude a matriarch encircled by men sniffing for influence) Sphinx acknowledged the cult of Elizabeth; whereas most *travesti* Hamlets visually denied the feminine, here the male elite claimed status by assuming female silhouettes. Older men and scholars wore dull gowns and Erasmus-like caps: Claudius' world dismissed them as sexless (Horatio) and redundant (Polonius). The Ghost was a Death figure with a genderless electronically-distorted voice. These costumes freed the company from the banality of 'playing men' and stated that definitions of gender shift like fashions. At the centre, however, Gertrude, Ophelia and Hamlet were dressed 'traditionally'. Asking why so many women played Hamlet, Parrish wrote, 'Shakespeare's Renaissance Scholar-Prince has become the human archetype. With the status of a myth, he is the perfect expression of the human condition in a fallen world' – a 'unique combination of "masculine" and "feminine" qualities'.[58] 'It is this "femininity" which has drawn many actresses, from the nineteenth century onwards.'[59] Yet Anne Mitchell was a physically powerful Hamlet and did not play for sensitivity at all. What she did present was a man *bewildered* by the 'feminine' – in his relationships and within himself.

Mitchell's Hamlet was rigid and monotonal and seemed nervous in the opening scenes. His difficulty finding a voice in public linked him to Gertrude and Ophelia, but Mitchell made him a misogynist, 'disgusted by his mother's fall from grace': 'Lines like "Frailty, thy name is woman!" have rarely resounded more damningly.'[60] When he mocked Polonius there was more ease – 'an engaging, melancholic youth, dallying with madness' – but Mitchell was strongest in the soliloquies, which she spoke plainly and fluently and with explosive emotion. Parrish cut Rosencrantz and Guildenstern. This diminished Hamlet – less comedy, danger, rage and moral complexity (no premeditated murder) – but heightened his status as a philosopher because 'What a piece of work is a man' became a new soliloquy. Mitchell's sober monologues were reasoned and decisive: Hamlet really believed he was a coward; only ignorance of the afterlife keeps an intelligent person from suicide; there can be no action unless the Ghost's words are proved true . . . Unlike *Lear's Daughters*, this project did not accuse Shakespeare of disseminating patriarchal distortions; it embraced *Hamlet* for women's theatre, and its most productive area of enquiry was Ophelia.

Parrish: 'Women have always lived alternative lives; but they have in some measure had to accept the status of Simone de Beauvoir's "other".' After the Court scene, Ophelia (Greer Gaffney) was alone. She threw a black cloak over her shoulder and secretly practised fencing, providing a startling glimpse of her 'alternative life'. The Ophelia-Laertes relationship was unusually warm: they looked similar – tall, fair and aquiline – and she gave him a flower for remembrance in France. Laertes' warning against Hamlet had rare force spoken woman to woman, with a sense of actresses taking control of the play, freed to give chosen lines more prominence. The secret Ophelia was a potential Rosalind – and like Hamlet 'in continual practice' – but in public all spark disappeared; she became a sullen, gangling Lady Di. Culturally maimed, she was almost immobile in the Nunnery Scene, but she was calm and Sphinx prioritised her viewpoint. She tried to make Hamlet see his cruelty but this confirmed his belief in women's treachery. He launched into despairing attacks to which she could not respond; she would not look at him; he exploded and Mitchell revealed a *male hysteric*, sneering, snarling, tearing off his doublet and seizing Ophelia's face – his gaze objectifying her – before he threw her down. Critics were not convinced –'Hamlet lacerates Ophelia as though fury will make up for the fact that such abuse comes oddly from a woman'[61]– but the reading was coherent. In an escalating frenzy Hamlet rushed off cursing, but Ophelia was not broken; her soliloquy was pitying and reasoned.

The all-male Players gained most from the all-female casting. The Player Queen was doubled with Laertes, so when Hamlet made 'Your voice is cracked in the ring' a dirty joke about virginity, we remembered Laertes' warnings to his sister. The 'mobled queen' speech brought out Hecuba's agony, not Hamlet's. The Play scene became transitional: it began with Hamlet's private torture of Ophelia and taunts to Claudius, but climaxed in Hamlet and Gertrude's mutual accusing stares. Followed by the interval, Hamlet's fantasy of confronting his mother, 'Now might I drink hot blood!', became the first-half climax.

For Diane Venora, playing Hamlet was not a matter of 'craft' but a process of immersion and self-confrontation – 'to challenge my own life, my own fears, my own spirituality, my own inner shadow and blackness.' Frances de la Tour offered a more liminal definition of acting: 'It is a question of becoming your fullest self through the part. . . The moments when you are closest to it are the moments when you are most in touch with yourself' – 'But you can say to yourself the person they're watching happens not to be me.'[62] She has described her approach as Stanislavskian and not, because the contradiction of performance involves self-exhibition while donning a mask.[63] But *The Roaring Girl's Hamlet* completely rejected the psychologising which had turned the female Hamlet into a literary Freudian symbol (and deterred Fiona Shaw from the role because there was nothing in her relationship with her father she wished to explore). Parrish: 'The modern method of building a character in a Stanislavskian way has nothing to do with playing Shakespeare. This is a play of language and ideas. . . [F]ind the truth through the verse.'[64] Thus in Acts 2 and 3, Mitchell made Hamlet increasingly frenetic; she played passion more strongly than most men preoccupied with registering 'sensitivity', and wore the

King's miniature in a ring on her sword hand. Mitchell never exposed herself like Teresa Budzisz-Krzyżanowska and never played subtext: Hamlet seriously feared a 'damned ghost' might infect his 'foul imaginations' and 'Now might I do it pat' was not ambiguous: this wretch belongs in Hell.

Parrish: 'There are two roles for women: Ophelia is iconised as the Madonna and Gertrude is demonised as the Whore.'[65] This Gertrude read the Bible, there was no bed, and nothing about the impassive Queen justified Hamlet's erotic ranting; she seemed a blank (as they were training Ophelia to be) onto whom he projected fantasies. Perhaps Shakespeare's silence about her inner life meant she had nothing to confess. Hamlet seized her face as he had Ophelia's and stared, objectifying her. Hamlet wept when she could not see the Ghost and Gertrude was moved, but to no purpose because he could not stop describing her 'honeying and making love'. Hamlet's excess of speech collided with Gertrude and Ophelia's silence; repeatedly Hamlet confronted socialised figures; their failure to react pitched him into frenzy. The detailed intentions in the scenes between Mitchell and the other actresses were sometimes unclear, but the production came into focus during Hamlet's exile: 'If "we are" at last "all Hamlet"', Parrish asked, 'who are Gertrude and Ophelia?'

Ophelia, an alternative Hamlet, travels the same road – the murdered father, madness and death – but like Shakespeare's Sister ends in suicide, shame and 'maimed rites'. Sphinx stressed the parallels. Ophelia became the one in black: raucous and accusing, the madwoman from the attic. She alarmed Horatio by dancing with him, stamped and yelled; she too seized Gertrude's face and her last 'goodnight' was a shriek; then she became a mourning bride with rouged cheeks and scarlet lips. Sphinx reversed the scene: Laertes showed her the purple flower she once gave him; beyond memory, she saw nothing in it now. The gender dynamics of the finale were mapped by the responses to her death: Gertrude at last found her voice and spoke 'There is a willow' *to the audience* while the men sniggered at more smut ('dead men's fingers'). Then it was Laertes' turn to explode in a Hamlet-frenzy, enraged by his tears because of what they revealed about him: 'The woman will be out!' Hamlet, Laertes and Claudius, the three men who despised the feminine, all became studies of 'hysterical' panic.

Plotting Hamlet's death, his enemies were scared and breathless, gesticulating uncontrollably. In contrast, exile gave Mitchell's Hamlet objectivity. He escaped from his limited vision, which had been based on a horror of intimacy and blinded him to the larger world – *en route* to England, the war took him by surprise. Alarmed by Yorick's skull (holding it as he had held the women) he reverted to machismo. 'Hamlet the Dane!' was an eye-to-eye challenge to Claudius, but when he removed the shroud and saw Ophelia's face for the last time, there was an Aristotelian recognition. Mitchell thought through the 'fall of a sparrow' sequence carefully: Hamlet finally confessed to 'Such a fear as would trouble a woman', accepting a female self:

Because of the circumstances of the theatre of his time, Shakespeare explored what made a human being, very often putting both male and female qualities into his male protagonists. Henry V, Hamlet and Richard II debate with their own female qualities.[66]

Hamlet's last minutes radiated objectivity and, at last, comedy. Diane Venora internalised Hamlet's humour – it was aggressive and strange, for his own benefit; Frances de la Tour was a unique Hamlet because of her fame as a comedienne but 'I didn't play the humour very much.' She felt she missed 'Hamlet's *enjoyment* of his own humour' – 'It was there but if anything I fought against it' – because laughter seemed inappropriate to the Hamlet myth, to 'this great part'.[67] Nonetheless, her natural gift gave Hamlet a biting, wrong-footing wit. Anne Mitchell's version lacked humour completely until the very end when she jammed Osric's hat on his head and was finally freed to play with gender roles, imitating the courtier's Lady Bracknell voice. The duel scene, from which the ashen King tried to exclude Gertrude, was high-spirited. Hamlet's escape from misogyny heralded a new balance: Laertes accepted punishment ('I am justly killed') and, in the device many end-of-the-century directors would repeat, Fortinbras was Ophelia reborn.

Fleet Street ghettoised the production, giving it even less attention than Bellamy's, and the radical press reviews were hostile. Carol Woddis called it 'the most unjustifiably hyped show in months. I feel positively defrauded... The reality is shockingly deficient: a three-minute prologue followed by a three-hour-plus version of *Hamlet*, virtually uncut and... stultifyingly unadventurous.'[68] For *Time Out's* Jane Edwardes it proved 'mundanely' that 'regardless of their sex... dull actors will leave us out in the cold.' Why was the response unsympathetic? *The Roaring Girl's Hamlet* was as in some ways a product of a Thatcherite theatrical crisis. The Women's Theatre Group's relaunch as The Sphinx ('female, classical, multiform, dangerous, organic, a woman's head, a lion's body') happened because the Arts Council selected the company as a 'centre of excellence', to be encouraged while others' funds were cut. The Sphinx launched several major feminist interventions including 'Glass Ceiling' conferences on opportunities in employment and the arts, and *Hamlet* was the perfect cross-boundary project: the company could position itself both with Moll ('dressed in men's clothes and putting two fingers up to the system') and Peter Brook (pursuing the 'universal truths in Shakespeare's masterpiece').[69]

But Mitchell could not resolve all the questions she raised and her resources fell short of her goals. Sharp marketing raised excessive expectations; many performers seemed inexperienced; the gender analysis was hard to read in a single-sex production since spectators soon took the cross-casting convention for granted; and it was misleading to advertise it as 'based around the life of Moll Cutpurse' since Luckham's new text was minimal. But it was symptomatic of British theatre in the early 1990s that a feminist company must be seen to do everything, to justify any funding at all. 'At least Parrish's production has stirred the waters', said Jane Edwardes, 'offering the actresses a rare chance to play complex parts who wield power and make an attempt to control their fate.'[70] *The Roaring Girl's Hamlet* mattered because it celebrated what was happening on small stages around the English-speaking world. As a prestige production it was disappointing, but as a statement of pluralism the story The Sphinx told was true.

Over the past decade, race and looks have become increasingly irrelevant in casting – no longer does Viola have to be beautiful or the house of Capulet exclusively white. But some directors are wondering whether gender is not also negotiable as men and women attempt, sometimes pitifully, to reconstruct themselves to include more and more aspects of both sexes.[71]

IV

Politics or theatre?

We believe that human beings look for role models, for mirrors in which to define ourselves. In the theatre we find a living mirror, and if the images reflected back are narrow and unexamined, our own minds and dreams and ideas narrow and we become disillusioned with ourselves. . . The mind of man is being explored in much greater depth than the mind of woman. The theatrical world is out of balance. (Footsteps Theatre, Chicago: manifesto)

In 1985 Erika Munk in the *Village Voice* condemned as reactionary the whole tradition of women playing Hamlet: 'Hamlet, stereotyped as a waffling neurotic prone to violent fits, is considered proper for women to enact, unlike Lear, Henry V, Caesar, Coriolanus, or Falstaff.'[72] She saw the tradition as proof of patriarchy's power over the imagination, stemming from producers' gimmickry and actresses' frustration, 'from the fact that most playwrights and most big roles are male; as long as men are not clamouring to play Mother Courage or Juliet. . . Hamlet as a woman re-emphasises the universalist pretensions of maleness, the specific limitations of femaleness, in our culture.' However, feminism, the gay movement, and growing interest in the politics of gender definition enriched the meanings of cross-dressing, and in the 1990s *Hamlet* became, especially in the USA, a site for sustained gender exploration.

Melinda Eades' 1991 production in New York State with Elizabeth Swain reversed the traditional gender bias with a mainly female cast; in February 1992 Julianne Ramaker played the lead in Lisa Juliano's all-female *Hamlet* at New York's Kaufman Theatre; and that April another opened in Chicago, staged by the Footsteps company, founded by actresses with an artistic/social programme and an open-door policy: 'We're trying to get women in here who maybe haven't had the experience and give them the opportunity to be creative.'[73] Their core audience was lesbian but since 'there aren't that many lesbian plays out there', in 1991 Footsteps launched its Classical Project with an all-woman *Two Gentlemen of Verona*. 'I just got tired of not being able to do what I wanted to do', the co-director Joan Adamak explained; she wanted to see how classically trained actresses could 'flex their muscles', and their success proved 'the boundaries are what you make them.' So Deya Friedman's *Hamlet* followed – a fast, undeclamatory production which encouraged actresses to use their own accents: 'The all-female delivery results in new sounds, insights and altogether different sensibilities.' (*Chicago Tribune*)[74] While Julia Fabris' Hamlet was described as 'passionate, fiery-tempered and moody', with 'the princely virtues of courage, chivalry, and compassion', the group explored the interweaving narratives democratically, creating a broad study of generational breakdown: 'It became people with problems working them out in the best way they could.' (Adamek)[75] Though the character readings were realistic, single-sex casting stylised them, abetted by formal designs: drapes and cowled robes that seemed Egyptian or Greek to reviewers, plus frozen groupings, gave *Hamlet* a hieroglyphic quality, with the cast suggesting 'philosophical concepts far removed from mundane gender differences and sophomoric Freudianisms'.

(*Chicago Reader*) 'Women are trained to like a lot of things that don't feature them, that don't express their full human range', said a company member, 'We get used to seeing ourselves in more circumscribed roles.' Footsteps' manifesto goal was to facilitate, to try to nurture 'a whole generation of women who revel in their own strength and creativity'.[76] They went on to stage an all-female *Romeo and Juliet* (1993), then *Richard III*, *Othello*, *Macbeth*, the *Shrew* and the *Dream*.

Other companies followed, including the multicultural Los Angeles Women's Shakespeare Company (founded 1993: *Hamlet*, 1995) and Women's Will in San Francisco (1998: *Hamlet the Melancholy Dame*, 2000). Women's Will 'promoted the idea that women can work together to create new possibilities for themselves and other women and girls of all ages, backgrounds and beliefs;' the Los Angeles group, led by Lisa Wolpe, used Shakespeare to explore dominant perceptions of 'violence, victimisation, power, love, race and gender issues and to provide positive role models for women and girls'.[77] Natsuko Ohama, the LAWSC Hamlet, said their production (paralleled by a girls' workshop version) investigated the 'special resonances, images and awakenings' that might result from an encounter between ethnic diversity – 'an all-female multicultural ensemble', 'this rainbow of women' – and 'this classic icon of eurocentric culture, *Hamlet*': 'diversity is nothing less than the truth as it manifests itself in the world around us'.[78] *Hamlet* broke the group's normal rule of locating Shakespeare in the Renaissance: 'We set our Denmark in the timeless now. Of our time, but not rigidly our time', to clarify 'relationships between men and women, mothers and sons, daughters and fathers, friend and friend, class and class, the feminine in Hamlet and the male in us'. LAWSC joined in the reassessment of Ophelia as the second protagonist: 'Why is it that Hamlet feigns madness and commits murder, and Ophelia becomes mad and commits suicide? Is the name of woman really frailty? . . . Who is nobler in the mind?'

An explosion of cross-cast *Hamlet*s offered shifting permutations of doublings and reversals as if in one extended collective workshop. In 1992 Melody Garrett and Brendan Corbalis shared Hamlet at Yale Rep. (Ophelia too was played by a man and a woman; two women played Gertrude.)[79] At Hope College, Michigan, six performers, male and female, were Hamlet; and in Texas actresses played Hamlet and Horatio.[80] In Wisconsin (1995), New Orleans (1996), New York (1996) and at the Cincinnati Shakespeare Festival (1997), Hamlet became a female *character*. This confronted Micheline Wandor's argument that for a woman in Hamlet's situation every value and problem would be different. In the modern-dress Cincinnati version (where as in *Angel of Vengeance* Rosencrantz and Guildenstern were women – the *Clueless*-style Rosancrantz stole the show), the decision to make Marni Penning's Hamlet a princess was taken in rehearsal. The director Jasson Minadakis told the press, 'She has one of the most feminine bodies in the company. She will be dressed as a princess would be dressed.'[81] The reversal reanimated old debates about plausibility and especially women and violence, and about the loss of 'Hamlet's defining quality of existential doubt' if an actress plays for anger and, as Minandakis said, 'dangerous lunacy': 'She is going to go over the edge at any minute.' However it was the relationship between the Princess and Ophelia that attracted interest, partly due to Minadakis' publicity tactics: 'Now Hamlet is a female people seem to want the answer: Are they or are they not lesbians? Have they slept together? I'm not going to tell you that.'

The gender-reversal caught on in colleges and some found the Cincinnati Polonius' now homophobic warnings to Ophelia intriguing. However Joanne Zipay, the director of New York's Judith Shakespeare Company (named after Shakespeare's Sister) objected: 'It didn't make any sense . . . I couldn't understand why Polonius and the king wanted this woman to marry this woman.'[82] Though the aesthetics of cross-casting are written into Shakespeare's theatre, 'I object very strongly to gender reversal without consideration of what it's going to do to *the dynamics of the play*.'[83] Zipay saw cross-dressing as an analytical tool grounded in defamiliarisation. Working with mixed-sex casts, her task was to uncover and critique the gender dynamics of a specific play, then devise new opportunities for actresses within it. In *Hamlet*, she suggested, the best strategy would be reverse-casting, with two men isolated and objectified as Gertrude and Ophelia. Zipay too saw Ophelia as a blocked protagonist: Hamlet was 'stuck in this infantile obsession' but Ophelia was not passive – 'fluttering against the glass . . . so her voice could be heard'. Judith's gender-swapped *Julius Caesar* tried to expose Rome's ruinous codes of masculinity, the vicious competition and fixation with male 'love'. When Zipay founded the group it was 'half men and half women . . . I didn't want . . . an all women company . . . I was concerned about the issue of ghettoisation.' In terms of cultural engagement, however, one of the most influential groups was the all-female Company of Women, founded in Boston by the leading voice teachers Kristin Linklater and Carol Gilligan. Though there were only two productions, *Henry V* and *King Lear*, they set a crucial example – Lisa Wolpe played Henry V and acknowledged her Los Angeles *Hamlet*'s debt to Linklater.

Regendering the Shakespearean voice, to which so many directors from
Zipay to Sue Parrish referred, was the core. In Shakespeare, Linklater
argued, 'archetypal' stories were slanted by 'an inevitable patriarchal
history' –

But when they're told through a different voice, through the psyches, the bodies,
the intellect and the emotions and the voices of women, they undergo an extraordinary sea change.

Taking on Shakespeare might 'help women to hear themselves and
speak themselves perhaps with more power and more strength
and more range. . .changing the harmonics in the cathedral of the
culture.'[84] For Gilligan and Linklater, the conjunction of women's
voices and Shakespeare animated 'the voice of individuality, of
iconoclasm. . .[O]nce the soul of the language has been discovered
by the speaker, the soul and voice of the speaker is liberated to tell his
or her story.'[85] The significance for work with girls and teenagers, they
argued, was immense: 'What we were plugging into was the incredible
strength, power and sense of adventure in girls at the age 8, 9, 10 before
they come to the edge of adolescence and have to go under, when they
either become silent or strident.'

In America the refiguring of gender ran alongside other issues of ethnic,
racial and cross-cultural empowerment. In Britain, the discourse was different. In Spring 2000 the Artemis Project was founded by a group of
experienced actresses committed to staging two all-female Shakespeare
productions in London each year, beginning with *Richard III*. Exploring
ambition and deformity was an unstereotypical choice, but after derisive
reviews the entire project folded in days. Networks of groups grew in the
USA, depending on the loyalty of volunteers and complex regional
networks of funding to make the work possible. Their output was
small, sometimes one production annually; Non-EQUITY actors and
free performances often characterised their work; and its political role in
the nurturing of personal development was never in question. British
cross-dressed Shakespeare never became symbolically significant or
socially instrumental in this way; sporadic productions still struggled in
the crowded marketplace for decent reviews and attention. After a history
of isolation, Cushman's American successors were in the vanguard, with
new structures of networking and support, and even official recognition
of their diversity of motives and goals.

In May 2000 New York City Council of the Arts sponsored a forum
on 'Expanding the Presence of Women in Shakespearean Performance'.

It focused on cross-gender performance in the context of women's social advances and gave it a triple significance – it was the 'expansion of the presence of women in Shakespeare. And it's also an expansion of Shakespeare through the presence of women, and it's also an expansion of women in their lives.' 'Gender issues are all about power', Zipay said: 'Shakespeare wrote about a man's world. We live in a man's world. It's a great world for us to play with.' The actress Jan Harding argued, 'When men cross-dress as women it's much lighter, and it's usually comedy. There's an easier acceptance of that. Because I think, politically anyway, that it's a step down . . . I think when women play men, there's more weight to that and it's more threatening.' Moreover 'When Shakespeare's women talk about being women it's as opposed to being a man. Whereas when men in Shakespeare talk about being a man it's opposed to being a god or opposed to being an animal.' Cross-casting exposed ideology: 'If you put women in men's roles you're automatically making a political statement whether you want to or not.'

At the NYCCA Gay Gibson-Cima (author of *Performing Women*) argued these practitioners were subversives – 'trying to create this queer body, this body that's fluid, this body that doesn't have to be locked into these sort of binary oppositions of male and female, black and white'. The Public Theater casting director Heidi Griffiths agreed: 'We're trying to create those kinds of new images.' 'Scrutinize the tropes', said Zimay, more analytically: 'You have to think like a man and you have to make choices about the way men behave.'[86] There were also questions of denial. Harding argued that 'When you play a man, instead of getting in touch with your male sexuality you almost have to drop your sexuality, unless you're playing the lover . . . I have to do just as much work in dropping the woman'; and Fanni Green argued one could erase too much: 'The best artist brings about a certain resonance to the role because of who they are . . . I don't want you to forget that I was a black woman that played that man. In the end I don't want you to forget. Because otherwise . . . I get invisible.'[87] Performing Shakespeare was not simply a question of empowerment through reversal, and gender was not, can never be, an issue in isolation. Collectivity was the most important issue. Lost pasts came into focus. To quote Leslie Jacobson, who ran a women's theatre company in Washington for over twenty years:

The movement of women artists, finding their voices, and being given voice, has happened before, and it will happen again. But what we want to do is find ways so that we can stand on the shoulders of those who went before, instead of not even knowing that their shoulders are there.[88]

Notes

1. Half Moon Theatre, London, directed by Robert Walker: 18 October to 17 November 1979.
2. Frances de la Tour interviewed by Peter Roberts, 'Tour de Force', *Plays* (March 1984), p. 14, and documentary, *Playing the Dane*, BBCTV 1994.
3. *Sunday Telegraph*, 15 July 1979; *Playing the Dane*.
4. *Sunday Telegraph*.
5. *Ibid.*
6. Personal correspondence.
7. *Guardian*, 19 October 1979.
8. *Time Out*, 23 October 1979.
9. *Plays and Players*, December 1979.
10. *Guardian.*
11. *Plays and Players.*
12. 'Tour de Force', *Plays.*
13. *Financial Times*, 19 October 1979.
14. *Guardian.*
15. 'Tour de Force', *Plays.*
16. *Playing the Dane.*
17. *Ibid.*
18. *Guardian.*
19. Following Tynan, Billington believed great male actors depended on an ability to release their femininity.
20. *Plays and Players*; *Guardian.*
21. Milton Shulman, *Evening Standard*; Wandor, *Time Out.*
22. *Time Out.*
23. Micheline Wandor, *Postwar British Theatre: Looking Back in Gender* (London: Routledge, 2001), pp. 17–21.
24. Sheila Rowbotham, Lynne Segal and Hilary Wainright, *Beyond the Fragments: Feminism and the Making of Socialism* (London: Merlin, 1979) pp. 191, 58.
25. Steed then appeared in the Royal Court revival of *Cloud Nine* and played several real-life male politicians in Walker's production of Howard Brenton and Tony Howard's satire *A Short Sharp Shock* (1980) which contrasted Thatcher with the generation of women who created the Welfare State.
26. Walker, who had lived in Germany, borrowed the bare-breasted Queen from Peter Zadek's iconoclastic Bremen *Hamlet* two years earlier. This was staged in a disused factory also littered with props and a players' cart. Ophelia's breasts were exposed in the Nunnery scene, Gertrude's were red-painted. Zadek introduced farcically cross-dressed actresses as gravediggers, pirates, Polonius, the Ghost, and a Guildenstern (sado-masochistically tied with Claudius) who also revealed his/her breasts. Gertrude was younger than Hamlet and Ophelia: in this iconoclastic *Hamlet*, so unlike Zadek's 1999 collaboration with Angela Winkler, 'one thing is denied absolutely: the unity

and beauty of a work of art . . . in favour of the openness, vitality and radicalism': Volker Canaris, 'Peter Zadek and *Hamlet*', *Drama Review* 24, 1 (March 1980), p. 62.

27. *Sunday Telegraph*, 15 July 1979; personal correspondence 1997.
28. Interview, *Observer*, 7 February 1993.
29. 'Tour de Force', *Plays*.
30. Interview, *Observer*, 7 February 1993.
31. Rowbotham *et al, Beyond the Fragments*, p. 205. Frances de la Tour in correspondence, 1997.
32. Speaking at Judith Shakespeare Company conference, 'Expanding the Presence of Women in Shakespearean Performance', New York 22 May 2000. Transcript on website: www.judithshakespeare.org.
33. *Hamlet Studies* vol. 6 (1984); *Shakespeare Quarterly;* vol. 34 (Spring 1983); *New York Times* 3 December 1982.
34. *New York Times.*
35. *Shakespeare Quarterly.*
36. All rehearsal quotations are taken from this documentary.
37. Interview, 'Diane Venora Plays the Lady', 15 May 2000: Theatermania.com/content/news.cfm.
38. 'Deep Inside TNT's Rough Cut. Q & As: Diane Venora', TNT website.
39. 'Diane Venora Plays the Lady'.
40. 'Rough Cut: Q & As'.
41. Warehouse Theatre, Croydon, 31 January to 23 February 1992. (Then national tour and Lilian Baylis Theatre London).
42. Charles Marowitz, 'An Othello' in *Open Space Plays* (Harmondsworth: Penguin, 1974), p. 292
43. *Observer*, 1 October 1967. The original director John Dexter had left the company.
44. *Vagina Rex and the Gas Oven* (London: Calder and Boyars, 1971), p. [5].
45. Quoted, *As You Like It* programme, p. 19.
46. See Gillian Hanna, ed., *The Monstrous Regiment Book* (London: Nick Hern, 1991); Gabrielle Griffin and Elaine Aston, eds., *Herstory: Plays by Women for Women* Vol. 1 (Sheffield: Sheffield Academic Press, 1991); Jane de Gay, 'Playing (with) Shakespeare: Bryony Lavery's *Ophelia* and Jane Prendergast's *I, Hamlet*', *New Theatre Quarterly* 54 (May 1998), pp. 125–38.
47. Reviews from *Sunday Today; City Limits; Guardian; Evening Standard.* Directed by Ian Thompson (his first major production), Young Vic Studio, London, 27 May to 21 June 1986. Fortinbras, Rosencrantz and Guildenstern were cut; the best-known actor, Lisa Daniely, played the Queen.
48. See Lesley Ferris, *Crossing the Stage* (London: Routledge, 1993), and 'Hamlet's Body', *American Theater* (March 1992), pp. 12–17. The Compass production opened in April 1988.
49. *City Limits*, 5 June 1986.

50. Holly Hill, *Playing Joan: Actresses on the Challenge of Shaw's 'Saint Joan'* (New York: Theatre Communications Group, 1987), p. 200; Carol Woddis, *Sheer Bloody Magic: Conversations with Actresses* (London: Virago, 1991), p. 69.

51. Woddis, *Sheer Bloody Magic*, p. 138.

52. Hill, *Playing Joan,* p. 208.

53. Parrish in Gwyn Morgan, 'The Britches Parts', *Plays and Players*, February 1992, pp. 16–17.

54. *Guardian*, 11 February 1992.

55. Parrish in Morgan, 'Britches Parts'. See Michael Billington, *Peggy Ashcroft* (London: Mandarin, 1989), p. 17.

56. Parrish, programme note.

57. Parrish in Morgan, 'Britches Parts'.

58. Parrish, programme note.

59. Sphinx publicity.

60. *Time Out*, 12 February 1992.

61. *Time Out*.

62. Interviewed *Guardian*, 19 January 2000; 'Tour de Force', *Plays*.

63. 'One can find a way emotionally. . . everybody at some time lost a loved one': de la Tour in Peter Roberts, 'East Meets West', *Plays International*, February 1993, p. 25.

64. Parrish in Morgan, 'Britches Parts'.

65. *Ibid.*

66. *Ibid.*

67. *Playing the Dane*.

68. *City Limits*, 13 February 1992.

69. Parrish in Morgan, 'Britches Parts'; Sphinx programme.

70. *Time Out*.

71. *Ibid.*

72. *Village Voice*, 12 March 1985.

73. In interview: Carrie L Kaufman, 'Expanding Visions', 22 April 1993: Footsteps website. For reviews of Lisa Juliano's New York production (14–28 February 1991) see *Stages*, May/June 1991; *Shakespeare Bulletin*, Spring 1991.

74. *Chicago Tribune*, 5 April 1992.

75. In Kaufman, 'Expanding Visions'; reviews from *Chicago Tribune* and *Chicago Reader*.

76. Manifesto. Joan Adamek: 'We do work to stay out of pigeon holes . . . We don't want to be labelled a lesbian theatre or a feminist theatre . . . Our goal is to open it up, open people's eyes and say, "Look how broad this can be." '

77. Company mission statements: www.womenswill.org; www.lawsc.net.

78. Directors' notes. Wolpe and Ohama co-directed. The LAWSC website contains enthusiastic press comments (*Los Angeles Times*: 'Wolpe's highly developed sense of irony persists until the last dying gasp. It's a compelling, convincingly sexy performance, whatever your gender.')

79. 8–31 October. Review: *Hartford Courant*, 17 October 1997. Michele Wade and Guy Manning split the lead and played other roles in Metin Marlowe's fringe *Hamlet*, Maison Bertaux, London 1993.
80. Winedale, Texas. Reviews: *Houston Chronicle* and *Dallas Morning News*, 8 July 1993.
81. *Cincinnati Post*, 17 September 1997. Review from *Cincinnati City Beat*, 25 September 1997.
82. Web interview with Joanne Zipay, *Director's Insight*.
83. Judith Shakespeare Company seminar, 'Expanding the Presence of Women Directors', 12 October 2000. Transcript on website: www.judithshakespeare.org.
84. Speaking at Judith Shakespeare Company conference, 'Expanding the Presence of Women in Shakespearean Performance'. Linklater played Lear: 'You just feel the transformation, the metamorphosis, the absolute alchemical shift that those words can do through your voice.'
85. Kristin Linklater, *Freeing Shakespeare's Voice: The Actor's Guide to Talking the Text* (New York: Theatre Communications Group, 1992), p. 195.
86. Zipay, *Director's Insight*.
87. There were debates because in the Company of Women's *Henry V* the three traitors were played by women of colour, who also played predominantly lower-class roles.
88. At Judith Shakespeare Company seminar, 'Expanding the Presence of Women Directors'.

CHAPTER II

Beyond silence, imagination

The history of gender crossing in *Hamlet* has also been a story of crossing media and national boundaries. In the mid-1990s two films, both adaptations of originals written in French, put actresses who play Hamlet at their centre and offered more ambitious explorations of the *topos* than cinema had seen since Asta Nielsen. These were *All Men are Mortal* (1995) and *Le Polygraphe* (1996).

I

Hamlet's scream: authenticity and the actress

All Men are Mortal was based on a novel Simone de Beauvoir wrote between 1943 and 1946. The film's screenplay was by the dramatist Olwen Wymark. It begins with newsreels of the Liberation, and a woman's voice: 'The war was over, but it was like a great unwashed corpse . . . It was as if we started in the year zero, everything had to be new. And different . . .'[1]

1945. Paris. Onstage: Elsinore is a Cocteauesque painted palace flanked by unicorns. All is elegant black and white, including a negro jazz trumpeter in white and a black-clad Ghost with white corkscrew markings; only his eyes show through a mask. The King is a uniformed Fascist. In this theatre of modern illusions, *Hamlet* opens with the play-within-the-play; it ends when Hamlet, boyish in black velvet and pallid aquiline make-up, steps forward as the curtain falls and tugs off a close-cut wig: the actress Mlle Regina shakes her hair free and takes five bravura curtain-calls.

'When the actor knows his job', wrote Sartre, 'We remain captive to Hamlet till the curtain falls. Captive to belief.'[2] Like Sartre's *The Flies*, this *Hamlet* is an Occupation allegory of remembered collaboration and resistance, but it is also, through Regina, an assertion of radical freedoms: *Life* magazine uses photos of her Hamlet to symbolise the birth of new

Europe from the ashes. But after Auschwitz, what are art and philosophy worth?

Simone de Beauvoir's novel appeared a year after French women gained the vote and three years before her epochal publication of *The Second Sex*; Olwen Wymark was an American-born writer who became part of the late-1960s wave of women playwrights in Britain. *The Second Sex* helped launch modern feminism; *Female Parts*, Wymark's hugely popular translation of Franca Rame's one-woman plays, gave British actresses a key resource in the 1980s; Beauvoir and Wymark both used Regina, the archetypal Actress, to explore the possibilities for self-definition open to modern women. In the novel she plays Rosalind; but in the 1990s Wymark substituted Hamlet, and she was played by Irène Jacob, an icon of European cinema after the Cold War.

'For three centuries', Beauvoir wrote in *The Second Sex*, actresses 'have been the only women to maintain a concrete independence in the midst of society. . . [M]aking their own living and finding the meaning of their lives in their work, they escape the yoke of men.'[3] Almost uniquely, they could 'find self-fulfilment as women' and 'self-realisation, their validation of themselves as human beings', through both profession and lifestyle: 'They are not torn between contradictory aspirations.' Furthermore, 'a great actress will aim higher yet: she will go beyond the given . . . she will be truly an artist, a creator, who gives meaning to her life by lending meaning to the world.' Since Beauvoir's fundamental charge was that the world cast women as Other, so 'the drama of woman lies in this conflict between the fundamental aspirations of every subject (ego) – who always regards the self as the essential – and the compulsion of a situation in which she is the inessential. How can a human being in woman's situation attain fulfilment? What roads are open to her?'[4] *All Men Are Mortal* was driven by Beauvoir's sense that every woman's existence is theatricalised, lived for spectators, and Regina knows it: 'She was playing the game of being mistress of the house, the game of glory, the game of seduction – they were all one single game: the game of existence.'[5]

Theatre might be an escape route but Beauvoir's attitude to the profession was complex: she also saw the Actress as one of the available victim-roles, the purest form of narcissistic 'self-worship' – 'vain, petulant, theatrical; she will consider all the world a stage.'[6] Beauvoir argued that insecure women were driven to perform – onstage or off – because they 'need eyes to gaze at them, ears to listen to them; as personages they need the greatest possible audiences.' Or again, 'The greater actresses – Rachel, Duse – are genuine artists, who transcend self in roles they create; but the third-rater, on the contrary, is concerned not for what she is accomplishing but for the glory it reflects on her.'[7] And she argued that in life's patriarchal theatre, most female artists are fated to be third-rate: 'It is because she has not been engaged in action that woman has had a privileged place in the domains of thought and of art; but art and thought have their living springs in action. To be situated at the margin of the world is not a position favourable for one who aims at creating anew.'[8] And here, perhaps, Beauvoir indicates the fascination, for so many actresses in this book, of Hamlet – the greatest theatrical example of the torn figure who is central yet marginal, dynamic yet passive, the spied-upon observer, inventing independence whilst chained to the paternal will.

In Beauvoir's novel, Regina is twenty-six, successful, and obsessively ambitious. Acting for her is what Beauvoir called a mere 'expressive art', the expression not the transcendence of self. So she experiences consuming jealousy; she feels a knife in her heart if another actress wins an ovation or if she compares the rapture of lovers to the short-lived adoration in her audience's eyes. For her Rachel is not a model but a threat: 'Was she much better than me?' (p. 69) She is a gifted but doomed egoist whose goal since childhood has been to be famous and loved – to which she now impossibly adds, 'To leave a faint memory in the hearts of mortal men which would gradually crumble into mortal dust.' (p. 32) Like Bernhardt she longs to become immortal through the legend of her acting but she is dependent on her audience, required to seduce them: 'I like the way your Rosalind remains so coquettish', says an admirer, 'and has such ambiguous grace beneath her man's clothes.' The book discussed the disguises a woman must don in a man's world – but all are masks for the dependent role of *amoreuse*. In fact Beauvoir's novel was harshly pre-feminist in its critique of Regina's narcissism ('She needed to look at herself. She loved her face'[9]) and more seriously in its structure. For after eighty pages another narrative, three times longer, pushes Regina's story aside.

She meets Fosca, an Italian nobleman, who actually *is* immortal. In the Middle Ages he renounced death in a bargain to save his city; now he describes the appalling periods of history through which he has lived, losing faith in ideologies and then the human race. He has spent most of the twentieth century in a madhouse. Beauvoir explained that in the face of Fascism 'I was obsessed by History' – that 'monstrous mechanism'. Faced by true experience, the actress shrinks, becomes Fosca's mute audience. This skewed structure was Beauvoir's comment on the historical marginality of women; however at that point she seemed to accept it as inevitable that men made history while women must be schooled out of triviality. The novel (which has been read as a reflection of the early Beauvoir-Sartre relationship) was a visible attempt to discard 'feminine' preoccupations and enter what Elizabeth Fallaize terms the 'masculine intellectual tradition'.[10] The novel valued writing (presented as exclusively masculine) over performance (the female condition) and as Regina admits, 'Books live on.'

Unlike Regina, Fosca narrates his story in the first person. Olwen Wymark however let Regina narrate the whole film and play Hamlet instead of the *amoreuse* Rosalind. Her script enriched Regina's tale and reduced Fosca's epic to a sprinkle of bleached-out images – most effectively a mass drowning photographed from below, History's victims envisaged as a collective Ophelia. Wymark organised the film around *Hamlet*, which became Regina's attempt to authenticate herself *through* performance. 'Newly come into the world of men, poorly seconded by them', Beauvoir wrote in 1949, the independent woman 'is still too busily occupied to search for herself,' but at the end of the century Wymark centred that search on Hamlet. Discussing *The Second Sex*'s origins, Beauvoir said 'It is both strange and stimulating to discover suddenly, at forty, an aspect of the world that has been staring you in the face.'[11] Wymark reconceived *All Men Are Mortal* in the light of Beauvoir's later insights, and the next generation's.

As usual in actress-Hamlet films, the spectacle of transformation is more important than the Shakespearean text; once again we scarcely hear Regina speak onstage; her Hamlet exists in the wings, rehearsals, silences and curtain calls but it binds the film together and proves her commitment. Beauvoir often refused to let her female characters succeed as artists, but Wymark's Regina colonises 'inappropriate' great roles ('Yes, you're too young to play Phèdre', says her director, 'and yes you're going to be superb,') and whereas Beauvoir's version wished to become a great actress, in the film she is idolised already. Beauvoir made her fame-obsession neurotic, Wymark has her battle the Absurd quite as much as Fosca, here a Beckettian derelict, does. Knowing her acts of creation are evanescent, she must rely for futile proof of her existence on others, whom she despises, and on memory, which fails: 'They'll all forget me.' Regina's adoring provincial public ('Just like playing to a herd of cattle') troop backstage to pay court:

POLICEMAN: The finest female Hamlet I have ever seen!
REGINA'S DRESSER: How many have you seen?
POLICEMAN: Err–

Her candle-lit dressing room is a shrine to Bernhardt – Wymark's Regina does draw strength from her forebears – but in the foyer someone sees Sarah's portrait: 'Who's that old fart?' Is acting Being-for-Others or Being-for-Itself? Is the actress who plays Hamlet a pioneering rebel or a pathetic simulation of a male ideal? If even Bernhardt is forgotten, what then?

Wymark made Regina dynamic. She toasts 'the Future', literally embraces *Life,* and seizes on cinema as a way to cheat death. But there are no solutions for someone with her cruel clarity of vision, a child of times horrifically out of joint – her cast call her a 'monster'. Her provocative acts offstage make her a 'crazy' (Jacob said) role-model for impatient women even younger than herself. She provokes catcalls ('Parisian whores!') by dancing with girls and starts a riot embracing her black lover. She uses *Hamlet* to shock:

MANAGER: Your fans won't understand all this avant-garde stuff.
REGINA: If they did it wouldn't be avant-garde, would it?'

But there is no clear future. Theatre symbolises impermanence, yet the new media will consume her ('It's cultural imperialism!'): *Life's* photographer disrupts the *Hamlet* rehearsals and a Hollywood producer expects sex in exchange for stardom – which also involves Regina firing the *Hamlet* ensemble. The price of becoming an icon is to be form without meaning: 'Now talk', the producer says at her screen test, 'Quote some of that Hamlet stuff you were doing. Or a shopping list.' So Regina finally refuses to be an object of desire. She destroys everything, from her photographs to her surreal *Hamlet* poster – her face flowering from a stunted tree – because 'I don't want any more lies.'

To quote Irène Jacob, *All Men Are Mortal* was 'about the survivors of the war who were unable to reinvolve themselves in life'. The men in Regina's company seek extreme experiences too – one recites poetry in a boxing ring – but the actresses experience deeper existential disquiet. They hurl themselves in random directions. One Ophelia abandons the theatre to have a child; her replacement, convinced 'an actress should experience everything', burns herself; and most of the actresses long to step into Regina's bed – stealing her lovers – or into her Hamlet costume. 'Nothing is less natural than to dress in feminine fashion' Beauvoir wrote: 'All little girls who are brought up conventionally envy the convenient clothing worn by boys.'[12] The *Second Sex* linked cross-dressing to a wary discussion of lesbianism, and when Beauvoir's Regina, high from playing

Rosalind, dances with an actress she scares her by moving 'obscenely'. Beauvoir condemned the imitation of men ('That is, men as they are today') and suggested that lesbian identity was a persona, as potentially imprisoning as any other, which could still not reconcile 'the active personality and the sexual role'. 'The "true woman"', she said, 'is an artificial product that civilisation makes, as formally eunuchs were made', and the gender trap was almost watertight: 'Whenever she behaves as a human being, she is declared to be identifying herself with the male.'[13] In the film however 'masculine attire, manner, language' positively symbolise hunger for empowerment, even though Wymark grants that Individuality is a harsh goal – when Regina is late for a performance, her thrilled understudy stands poised in the wings; then the star arrives and shoves her aside.

In *The Second Sex* Beauvoir argued that Hamlet, the West's archetypal male Subject, demands that Woman embody his idea of perfection and when that fails, as it must, he rails against the whole sex's 'mediocrity' and 'falsehood'. Shakespeare and his heirs, she argued, infantilised women as the *'petite fille'* Ophelia, capable of only domesticity and 'small, common remarks'; she cited Auguste Compte's definition of femininity as 'prolonged infancy'.[14] But the second part of her novel reduced Regina into just that – a *naif* mesmerised then rejected by a father-lover. Given this, it was interesting that the film cast the young Swiss actress Irène Jacob as Regina. Where Beauvoir's heroine suggested France reinventing herself, Jacob had become an emblem of Europe after the Wall thanks to Kieślowski's *Double Life of Véronique*, where she played two spiritually twinned girls, Polish and French. In the next few years almost all her films were international co-productions, many with ex-Communist states, typified by *All Men*: a British-French-Dutch project shot in Hungary with Swiss, French, British, Irish, German and Italian leading players and co-funded by the Council of Europe. Amidst such diversity, Jacob's androgynous Hamlet was a universally legible sign – a call for new evolved identities in complex times.

However, male directors repeatedly cast Jacob as an outwardly independent young woman spied on by a nihilistic 'experienced' man who shows her the world's brutality, exposing her calm as saintly ignorance: she must redeem him (Kieślowski's *Red*) or perish (Desdemona in Oliver Parker's *Othello*), or follow Hamlet's advice and join a convent (Antonioni's *Beyond the Clouds*). This signature-narrative repeatedly objectified Jacob – as in what she called the 'boy's film' *Othello* where

she was required to act out Othello's sexual fantasies – but Jacob defended
the pattern. 'Basically, we are alone', she argued: 'We don't know who we
are until we meet some other person. Sometimes we're ready for them,
sometimes we're not, but we depend on these meetings in the quest to
discover ourselves.'[15] Jacob's Regina cannot know what each spectator
makes of her Hamlet: Fosca stalks her, seeing her as the reincarnation
of his lost loves; for him the weird poster that asserts her nonconformity
locates her in a perennial pattern, the latest brief bud on the tree.
Jacob was more intrigued by Fosca ('Such a chance for her,') than by
what Beauvoir called Regina's 'proud solitude': 'He has lost too many
loves, seen too many sons die.'[16] Our unforeseen encounters, Jacob
argued, open the 'inner dialogue. . . between all the expectations we
have when we are young – our hope, our beliefs – and the disbelief
and distrust that comes with experience. This dialogue is kept
alive inside us.'[17] Many of Jacob's films were millennial. In tired patri-
archies, envious men spied on the Young Woman hoping her faith and
introspection promised renewal. When Regina meets Fosca, the question
seems to be whether she can achieve immortality via his memory; both
Beauvoir and Wymark revealed this as a false issue, but for opposite
reasons.

In 1946 Fosca's knowledge of death exposed Regina's concerns as infantile: let her paint an inch thick, to this end she would come. But Wymark
reversed the balance so historical understanding deepens art: her Regina,
playing the Ghost scene, hallucinates Fosca's charnel-house memories,
and in a reconceived ending she rejects his nihilism. The 1946 finale
replayed *Hamlet*, with Regina reduced to Ophelian helplessness:
'She becomes the victim of Fosca's perspective on human activities
which abolishes her uniqueness, converts her into an anonymous blade
of grass, a feverishly active ant with no weapon against the futility of
death.'[18] He abandons her by a river and her end is madness: 'It was
when the bells began to chime the hour that she let out the first
scream.' (p. 406) Wymark's heroine also absorbs Fosca's Absurdism –
'All this will become ruins' – and lets out a tragic cry, but then she rejects
despair for the concrete moment: 'Slowly, I began to feel the beauty of the
day surrounding me. This day. This world.' The sudden pastoral existen-
tialism seems arbitrary, but if Regina and Fosca are both Hamlets,
Wymark insists that she who selects her identities can learn to step
from the grave. Two last quotations focus the differences: according
to Simone de Beauvoir in 1949, the actress is like the mystic, she tries
'to achieve individual salvation by solitary effort,' so her Regina despises

other actresses as '*petite filles*'.[19] According to Irène Jacob in 1994, 'In my profession, you never do anything on your own.'[20]

11

Hamlet's autopsy: the heterogeneous body

1996: *Quebec City. Underground.* In a long cellar floored with red earth, candles glow in darkness and Hamlet, played by Lucie Champagne (Marie Brassard), holds a skull, her clothes wrapped round her against the cold. She wears stout boots, her cropped hair dyed red. Her words echo through the catacomb:
  Hélas pauvre Yorick! Je l'ai connu, Horatio! . . .
Her voice is a passionate whisper. Speaking Yorick's elegy, the actress seems younger, more confident and powerful than in daily life. She passes the skull to Horatio. The shivering audience stand like eavesdroppers.

Robert Lepage's 1996 film *Le Polygraphe* was based on a brilliant performance piece he and Marie Brassard co-wrote and acted in eight years earlier. Théâtre Repère's production premiered in French in Quebec and was reworked into a bilingual English/French version.[21] This toured and Brassard played Lucie/Hamlet in London in 1989. Play and film were both pastiche *film noir*. The film added a large cast but the play studied three intertwined lives; in every version Brassard played Lucie, a quirky, 'sensitive and almost child-like' actress playing Hamlet.[22] But Lucie is also in an exploitation movie, cast as a victim of rape and murder, and this film is based on an unsolved case in which, unknown to her, her friend François was a suspect. (Following a close friend's murder, Robert Lepage was once a suspect himself.) Coincidences bind the characters together as the actress-Hamlet literally leads us down subterranean labyrinths. Lucie witnesses a suicide on the metro; she is helped home by a stranger and they begin an affair; he is Hausmann, the coroner/criminologist who operated the polygraph lie-detector during François' interrogation. Though the test cleared him, Hausmann implied the opposite – like Hamlet he believes the 'ultimate proof' is to observe 'the spontaneous reaction' of an accused man. In a state of shock, François now doubts his own innocence. Hausmann haunts his dreams, and in the play François drives himself into extreme masochistic situations, every sexual act becoming a gamble with death. In the original François is homosexual, seeking violent partners; he finally kills himself. In the film he is not gay, the victim was his girlfriend, and he is saved when a jealous woman is revealed as the killer. 'This film has mainstream crossover potential due to its more standard, whodunnit storyline.' (Distributor)[23]

In both versions plot was only the spine. The play surrounded the intense athleticism of the actors with complex technology, building on the idea of the polygraph as a machine that reads bodies but must itself be decoded by confused beings. Stealing the grammar of film – fast-motion, slow-motion, overhead shots, projected credits, subtitles and even holograms – Lepage and Brassard excavated the past and the unconscious. Their montage spliced flashbacks and dreams: here was 'the emotive body's confrontation of things which are man-made but, like persons, are involved in inexorable processes beyond human volition'.[24] As the script was reworked, the *Hamlet* parallels developed and when the Berlin Wall fell the political metaphors sharpened. The stage set was dominated by a brick wall – the ramparts of Elsinore and a French-Canadian city; the Berlin 'Wall of Shame'; a blank slab of secrecy and alienation. The opening intercut a lecture on Berlin – dissected, haemorrhaging exiles – with a murdered woman's autopsy. History, topography and human biology became elusive metaphors for each other. The naked corpse was Brassard: anatomical images were projected onto her: *'muscles, veins, organs and bones superimposed on her flesh, as though she is transparent'*.[25] *Le Polygraphe* displayed Brassard's body as a generic object for dissection and yet uniquely mysterious: what was the link between the corporeal and consciousness?

Like Hamlet the three characters saw death everywhere. Hausmann picked up a skull (*'assuming the cliché position of Hamlet'*) and Brassard materialised with another: *'Hélas, pauvre Yorick! . . . Je l'ai connu, Horatio!'* The Actress, the Suspect and the Coroner (an East German defector) all lived multiple lives; and speaking Shakespeare turned Lucie from the ultimate Object, the naked corpse, into the eternal philosopher, reclaiming mortality from the language of forensics. It was also important – taking us back to Bernhardt – that she was claiming Hamlet's thoughts for the French language; Lepage had directed a bilingual French-English *Romeo and Juliet* commenting on Canada's political and linguistic schisms. In *Le Polygraphe/Polygraph*, Body, City, Country and Language are all cut, divided, yet struggle to communicate and reform. It was a far more effective attempt at creating philosophical theatre than Iris Murdoch's adaptation of *The Black Prince* because Lepage and Brassard expressed ideas directly through image and action. The only conventional poetry was Hamlet's – which, revoiced by French-speakers, could not claim to be innocent.

Brassard and Lepage explored the axis of intention and effect. François and Hausmann understand Lucie's Hamlet differently. The pathologist ('Well, I thought it was quite interesting') is more drawn to the skull, stroking it in her dressing room: 'It must be difficult to pronounce "To be or not to be", and to question the fundamental things of life: love, honour. . . death.'[26] Mordantly, he sees Yorick as 'the only character who isn't killed at the end of the play'; his familiar motive (Eros/Thanatos) for seeing Lucie as *Hamlet* is sex. But François and his boyfriend relate passionately to her from the margins: 'We thought it was brilliant to cast a woman as Hamlet; some of those questions take on real significance coming from a woman; especially for today – more so than from a man.'[27] Haussman analyses her Hamlet in English, she and François respond to it in French. Like Julian in *The Black Prince*, Lucie's link with Hamlet is non-neurotic. She sees no significance in it ('I'm playing a guy in a show') save as a random anecdote in a chaotic trade: 'It wasn't planned that way originally. They called me at the last minute. The guy who was playing Hamlet got sick and the director had this strange idea of casting a woman for the part.' She debunks her art, explaining she did not have time to learn the lines and wrote the Yorick speech on the skull. Yet: 'Death – it's on my mind.' Marie Brassard's force challenged Lucie's flippant vision of acting, especially in the screen version where – finally, a century after Bernhardt – a film audience hears an actress speak Hamlet's thoughts in production. By speaking them in French, she redefines them as both Shakespeare's and her own. 'It's all fake', Lucie says, 'Sometimes.'

François' interrogation parallels Lucie's audition for the role of victim. When she offers a speech from *Hamlet* the Anglophone movie producers assume she means Ophelia and – as in *All Men are Mortal* – do not want Hamlet's words: 'Oh, you would prefer an impro. . . To imagine myself in a tragic situation. . . To imagine myself in a state of absolute panic. . . Don't you think I'm panicking enough here?'[28] Chance gave her Hamlet; capitalist culture reduces her to flesh again: she wins the film role and her reward is to be nude and terrorised. In the stage version a robot camera dollies in on her 'maniacally', take after take, a voyeuristic assailant demanding 'truth'. Cinema, which began gazing respectfully at Bernhardt's Hamlet, has evolved intricate technologies of commodification:

HAUSMANN: But aren't you used to being watched?
LUCIE: In theatre, it's different. When you perform, the audience is watching the whole you. . . But today, I felt that they were taking me apart.

Yet as she re-enacts the victim's death, she makes the wall bleed. With 'a bravura display of emotional arpeggios' Brassard made the Actress an existential detective who learns (cf Venora) by submitting herself to feeling.[29] And when she and François make love, she reads his innocence in his flesh.

The play finally intercut François' desperate suicide with Lucie's return to *Hamlet*. His elongated shadow (cf Goncharova) awaits the last metro. Above the wall, Lucie-Hamlet reappears in Hamlet's black, but now she holds a knife – no longer bait for the Gaze. Peter Zadek: 'Today, in a world in which science and politics want us to believe that all questions can be answered, our instincts tell us this is all wrong . . .' Lucie-Hamlet paces, asking 'those questions' that 'take on real significance coming from a woman; especially for today', that 'question the fundamental things' – 'the famous soliloquy'. As Hausmann said, 'It must be difficult.' '*Etre ou ne pas être . . .*': Lucie/Hamlet's questions are the closest *Le Polygraphe* can come to truth. '*C'est cette / réflexion là qui nous vaut la calamité / d'une si longue vie*' is the play's linguistic terminus, whereupon François throws himself under a subway train/through the wall. Lepage and Brassard frequently reworked the ending. In one version (published 1990) the actors reprised key images round the mortuary table until, in a rhapsodic transformation of *Hamlet* iconography, Lucie slit open François' shirt, drew a flame from his chest, and held it aloft. The play described itself as 'an autopsy on the living which lets the dead rest in peace'.

'I hate naturalism', Lepage has said, 'I'm interested in what's artificial,' yet 'you have to be extremely eager to explore your own ambiguities.'[30] Proving 'there are more things in heaven and earth', all *Le Polygraphe*'s characters unwittingly re-enact Hamlet's ontological encounters. In the film Hausmann lectures students on mortality inside a hall shaped like a bloody ribcage: the intellectual, oblivious, is not outside his topic. Though Lucie/Hamlet walks the wall in the stage version, looking down on the sea of troubles, in the film s/he must go underground (see Figure 20). The film denied her the last word, though. Theatre is the realm of the performer, where experiment and transformation are the grammar of acting, whereas cinema gazes more starkly. And perhaps because Western film language is so dominated by a particular set of fantasies, Lepage remade *Le Polygraphe* in terms that favoured the men. The stories of the suspect and the coroner (his Berlin life now shown at length) were expanded, but Lucie's was not; instead Lepage included four new women – the German's wife, the movie director, the victim,

Figure 20   The shadow of Lucie-Hamlet (Marie Brassard) and the suicide of François:
Le Polygraphe, Montreal 1988. (*Photo*: Claude Huot).

and the killer – two of whom commit suicide. In a ghastly rethinking
of the Flame, the murderess, who killed in *travesti*, douses herself in petrol
and burns to death, a nightmare travesty of Ophelia, in the bathroom.[31]
On the other hand, the three central characters return to normality, and
life wins. If 'We know what we are, but we know not what we may be',
in *Le Polygraphe* François does not even know who he *was*; but as
Iris Murdoch argued, one function of drama is to offer a house of archetypes where, because *all* roles are false, we may understand better
the constructed or fortuitous nature of what seemed inevitable. Here
identities are made and unmade from zero nightly, as the actress who
plays Hamlet demonstrates every time.

Hamlet's enduring importance is as the observer-actor-speaker, an
amorphous being compelled to deconstruct everything, probing surfaces
and uncovering lies until life is exposed as death's mask, death as life's
dream, and there is no distinction between action and submission to
whatever force wills the fall of a sparrow. Hamlet became the medium
for audiences' collective enquiries and 'To be or not to be', quite apart
from its particular meanings, context or theatrical function, became the
universal signifier of Thought. We, men and women, project onto it and
Hamlet's body whatever meanings and anxieties we will. Mlle Regina
strains to resolve her existential crisis through Hamlet; Lucie

Champagne, simply responding to circumstances, climbs then burrows towards truth. Wymark and Brassard's Hamlets offered feminised versions of history, acknowledging but not defined by violence, honouring the continuity of experience: 'Remember me.' Sometimes unwittingly, sometimes polemically, often on some level putting themselves at risk, actresses have contested the dominant traditions and created a Shakespearean subculture that, across two hundred years and several continents, has emerged in small spaces and unrespectable films, in the wings, the regions, underground. These gendered tales of transformation, from Civil War America to Stalin's Russia or from Franco's Spain to millennial Berlin, cannot be dissociated from cultural and political forces. Nor can the starkness of Hamlet's story be ignored: whereas comic *travesti* celebrates confusing freedoms, tragic cross-dressing compounds liberation with defeat. Hamlet is a strange route to self-definition because however triumphant the performer, Hamlet is forever imprisoned and must always die. 'History is painted in blood' is daubed on a wall in Lepage's film; this was Fosca's message in *All Men Are Mortal* and in 1946 it drove the heroine mad, but in the 1990s it deepened Regina's resolution to oppose seas of troubles at whatever cost.

In Lepage's film, François gives a lecture on the division and reunification of Berlin (to students bored by what they already think ancient history), explaining his belief in *the heterogeneous body*. For François, Brassard and Lepage – and for this book – the histories of the human body and the body politic are inseparable, and the performer who crosses barriers of gender challenges a community's ingrained assumptions about power. S/he enacts in specific situations and in microcosm our common need to demolish walls. Thus as we have seen, Fatma Girik's Hamlet took most of its meaning from its Turkish origins – then an unstable, secularised Muslim 'democracy' dominated by the Military and seeking to ally itself with the West, offering a 'liberty', especially for women, that could just as easily mean intellectual empowerment (Hamlet) or commodification (Rosencrantz and Guildenstern in bikinis) – and yet the surname of Girik's rebellious Hamlet is *Evren*: 'Universe'. Women have played Hamlet the child, the adolescent, the misogynist, the rebel, the thinker, the sister, the saint. Hamlet can be, has been, a symbol of (painful) empowerment for woman as well as man almost anywhere and at any point from childhood (the Bateman sisters, Wednesday Addams) to old age (Dame Judith Anderson, Nora and Dora Chance). 'Whence came we? Whither goeth we?' writes Angela Carter's Nora: 'I know the answer to the second question, of course,' but the first is more important because lost facts can be retrieved. Carter quoted Ellen Terry – 'How many times Shakespeare draws fathers and daughters, never mothers and daughters,' – and Nora asks: 'If the child is father of the man, then who is the mother of the woman?' As Leslie Jacobson said in New York in 2000, 'What we want to do is find ways so that we can stand on the shoulders of those who went before, instead of not even knowing that their shoulders are there.'

In recent years, scholars – Joel Berkowitz, Jill Dolan, Lisa Merrill, Elizabeth Reitz Mullenix, Annibell Jenkins, Gerda Taranow, Anne Russell, Monika Seidel, Robert A Schanke, Kristina Straub, Ann Thompson and others – have reanimated the history of the actress-Hamlets and the complex traditions of cross-dressed performance. And so have artists. For example Carolyn Gage's 'One-Woman Lesbian Play' *The Last Reading of Charlotte Cushman* recreated moments from Cushman's Hamlet and Romeo; it was widely seen in the USA, especially in Debra Wright's performance, and was published in 2003.[32] In 2004 Imogen Stubbs' *We Happy Few*, inspired by Nancy Hewins' Osiris Players, showed an all-woman theatre group touring wartime Britain; Juliet Stevenson (who had often stated that she entered acting hoping to play Richard II and Lear) was glimpsed in roles from Henry V to Macbeth. Though its West End run was brief, this tragi-comedy about actresses taking Shakespeare to 'the masses' while discovering 'the man in us' directed considerable attention to Osiris and to Hewins (Beatrice Webb's god-daughter), whose repertoire included eighteen Shakespeare plays. Lynn Redgrave's *Shakespeare for My Father* (seen in America and – 1997 – London) retraced Charlotte Charke's steps but in a totally different spirit, exploring her tense relationship with her father Michael Redgrave – the greatest English Hamlet of the postwar decade. Part recital, part therapy, it explored her father's lack of interest in her; watched by giant blow-ups of his Shakespearean roles, she explained that he only seemed to come alive in them, or in passing sexual relationships with men. As Lynn Redgrave re-enacted a familiar memory – a girl entering her father's study, hoping to find the secret of his identity there – it became the *Hamlet* Ghost scene, and she fled Michael Redgrave's recorded voice. But hearing her father's Hamlet, Lynn Redgrave took over 'To be or not to be'; she used it to dramatise the moment when she determined to become an actress rather, she said, than kill herself: she declined to be Ophelia.

In December 1999 Diane Venora, playing Gertrude, walked across the New York Public Theater stage carrying a huge photo of another Hamlet – herself. Andrei Serban directed many scenes in this production as pastiches – from Elizabethan to Kabuki, Stanislavsky to Meyerhold – 'trying to mirror life': 'It's hard to say that life has a style.' When Hamlet said 'O there be players that I have seen', the stage filled with actors carrying blow-ups of historic Hamlets, including Olivier and Barrymore, Bernhardt and Venora. Cross-casting assumed a last millennial flourish as twin androgynous Fortinbrases entered, a Saint Joan and an 'Archangel Gabriel . . . a caressing kind of hope'.[33] Peter Zadek's concurrent German version was more cynical here – though Ophelia reappeared as Fortinbras, s/he was aggressive. As s/he walked round the corpses s/he noticed a repressed court lady, dressed exactly as Ophelia had been. The victims of Elsinore were infinitely recyclable, and in Zadek's hands Ophelia's transformation posed new questions. Here feminist perspectives and androgyny did not necessarily register as hope. And yet as we saw at the start of this book, the centre of that production, Angela Winkler's Hamlet, in its complexity, skill and humanity contradicted everything Zadek's defeatest, cartoonlike direction (where male effeminacy denoted an abyss of decadence) seemed to say. It was apt that at the 2000 Frankfurt Expo where Winkler's Hamlet played, Asta Nielsen's Hamlet was screened in the streets.

Nielsen's *Hamlet* also appeared in 2000 in London at the National Film Theatre, presented by Shakespeare's Globe with a new live score by Claire van Kampen. Her husband the actor-director Mark Rylance was exploring all-male casting at the Globe for historicist reasons, playing Cleopatra himself; but he understood both that modern actresses needed to be afforded similar opportunities and that in the anti-illusory new Globe *every* 'reality' was simply the product of a collective act of imagination embracing spectators and performers. A few months after the *Hamlet* screening Vanessa Redgrave played Prospero at the Globe, the most publicised cross-dressed Shakespearean performance in Britain since Bernhardt. In 2003 and 2004, the Globe created all-female companies to play *Richard III*, the *Shrew* (Janet McTeer's magnetic Petruchio simultaneously radiated and mocked supercharged *machismo*) and *Much Ado*. Fiona Shaw played Richard II at the National Theatre (1993), and at Leicester and the Young Vic Kathryn Hunter played King Lear (1997) – one of many actresses across the world to do so since the early 1990s.[34] *Richard, Lear* and *The Tempest*, all directed by women, were significant not only because the actresses progressed in a sense from Hamlet, the 'hysterical' displaced heir, to the dramatisation of power and the meaning of its abuse, but because all these productions considered *the heterogeneous body* – Shaw's Richard was an idol of sacred monarchy as close to the

Pharoahs as to Elizabeth I, and both *The Tempest* and *Lear* were direct responses to the experience of war – the first directed by a Serbian and the second by a Pole, who dedicated the production to the memory of her mother who had lived through almost a century of fallen ideologies, invasions and flight. Hunter's Lear seemed shrunken by age, scarcely human, let alone female or male; Redgrave made Prospero gruff but benign (she found his vindictiveness difficult) and though she whirled her staff like a martial artist – condensing masculinity into a gesture – she joined in the spirits' dance.

Exploring that heterogeneous body, the identity which is political and collective as well as personal and is always in transition, such productions involved women exploring aspects of power and domination, the kaleidoscope of strengths and vices within the plays. The gates are open but Hamlet was the Trojan horse and remains the most extensive challenge for women as it always has been for men. Three actresses played Hamlet in fringe productions in London alone in 2001–3.[35] Hamlet represents complex consciousness, personality defined through diversity – through the family, through education, friendship, sexuality, and politics – and yet remains irreducible to other characters' explanations, or those of a thousand critics: 'You would seem to know my stops, you would pluck out the heart of my mystery, you would sound me from my lowest note to the top of my compass.'[36] This amplitude remains whether Hamlet is seen as a 'person' or a literary construct, since 'his' text is a multivocal montage of rhetoric, soliloquy, prose, rhyme, quotations, allusions, prayers, jokes, outcries and rants. The technical challenge and the technical freedom the role offers are inextricable. To play Hamlet is to be for a while the voice of agnosticism and belief, love and obscenity, insight and madness, and to map them one's own way. The result is a tangible dialogue – or a palpable battle – between character, actor and audience.

Nothing proceeds in straight lines. In the 1990s Italian television used a Hamlet-housewife to advertise pasta sauce. Systems can assimilate anything. Nonetheless, in the shadows of Siddons, Cushman, Bernhardt and Nielsen, scores of actresses made Hamlet a symbol of change. It is part of the constitution of human beings that we need art, and theatre above all, to find models for ourselves – roles to act in life, roles to explore in the imagination. Hamlet is a consciousness facing everyone's dilemmas – to try to confront the *status quo* or withdraw from it, to work with words or violence, to blame the world's malaise on others or face a sickness in oneself, to understand death – and these actresses added new layers of meaning to them all. Though we all seek simple explanations and yearn, though few would admit it, for the reassurances of propaganda, individuals, generations and cultures find themselves drawn to complex mirrors, to the art which confronts us with questions, and for many – increasingly, many women – this mirror has been Hamlet. *Hamlet* is about responsibility to the past and possibilities for the future: will Fortinbras protect either?

This book has been an attempt to uncover some partially forgotten histories and is a tiny part of the process of reclamation that ensures that somehow the ephemeral art of theatre is not always lost to time. In 2000 at the Oval in London, the Fifth Column group explored Meyerhold's abandoned *Hamlet*, in which Zinaida Raikh and a male actor would have split the Prince. Though Bob Curry originally planned to cast a man and a woman (Rodin's 'Kiss' was the publicity image) he decided that the female Hamlet would be read as either stereotypically weak or strong; he cast two men instead. However in 2001 at the Budva Festival, Portugal, Alla Demidova of Moscow's Taganka Theatre appeared in *'Hamlet': A Lesson*. With her Greek director Theodoros Terzopoulos, she worked on the *Hamlet* translation Pasternak had been preparing for Meyerhold and Raikh before their murder. Demidova explored the history of that project in the form of a master-class, working with two local actors and building on Hamlet's advice to the Players. Alla Demidova had acted in the Taganka *Hamlet* that inspired *Hamlet (IV)*, and Terzopoulos called her 'the greatest actress of our time. She possesses the complete Russian tradition, Stanislavsky, Meyerhold, constructivism, pure treasure. I think that she is the last representative of the old school.'[37] It lasted an hour, half demonstration, half rite. Demidova slipped between Hamlet's world, the 1930s and our time, exploring the multidimensionality of the theatrical act. She lectured as she wielded Hamlet's sword, held a diva's scarf in one hand and the skull in the other, donned a white dress like a straightjacket over her own dark gown. She acted the encounters of Hamlet and Ophelia, Hamlet and Gertrude (presence suggested by a glove). She acknowledged the applause on the floor, still half within the role. Theatre is a network of influences, often so intricate that they cannot be traced with confidence or clarity, usually so intricate that they warn us against simple conclusions or theorisations. What matters is whether we have attempted to understand what these Hamlets experienced. If not, and the past is silence, then silence is the future too. It need not be. *Hamlet* is our culture's greatest memory play, and finally a meditation on succession.

In May 2001 at the Darul Ihsan University, Bangladesh, after 'a recitation from the holy Quran' came 'an announcement for a recitation from

Hamlet . . . Naturally, the passage chosen was the famous "To be or not to be" speech. The choice of reader, however, seemed unusual. A female Hamlet in a black velvet evening gown with a black headscarf was . . . a surprise. She delivered the passage with great solemnity and grace and mesmerised the audience . . .'[38]

Notes

1. *All Men Are Mortal* (1997; director Ate de Jongh). The film was poorly directed and critically dismissed, but the script is as fascinating as the novel.
2. Jean-Paul Sartre, *Sartre on Theater* (London: Quartet Books, 1976), p. 161.
3. Simone de Beauvoir, *The Second Sex* (Harmondsworth: Penguin, 1983), pp. 711–12.
4. *Ibid.*, p. 29.
5. Simone de Beauvoir, *All Men Are Mortal* (London: Virago, 1995), p. 73.
6. *Second Sex*, pp. 712–13. 'The roles women are called on to play are thus fraught with danger . . . It is they, more than any biological or psychological determinism, which create women's situation, block their freedom, and encourage them to remain locked in femininity. The only way out, for Beauvoir, is the refusal of these roles.' Elizabeth Fallaize, *The Novels of Simone de Beauvoir* (London: Routledge, 1988), p. 15.
7. *Second Sex.*, pp. 646–7.
8. *Ibid.*, pp. 163–4.
9. *All Men are Mortal*, p. 4.
10. Quoted Fallaize, *Novels of Beauvoir*, p. 184. Fallaize quotes her on the 'monstrous mechanism'.
11. Simone de Beauvoir, *Force of Circumstance* (Harmondsworth: Penguin, 1985), p. 195.
12. *Second Sex*, p. 429.
13. *Ibid.*, pp. 428–32.
14. *Ibid.*, p. 142.
15. Jacob on *All Men are Mortal*: 'The only thing I learned from this movie was not to trust directors who say, "Don't worry, we'll work on the script while we're shooting."' (*Guardian*, 10 January 1997)
16. *The Face*, December 1995.
17. *San Francisco Weekly*, 14 December 1994.
18. Fallaize, *Novels of Beauvoir*, p. 190.
19. See *Second Sex*, p. 639.
20. *Journal de Brasil*, 30 October 1994.
21. Originally Lepage played François, replaced in the film by Patrick Goyette. An early version was published in *Canadian Theatre Review* (Fall 1990) and a later text was published by Methuen in the UK in 1997. The latter – set in Montreal – is normally quoted here. The third character was called David on stage.

22. *What's On*, 1 March 1989.

23. 1996 Venice Film Festival programme. There is no room to discuss the narrative changes from play to film fully. The film begins with François (resembling Christ crucified) taking the polygraph test, followed by Lucie's tense audition. She is surrounded by recycled images of her face on video monitors and in both scenes Authority controls their gaze ('Look down', 'Look in the camera'). The stories of François and Hausmann are elaborated: there is a great deal about the coroner's defection from East Berlin and the suicide of his wife; François is embroiled with many heterosexual lovers.

24. Lepage juxtaposes the body to 'the hard surfaces and shapes of things – and the words of various languages treated also as shapes and textures – that it must negotiate, or succomb to'. Michael J Sidnell, '*Polygraph*: Somatic Truth and an Art of Presence'. *Canadian Theatre Review* 64 (Fall 1990), p. 46.

25. Robert Lepage and Marie Brassard, *Polygraph* (London: Methuen, 1997), p. 5.

26. *Ibid.*, p. 14.

27. *Ibid.*, p. 8. Spoken in French.

28. *Ibid.*, pp. 9–10.

29. *Evening Standard*, 23 February 1989.

30. Andy Lavender, *Hamlet in Pieces: Shakespeare Reworked by Peter Brook, Robert Lepage, Robert Wilson* (London: Nick Hern Books, 2001), pp. 125, 128.

31. It could be argued that *Elsinore* (1995) – Lepage's solo *Hamlet* in which he played Ophelia and Gertrude – marked an appropriation of the feminine. That year the director Robert Wilson appeared in *Hamlet – a Monologue*, travelling the same expensive international circuit. See Andy Lavender, *Hamlet in Pieces*. But Lepage's company also toured Brassard's own solo piece *Jimmy* (seen London, 2004) where she played an American general. She drew this work from dreams.

32. In Lynn Miller, *Performing Autobiography* (Madison: University of Wisconsin, 2003).

33. *New York Times*, 19 December 1999.

34. On Hunter's Lear, directed by Helena Kaut-Howson, see Elizabeth Schafer, *Ms-Directing Shakespeare* (London: Women's Press, 1988), pp. 141–7: 'Katherine has that unique ability to transcend gender, to transform, but the reason I wanted her to play the role was that intellectually and emotionally she was capable of the leaps of imagination towards old age and towards death.' Female Lears also appeared in Robert Wilson's German production (1985) with Marianne Hoppe; Mabou Mines' gender-reversed version set in the Deep South (1988); Bernard Sobel's *Threepenny Lear* (Paris 1993) with Maria Casares; and Shakespeare and Company's *Lear Project* (Boston 1998) with Olympia Dukakis.

35. Horla company at Rose & Crown Theatre (3 July 2001). Directed by Alistair Green with Sally Orrock as Hamlet, a spartan, intimate, Berkoff-like version. Outlook Productions played at Hackney Empire (9 April 2002) directed

by Ed Richardson: 'Hamlet is played by a woman . . . to examine the relationships between Hamlet and Ophelia and Hamlet and Gertrude, when, as originally intended, all were played by actors of the same sex.' Meanwhile 'another set of stock characters, those of the Italian Commedia dell'Arte, are woven around them. A strange, abstracted world evolves; an abandoned fairground, by turns glittering and eerie, a world where the narrative unfolds through the power of imagination.' (Publicity) Stephen Jameson directed Miranda Cooke in an all-female version (Wild Thyme at the Gatehouse, Highgate; 2 July 2003): 'The theatre world has suddenly realised that it is incredibly enlightening to witness women exploring more than two main characters in the world's greatest pieces of dramatic literature . . . The sensibilities that women bring to traditionally male roles are unencumbered by expectations, giving rise to a whole set of new meanings. It's like seeing *Hamlet* for the first time.' (Publicity). See Mark Rylance, 'Unsex Me Here', *Guardian*, 7 May 2003.

36. *Hamlet,* III. ii., 152–4.
37. Press release Budva Festival 2001.
38. *Daily Star* Internet Edition, 15 May 2001.

Index